EL MISTI

This extinct volcano, with its snowy top rising 21,000 feet, is the imposing background of the Harvard Observatory at the white city of Arequipa, Peru

LATIN AMERICA—
MEN AND MARKETS

BY

CLAYTON SEDGWICK COOPER

AUTHOR OF " FOREIGN TRADE MARKETS AND METHODS," " UNDERSTANDING SOUTH AMERICA,"
" THE BRAZILIANS AND THEIR COUNTRY," " UNDERSTANDING ITALY," ETC.

GINN AND COMPANY
BOSTON · NEW YORK · CHICAGO · LONDON
ATLANTA · DALLAS · COLUMBUS · SAN FRANCISCO

𝕿𝖍𝖊 𝕬𝖙𝖍𝖊𝖓𝖆𝖚𝖒 𝕻𝖗𝖊𝖘𝖘

GINN AND COMPANY · PRO-
PRIETORS · BOSTON · U.S.A.

PREFACE

This book has been written in order to promote a clearer understanding of the main characteristics of Latin-American business men and a better knowledge of the trade relationships existing between the United States and Latin America. While here and there in the book the author has made some attempt at interpretation and analysis, his main object has been to present briefly the fundamental facts relative to trade and business conditions in each of the Latin-American countries, so that the student, the business man, and the general reader may secure some comprehensive knowledge of Latin America as a whole, particularly with regard to the close commercial relations existing between the two parts of the Western Hemisphere.

The vital and growing economic relationship between the United States and the Latin-American countries is hardly appreciated in this country, even by those who have traveled more or less extensively in both Americas. Our lack of knowledge as to our Latin-American neighbors and our consequent lack of sympathy with many of their problems have been at the root of much of the misunderstanding that has existed in the past.

In this book the author has tried to stress the importance of a sympathetic point of view on the part of the reader; to cause him to realize among other things the fact that a Latin-American business characteristic or practice may be different from ours without necessarily having less merit. Take the sense of business honor, for example. Some writers have given the impression that in this respect the Latin-American business man has not advanced so far as his North American neighbor. The testimony of many intelligent American traders in Latin-American countries, however, does not bear out this opinion.

There is still a decided ignorance among the people of the United States as to the magnitude of our economic relations with Latin America. A half century ago Latin-American coun-

v

tries took from the United States imports valued at $28,628,000, while exports to this country reached the sum of $79,292,000. In 1900, or twenty-five years later, Latin-American imports from the United States had tripled, and exports to this country had nearly doubled. During the next twenty-five years, which included the years of the World War with their radical effect on American trade, far more startling changes were brought about. In 1925 Latin-American imports from the United States were valued at $960,393,000, while Latin-American exports to this country were valued at $1,133,802,000. The contrast is most striking, however, when the total value of Latin-American trade with the United States fifty years ago is compared with the total value in 1925. An increase in fifty years from $100,000,000 to $2,000,000,000 leaves no doubt as to the importance of the economic relations involved.

Whether the United States will maintain a dominant position in Latin-American trade is a question that depends largely upon the extent to which our business men study the psychological factors entering into successful trade relationships, and upon the emphasis which they give to the mastery of the languages of Latin America. Business methods must be adapted to the traditional and inherent racial tendencies of the Latin Americans.

The huge sums of money, amounting to many millions of dollars, which the United States has invested in Latin America, particularly in the northern countries, are indicative of another of our spheres of influence in the growth of these countries. When it is appreciated that in 1925 our investments in Latin America were nearly twice as large as our investments in Europe, the need of more complete knowledge concerning economic conditions in Latin America becomes even clearer. It is estimated that approximately 43 per cent of all the money invested abroad by the United States is invested in the countries of Latin America.

The various phases of our influence in these countries entail both privileges and obligations of exceedingly great moment. The reciprocal relations existing between the two Americas cannot be denied. Unless both prosper, neither can prosper permanently. More than a century ago John Quincy Adams defined the elements necessary for friendly Pan-American relationships as "disinterestedness, cordial good will, and fair and equal reciprocity." If we are to maintain and increase our hold on Latin-American commerce in conformity with such principles, the training of our present-day business representatives and of the youth in our schools, who will enter into the heritage of our vast investments in Latin America, must be given immediate and increased attention. It is the hope of the author that this book may be enlightening to those who are to be our future traders, diplomats, and teachers in Latin-American countries, and that it may promote a better understanding of the problems which are so vital to the growing and ever-expanding life of these countries. The questions and the bibliography at the end of the book are presented as suggestions for the use of teachers and students.

The author desires to express his grateful appreciation to Mr. B. L. Hunt of Washington, D. C., for his criticisms and suggestions in connection with the manuscript; to Mrs. Florence Pegram for work on the manuscript and proofs; and to many correspondents and friends in the United States and in the Latin-American countries, who have greatly assisted by furnishing varied information and counsel.

He wishes also to acknowledge his indebtedness to the various reports and literature published by the Bureau of Foreign and Domestic Commerce of the United States Department of Commerce, to the pamphlets and literature furnished by the Pan-American Union, and to the many publications for which specific acknowledgment is made throughout the text.

That the student and the general reader of this book may gain an increased realization of the fact that the commercial and economic relationships existing between the northern and southern portions of our Western Hemisphere are basic factors for Pan-American growth and harmony is the earnest wish of the author.

CLAYTON SEDGWICK COOPER

Miami Beach, Florida

CONTENTS

CHAPTER   PAGE

    I. Understanding Latin Americans 1

   II. Historical Background 25

  III. Ecuador 36

  IV. Peru 59

   V. Bolivia, the Mountain Republic 90

  VI. Chile 110

 VII. Argentina, the Landed Republic 135

VIII. Uruguay 166

  IX. Paraguay 181

   X. Brazil, the Leviathan Republic 195

  XI. Venezuela 251

 XII. Colombia 267

XIII. Panama — the Providential Republic 282

XIV. Central America 300

 XV. Mexico 342

XVI. The West Indies 367

XVII. Foreign Possessions in the West Indies and South America 390

XVIII. Trade Problems 430

Bibliography 447

Index 455

LATIN AMERICA—MEN AND MARKETS

CHAPTER I

UNDERSTANDING LATIN AMERICANS

I know the attractiveness of the Spanish-American; I know his high-born courtesy, I know his love of art, his poet nature, his response to generous treatment, and I know how easily he misunderstands the thoughtless bluntness of an Anglo-Saxon diplomacy, and the too frequent lack of regard for the feelings of others that we have inherited. — Ex-President Taft [1]

LATIN AMERICA AND THE UNITED STATES

The term "Pan-American Union" has a basis in fact. Geographically Latin America and the United States are contiguous neighbors; politically they are much the same, with a similar form of government; commercially they have mutual and, for the most part, noncompetitive markets. Their natural and material resources are complementary. The same is true of their culture, their philosophy of life, and their prominent characteristics.

The Honorable Elihu Root has shown how the Americas are complements of each other, and how they are therefore bound together by the natural ties of mutual relationship:

The South American is polite, refined, cultivated, fond of literature and of expression and of the graces and charms of life, while the North American is strenuous, intense, utilitarian. Where we accumulate, they spend. While we have less of the cheerful philosophy which finds sources of happiness in the existing conditions of life, they have less of the inventive faculty which strives continually to increase the productive power of man and lower the cost of manufacture. The chief merits of the people of the two continents are different; their chief defects are different. Mutual intercourse and knowledge

[1] In the *Independent*, December 18, 1913. Used by permission.

cannot fail greatly to benefit both. Each can learn from the other, each can teach much to the other, and each can contribute greatly to the development and prosperity of the other. A large part of their products find no domestic competition here; a large part of our products will find no domestic competition there. The typical conditions exist for that kind of trade which is profitable, honorable, and beneficial to both parties.

Need of better understanding. The first step toward enlarging commerce — that is, closer social and political relationship between peoples — is a thorough knowledge of the traits, or characteristics, of the parties concerned. In spite of the fact that the people of the United States have lived so long in close geographical relation with the Latin Americans, the one group still shows a surprising lack of knowledge of the other. Until a comparatively recent date both have known Europe better than they have known each other.

The South American republics were influenced by North American precedent in their revolt against Spain, but for many years this relationship was not advanced. Latin-American countries, like the United States, sent their raw products to Europe and bought manufactured goods in return. European rather than North American bankers furnished money for the development of Latin-American industries, cities, railways, and harbors. The people of the Latin race also sought their intellectual life, their educational systems, their fashions, and their modes of thought from France, Spain, Portugal, and Italy, rather than from the United States.

The reason for this lack of knowledge and association between the two countries was that ties of language and kinship drew the people of South America to Europe. The principal slopes and great commercial rivers of the continent were on the Atlantic side, many degrees east of the longitude of New York, and thus favored commerce with Europe. The United States was occupied at home with her own industrial development and had inherited an unwritten policy of staying at home and of avoiding entangling alliances with other nations.

Even before the World War, however, signs were apparent that the United States had reached a period in her commercial history when additional foreign markets had become a necessity for her expanding trade and commercial well-being. During the past decade her ever-increasing import trade, in which agricultural and mineral products from South America have constituted a considerable share, the establishment of American banks in Latin America, the investment of huge sums of American capital in every Latin republic from Mexico to the Argentine, the inception of new steamship lines connecting the two parts of the American hemisphere, and notably the opening of the Panama Canal, which forms a crossroad of commerce for the entire world, have all helped to lay a new basis of trade relationship. Moreover, the new place that the United States has taken in the financial world as a creditor since the war has changed relationships with more than one of the republics to the south of us.

In view of such radical changes, and in order to take advantage of so many new opening doors, it has become increasingly necessary for North and South Americans to know and understand each other. Such knowledge and understanding is the basis of all future successful trade, and without it the two Americas will remain strangers, no matter how much business may be conducted in a utilitarian manner.

Permanent ties, national as well as individual, are made through the means of sympathetic understanding and the mutual will to know the ideals, customs, and modes of thought and business procedure of the other nation.

THE LATIN AMERICANS

It is by no means an easy task to answer the question What are the Latin Americans? While to a marked degree the same characteristics run through the races of men in these southern republics, in another sense the people differ decidedly from each other. The Mexican and Argentino, with the same general strain of blood, are quite different types of men, while the inhabitant of Rio de Janeiro would feel as strange in Guatemala or in Quito as would the inhabitant of a North American city.

Difficulty in analyzing. Furthermore, Latin-American citizens are difficult to analyze, especially to a foreigner, not merely because they are of such varied race but by reason of their rapidly changing moods. Like the Oriental, the inhabitants of Latin-American republics are quite likely to disarrange the customary characterization of the foreigner by unlooked-for manifestations of traits as puzzling as they are complex. The Latin American is a man of surprises, but our very great need to know and understand him makes the attempt to analyze his traits and the conditions of his country a worth-while proceeding.

Sensitiveness. One of the first characteristics of the Latin Americans that must be recognized by those who would have successful dealings with them is a keenly sensitive disposition. There is a pride of person, a disinclination to accept adverse criticism, and what would seem to the North American an almost foolish vainglory, all of which is a part of the Latin inheritance. In Latin lands feelings lie near the surface. Criticism of Latin-American habits or life, or of the procedure of government or business, has lost trade for foreigners indulging in it.

Latin Americans are devotees to form and are courteous at all times. Even the laborer and the servant are seldom forgetful of those forms of politeness that invariably accompany Latin-American conversation and business contacts. The brusque directness of the Northerner is anathema to the Latin American.

The business success of the Germans in these regions has been due in large measure to their adaptability to the conditions in which the Latin American desires to live and to work. The Germans have carefully studied the latter's temperament, his business habits, and his mode of life, as well as his requirements as to products for export and import. They have studied seriously the question concerning the "what" and the "how" of Latin-American business. They have been careful not to offend their prospective customers, realizing that these Latins, with their great territorial expanse, their ability to support themselves wholly, and their endowment of a rich racial heritage and pride of birth, are not obliged to trade or to associate with people whom they do not like.

Attitude toward time. The Latin-American's attitude toward the use of time differs greatly from that of the people of the United States.

In the United States the penchant for saving time is almost a mania. Specialists for organizing and eliminating and systematizing have created here a profession, — efficiency engineering, a new vocation of time-saving, a brand-new germ, working as methodically and fatally as natural laws against the national octopus of waste and extravagance. The idea is popular among people who are always striving to get ahead, even of themselves. In this Northern world of ours, eminent for its forehandedness and progress, where people read the evening newspapers at noon and the morning newspapers before the previous midnight, where the September magazines appear early in August, the lines of Seneca are appropriate:

> Who murders Time
> He crushes in the bud a power ethereal,
> Only not adored.

The American free translation of these lines reads somewhat more practically than the Roman original, and was exemplified in the rules nailed up in the printing office of Benjamin Franklin: "Lose no time; be always employed in something useful; cut off all unnecessary actions."

The "Yankee notions" of our fathers' days were in the majority of cases time-saving or material-saving notions. The inventions of the Yankee sons have enlarged these ideals of time preservation until we sow and reap and gather into barns to the tune of time-saving machinery; we print, we manufacture, we sew, we wash our clothes, we write our letters, we clean our cotton, we light our homes, we talk to our distant friends by means of time-saving devices. We annihilate space by airplanes, limited trains, telephones, and ocean liners, all of which are made in the United States. We have carried our individuality in these inventions around the world, and our steam plows, sewing machines, typewriters, telephones, cotton gins, and incandescent lights—all time-saving machinery—are omnipresent indications of the North American characteristics and the desire to save time and to quicken life in general.

If we should go to any part of Latin America and endeavor to introduce summarily these ideas of alacrity and the careful use of time, there would surely be misunderstanding and lack of coöperation. The Latin American is antipodal to us in his ideas as to the use of his time. More theoretical and less direct, less practical, less scientific, he more often finds satisfaction in the quiet, romantic, and sentimental sides of life. He is artistic, a lover of music and art, an adept in languages, a student of literature and history, and inclined to professional and cultural matters rather than to the scientific and material activities exercising the genius of the Northerner. Moreover, the climate of many of the Latin-American countries is not conducive to a strenuous life.

While habits of delay in keeping appointments are not the heritage of any one nation, the Latin American is probably quite as dilatory as any, save possibly the Oriental, in his attention to time and place. When one of our state officials visited the Republic of Bolivia a few years ago, a large reception was held at La Paz, invitations for which were sent out to all natives for three o'clock, and to foreigners for four o'clock, with the result that natives and foreigners arrived at approximately the same time, that is, about four o'clock.

It is necessary to study the hours for doing business in Latin-American cities and towns, as in many sections these are quite different from the business hours in the United States. Salesmen's methods that succeed at home often meet with failure in the Southern republics. It is necessary to discard haste and the tense attitude of "Do it now!" when dealing with Latin Americans.

BUSINESS DEMANDS

In addition to these general traits of delay and intermittent energy there are certain methods of doing business in Latin America that must be understood by Northern people going south on business.

Need of credentials. The necessity of proper introduction on the part of salesmen who go to Latin-American cities and towns cannot be overestimated. All the republics of Latin America have been exploited more or less by irresponsible "fly by night" concerns, and there is usually a demand that business representatives from the North shall be properly accredited from the start. A letter of introduction from the firm, if the firm is well known, is desirable, and a letter from a well-known bank is often found to be of real value. In fact, anybody going to Latin America — for business or investigation, on a political mission, or purely for pleasure — will find it to his advantage to carry credentials from the State Department at Washington or from the Department of Commerce, and from half a dozen or more well-known firms or individuals having a good reputation in various parts of Latin America.

Acquaintance of ambassadors and consuls. The good offices of the Pan-American Union at Washington have been helpful in the way of introductions, while letters of introduction from prominent South or Central Americans living in the United States are always to be desired. Since the Latin American is usually a stickler for form, it is often advisable for the business agent or manufacturer, upon arrival in a city or town, to call first on his consul, and also upon the United States minister or ambassador, who will be able to give him local suggestions of real value as to the particular methods of doing business in that region. Often the consul's note of introduction will be of use in addition to the credentials carried by the foreigner. It should always be remembered that Latin Americans like to do business by appointment, and that to "blow in" abruptly to a Latin-American's business office is never a successful means of approach.

Formality in dress. The Latin punctiliousness in dress plays an important part in business deportment, and it is wise when in Rome to do as Romans do. A United States official who was the guest of honor at a formal reception in Latin America a few years ago caused great consternation by appearing in a light business suit and wearing an American straw hat. While this, of course, would be quite permissible at certain gatherings in the United States on such an occasion, yet when all the native government officials were clad according to the customs of the country in regulation black clothes and high hats, the dress of the Northern official struck a false note and gave the impression of a lack of good taste. While these matters are generally considered dilettante and artificial by the intense, direct, and practical business man of the North, it must be remembered that they do not appear thus trivial to people who have been reared in the atmosphere of ceremonial and of formal procedure.

Observance of holidays and mail days. It is a mark of courtesy for the foreigner to acquaint himself with the many holidays and saints' days observed throughout Latin America, when business offices are closed or running with a diminished office staff. "Mail days" are matters of importance, too, and it is wise for the foreign representative to refrain from calling in behalf of new business on the days when mail steamers arrive, bringing, naturally, unusual business activity.

Type of man in business in Latin America. In Latin America the heads of the large business houses are quite frequently men of the aristocratic class who have inherited wealth or who have gone into business sometimes from the professional ranks; they are, as a rule, older men, who regard their dignity and standing as a matter of some importance. These men neither understand nor enjoy meeting the type of salesman with a minimum of courtesy who is interested only in "putting over" an order in double-quick time. Frequently such salesmen will be received courteously enough, but they will never be asked to return.

Requirements for good salesmanship in Latin America. It is becoming more and more vital to successful business dealings between North and South Americans to have the representative whom we send southward fitted by gentlemanly training and general education to do something more than sell goods. He should be a salesman plus, and the "plus" is quite as vital at times as the salesman, since only the man who has given some attention to the social niceties in Latin-American business gets proper entry or even a hearing.

A successful representative of a North American business house relates the following incident concerning his first experience in selling goods in South America, in accordance with the desirable method of one section. He was fortunate in possessing, to begin with, a polished training, which is especially desirable for business success in South America, though not, of course, absolutely essential. He was also wise enough to study carefully business procedure in foreign countries, mastering the various books on the subject and conversing with a large number of American traders who had lived in Latin America and had learned, often from bitter experience, how *not* to try to do business with these people. Many of these experienced business men told him that the South American desired to trade with people who were *simpático,* — people whom they liked, — and that it was sometimes important in a case of large business transactions to be in no hurry whatsoever to make sales. Getting acquainted first and doing business afterward, therefore, was a motto that he chose in dealing with his first customer.

This agent called upon a large landowner of Argentina, making it a point to interest himself in almost anything except the selling of farm machinery, which was the object of his visit. He presented his letters of introduction, evidently made a good impression socially, and was invited by the landowner to his club for luncheon. After several other meetings, all of a social nature, in which the men became interested in each other by reason of a common interest in books on nature study, the landowner invited the American to his country estate, where he met his family and was entertained most hospitably. It must always be remembered that the Latin American rarely, if ever, invites a foreign stranger to his home until he has tried him out, so to speak, by personal acquaintance, and has decided that he is a proper person to introduce to his wife and family. In this particular instance the American saw a great deal of the newly found Argentine acquaintance and was treated so courteously that he felt almost ashamed, when obliged to leave, to broach the matter of business. As luck would have it, on the day before he was to depart his friend said to him, "By the way, we have been a bit curious concerning the object of your visit to the Argentine," stating at the same time that he had enjoyed the acquaintance so much that he hoped it might be maintained through correspondence. The American then explained that he had come down with the express purpose of selling farm machinery for a firm in the Middle West. The Argentine replied, "Why, that is a matter in which I am particularly interested just now. Come up to the office and we will talk business."

As a result the young salesman left the Argentine with an order for $100,000 worth of farm machinery, and the South American landowner wrote to the president of the company in the United States, saying, "Mr. X, your representative, has just sold me $100,000 worth of machinery for my hacienda, and I take the privilege of adding that he is the only American representing an American business house whom I have ever met who knows how to do business with the Argentines. I like him and hope you will send him to us again."

While, of course, it is not always necessary or wise to preface a request for selling American goods by several weeks of social acquaintanceship, in this particular case the American salesman felt that his time was well spent.

The principle illustrated, in his case at least, is that the *approach* in South American business transactions is quite as important as the knowledge of one's goods and the ability to close the transaction.

INTELLECTUAL AND ARTISTIC TRAITS OF THE LATIN AMERICAN

The contribution of the Latin American to the intellectual, artistic, and cultural resources of the world has already been notable. During the last decade people of the United States, by better means of communication with Latin America, through the exchange of professors and students, and by a better knowledge of the Spanish language, have become more and more impressed with the fact that the Latin Americans, although wanting in certain of the scientific qualifications required for commercial and industrial progress, reveal, nevertheless, marked characteristics of strength in the realm of the intellectual and social requirements for a high type of civilization.

Universities. The educational facilities of these republics are apparent in the universities of long standing, where professional men, scholars of literature, and jurists have been trained. Latin Americans affirm that the first university in the New World, Santo Tomás de Aquinas, was founded at Santo Domingo in 1538. Since this university is no longer extant, the University of San Marcos, at Lima, Peru, established in 1551, is the oldest seat of learning on the South American continent. There is also the University of Mexico, founded in 1553, which was dissolved in 1862 and reëstablished in 1910. This institution was originally known as the Royal and Pontifical University of Mexico, and was perhaps the most famous of the colonial institutions of learning. The prologue of its constitution of 1775 states that the university had granted 30,000 degrees. In addition to other subjects taught at this institution, Indian dialects were studied.

Schools. Primary and secondary education has been neglected in many of the Latin-American states, but now these defects are being repaired in South America. Several of the republics have called upon trained educators, both in North America and in Europe, to assist in the establishment and general organization of their schools and institutions giving special training. Peru has been assisted by North American educators; German instructors are found in a large number of the educational institutions; while many private and secondary schools have been established by foreigners in different parts of Latin America. The awakening of the commercial and industrial life in these countries has brought into being various kinds of training schools and social institutions. Military schools are popular, and considerable attention is being given to schools having as their aim cultural and artistic training.

Modern educational institutions for the Indian and negro population are sadly infrequent, though here and there, notably in Brazil, practical education for the Indian has made progress.

Printing and literature. In addition to establishing universities, Latin America pioneered the use of printing presses in this hemisphere, introducing into Mexico the first printing press, and, in the year 1536, printing the first book published in the New World. This book, by Father Las Casas, was a plea for a higher idealism. Printing presses were introduced at Cartagena, Colombia, in 1560, and in Peru about 1584, where the first book published in South America is said to have been printed.

The Jesuit missions furnished no little inspiration for education in Brazil and Paraguay in these early centuries. The desire for learning and the habit of study has thus been a heritage of the Latin-American people, and while this culture has at times been tinged with ecclesiastical and medieval learning, there have been, nevertheless, a long line of scholars, historians, jurists, orators, physicians, musicians, painters, sculptors, poets, and playwrights.

The traveler to South America is astonished to find, often in the out-of-the-way towns as well as in the large cities, book stores supplied with works of fiction, history, and art that have been translated into many European languages and are well known to Spanish and Portuguese scholars, although they are utterly unknown to the majority of the inhabitants of the United States. For years the Brazilians have been industriously turning out books of extraordinary merit. Here are to be found the works of such Brazilian poets as Francisco Octaviano and Raymundo Correa, which have met with great popularity throughout the Portuguese-speaking world, and the books of Doctor Ruy Barbosa, a writer on politics and jurisprudence, of whom a contemporary said not long ago, "The purity and correctness of the language alone assures his works and his discourses a permanent place amongst the classics."

The Brazilian Academy, modeled on the French Academy, has its "forty immortals," among whom is the popular woman writer and novelist, D. Julia Lopez de Almeida, and the short-story writer Coelho Netto, who has seventy volumes to his credit and holds a leading place in the estimation of the public. Among literary critics José Verrisimo is a well-known figure, occupying a place in the realm of national literature similar to that of Émile Faguet in France.

Brazil was also fortunate in having in its former emperor, Dom Pedro II, an eminent book-lover and scholar, who donated fifty thousand volumes from his own collection to the large and well-equipped library at Rio de Janeiro. It is significant of the breadth of learning of these South Americans that the languages represented by the books of this library number fourteen. The library is one of the most popular places in the city.

What has been said concerning scholars and intellectual development in Brazil may be said of at least a dozen of the Latin-American republics. The cities of Buenos Aires in Argentina,

FIG. 1. Pan-American journalists on a visit to Philadelphia. (Courtesy of the Pan-American Union)

Santiago in Chile, and Rio de Janeiro and São Paulo in Brazil contain opera houses more elaborate and beautiful in construction than those found in any North American city. The governments of many Latin-American countries reflect the desires of the naturally music-loving population by subsidizing opera troupes and paying large sums to obtain the best singers. Many a celebrity of the Metropolitan Opera Company of New York began his musical career in Latin America, while it is a well-known fact that the summer trips of our Metropolitan Opera singers to Latin-American cities have almost invariably met with a success unsurpassed by such trips in many portions of the United States.

Linguistic attainments. As linguists the Latin Americans are cosmopolitan to a far greater degree than their United States neighbors. The leading men of affairs, as well as scholars, will turn easily from Spanish or Portuguese to fluent French or Italian and give evidence of being entirely at home. The Latin-American newspapers, especially those found in the large centers, are unusually notable for the literary talent displayed; and while the weekly and monthly publications have not been greatly developed, they are rapidly increasing. Many North American publications find that their Spanish editions circulated in South America are as profitable as many other products that we export to these countries.

All this emphasizes the fact that the Latin, wherever found, turns most readily to the literary, artistic, and political side of life. While the people of the United States were devoting their energies to the taming of their rugged country and building up their industrial civilization, the educated classes of Central America and South America, inheriting from their ancestors a natural distaste for agricultural and industrial careers, were turning out from their schools and universities lawyers, doctors, poets, and devotees of literary and artistic pursuits, leaving the manual work of the country to be carried on by ignorant but industrious Indians, negroes, and such mixed races as the cholos and mestizos. Foreign capital has gone to South America, to Central America, and to the West Indies, and, in the hands of foreigners from Europe and the United States, has become the leading force in material development. This is because the Latin American, while not lacking in intellectual ability, has for generations been turning his attention to matters more in line with his natural aptitudes and his aristocratic inheritances.

The Latin Americans have been called, and justly so, impractical, and those who would know them must appreciate this fact. But it must also be realized that as poets and dreamers they have made a real contribution to life in the realm of beauty and imagination, even though they may have found such characteristics a handicap in subduing a vast continent rich in physical and material possibilities.

The late Francisco J. Yánes wrote as follows:

We inherited from our forefathers the love of the beautiful and the grand; the facility for expression and the vivid imagination of our race; from them we inherited the sonorous, majestic Spanish, the flexible, musical Portuguese, and the French language of art, and a responsive chord to all that thrills, be it color, harmony, or mental imagery; we inherited their varying moods, their noble traits and their shortcomings, all of which we have preserved, and in certain cases improved, under the influence of our environment, our majestic mountains, our primeval forests, the everblooming tropical flowers, the birds of sweetest wild songs and wonderful plumage; under magnificent skies, and the inspiration taken from other poets and writers, be they foreign or native, who have gone through life like the minstrels of old with a song on their lips and an unsatisfied yearning in their hearts.

THE INDIVIDUALISM OF LATIN AMERICANS

A trait which has greatly retarded the corporate life of Latin America, and postponed coöperative organization, has been the intense individualism of the people, — a heritage from the old aristocratic social order. The Latin Americans, like the Italians, have been followers of individual leaders rather than of political principles. The names of Bolívar, San Martín, and Francisco Miranda are as representative of the days of independence of the Spanish-American republics as the names of Pizarro, Hernando Cortez, De Soto, and Almagro — eminent *conquistadores* e representative of the days of Latin-American discovery and conquest. In fact, it is quite possible to write the history of Latin America around the names of its individuals, — conquerors, military leaders, and statesmen.

Emerson said "History is biography." This statement is particularly true with regard to the countries of Central America and South America. Professor William Spence Robertson, who has written of the rise of the Spanish-American republics as told in the lives of their liberators, states in the preface of his work, "I firmly believe that the history of the Spanish-American revolution can be clearly told in the lives of its notable men."[1] If you take pains to read carefully the biographies of such Latin Americans as Santander, Artigas, Francia, Bernado O'Higgins, Antonio José de Sucre, Hidalgo y Costilla, and Mariano Moreno, as well as the more familiar biographies of Spanish-American adventurers and liberators, you will inevitably become acquainted with the political, social, and colonial development of these Latin-American republics.

In politics. It is because of this individualism that Latin America has lacked coöperative movements and those political elements that make for the solidarity of democratic states. It is also true that the numerous mountain ranges which traverse South America divide communities and prevent ready communication, thus greatly hindering the development of national public opinion. The tendency of these geographical barriers has been to circumvent efforts toward national unity. A greater obstacle, however, lies in the character of the Latin American himself, in his excess of personal pride, in his exaggerated idea of personal dignity, in a certain sensitiveness and self-will, all inveterate enemies of compromise and coöperative development.

Ex-President Taft, speaking at Habana some years ago, stated that, so far as politics go, the peoples to the south of us are poor losers. In other words, one explanation of the frequent revolutions of South America is that the losers have too much pride to submit to electoral defeat.

In college spirit. One finds even in the student communities a decided contrast to conditions in the United States in the

---

[1] From " Rise of the Spanish-American Republics," by William Spence Rober'ᵉ'·ᵉ·ᵉ D. Appleton and Company, New York.

lack of so-called "student activities," of class feeling, and of that vital element known in our universities as college spirit. The ability of the Latin-American student to sink his own individuality in a democratic fraternalism, such as is evidenced in the colleges of the United States, is usually conspicuous by its absence. The comparatively small number of literary and fraternal orders in the colleges is at once noticeable. The students do not like to compromise and do not seem to understand the spirit of giving up nonessentials for the sake of teamwork. Although interest in athletics is growing, the spirit so sensitive to defeat has handicapped contests.

In sport. Some years ago the author witnessed a football game at one of the foreign colleges in Egypt. As soon as one team began to forge ahead, the opponents, who feared defeat, came to the principal of the school and announced that they were going to stop playing; as they expressed it, "It shames us to play any longer." While the South American youths are far more vigorous in many ways than were these Egyptian boys, there is apparent, nevertheless, the same dislike of what the Chinese would call "losing face."

In attitude toward manual labor. Add to this trait of individualism the disdain of manual labor inherited by the Latin Americans of today from their ancestors, and you have two rather serious weaknesses in the Latin-American character. It is said that in Peru the people would starve were it not for the Indians, who, having no false pride concerning manual work, are both industrious and effective as agriculturists. It is true that the Spanish Americans have inherited, along with a mild scorn of industry, some of the indolence characteristic of the Spaniard, and there is no doubt that these characteristics have been deterrent elements in the Latin-American civilization.

In racial inheritances. Streams of immigrants from the working classes of Europe, the constant increase of British, German, Belgian, French, and Italian investment and industrial interests in South America, and a constantly growing commercial and shipping relationship with the United States are forces bringing in new tendencies and fresh vitality to many of the South American and Central American countries. The opening of the

Panama Canal and the increase of American interests in Cuba, Porto Rico, and certain of the West Indian and Central American states have brought this section of Latin America into close touch with the modes of life, as well as with the organization and methods of business, of the United States. In recent years a large number of Latin-American leaders of big business have developed, throughout South America particularly, and in Chile, Argentina, Uruguay, Peru, and Brazil one finds in ever-increasing numbers astute and successful business leaders in virtually all lines of trade. If these people are inclined at times to be ultra-individualistic, to disregard the elemental necessity of working at any kind of honorable toil, to be "good beginners but poor finishers," and to follow the theory that the end justifies the means, it must always be remembered that one finds a reason for most of these traits in racial inheritance. In the larger cities and in connection with the more important undertakings, however, there is evidenced the influence of contact with the larger world of trade and travel, which is helping to counteract the defects of medieval tendencies. It has been said concerning the South Americans that one must know their conditions before passing judgment on their defects.[1] The more thoroughly one acquaints oneself with the background of Latin-American history and contrasts the conditions existent one hundred years ago with those of today, the more truly does one learn to believe in the future destiny of these people.

In home life. A characteristic to be noted by those who desire to have relations of any kind with our neighbors in the South lies in the realm of the Latin-American's love for his family and his home and the various customs inhering therein. The home life of the Latin American is based on the patriarchal idea, with strong evidences of Oriental influence. The attitude toward women in the home is quite different from that in the North. There is no such freedom on the part of either the wife or the daughters as is known in the United States or in most of the countries of Europe. Happy-go-lucky, jolly camaraderie between boys and girls and between men and women is con-

[1] From " Rise of the Spanish-American Republics," by William Spence Robertson. D. Appleton and Company, New York.

spicuously absent in Latin America. On the west coast of South America one finds a semiseclusion of women, and rarely is a woman seen on the streets alone. Only in recent years has there been a tendency for women to engage in business life as clerks or stenographers, and only very recently have women begun to take part in civic or public affairs. There is a general feeling throughout Latin America that the place for the woman is primarily and exclusively in the home, and rarely does a foreigner find the home of a South American open to him on short acquaintance.

When an American who had lived for a long time in Brazil was asked why so little was heard from foreign travelers regarding Brazilian homes and home life, he replied, "There are at least seven reasons why they don't talk about Brazilian homes; the first is because they never get inside of one, and the other six reasons don't count." It is the Latin-American home life which, to those who know it best, gives one of the richest promises for the future of these countries. A nation is what it is in its home. It is within home circles that the Latin American spends his happiest hours, and few, if any, customs are cherished more sedulously than those associated with the family and home.

The families are large, and love of children is widespread. Of course there is a great difference between the home life of the better class and that of the laborers, many of whom are of mixed race. The aristocratic South American woman is often a revelation to the Northerner, not only in her homemaking characteristics, but in her mode of dress, taken directly from Paris, Genoa, and Lisbon, in her linguistic ability, in the scope of her reading, especially upon subjects relating to art and music, and in the upholding of aristocratic traditions.

The Latin American is fond of family reunions, and resembles the French in his devotion to the simple pleasures of family life, outings, and the cultivation of music and the social graces. Life in general flows along in Latin America with fewer of the social problems than with us in the United States. The climate forbids overstrenuousness, and one finds fewer sanatoriums for the healing of broken nerves. The Latin American is decidedly a social being, and the spirit of good nature and friendliness is an important adjunct to him in all his relationships. Bachelors are so rare as to be almost suspicious characters in South America. The prevailing Catholic faith forbids divorce, and while in the judgment of some this makes for laxity in the morals of the men outside the home, it also tends to perpetuate and hold together the family circle, while the loyalty between members of the same family and their numerous relatives is a strong bond among these people.

In friendships. The multifold anniversaries, birthday parties, family gatherings, and banquets in honor of distinguished personages are played upon in the daily papers with a wealth of congratulations unknown in the North. The stress laid upon friendships, and the lengths to which the Latin American will go in doing a favor for a friend, are well known by all those who do business with him. Friendship is no glittering generality south of the Rio Grande. In nine cases out of ten the Latin American will trade with a personal acquaintance or with the friend of a friend or relative, often even in the face of economic loss, rather than engage in business with a stranger of whom he is inclined to be suspicious until he knows him.

The following incident, taken from "The Brazilians and their Country,"[1] illustrates the characteristic sentiment entering into the entire life of the Latin Americans:

During my sojourn in Brazil, I recall particularly a complimentary dinner given to a distinguished Brazilian diplomat, author and prominent member of the Brazilian Academy of Letters. There were present seventy of the gentleman's friends and admirers. There was a profusion of flower decorations as always at such functions here; even the tables were rimmed with Brazilian roses. In spite of the proverbial "excitability" of the Latin temperament, there were no emotional outbursts, nor any "He's a Jolly Good Fellow" songs and wild cheers. There was a natural restraint, which in some other countries might be taken for lack of interest. Everything from the reading of telegrams (everyone sends telegrams in Brazil when congratulations or social events are in progress) to the partaking of the five kinds of wine served, was done decently and in perfect order.

[1] Clayton Sedgwick Cooper, The Brazilians and their Country. Frederick A. Stokes Company,

Good form and gentlemanly decorum, no loud talking or undue excitement anywhere. After the congratulatory addresses had been made by a number of eminent men, government officials and well-known scholars, some in French, others in the national tongue, both of which were evidently understood equally well by all the guests, the gentleman in whose honor the banquet was given rose, and with utter simplicity spoke substantially as follows:

"I have tried to serve my country in diplomacy; in that I have not been eminently successful. I have done some literary work; but there are many other younger and more successful writers than I have been. I have also tried to make friends. Although I may have failed in the first two mentioned ambitions of my career, this gathering has convinced me beyond any doubt that I have succeeded in friendship. Therefore I am tonight exceedingly happy and content."

It is very evident that this was no speech to the "gallery"; no one could have heard it and seen its effect upon the hearers without being impressed by its sincerity. It represented an ambition and a triumphant result that bulk large in the hearts and aims of Latin America. If Emerson, the sage of Concord, was right in his estimation of values when he said "Life is simply a means for expressing a sentiment," our Northern nations, with their all-too-exclusive devotion to the "business is business" policy, may well go to school to these Latin-American nations.

In attitude toward religion. The prevailing religion throughout Spanish and Portuguese America is that of the Catholic Church, and the characteristics of this church in Latin America exemplify the European characteristics of that faith more truly than do those of the United States. In certain sections, particularly in the region of the Andes, one finds monasteries and medieval reminders of a day in which the Inquisition was a potent fact. The Catholic Church has inherited large estates in some parts of Latin America, and many of the priests, monks, and officials are imported directly from Spain.

As to the influence of the Church upon the modern business man, it is, of course, difficult to generalize. The Latin American has a strain of religion along with his strong feeling and sentiments, and the ceremonial and forms of the Church are a part of his inheritance. There is apparent throughout Latin America, however, especially among men, an indifference to the avowed forms of religion that is found more or less in the United States and in other countries of the world.

In no other part of Latin America are religious conditions so backward as in the Andean region, where futile attempts have been made on the part of the Catholic Church to convert the ignorant, superstitious Indians to the forms of a faith more or less foreign to their natures. Here also are found certain Protestant missions, but there is not the best of feeling between the two types of Christian faith. It is pathetic to realize that the millions of Indians living upon the desolate slopes of the Andes in their small mud villages, or on the borders of the larger towns in their primitive huts, are in a worse predicament now, from almost every point of view, than they were when the Spanish conquerors came to Peru. There is ample opportunity and need for the inauguration of modern schools among the Indians, and for the introduction of up-to-date training in living conditions in general, as well as in agriculture and mining. In such reforms, while small beginnings have been made in scattered places, there seems to have been little interest on the part of either the Church or the State.

While the Catholic faith is supported by the leading classes of both men and women in Latin America, as well as by the government in certain states, there seems to be a growing tendency toward freethinking and agnosticism, especially among thoughtful men and students in the larger universities. In almost every section of the continent one is usually impressed, upon entering a church, with the absence of men, — a condition not characteristic of Latin America alone.

In speaking of religious training as a force in shaping Latin-American civilization, it should be stated that certain North American educational institutions are accomplishing excellent results in giving the youth of these regions first-class modern educational advantages. The excellent school for young men and also one for young women, conducted under the auspices of the North American Presbyterian Church in Santiago, Chile, are examples of the real contribution that Protestants are making to the up-building and educational development of some of these Latin-American countries.

In love of pleasure and amiability. Despite the fact that the Latin Americans are not conspicuous as a highly scientific and practical people, they nevertheless possess traits of amiability and devotion to the kindlier and more pleasurable side of life which other peoples would do well to imitate. Foreigners who live for any length of time in Latin America usually bear witness to the fact that these people are pleasant folk with whom to live, that they will go out of the way to help or to do a favor, and that they make good friends; but it must be added that they also make bad enemies.

The Latin American makes it his business to enjoy life. He can hardly understand how people in other parts of the world can devote themselves so strenuously, at the expense of health, and often of home life and happiness, to money-making. Gambling, horse-racing, and football are some of the chief recreative exercises, the first two being much more general than in the United States.

While money "talks" in Latin America as elsewhere, one usually finds that in the best circles more attention is paid to the social, cultural, and romantic sides of life than in the North.

THE LATIN-AMERICAN IDEA OF THE AMERICAN BUSINESS MAN

A play that was very successful at one of the theaters in Rio de Janeiro a few years ago had as one of its principal characters a typical business man of the United States. This business man, who was represented as comparatively young, dressed in a checked business suit, brusque in manner, and direct in action and speech, was supposed to be in love with a young lady. As an evidence of this love the Brazilian playwright caused the "all-business" young American to rush madly upon the stage at frequent intervals, confront the young lady, and exclaim while looking at his watch, "I love you very much, but I must get back to my office; I have an important business engagement." Each time the American appeared, always in a state of hurry and always with a watch in his hand, the audience would applaud uproariously. A Brazilian was heard to say to a man from the United States: "Isn't that the way it is with you people? We understand that you are all so busy making money and attending to business that you do not even have time to make love."

The tendency to exercise the emotional and enthusiastic temperament in the more pleasurable side of life has brought certain criticism upon the Latin American. We are often told that this chivalrous and gentlemanly type of man may be all right in the drawing-room, but that he lacks the Anglo-Saxon seriousness and power to hold out in the face of obstacles. Many foreign residents in Latin America will tell you that the Latin American is usually keen to begin new ventures, but often fails to "carry through." He lacks what Napoleon called "two-o'clock-in-the-morning courage."

There may be some truth in this, but the law of compensation holds. It is easy enough for Northerners to criticize Latin Americans for the things which they have in abundance; it is not so easy, in a spirit of genuine good will, broadmindedness, and sympathetic imagination, to be taught by these people out of their wealth of kindliness, strong feeling for friends, and attention to those amenities of daily intercourse without which money and success are alike inadequate to make the world a pleasant place in which to live. James A. Garfield received from an old lady who knew him intimately one of the highest compliments that was ever paid him. Shortly after the martyred president's death this lady said to a friend, "I liked him; he was so pleasant."

Latin Americans are still learners in the school of practical, commercial, and industrial progress, though it must be admitted that they are rapidly advancing in the realm of mastering practical business, doing it always in their own way and in accordance with their particular modes of traditional procedure; but in the realm of agreeability and in the fine art of living pleasantly with their fellow men the Latin Americans are far superior to their Northern neighbors.

CHAPTER II

HISTORICAL BACKGROUND

The tendencies of a nation are all that count. — ELIHU ROOT

Latin America is often thought of as a geographical unit, with a more or less homogeneous population and with similar climate, history, and habits of life. No conception could be farther from the facts.

Here is a vast area of approximately 8,500,000 square miles, or nearly one sixth of the earth's surface, with about 86,000,000 inhabitants, who have been profoundly influenced not only by their racial inheritance but also by climate, topographical conditions, natural resources, and the native populations with whom the early settlers came in contact. While most of the twenty Latin-American republics, with the notable exception of Brazil, were originally discovered and colonized by the Spanish, and while Spanish is the language generally spoken, there are marked differences in the life, customs, and characteristics of the peoples of the various states.

It is apparent that no one can satisfactorily understand Latin-American people or markets who has failed to study first the historical background of the people as a means of interpreting their present development. Latin-American trade with the United States, as well as with other nations, did not begin with the breaking out of the World War. It has been in existence for several centuries, and the influences which have governed it still persist today in many phases of our inter-American commerce.

THE FOUR PERIODS OF LATIN–AMERICAN HISTORY

The history of Latin America may be roughly divided into four periods.

The period of discovery. This portion of the history of Latin America belongs to the latter years of the fifteenth century and is associated with such outstanding names of discoverers and adventurers as Columbus, Pizarro, and Hernando Cortez.

The colonial period. This is a vexed era of three centuries, during which Spanish and Portuguese America was ruled by a diverse line of royal representatives, viceroys, and captain-generals, — a period marked by many political misunderstandings and a very small amount of constructive nation-building.

The liberation period, or the period of independence. This part of Latin-American history covers the period between 1783 and 1830. During these years virtually all of the larger Latin-American states threw off the yoke of their mother countries, Spain and Portugal, and set up independent governments. All of them, except Brazil, chose the republic as their form of government. Brazil continued under an emperor until 1889.

The republican period. During the years between 1830 and the present time — nearly a century for most of the Latin-American republics — these states have been endeavoring, with varying degrees of success, to build up a representative form of government similar to that of the United States. It must be appreciated, however, that the historical background, and in fact the entire foundation upon which the Latin-American states reared their republican institutions, is entirely different from that afforded by the more fortunate conditions and experiences falling to the lot of their sister republic of the North.

SEARCHING OUT NEW SEA ROUTES

The discovery of Latin America was a result of the era of trade and transportation that opened on the high seas in the fifteenth century. During this period the Portuguese were developing a coastal trade to the north, vessels from Genoa and Venice had found a seaway as far as Antwerp, and the Hanse traders, who had already opened sea trade with Iceland, were in turn pressing southward. Larger ships, which were better able to cope with the rough seas of the Atlantic, were replacing the coasting galleys of the Mediterranean and the other lighter vessels of the period, and the compass and astrolabe had come into use.

The greatest impetus to the spirit of maritime progress, however, was given by the increasing Turkish control of the eastern Mediterranean and consequently of the land routes to India and the Indies. It was necessary to seek at once for a new route to the Indies, for the trade in silks, spices, and other products of the Far East was the basis of the prosperity of the western Mediterranean cities.

The first possibility to be thought of was, naturally, a route around the great unknown continent of Africa, and many adventurers set out in search of such a route. The dream of Columbus, the Genoese seaman, of sailing west into the sunset until he reached the Indies was ridiculed as the madness of a visionary. To the people of his time his idea was as sensible as an air voyage to Mars would seem today. But Columbus persisted in his idea, influenced by the writings of Marco Polo and other travelers and by a careful study of all the available information on navigation. Eugene O'Neil, speaking of the dreaming Columbus, says, "His eyes were full of golden cities."

After repeated attempts to get boats from Portugal and England, Columbus obtained his three historic ships in 1492, his only deck ship being the *Santa Maria*, a vessel of one hundred tons, and the total complement of sailors numbering eighty-eight. After sailing southward to the Canaries and then heading west over unknown and uncharted seas for two months and nine days, on October 11, 1492, Columbus saw land ahead, and early the next day he and his men knelt on the shores of an island which they thought was one of the Indies. Columbus did not realize then that he had discovered a new world.

The later voyages of Columbus established the claims of Spain more firmly in the New World, and during the immediately succeeding years a swarm of Spanish adventurers and gold-seekers descended upon the new lands. The hunt was on, not for lands to cultivate and to colonize, but for gold and material treasure.

In addition to their passion for gold the Spanish brought another handicap to the early history of discovery and colonization of Latin America in their religious bigotry, born of their recent war with the Moors. These two dominant traits did not make for peaceful relations with the native peoples or for a well-ordered civilization. In his "Outline of History" H. G. Wells describes their methods of dealing with the natives thus: "They made few intelligent observations of the native methods and ideas of these primordial people. They slaughtered them, they robbed them, they enslaved them, and baptized them; but they made small note of the customs and motives that changed and vanished under their assault." [1]

SPAIN'S FAILURE IN COLONIZING

Latin America's late start. In a noteworthy moving-picture production entitled "The Covered Wagon," adapted from the novel of Emerson Hough, the long, winding wagon trains of the early pioneers of the West are shown moving out of the dreary plains of Wyoming, after many tragic vicissitudes, and coming to a signpost. The arms of this signpost point in nearly opposite directions, the one "To California and the gold fields" and the other "To Oregon and the farm lands."

Here the caravan divides, the bulk of the settlers heeding the speech of the pioneer leader, which is to this effect: "You may go to the California gold fields, but only a few lucky ones can win, while out there to the northwest are thousands and thousands of acres of free lands waiting for our plows. There we will build our houses, there we will turn the prairies into wonderful wheat and corn lands, there we will settle and rear our families, there we will make our homes and our fortunes. We go to the Oregon farm lands!"

In this speech we have the key to the difference in the early histories of the two Americas, which were discovered at about the same time. The Latin pioneers of the southern continent, led by adventurers like Pizarro on the west coast, and by Cortez in Mexico, were like the men who followed the signpost to the gold fields, caring nothing for cultivating the lands and less for home-making. For more than two centuries it was the desire for gold and treasure that lured the Spanish and the Portuguese to

---

[1] From H. G. Wells's "Outline of History." By permission of The Macmillan Company, publishers.

these Central American and South American regions to search for the garnered wealth of the Inca and the Aztec. Gold-hunters and freebooters of the buccaneer type, these men were brave beyond compare on both land and sea; but they were not conquerors of the soil. The civilization that they erected was only superficial, based as it was on exploitation and personal aggrandizement. It is not strange, therefore, that the foundation they laid furnished a poor basis for a unified government, and that the epoch was a sorry one, with its conglomerate attempts at colonizing and its numerous revolutions.

In the northern continent, on the contrary, the pioneers followed the example of the men who were guided by the signpost to the farming lands. First wresting their livelihood from the lands along the Atlantic coast, they later pushed farther and farther west, and as they went they laid the foundations of a great and united nation, based on the land and its cultivated products. By the time the Latin-American countries had finally achieved their independence and had entered upon their constructive period, the United States had already risen to union and power.

It was not until the countries from Mexico to Patagonia were released from the leading strings of Old World kings, with the breaking down of Spanish and Portuguese power in the first part of the nineteenth century, that they began their modern history of accomplishment. Though the past hundred years have witnessed tremendous forward strides in government and in industry, no one can truly understand these great potential countries who does not visualize the story of the signpost and the people who turned in opposite directions to establish new nations.

Extent of Spanish possessions in America. When the Spanish colonies rose up to claim their independence during the first quarter of the nineteenth century (an act coincident with the Napoleonic usurpations in the Iberian Peninsula), the territory that Charles IV, king of Spain, claimed for his country comprised nearly half of the entire area of the three Americas. His royal claims began with the region near the sources of the Mississippi River, and reached to Cape Horn, including

7,000,000 square miles of territory. According to Alexander von Humboldt this vast stretch of land, representing the greatest potential colonial empire the world has ever known, was inhabited by 17,000,000 people.

"Within this vast region," said Henry Clay, "we behold the most sublime and interesting objects of creation; the loftiest mountains, the most majestic rivers in the world; the richest mines of the precious metals, and the choicest productions of the earth." Well might the Spanish minister, Manuel de Godoy, immortal at least for his astute diplomacy, exclaim that this magnificent domain made Spain "the Queen of the Two Worlds."

Spain's colonial policy. The title of this richest of earth's possessions lay in the name of the Spanish monarch and not with the Spanish people. His Catholic Majesty was the connecting link between Spain and her American colonies, — a fact that did not, for various reasons, result in a beneficent policy or an efficient governmental régime.

No greater tragedy is recorded in history than Spain's failure to meet the needs of the people of these richest lands of the earth. From the early sixteenth century to that eventful day when Admiral Dewey sailed into Manila Bay, the colonial government of Spain was neither a credit to the country nor to the men who were called upon, through these centuries, to represent the Spanish crown in distant parts of the earth. It was notable for its complexities, its overlapping authorities, and the venality of its officials. There were governments within governments and checks and counterchecks on officials, showing that no one trusted anyone else. The result was conflicting jurisdiction, jealousies, and political intrigue, while the land missed its rightful development, and industries failed to appear in constructive sequence.

In a stirring pamphlet quoted by Professor William Spence Robertson in his book "Rise of the Spanish-American Republics,"[1] Father Juan Pablo Viscardo y Guzmán, a Jesuit exile, declares that the history of Spanish rule in America could be

[1] From " Rise of the Spanish-American Republics," by William Spence Robertson. D. Appleton and Company, New York.

epitomized in four words, — "ingratitude, injustice, slavery, and desolation." The following excerpt from this remarkable pamphlet is a scathing testimony to the manner in which Spanish rulers threw away their priceless opportunities and rights to govern the new America.

The pretension of Spain to blind obedience to her arbitrary laws is based mainly upon the ignorance which she has permitted and encouraged, especially in regard to the inalienable rights of man and the imprescriptible duties of every government. Spain has attempted to persuade the common people that it is a crime to reason upon matters of the greatest importance to every individual; and consequently that it is always a duty to extinguish the precious flame which the Creator gave us for enlightenment and guidance. But despite the dissemination of such fatal doctrines, the entire history of Spain bears witness against their truth and legitimacy. . . . Nature has separated us from Spain by immense seas. A son who found himself at such a distance from his father would doubtless be a fool if, in the management of his own affairs, he constantly awaited the decision of his father. The son is emancipated by natural law. In a parallel case should a numerous people, who are not dependent upon another nation whom they do not need, remain subject to it like the vilest slave?

Our distance from Spain, which proclaims our independence, is, however, less significant than the difference in interests. We imperatively need a government in our midst for the distribution of benefits, the object of the social union. To depend upon a government two or three thousand leagues distant is to renounce these benefits; for such is the policy of the court of Spain that it aspires only to give us laws which monopolize our commerce, our industry, our property, and our persons, and which sacrifice them to her ambition, her pride, and her avarice.

That these Spanish colonists were influenced by the example of the United States in their struggle for freedom is brought out by the same writer when he exclaims, in his effort to arouse his countrymen from their lethargy:

The free enjoyment of these natural rights [of personal liberty] is the inestimable heritage which we ought to transmit to our posterity. . . . The valor with which the English colonists in America fought for the liberty that they gloriously enjoy shames our indolence.

Peoples. The population over which Spain was called upon to rule doubtless added to the officious and capricious character of her conduct in the New World. Of the 17,000,000 or more inhabitants which Alexander von Humboldt gives Spanish America at the opening of the nineteenth century, he estimated that about 7,500,000 were Indians, 3,250,000 were whites, 750,000 were negroes, with something like 5,250,000 composed of mixed races.

As a matter of fact the Spaniards recognized only two classes, the freemen and the slaves, the whites and the Indians being free and the negroes and their descendants slaves. As to the Indians, a study of the first three centuries of Spanish rule in the Americas reveals the fact that the red men of the southern American hemisphere complicated and at times (notably in Mexico) severely menaced the existence of Spanish rule.

No one can fully understand the Latin-American republics and their history without knowing the ethnic strains and types out of which the present population has sprung. The mixtures in general are whites, especially of Spanish blood (Portuguese in Brazil), with Indians and negroes. When Indians and whites mixed, the resultant strain was generally called mestizo (caboclo in Brazil), while the white and negroid blood intermixture brought about the so-called mulatto strain. Other examples of mixtures were the sambos, the descendants of Indians and negroes, and the pardos, the descendants of whites and mulattoes.

There were also the creoles, people of Spanish descent born in the Americas, between whom and the Spaniards there was a constant feeling of jealousy because the Spaniard born in Spain was preferred to the creole in the giving of royal and clerical patronage and offices. It is significant that the majority of the great liberators of the Latin-American republics were creoles, — such men as Simón Bolívar, Francisco Miranda, José de San Martín, Mariano Moreno, Miguel Hidalgo y Costilla, Agustín de Iturbide, and Antonio José de Sucre. In those early days, as at present, the leading Latin-American families of creole origin traced with pride their descent from the historic *conquistadores*. Even today one finds inhabitants of Lima,

Peru, who proudly trace their lineage back to Pizarro. These descendants of the South American conquerors and pioneers were persons of noble and aristocratic descent called *hijosdalgo*. They were the aristocrats of the New World, corresponding to the nobles of Castile.

Spaniards and their descendants were entitled to special privileges, particularly with regard to the learned professions. Certain of the lower caste, however (for example, the sambos and mulattoes), were debarred from the legal profession in Peru by a royal *cédula* to the viceroy of Peru, July 14, 1758.

Conditions in the early nineteenth century. Immediately before the uprising of the colonists for independence, Spanish America was well-nigh smothered by the weight of her own numerous and conflicting ordinances, if not actually buried beneath it. The current of the river of royal authority was clogged by a multiplicity of legislative decrees, while it was beginning to be further swollen by the inflow of small streams of colonial legislation smacking of independence. The complicated and burdensome system of royal taxation and the shortsighted commercial policy of Spain which insisted that the colonies trade only with herself, together with the attempts of the mother country to extend the influence of the Church so that the colonies might be under her control in spiritual matters as well as temporal, all combined to increase the misrule tremendously. The Spanish ship of state was being caught in the swirl of forces old and new, the old forces having the advantage of tradition and royal prerogative and a certain kind of unity, while the fresh power of youth and self-government dominated the new forces at work and spelled the doom of Spain in the Western world.

Not all at once does a nation or an individual founder. Small leaks in the ship and the corroding of antagonistic forces, the lack of attention to the elements of repair and reconstruction, these lay the seeds of dissolution and decay. New governments appear upon the ruins of old and worn-out governments, and never take the place of vigorous and upbuilding institutions. The Spanish republics of the New World rose upon selfishness, arrogance, inattention to the psychology of youthful colonies, and the conflicting authorities of Spanish colonial government.

The main tree was dying at the top when the new shoots of young life appeared at the base. When a government gets bad enough, there is hope for renewal. It is the half-and-half rule that paralyzes a country and saps the energies of a people. Take away the rightful opportunities of a people, show them a blank wall of arbitrary authority, confront them with sheer injustice, and you will find a people rising in their God-given strength to carve out their own chances and determine their own destiny.

THE LATIN-AMERICAN REPUBLICS

It was not without cause, therefore, that the people of the early Latin-American colonies of Spain and Portugal dreamed and worked for liberation from the mother country. Virtually every mistake that could possibly be made in colonizing was made by Spain during these centuries of her world-wide sovereignty of trade upon the seven seas. Meanwhile the example of the early pioneers and the development of republican forms of government in the United States were having their effect upon the people of the countries of Mexico, Central America, the West Indies, and South America. New leaders in the cause of independence arose, notably San Martín, who, after helping to gain independence for Argentina, extended his services to Chile and the west coast of South America, and Simón Bolívar, justly called "the Liberator," who worked from the northern Caribbean countries to the west and south. During the early part of the nineteenth century nearly all of Latin America became independent of its Iberian rulers and started to emulate the example of its sister republic, the United States.

Brazil (a notable exception to the other sections of Latin America, where the republican form of government began immediately), after freeing herself from Portugal, still retained her emperor until the year 1889, when this leviathan country sent Dom Pedro II back to Lisbon and followed her sister republics in forming a free state, with a constitution modeled on that of the North American commonwealth.

While at present virtually all of the Latin-American states have a form of government that is republican in name, they have yet far to go in making representative government a successful fact. There are still revolutions in certain of the smaller republics, and in many parts of Latin America domineering dictators have taken the place of presidents even during the last century. In Mexico General Diaz, with his long and firm control of that republic, brought about a certain amount of prosperity. The failure of his régime to afford an opportunity for a real democratic self-government, however, delayed for a generation the inception of representative rule.

The Spanish-American War, resulting in new responsibilities in the West Indies for the United States, brought that country into increased prominence in Latin-American affairs, while the building of the Panama Canal and the almost enforced trade of Latin America with the United States during and immediately after the World War opened new avenues of commerce between the two Americas. The need for a thoroughgoing acquaintance with Latin-American men and markets is therefore increasingly evident, and it is equally evident that such an acquaintance must necessarily be based upon a careful study of the historical background of these peoples, extending over four centuries, and of their evolution through checkered and stormy careers.

Much water will flow under the bridge before the countries of Latin America will fully recover from the exploitation of unscrupulous explorers and adventurous pioneers, from the devastation of the wars of independence, and from the mistakes of commingled monarchy and democracy in the last century. The result of this historical evolution, as it is becoming evident today, lies in the growing prosperity, both commercial and political, of these South American and Central American states. They are still depending to a large degree upon foreign initiative and foreign shipping for their industrial, scientific, and agricultural progress, but in an increasing number of cases Latin Americans themselves are coming forward to grasp the helm of leadership in the institutions and trade relationships most compatible with their temperament and manner of life and with the growing needs of their countries.

CHAPTER III

ECUADOR

GEOGRAPHY

With the exception of Uruguay, Ecuador is the smallest of the South American republics. Its area is computed to be all the way from 100,000 to 275,000 square miles, depending upon unsettled boundary disputes, dating from Spanish colonial days, over land that Ecuador is claiming from Peru. The area of the republic, however, is generally considered to be about 116,000 square miles, or a little more than the area of the state of Nevada or of Arizona.

Within this area the Andes attain their most abrupt and sustained altitudes. Here are the two noted peaks Chimborazo and Cotopaxi, each of which reaches an altitude of about 20,000 feet above sea level. Nowhere else in the world are there so many volcanoes in so small an area.

Two roughly parallel ranges of the lofty Andes, crossing the country from north to south, divide Ecuador into three distinct regions, easily recognized by the differences in topography, climate, vegetation, and animal life.

The first of these regions, the littoral, comprising the country between the foothills of the western Cordilleras and the Pacific Ocean, has an altitude varying from sea level to 800 feet above. Far from being a desert, this coastal region, from 150 to 200 miles in breadth, is a rich agricultural land, through which flow several rivers, chief of which is the Guayas. The plantations that border this river and its tributaries for many miles produce a large part of the world's cacao, vast amounts of sugar cane and rice, and various kinds of tropical fruits. This western lowland furnishes the straw from which Panama hats are made. These hats are the one important manufactured article of the whole region.

FIG. 2. Cacao beans drying in the brilliant sunlight on flat cars which are taken into sheds at night. A familiar scene in Ecuador. (Photograph by Ewing Galloway, New York)

The second region, or zone, of Ecuador is what is called the central or inter-Andean region. This consists of the mountains and plateaus with their interlying valleys. The eastern and western ranges of the Andes are joined transversely by other ranges called *nudos*, or knots, and between the *nudos* are basins. In the Ecuadorian Andes there are several *nudos* and their corresponding basins, all of which may be considered as one vast plateau, 300 miles in length from north to south and 20 to 30 miles in width, with an altitude ranging from 6900 feet to nearly 10,000 feet above sea level.

Here most of the white people and a great many of the natives live. A large part of the region is cultivated, and crops similar to those grown in the north temperate zone are raised.

The third region, in the eastern portion of Ecuador, is known as the trans-Andean country. It is a lowland region of forests and rivers. On the eastern side of the Andes the descent to the plain is less gradual than on the western side, and frequently a fall from 18,000 feet to 500 feet above sea level, or from the eternal snows of the Andes to the hot and steamy jungles of the Amazon valley, occurs within a few miles. Hundreds of swift-flowing rivers rush down from the Andes across this eastern lowland to the Amazon. Some of the rivers are navigable and thus open up large areas of forest and plains.

In spite of the fertility of the soil the trans-Andean region is largely unexplored and uninhabited by white men. The land has little value at present, chiefly because means of communication are lacking. It is only recently that any serious attempts at railway construction have been made.

In this forest lowland lies the territory disputed by Peru; but as it has produced only a comparatively small amount of rubber so far, the government of Ecuador apparently considers the territory scarcely worth fighting over.

Although the Republic of Ecuador derives its name from the fact that the equator passes through it, yet the word "equatorial," as usually conceived climatically, is scarcely a fitting adjective with which to describe this country. More kinds of climate are encountered in Ecuador than in any other South American country, — a fact explained by the marked differences in altitude. Only in the lowlands of the east and west can the climate be considered tropical, for in the high plateaus lying between the two parallel ridges of the Andes it is cool and pleasant, and high above the plateaus the lofty mountain peaks rise into a land of eternal snow.

The coastal region of Ecuador has a temperature ranging from 66 to 95 degrees Fahrenheit. It lies in the belt of equatorial rainfall, and, unlike the coastal region of Peru and northern Chile, the coast strip of Ecuador is wet. The cold Humboldt current, sweeping up from southern seas, absorbs the moisture of the sea winds which blow toward the Peruvian shore, but sheers to the west near the southern boundary of Ecuador, thus lessening its devastating effect on the winds and rains of that country.

The climate of the plateau is cool, and the rainfall is generally ample, amounting to 40 inches in Quito.

In the forest lowland the temperature is high, and the rainfall is sometimes as much as 150 or 200 inches a year. A large part of this rainfall occurs between the months of February and June.

HISTORY

Modern Ecuador can hardly be understood without a glance at its historical background. In the beginning of the sixteenth century Francisco Pizarro, after conquering the Inca empire and executing the Inca king, turned his attention to Ecuador. The Indians here resembled the Incas in their social and political institutions, and the type of country and occupations was virtually the same, especially in the elevated interiors. On December 6, 1534, the Spaniards entered Quito as conquerors; Gonzalo Pizarro, the brother of Francisco, was appointed governor of the province of Quito; and the Spanish custom, inherited from feudal times, of dividing the land among themselves and establishing feudal estates was put into practice.

After several arrangements and rearrangements of territory, by which Ecuador was included first in the viceroyalty of Peru and subsequently, in 1717, in the viceroyalty of New Granada, the movement for independence began, on August 10, 1809, when the citizens of Quito deposed the Spanish governor and established a revolutionary junta, or council. The Spaniards soon regained control, but in 1820 the citizens of Guayaquil declared their independence, and after a two years' struggle, in which they were aided by General Sucre of Venezuela, they succeeded (after the battle of Pichincha, on May 24, 1822) in making this independence an established fact. Although many of the people wished to join the Republic of Peru, Ecuador then became a part of the Republic of Colombia, which also included Venezuela and New Granada. After eight years of internal warfare, however, the union was dissolved. On August 14, 1830, a constitutional assembly was held, and Ecuador was declared a republic.

Since the coming of independence the country has had to battle with old and traditional Spanish ideas, and an ancient Spanish régime still reveals its influence in many of the customs of the inhabitants. Three centuries of misrule leave a decided imprint on any country. Spain's prohibition of immigration, together with her limitation of foreign trade, had an injurious effect on Ecuador, as it did on other Latin-American countries. There was a multiplicity of privileged classes here, including priests, friars, and nuns, and here the Spanish régime included elements of force, bribery, intrigue, cruelty, treachery, and rigidly prescribed religion, all forming doubtful aids to progress and industry. One of the Mexican viceroys expressed the policy of the Spanish rule, the effects of which are still evident in Ecuador today, by the following words: "Let the people of these dominions learn once for all that they were born to be silent and to obey, and not to discuss or to have opinions in political affairs."

Undoubtedly Ecuador will be long in attaining a constructive national organization worthy of her resources, for the country is more isolated by nature than the other South American republics, and is slower to accept modern progress. Ecuador has still to learn that revolutions are not the proper instruments for bringing about the sort of government desired by the people of a republic. The appeal to the ballot instead of to arms, the building up of self-confidence and self-reliance, the bringing of stability both to business and to legislative affairs, are results that cannot be attained quickly, and certainly not by the mere writing of a constitution full of high-sounding words. Republics develop from within out, and not in the opposite direction. Republican institutions must grow; they are never born full-grown.

Remembering these days of checkered history and the rapid changes of government secured, not without revolution in many cases, it was not astonishing to hear a prominent Ecuadorian reply, when asked what he considered to be the chief needs of the people at present, "Discipline, — personal and national discipline."

PEOPLE

The population of Ecuador, estimated at about 2,000,000, is made up of three distinct elements, — whites, mestizos, and Indians. The character of the Ecuadorians varies widely according to the particular class under discussion. Spanish is the language of the country, although many of the Indians of the interior speak Quichua.

Spanish. Most of the educated upper class are of Spanish descent. All the political offices are held by this class, though it represents hardly more than 2 per cent of the whole population. One finds among the wealthy and cultured Spanish-American families in Quito, the capital, the same type of customs and manners as in the larger Latin-American cities. The sons of the better families are frequently sent abroad for education, and many travel in Europe. Courtesy and ceremonial are everywhere evident among the higher classes of the Latin races, and there is a strong adherence to the dignity of historical associations connected with Quito and its institutions.

Mestizos. The mestizos, the race formed by the mixture of Spanish and Indian blood, make up about one fourth of the population, and are for the most part the artisans and small shopkeepers of the country. Some of them attain to position and wealth, and intermarry with the white people, but those dwelling in remote regions are likely to revert to the mode of life of the Indians with whom they associate.

Indians. The Indians, the largest element of the population, vary in type according to their place of habitation. The Indians of the coastal regions show signs of superficial advancement and Christianization, being, as a rule, hospitable and approachable. Those occupying the high plateaus, who form the bulk of the Indian population, are similar in appearance to the Indians found in Peru. They are called Quichuas and are descendants of the Incas. In color they closely resemble our North American Indians, but their features are less stern and warlike, and their stature is rather short and stocky. They compose the laboring class, and often their condition is lamentable because of lack of education and the necessities of civilization. They serve as porters, drovers, and farmers, and the women work as hard as the men.

It is said that the Indian laborers lack ambition, and care for little more than the barest necessities of life, but the conditions under which they work are the chief explanation of their attitude. Most of the land in Ecuador is still divided into large estates upon which the Indians and negroes are employed. The laborer buys his supplies at the plantation store. His wages are so small and his ignorance so great that he constantly falls into debt and becomes a victim of the law of the land, according to which no laborer may leave an employer to whom he owes money. Therefore he soon becomes little more than a slave, hopeless and forlorn.

The Indians of the Oriente, or eastern part of Ecuador, consist of some forty-six tribes, most of them wild and savage, but quite diverse in habits. Of these tribes are the famous Jivaros, or head-hunters. Though nominally under the government of Quito, they live so far away that the law of the land hardly affects them, and they are as primitive today as they were before the Spaniards arrived. The interest shown by collectors in the shrunken heads produced by the Jivaros created a great demand for them as curiosities, with such dire results that the Ecuadorian government strictly forbade traffic in these objects. The seeker after strange customs will not be disappointed if he visits these people.

The Jivaros live in scattered villages along the streams flowing into the Rio Napo and the Rio Paute, seldom venturing up the slopes of the Andes and always remaining below the 3500-foot elevation. The tropical climate has eliminated the question of clothes, with the exception of the loin-cloth. The principal weapons are bows and arrows, lances, and the dreaded blowpipe.

In other districts are found well-informed Indians of a somewhat lighter color than those of the west coast. Certain of these tribes have a strain of Spanish blood, and they attribute their treachery and cruelty to the fact that they would retaliate for the countless wrongs inflicted upon the race by the white men.

Negroes. In addition to the three races just discussed, there are some negroes, mulattoes, and sambos in Ecuador, the latter name being given to those who have a mixture of negro and Indian blood. The negroes were originally imported for labor in the coastal plain, where white men and the Quichuas could not endure the humidity and heat.

CITIES

Ecuador's chief handicap, which has continued through a century or more, has been the fact that its sole large entrance port, Guayaquil, has been disease-ridden. Until recently it was infested with yellow fever or bubonic plague, and, surrounded as it is by marshes, with malaria. There was little or no attempt on the part of the inhabitants to improve this condition, because of the fear that if the port became usable by foreigners to any great extent, local business would be ruined and the country overrun with outsiders. This fear of the *gringo* is still found in certain remote sections of Latin America.

Through the notable efforts of the Rockefeller Foundation and a more up-to-date local government than is usual for Ecuador, these unhygienic conditions have been abolished, and Guayaquil is now a perfectly healthy port. Since its cleaning up there remains no important city or district in all of South America where unusual dangers of disease menace foreigners or natives. With this accomplishment Ecuador has opened a door through which new business, travelers, and foreign capital and industry may safely enter, and has given promise of future accomplishments like those of other sections of the west coast.

Guayaquil, founded in 1535 by Sebastian de Benalcazar, has undergone a wide range of vicissitudes, having been sacked by buccaneers, shaken by earthquakes, and nearly destroyed by fires several times. Today it is Ecuador's chief commercial city and harbor.

When one approaches Ecuador from the south and sails up the Guayas River to Guayaquil, one is impressed by the contrast between the tropical and picturesque surroundings of the city and the dull and rainless coast left behind. The river is deep enough to admit vessels drawing twenty-three feet of water as far as Guayaquil, and along its shore, for a considerable distance about the city, is the *Marina*, or quay wall, which is capped with stone.

The port proper is about 3 miles long and from $\frac{1}{2}$ mile to 1 mile broad, with a depth of water varying from 12 to 40 feet. Above Guayaquil several rivers unite with the Guayas, among them the Daule and the Babahoyo. Here the tide is very strong, running at eight knots an hour both up and down the river. Boats going in either direction take advantage of this tide, which is felt for a distance of from 50 to 80 miles up the rivers.

The harbor of Guayaquil is picturesque, for many small sailing vessels and boats bring native products from the interior. The merchandise of the larger ships in the harbor is transferred to the shore by lighters at the rate of about eight tons per hour from each hatch of the ship. Attention is being given to the dredging of the river and the construction of docks, both of which will greatly facilitate trade operations.

Guayaquil is the capital of Guayas, the largest province of Ecuador, and is the Valparaiso of the country. It has a population of about 100,000. The municipality is now provided with very good streets, an excellent water supply, and other modern improvements. Reënforced concrete is being used in the construction of the buildings as a protection against earthquakes. Most of the sidewalks are protected by arcades from the heat of the sun and also from the tropical rains. The sanitary improvement of the city and harbor will change its whole future commercially.

The wide range of industries in Guayaquil is indicated by its sugar mills, breweries, distilleries, shipyards, sawmills, tanneries, and factories for the manufacture of shoes, ice, candies, soap, and candles.

The commerce of the city is associated with the banks (established with national capital), with the export houses, and with retail trade. A number of wholesale importers and exporters "cover" the entire republic, including Quito, from Guayaquil. Direct importing is carried on by certain retail merchants, among whom may be found representatives of many nationalities, including Americans, English, French, Germans, Spaniards, Italians, and Syrians. There are also Chinese traders here.

The large import houses of Guayaquil send their agents to visit the principal houses of the interior, selling their goods against *pagarés*. The larger firms keep these documents in their safes until the customer pays, but the smaller houses, which cannot afford to have so much money outstanding for so long a time (especially as many of the payments are delayed for as long as a year from the date of purchase), have the *pagarés* discounted at the banks, at the rate of 9 per cent. A considerable amount of goods is sold on stricter terms in the city itself and also in smaller places on the coast. The coast towns are good buyers of provisions, clothing, and hardware for the use of the laborers.

The principal products exported through Guayaquil are cacao, coffee, vegetable ivory, gold, cotton, and Panama hats.

Guayaquil maintains telegraphic connections with the outside world through the All-America Cables, and with the principal places of Ecuador through the Compañia Nacional de Telégrafos. There is also a telephone system which aids trade communication with the interior. Traffic on the Guayas River is carried on by steamboats and smaller boats.

Guayaquil is reached by steamers from Colon (Panama), about 800 miles to the north, and from Callao (Peru) to the south. It is connected by railway with Quito, 297 miles to the northeast. The greater part of the import merchandise for the interior passes through this port, and the customhouse here constitutes Ecuador's chief source of revenue.

Quito. Situated on the plateau between the two mountain ranges, more than 9000 feet above sea level, Quito, with its 100,000 inhabitants, is one of the loftiest capitals in the world and shares with Mexico City and Cuzco (Peru) the glory of having a civilization older than that of the Spanish-American era. In spite of the fact that the city lies almost on the equator, the days and nights are pleasant throughout the year and the climate is healthful, owing to the altitude.

Quito and Guayaquil are by far the most important centers of Ecuadorian life. Today Quito does not resemble the old Indian city so much as it resembles a Spanish city of the colonial type. It is supplied with electricity, but still no heating is provided for the houses, although the temperature often drops to the freezing point. Water is obtained from the adjoining mountains and is delivered to the city through the public fountains or brought to the houses in earthen jars. Ice too is brought from the mountains, but it is also manufactured in the city. A tramway is now being operated in Quito, and such modern improvements as sewers and pavements have been installed, all of which were sorely needed.

Among the conspicuous buildings of the capital are the governor's and president's palaces, the archbishop's palace, the municipal buildings, the national library, the Sucre theater, and the astronomical observatory. Most of these are worthy of the Spanish tradition for ornate architecture.

A number of retail and some wholesale firms which do a general distributing business are located in Quito, but the volume of trade transacted here is far less than in the city of Guayaquil, Quito being the political rather than the commercial center of the country.

The principal products of the region around Quito are cereals, sugar, and cattle. The industries are mainly agricultural, cattle-breeding being especially important. Other industries that are notable are ivory-carving, weaving, embroidery, and lace-making.

Cuenca, the capital of the province of Azuay, is situated about 9000 feet above sea level on the Matadero River, 70 miles southeast of Guayaquil and 190 miles south of Quito. It has a population of about 30,000. While it now ranks third in importance in Ecuador as a commercial center, it will easily take second place when its railways are completed. A survey has been made for a railway between Cuenca and Huigra, the nearest railway station, — a distance of about 92 miles.

There are several important manufacturing plants at **Ambato**, a town situated on the Ambato River near the northern side of Chimborazo and having a population of about 20,000. Among its industries are wine-making, textile manufacturing, and tanning. The cities of **Loja** and **Latacunga**, with populations of about 10,000 and 16,000 respectively, are engaged in agricultural industries. The products of **Ibarra**, 60 miles north of Quito, are cotton, sugar, cereals, fruit, cattle, and salt. This city has 5000 inhabitants.

The coast cities, **Bahia de Caraques**, with a population of about 3000, and **Esmeraldas**, with about 5000, are located in fertile regions. Bahia exports a considerable volume of cacao beans and ivory nuts. A railway runs from here into the interior, and consequently the city is an entrepôt for a rich district. The trade depends largely upon the business houses of Guayaquil. Esmeraldas, 90 miles northwest of Quito and about 300 miles north of Guayaquil, is also a center of exchange for a rich agricultural section. It is the headquarters for a number of exporting houses and mining companies, and considerable business is carried on. Although the products of this section are largely agricultural, straw hats are manufactured and gold is mined here. Raw products shipped through these ports have to be loaded by the old method of small boats and lighters.

In several of these smaller places railways have been started, the aim being to carry them back into the country, and eventually to Quito and even across the mountains into the Amazon region. With increasing facilities for transportation these ports will be enlarged and modernized.

GOVERNMENT

Ecuador is a centralized republic under a constitution promulgated December 23, 1906, and having the usual legislative, executive, and judicial branches. Foreigners are guaranteed equal rights with citizens under the constitution, and there is both freedom of worship and of the press. The provision that women may exercise all rights granted to Ecuadorians and have the free administration of their property even when married is notable. The privilege of establishing banking institutions and the holding of lands is granted alike to aliens and to Ecuadorians. The provinces are administered by governors appointed by the president. The departments, or cantons, have political chiefs; the parishes have political lieutenants; and the municipalities have presidents.

The president of Ecuador is elected for a term of four years by direct vote. He may not be reëlected until after two terms have elapsed. The national Congress is made up of the Senate and Chamber of Deputies, there being thirty-four senators, two for each province. There are fifty-three members of the Chamber of Deputies, one for every 30,000 citizens. Both senators and deputies are elected by direct vote. Every male citizen over twenty-one years of age who is able to read and write has the right of suffrage. Congress, meeting each year, is in session at Quito, the capital, for sixty days.

There are seventeen provinces and one territory. The Galapagos Islands, 600 miles from the mainland, form the only territory.

ARMY AND NAVY

The Ecuadorian army consists of about 5000 officers and men, with 100,000 men in the first and second reserves. There is a mining and torpedo section, a telegraph and telephone corps, and a sanitary section; all these were created during the year 1910. The navy is almost negligible, consisting of only a few small vessels.

CURRENCY

The *sucre* is the unit of value and is equivalent in normal times to $0.487 in United States currency; it is subject to fluctuation, however. One hundred *centavos* equal one sucre, and ten sucres make a *condor*, which is equivalent to one pound sterling. Smaller coins of silver and nickel are current. Ecuador adopted a gold standard in 1898.

EDUCATION

Higher education is provided by a university at Quito (which was founded in 1787), by universities at Guayaquil and Cuenca, and by a law school at Loja. There is also at Quito a military school, the National Conservatory of Music, the National Academy of Fine Arts, and provisions for commercial instruction. An agricultural school is maintained by the government at Ambato.

A reorganization of public instruction was begun in 1915, and there are now about 1500 public and private schools in Ecuador, with more than 100,000 pupils. Each province has at least one secondary school, while in the country there are a number of special schools. About one person in sixteen attends school.

In spite of the preponderance of the Indian population the children of the Indians are receiving practically no schooling, and only one fourth of the children of the peons receive any kind of instruction. According to the Ecuadorian law a proprietor having ten or fifteen children on his estate is required to have a school for them ; the enforcement of this law, however, is something of a fiction. As in India, parents are loath to give up their children for school attendance, especially in the country, where there is little appreciation of education and where the whole civilization is backward. The wages that children receive for shucking ivory nuts usually outweigh the attraction of school in the mind of the Ecuadorian agriculturist.

PRODUCTS AND INDUSTRIES

AGRICULTURE

Ecuador depends entirely upon its agricultural resources, being less fortunate than the other Andean states in the matter of mineral wealth. The leading product is cacao, of which Ecuador produces an important part of the world's supply. Other products are the tagua nut, or vegetable ivory (one of the principal items in the export trade of the country), sugar, oranges, cotton, and tobacco ; in addition a considerable number of coconuts are exported from the coastal lowlands. The plant yielding the straw from which Panama hats are made grows abundantly in Ecuador, and consequently the straw-hat industry is most important.

Cacao. The chief industry of Ecuador is the cultivation of the cacao tree, which is indigenous to tropical America. This tree was cultivated in Mexico and in Peru at the time of the Spanish conquest. It is found wild in the forests of the Amazon and Orinoco basins up to an altitude of about four hundred feet. The cultivation and curing of its fruit is a somewhat complicated process, and Ecuadorian cacao is noted for its quality.

The alluvial section of the Guayas River system is the principal locality for the growing of cacao, with a large part of the suitable lands available still unused. The increasing use of chocolate in all its forms throughout the world has directly affected the cultivation and export of this product. For example, when the product known in the United States as "Eskimo Pie" became popular, the amount of cacao exported by the large trading houses increased appreciably.

The cacao tree bears after seven or eight years, and if it is in good condition it yields from one to two pounds of the dried beans at each harvest. The tree has a life of from seventy to eighty years, and before it dies it sends forth a new growth from the root, which, with proper pruning, continues to grow for another seventy or eighty years. This tree is being planted in increasing numbers throughout Ecuador. There are about 6000 cacao farms in the country, with a total of 80,000,000 trees and a yearly production of nearly 100,000,000 pounds. Guayaquil cacao is characterized by the shape and aroma of the bean, and is easily distinguished from the cacao of other districts. The better grades of cacao contain a large percentage of theobromine, which greatly increases their value.

Coffee. Among the cultivated crops of Ecuador coffee is next to cacao in importance, and the yearly production ranges from 4000 to 5000 tons. More than half of this amount is exported, chiefly to Chile.

Ecuador is peculiarly suited to coffee-growing, and with an increased labor supply will become a great coffee country.

Coffee cultivation requires much more care and more costly machinery, however, than the cacao industry, and therefore necessitates a larger population than Ecuador now has.

Vegetable ivory. Vegetable ivory, or ivory nuts, is another of the chief products of Ecuador. This ivory is used as a substitute for the elephant-tusk product in the manufacture of buttons, umbrella handles, chessmen, poker chips, and similar articles. The manufacture of ivory-nut buttons is an important industry, giving employment to many workers in Europe and in the United States.

Vegetable ivory is the fruit of a stunted palm fern called the tagua palm, which grows to a height of from ten to twenty feet and has a short trunk and fronds of large, bright-green, feathery leaves. The blossoms of the tree give off a strong perfume. Each tree bears from four to nine drupes, which are pulpy fruits somewhat similar to the coconut. They are about the size of a man's head and weigh nearly twenty pounds. In them, inclosed by a woody, fibrous wall, are the ivory seeds, which are of a hard, white composition, fine in grain, and very similar to real ivory. The development of the tagua palm is affected by climate, and there is a considerable difference between the fruit grown in a region of excessive rainfall and that of a drier region.

Vegetable ivory is found only in Colombia and Ecuador. In Ecuador the trees of large size grow in the provinces of Manabi and Esmeraldas. The average annual export is about 40,000,000 pounds, which is taken by the United States, Italy, and Spain; formerly the bulk of this trade went to Germany. The nuts used to be harvested whenever the Indians "saw fit," in the phrase of a Guayaquil trader. Of late years, however, the government has issued a decree outlining the conditions of cultivation and harvest of the crop in the different districts, thus guaranteeing to the exporter some degree of certainty as to the time of delivery of this product.

Panama hats. Panama hats were originally produced in Ecuador, and this country still leads in their manufacture. The reason why the name *Panama* is given to these hats is explained thus by one authority [1]:

[1] Pan American Union, Ecuador — General Descriptive Data

The name originated during the gold rush to California seventy or eighty years ago. Returning prospectors purchased the hats in Panama, and so they became known as Panama hats, in the same way as hats purchased in Paris are known as Paris hats. At first no attempt was made to disguise the origin of the hats. Everybody in Panama knew them to be made in Ecuador (or in northern Peru), and sold them as such. The name of Panama, however, attached itself to the hats in the United States, and is still used. Hats made of toquilla straw are now made in Colombia, Panama, and Central America, and all of them together, with the Ecuadorian and Peruvian hats, are indiscriminately known in the United States as Panama hats.

The plant yielding the straw from which these hats are made is known as *paja toquilla*. It grows wild in the low, damp forests of Ecuador and is extensively cultivated in some localities. The shrub grows from six to ten feet in height, is fanlike in shape, and resembles the saw palmetto.

It has been said that Panama hats were woven under water. This is not strictly true, but the straw is kept moistened while the weavers are plaiting it. Most of the weaving is done by native women and children, and the industry is especially well developed in Jipijapa, a town in the province of Manabi. The monthly production of hats in this province runs into hundreds of dozens. The hats are exported from the ports of Cayo and Manta to the United States, Mexico, Cuba, and Europe. Some hats, also, principally those manufactured in Cuenca, are sent to Guayaquil and exported from that port.

Cotton. Cotton exports from Ecuador have been increasing since 1917; before that time there was almost no production. Cotton cultivation, however, has been affected by the lack of experienced workers. There are a number of cotton mills operating in Ecuador, as well as ginning mills, and others are being constructed. High prices for all kinds of cotton goods are greatly stimulating cotton-growing, as is also the policy among exporting firms that have ginning mills. These firms distribute cottonseed free of charge to all applicants desiring to grow cotton.

Kapok. Kapok, or "lana de Cibo," is the product of a tree of the same name which grows in all the river districts near

FIG. 3. Packing Panama hats for shipment

Guayaquil, attaining a great height. It is used in France and Germany chiefly for stuffing pillows and mattresses, but of late years, because of its light weight, it has been found to be an excellent material for use in life buoys. The better quality is cleaned by hand rather than by machinery, and is used in the manufacture of silk articles. It is also mixed with cotton textiles. In the United States interest has been aroused in this product, and it is probable that the entire Ecuadorian export will be taken by American manufacturers. The amount exported in a recent year was more than 200,000 pounds.

Other agricultural products. Tobacco is cultivated in the lowlands of the rivers, and up to an altitude of 3000 feet rice, manioc, bananas, quinine, breadfruit, and other tropical products are grown. All these articles are exported from the country.

LIVE-STOCK INDUSTRY

Cattle are raised throughout the country, and several hundred tons of hides are exported yearly, the bulk of these going to the United States. Goatskins and alligator skins are also exported. A considerable number of sheep are raised in the highlands.

Ecuador possesses excellent grazing lands, both on the coast and in the interior, and the cattle industry is bound to expand. Before the railroads connecting with the interior were built, Ecuador imported many cattle from Peru; now it is possible to bring down the cattle of the mountain regions, which are of better quality than those of the coastal regions.

FOREST INDUSTRY

Balsa wood, a well-known product of Ecuador, is distinguished by a remarkable lightness of weight. It weighs 7.3 pounds per cubic foot, while cork weighs 13.7 pounds, spruce 27 pounds, and ebony 73.6 pounds. The South American quebracho, which is the heaviest and hardest wood known, weighs 91 pounds per cubic foot. The significant feature of balsa wood is the fact that its cell structure is such that the transmission of heat is prevented. It is used for lining ice boxes and the refrigerators of vessels, and in making life preservers and rafts.

Rubber production in the trans-Andean region of Ecuador, while not large, is sufficient to be encouraging for the future of this industry.

MINING

Gold. Gold is the only mineral produced to a considerable extent in Ecuador. This mineral has been found in all parts of the republic, but the most important mines are at Porto Velo. Almost the entire output of these mines is exported to the United States.

In the province of Esmeraldas several enterprises for gold-mining were established between the years 1899 and 1905, but in spite of a large expenditure of capital there were no important practical results. The river Sapato is said to have the richest deposits of gold, although it has not been exploited; platinum has been found there combined with the gold deposits. The other rivers containing gold in profitable quantities are the Caypas, the Bogotá, and the Cochavi. Modern mining machinery, including powerful pumps, is being imported from the United States.

Petroleum. Crude petroleum and pitch wells are found near Santa Elena, the wells belonging to private individuals, who dispose of their products, without refining, for fuel to the Guayaquil factories. The actual production covers only a small part of the home consumption.

A recent law in Ecuador taxes all petroleum mines in operation 6 per cent of the value of gross production, estimated at prevailing prices in Guayaquil. Undeveloped mines are also taxed.

Coal. Valuable coal deposits are known to exist south of the Huigra, but a railway is necessary for their proper development. Most of the coal used in Ecuador is imported from foreign countries. The principal importers and users are the Guayaquil-Quito Railway, the two cruisers belonging to the government, and the gas company at Guayaquil.

Other minerals. Besides the minerals mentioned Ecuador has rich deposits of mercury, copper, iron, lead, and silver ore, but these have been only slightly developed. Platinum has been discovered north of the Gulf of Guayas. There are deposits of sulphur in the Pichincha and Chimborazo districts, and a small amount is obtained from volcanic deposits on one of the Galapagos Islands.

EXPORTS AND IMPORTS

Ecuadorian exports in 1924 amounted to $29,800,000, cacao furnishing about one half of the total. The principal exports to the United States, in addition to cacao, were mineral earths, ivory nuts, Panama hats, and crude rubber.

Before the World War European countries supplied the bulk of Ecuador's imports, but during the war and since that time the United States has led all other countries. In 1924 Ecuador's imports amounted to $25,000,000, and of this amount imports from the United States made up $10,000,000. The United Kingdom came next with $6,000,000, while Germany, Italy, France, the Netherlands, Belgium, and Peru, the countries next in order, furnished imports valued at about $7,500,000. The chief articles of import were textiles, foodstuffs, hardware, and machinery.

TRANSPORTATION AND COMMUNICATION

Waterways. There is an active coast and river service with excellent means of transportation on a number of navigable rivers, twenty or more steamers and some sailing vessels being employed in this service. The Guayas River, navigable for river steamers as far as Bodegas, 40 miles from Guayaquil, is the most important waterway. The Daule River is navigable for 60 miles and the Vinces for 50, while the Esmeraldas, Santa Rosa, Santiago, and Mira rivers are all used for short distances, especially in the rainy season. The Amazon River, called in Ecuador the Marañon River, is navigable for almost its entire length, making it possible to reach the eastern slope of the Ecuadorian Andes by way of Brazil on the Amazon River and its tributaries.

Railways. The railway communications of Ecuador are for the most part by the Guayaquil-Quito Railway, which was com-

pleted between these two cities in 1908. This line carries the
largest part of the traffic existing in the country. The regular
passenger trains, running only in the daytime, make the trip of
297 miles in two days, whereas formerly fifteen days were
commonly required for the journey by mules or on foot. An
extension of this line is being made to Ibarra and Tulcan, and
thence west to Esmeraldas. Several short lines run up into the
interior from the ports, and the total extent of railway lines in
operation is about 500 miles. Commercial development in
Ecuador, as in many Latin-American countries, is waiting for
better internal communication. A number of railways are in
the process of construction.

Roads. Transportation in the interior is carried on by mules,
burros, or *carretas* (carts), as there is a good road from Ambato
to Quito. Until the advent of automobiles, omnibuses were used
on this road for carrying passengers. As the roads to Quito are
continually mountainous, freight carriage is considerably less
costly on the trip back from the city than on the trip to it;
moreover, there is less demand for cargo to the coast, and proprietors of mule transportation are glad to accept any freight
at a much lower rate.

Wireless and telegraph service. Wireless stations have been
established in Quito, Guayaquil, and at other points. There is
a station on Chatham Island, one of the Galapagos group. A
long-distance telephone service connects Guayaquil and Quito,
and there are more than 5000 miles of telegraph lines in the
country, with some 200 offices.

ECUADOR'S COMMERCIAL FUTURE

The two events which have already begun to change radically
the commercial and industrial life of Ecuador are the opening
of the Panama Canal and the thorough renovation of the port
of Guayaquil. The extent and quality of Ecuadorian resources,
hardly yet discovered and inadequately developed, calls for a
large expansion in investment during the next decade. Exporters and importers no longer need to depend upon transient
and irregular sailings for the conveyance of their commodities.

The foreign commercial man or traveler no longer needs to fear quarantine in an unhealthy port. Ecuador, perhaps more than any other rich Latin-American country, will have its commercial achievements in the future. Judging from the many indications of progress at the present time, it would seem that this future will not be long delayed.

THE GALAPAGOS ISLANDS

A part of Ecuador seldom considered as such is the group of Galapagos Islands which lie about 600 miles off the coast, almost on the equator. Together they have an area of 2870 square miles, and their population is estimated from 500 to 600. Of the sixteen islands in the group only two, Albemarle and Chatham, are inhabited to any extent. Originally the islands had Spanish names, but, being used as a place of refuge for English buccaneers and whalers, they were later given English names.

The islands are so named because huge tortoises (*galápagos* in Spanish), some of them weighing 600 pounds and said to live 200 years, are found there. The only other place where such tortoises exist is the Mascarene Islands, in the Indian Ocean east of Madagascar. Although there are great numbers of them, they are being exterminated because they are good as food.

The group is volcanic, and the fertile areas are on the southern and eastern sides, where the benefits of the moist trade winds are obtained. The climate is tropical, although the cool Humboldt current moderates it.

There are several good harbors and opportunities for ship shelter among the islands. Albemarle Island, with an area of 1650 square miles, has considerable grazing land where herds of wild cattle are found; and on Indefatigable Island, with its 390 square miles of area, there is well-watered land suited for agricultural purposes. Chatham Island has been settled since 1839, having been originally a convict settlement. It now has a governor and a population of some 500 people.

Cane sugar and other agricultural products are cultivated here, and in some parts there are large herds of cattle. Other products of the islands are hides, fats, and sulphur.

CHAPTER IV

PERU

Peru needs capital and increased population, through immigration, to develop the boundless resources of this country. Here are vast coast lands which may be made most productive through proper irrigation; a supply of water almost inexhaustible, capable of supplying power and energy for industrial development; immense natural pasture lands; mountains containing almost every known mineral; forests timbered with rare woods; rivers with thousands of miles of navigable water, connecting the heart of the South American continent with the Atlantic Ocean. Here is some of the best possible fuel, both in anthracite and petroleum; also guano, phosphates, and nitrates. Here is a seaboard extending 1300 miles, along an ocean stocked with an abundance of sea food of all varieties, and here is a remarkable climate, extraordinary in its possibilities of securing many crops on the same land throughout the seasons. — G. K. MORKILL, former manager of the Peruvian Corporation

A LAND OF SPLENDOR AND TRAGEDY

For many people Peru exerts a stronger dramatic and historic appeal than any other Latin-American republic. It is the tragic land of Spanish conquest, attended with every cruelty of the Middle Ages, over the most advanced and peaceful race of Indians known to the Western Hemisphere. It is the land which, more than any other, by its illimitable treasures of gold excited the cupidity not only of the Spaniards but of the buccaneers of every land.

It was no uncommon thing for English buccaneers to intercept Spanish vessels heavily laden with gold and treasure. No less an adventurous seaman than Sir Francis Drake, sailing in the *Golden Hynde* and accompanied by sixty ships, all heavily armed for battle, scoured the Pacific for treasure. Of him it is said: "His ballast was silver, his cargo gold and emeralds. He dined alone with music." [1]

Humboldt records that between the discovery of Peru and the year 1800 the Old World took more than $2,500,000,000 worth of treasure from the New World of Latin America.

[1] Millicent Todd, Peru — A Land of Contrasts, p. 92. Little, Brown & Company.

Peru is one of the most tragic lands in history. Tens of thousands of the bravest of the *conquistadores*, infused with religious fanaticism and greed for gold, here laid down their lives, battling not only against the native races but among themselves, and against the cold of the mountains and the heat and thirst of the desert. Almagro, the doughty lieutenant of Pizarro, is said to have lost 10,000 of his army of 15,000 through the hardships of a single campaign. One historian states: "In twenty-five years more than 8,000,000 Indians were worked to death in the mines of Peru. . . . In a century nine tenths of the people had been destroyed by overwork and cruelty." [1]

The era was, as Millicent Todd has aptly put it, "an extravaganza of destruction matched only by the scale of nature's waste."

Upon Peru the heavy hand of the Spanish Inquisition fell with all its lurid, terrorizing cruelty. The crimes committed in the name of religion in this ancient land stagger the imagination of later civilization. In the year 1570 the "Blessing of the Inquisition" had been conferred upon Peru by Philip II. "At first heresy, then blasphemy, polygamy, insulting servants, and opposition to jurisdiction, were punished by whipping, banishment, prison, and death by fire. In all the cases the goods were confiscated." [2]

Lima, the "City of the Kings," witnessed the splendor of the viceroys to an extent beyond that of any South American or Central American city in the years when these loyal representatives of Spain ruled all of South America from Guayaquil to Buenos Aires "as by the divine right of kings." The following graphic description by Millicent Todd, in her book "Peru — A Land of Contrasts," [3] gives a glimpse of the extravagant pomp and royal ceremony practiced here in the seventeenth century, — all at the expense of the Inca treasure.

The viceroy was served only by titled Spaniards. He was drawn about by six horses, with sounding of trumpets, and a personal guard of two hundred Spaniards, "for the safety of his person and to support the dignity of his office." The royal seal, his insignia, rode under a royal flag upon a horse saddled with black velvet and a gold

[1] Millicent Todd, Peru — A Land of Contrasts, p. 91. Little, Brown & Company.
[2] Ibid. p. 92.   [3] Ibid. pp. 85–87.

tissue foot-cloth, and was received with deep bows. The viceroy was allowed three thousand *pesos* to go to Callao, five miles away, and sixty thousand ducats a year for personal expenses.

Greeted with a jewel sent to meet him halfway, the viceroy reaches the bay of Callao. Throughout Lima, the City of the Kings, — founded "with God, for God, and in His name," — the streets are hung with rugs and tapestry and adorned with green boughs and triumphal arches. (On the arrival of the Duque de la Plata, in 1682, eighty million *piasters* were spent to pave the streets with bars of silver.)

"First comes a host of Indian warriors in feather pomp. The city militia with pikes and weapons glittering, the stocks of their guns embossed with gold, the noble guard on horseback, ... university professors in brilliant gowns, the royal council and officials, the magistracy in crimson velvet lined with brocade of the same color ... the chamber of accounts, the audience on horses with trappings, the scepter-carrier, heralds in armor with uncovered heads, the master of the horse with drawn sword, accompanied by four servants in livery, pages with the captain of the watch, and lastly, on a throne of red velvet whose silver staffs are carried by the members of the corporation, while the *alcaldes* hold the cords, all in velvet caps and gowns of incarnation color, rides the viceroy under the royal banner and a canopy of cloth of gold. Officers of the royal household, the royal guard in full armor with spear and shield, bring up the rear on horseback."

The procession moves between companies of halberdiers in a blaze of trumpets, bells, and drums, under showers of flowers thrown from carved balconies.

"When they reach the plaza the whole company faces the cathedral and is received by the archbishop and by the superiors of the religious orders; trumpets cease, knights dismount, and the multitude sings a Te Deum.

"The procession again mounts and accompanies the viceroy to the palace gates.

"Five days of bull-fights follow, and prizes are bestowed upon those who make the most ingenious compositions in praise of the viceroy. . . ."

As if the wholesale destruction of both Indians and Spaniards — a veritable holocaust of calamity, the fruit of inordinate vanity in extravagant display — were not enough, Lima, the most gorgeous and beautiful city of the world at that period, was utterly destroyed by an earthquake in the year 1746. If one were superstitious, such a calamity might seem the natural consequence of all this saturnalia of human cruelty, greed, and fanaticism. In its effects the earthquake equaled the Japanese disaster of 1923, when the city of Yokohama and a part of Tokyo were almost entirely destroyed. The proud city of Lima was demolished in four minutes, except for twenty buildings said to have remained standing. Callao, with its 5000 inhabitants, was destroyed by a tidal wave induced by the same seismic upheaval. Famine and fever followed in Lima, and historians record that in the ensuing year five hundred and sixty-eight lesser earthquakes shook this stricken city.

Seventy earthquakes of a more or less destructive nature have occurred in this region since 1870; and while the tremors and quakes in recent years have not been serious, there is always the fear that these lesser shocks may portend another wholesale disaster like that of the eighteenth century.

A LAND OF EXTREMES

Any study of modern Peru must always take into account not only the dark background of three centuries of scourges and destructive forces but also the fact that Peru is a land of violent extremes. Ten times the size of New York State, with an area nearly as large as the entire Atlantic slope of the United States, it has jungles and icy table-lands; tropic sun and arctic frosts; rainless lands and reeking equatorial swamps; misty seacoasts and the rare atmosphere of mountain fastnesses. In the central Cordillera rises the greatest river in the world, while much of the coast is a barren desert, craving water.

The natural resources of Peru offer another example of an extreme in their very abundance. In the past, however, they have often been the source of trouble rather than of profit. The gold in the mountains of Peru attracted the early Spaniards, who swept the land of treasure; guano islands provided riches without requiring great initiative, and caused all kinds of complications with other countries; while nitrate fields induced the

War of the Pacific, in which Peru lost her valuable deposits to Chile. These have never been regained.

Some countries, like some individuals, are destroyed by their inheritance. That Peru is today a prosperous republic proves beyond a doubt the virility of the new race of men whose fathers achieved the emancipation of the country from the heavy yoke of Spain on July 28, 1821. From that time onward Peru really began to live and to fashion her future destiny. Her greatest tragedies and her saddest misfortunes seem now to be behind her. She is facing the morning, and the day ahead should be her brightest, most stable era.

GEOGRAPHY

Peru is divided into three physiographic regions, out of which it would seem at first sight difficult, if not impossible, to carve any worth-while, unified civilization.

The desert region is a long and narrow, arid, sandy waste, almost rainless and sunless, lying along the coast. In one of its fertile valleys is Lima, the Peruvian capital. The cold Humboldt current sweeps along this Peruvian coast, while the moist winds from the eastern jungles lose their vapors in the dry or frozen ridges of the Andes. Thus the Peruvian littoral is abandoned to a dry and cheerless climate. In some places the mountain spurs almost crowd Peru into the sea, the width of the coastal region ranging only from twenty to about eighty miles. With no natural harbors like those of Brazil, Peru is obliged to have her cargoes loaded and unloaded in open roadsteads, while in many places passengers land almost literally upon sand dunes, where a few storehouses and huts are the only semblances of civilization.

The great Sierra plateau rises to an altitude of from 10,000 to 14,000 feet above sea level. Although it lies in southern latitude comparatively near the equator, its elevation makes existence for white men almost impossible. On both sides the vast Andean Cordilleras, consisting of three fairly well-defined ranges, — maritime, central, and eastern, — drive their barren ridges straight through the midst of the country from north to south, rising to an average height of about 17,000 feet. In places there are snow-white peaks which reach the prodigious altitude of more than twenty-two thousand feet.

Beyond the mountain barriers and the plateau is the Peruvian jungle, called the Montaña, which stretches 800 miles from north to south. This largest geographical section of Peru has great rivers and is luxuriant in forest and tropical growths, but is so thoroughly sequestered from the world by the lofty Andes on the one side and the steaming Amazonian wilderness on the other that it has not as yet been fully explored. In this perfect tropical garden of possibility, securely locked away from Peru herself by the devices of nature, live wild and savage Indians, with only a few white men in the rubber section.

The area of Peru, estimated according to the way one considers the various boundary disputes to be settled, embraces between 533,916 and 722,000 square miles. Most of this territory is useless for agriculture without irrigation. The elevated plateaus contain the largest portion of the population, for the most part Indians, and are fertile; but they are so securely shut in by mountains and so lacking in railways as to have a retarded development. The tropical Montaña, on the sunny side of the ranges, requires an altogether different type of workers and methods of cultivation, revealing the same general conditions as prevail in tropical Amazonian Brazil.

Nature seems to have raised effective barriers on all sides to prevent the growth of Peru. Inaccessibility and inadequate communications are severe handicaps to progress, and make unity of civilization and national feeling very difficult.

Although the country lies within the tropics, Peru has almost every type of climate. At Lima the mean temperature is about 66 degrees Fahrenheit, but during the summer (from December to March) it rises at times to about 80 degrees. The winter temperature never falls much below 50 degrees. Lima has a damp and disagreeable atmosphere, more or less sunless and chilly in winter. The lack of heating apparatus increases the discomfort of foreigners who are accustomed to steam-heated houses.

As one climbs to such points as Arequipa, nearly 8000 feet above the sea, the sun is discovered again and the climate is

FIG. 4. Llama pack train starting from a mine yard on one of the high peaks of the Peruvian Andes. Each llama has strapped on its back a small but heavy bag of copper concentrates. (Photograph by Ewing Galloway, New York)

delightful. The temperature ranges from 50 to 60 degrees, and there are many signs of tropical foliage and luxuriant vegetation.

The climate farther up the Andean summits on the lofty plateaus is California-like in the valleys by day but cold, cheerless, and bleak by night. Those who visit this section are bound to admire the Inca's good sense in worshiping the sun. It is the only ray of comfort in the Andean Cordilleras. When *soroche* (mountain sickness) adds its discomfort to those of the baneful variegated climate, one discovers reasons enough why these vast spaces, so rich in agricultural possibilities, have been so long unoccupied save by Indians, and never fully explored.

The Montaña affords a variety of climate such as would be expected in an equatorial country where the altitudes range from heavily wooded mountainsides, from which streams run down into the valley of the Amazon, to jungles and swamps that are not more than 1000 feet above sea level.

The climate of the west coast of Peru is in decided contrast to that of the west coast of Europe. To the latter the Gulf Stream brings climatic health and prosperity, while to Peru the cold Humboldt current seems to be only another count of nature against the country. From Tumbez, where Pizarro landed, to Coquimbo, Chile, a distance of 2000 miles, is found one of the driest and most sterile regions in the world, — sunless, rainless, and at first sight seeming unfit to be the habitation of men. That in such a barren stretch of land there have been already notable material and cultural accomplishments is an assurance of the future of this race of men and their country.

HISTORY

The historical story of Peru, from the time when Francisco Pizarro landed on its coast, in 1532, to the battle of Ayacucho, on December 9, 1824, when, through the efforts of Simón Bolívar and his able lieutenant, General Sucre, the last Spanish royalists were defeated and driven from the field, reads like a story of the "Thousand and One Nights." Those who are familiar with Spanish will find the momentous events of these three centuries graphically narrated by the historian Garcilasso de la Vega and other able Spanish writers; the classic story in English of the *conquistadores* and the long-suffering Incas is found in Prescott's "Conquest of Peru." Without a careful reading of this remarkable piece of historical narration, which gives, detail upon detail and character upon character, a vivid picture of these fighting years, no one can be fully equipped to understand this weird and mysterious country or its people of Indian or Spanish ancestry.

When Pizarro landed, the Inca empire embraced fully one half of the entire South American continent, and the Andean region could boast of a civilization which it has never seen since that time. In fact, the deterioration (when it has not been utter destruction) of the Peruvian Indian by the cruel practices or the inaction of the Spaniards has been steady throughout the years, from the time when Pizarro treacherously put to death Atahualpa, the emperor of the Incas (on August 29, 1533), took possession of his enormous treasure, and enslaved his people, whose abilities had been devoted to the peaceful arts of agriculture and mining rather than to the arts of war.

Pizarro, having been appointed governor of the newly conquered territory, founded the city of Lima, on January 18, 1535, and named it "the City of the Kings." Here he governed the country until his death on June 26, 1541. Immediately after Pizarro's death, Don Cristóbal de Vaca ruled as governor for three years, and then, in 1544, the famous viceroyalty of Peru was established, the first viceroy being Don Blasco Nuñez Vela, who arrived at Lima on May 17, 1544. At first the viceroy had jurisdiction over the entire continent of South America, but later the viceroyalty was divided into three sections, New Granada being created in 1718 and Rio de la Plata in 1776.

During the next century and a half forty viceroys came and went. Each one of these added something to the royal extravaganza of waste, and each one agreed with his predecessor in the policy of enslaving the Indians, destroying their civilization, and failing to replace it with anything that could rebuild a fallen nation. There were occasional uprisings of Indians meanwhile, especially that notable one of 1780, during which Tupac Amaru, a descendant of the Incas, was ruthlessly beheaded and his head stuck on a pike in the famous old Plaza at Cuzco. This terrorizing spectacle was authorized and enforced by the Spanish viceroy Francisco de Toledo. Another Indian uprising occurred in 1781, when an even more frightful slaughter was visited upon the Indian leader and his family. These atrocities were, in a way, a presage of the fall of the Spanish rule, for twenty years later began the first conspiracy against the authority of Spain, which ushered in the Peruvian war of independence.

The famous Argentine general, San Martín, who assisted Chile to free itself from the Spanish power, came to the aid of the Peruvians in 1820. Admiral Lord Cochrane, commanding the Chilean fleet, assisted him, capturing and destroying the Spanish force and attacking the fort at Callao. On July 9, 1821, San Martín made a triumphant entrance into the city of Lima, and on July 28 the independence of Peru was formally declared.

The first constitutional congress of the present Republic of Peru met on September 20, 1822, and the first president of Peru, Don José de la Riva Aguero, was inaugurated on February 28, 1823. From this time forth the modern political history of Peru has been checkered. Many revolutions have occurred, some of them attended by considerable bloodshed. For the last two decades, however, the country has received large numbers of foreign industrialists; foreign business houses for export and import have been established; and despite political unrest property has been safe and business has proceeded with little interruption on the part of politicians and revolutionists.

PEOPLE

The present population of Peru is estimated at about 4,500,000, the number being somewhat dependent upon the permanent fixing of the boundary lines between Peru and neighboring states. This population includes about 900,000 whites, 1,200,000 mestizos, about 2,000,000 Indians, 100,000 negroes, and 50,000 Chinese. There is an increasing number of foreigners in Peru, among whom Germans, British, and Americans, employed in mining, agricultural, and industrial enterprises, are prominent.

Whites and mestizos. The white people, for the most part of Spanish descent, naturally form the upper class of the population. They control most of the wealth and government offices of the country. The mestizo race is the result of intermarriage between whites and Indians, and the line of distinction between them and the whites is not always sharp.

. **Indians.** This race constitutes the preëminent problem in Peru, as far as the inhabitants are concerned. The Indians are not only an important factor numerically, but upon their labor and industry the vast majority of the population depends. "All Peru lives off the Indians" is a common saying in this country, for the Indians cultivate the land and make a living for the remainder of the inhabitants, so that anything that affects their condition, or notably increases their value, directly affects the Republic of Peru. They constitute the chief asset of the farm, and assure constant labor without fear of strikes or fluctuation of wages.

To be sure, the Peruvian Indian of today is a far lower type of being than the Indian of the time of the Incas; but his suspicion of the white man, his blank ignorance, dishonesty, and intemperate habits are traits that are traceable to the conditions to which he has had to submit for more than four hundred years. It is significant that during the old Inca régime the sins of lying, stealing, and adultery were punishable by death, the resulting conditions of that time forming a rare contrast to the pathetic conditions existing today among the rural population of the mountains of Peru. The Indian still speaks his own tongue, Quichua, maintains his own native customs, and goes to his favorite chicheria, where he drinks his chicha, the national drink. Chewing the ever-present coca leaves, he plods along in his sullen, monotonous way, more or less indifferent to the few white rulers who, for the purpose of farming, have established themselves in the plateaus of the Andes.

The Indians are hard-working and frugal. Many of them have small holdings of land on the slopes of the Andes, where they can raise enough to feed their families. They have markets in the chief towns of the Andes, and there are no more picturesque sights in any other part of the world than the scenes in these markets. Indian women sit by their little mats on which they display their goods for sale, — the socks which they have knitted or the ponchos which they have woven, — with the little spindle on which they are spinning the wool for their clothing always dangling from their arms.

Many of the Indians live on small patches of land frequently owned by the community or by a large landholder. When the land is sold, the Indian passes to the new owner along with the other chattels. His wages are a mere pittance, often no more than fifteen cents a day; but in some cases, on the great estates, he is given a small plot of land for his own use. On some of the large haciendas there are as many as four hundred families, who live there as did their fathers. The Indians with their llamas carry the produce of the estates along the winding Inca highways to the market and to the nearest shipping point, often many leagues away.

Throughout the valleys around Cuzco one sees these descendants of a noble race herding their sheep on the hillside, or, in the cities and towns, carrying immense burdens on their backs and trotting along by the sides of their llamas or mules, literally like cattle. There is here a striking absence of any determined or widespread attempt, like that made by Colonel Rondon in Brazil, to train the Indian industrially or to fit him to be a more intelligent and useful factor in the coming commercial, industrial, and mining development of the country.

Among the Indian population must be numbered the 200,000 or more inhabitants of the Montaña region. These Indians, however, are savages, and have little or nothing to do with the rest of the country.

Negroes and Chinese. The people of these races are employed on the sugar and cotton estates of the coast, but as a rule they are inferior to the Indian laborers.

Peruvian characteristics. The traits and culture of the upper-class population stand out in decided contrast to those of the Indian population. In Lima particularly one finds the remnants of a Spanish aristocracy probably unsurpassed, in all Latin America, in culture or in the use of the pure Spanish tongue. For many years Lima, long the seat of the viceroys, was the

Fig. 5. An Indian market place at Juliaca, Peru. Juliaca is a railway junction and trading post halfway up the Andes

chief city of the Spanish colonial possessions in the New World. One still finds here old Spanish families who proudly trace their ancestry back to Pizarro and the *conquistadores.*

Here is society life, gayety, and the penchant for pleasure, all of which are quite incongruous with the life and occupations of many of the small towns of the country, which are largely given up to mining and commercial enterprises. There is more of the old Spanish atmosphere in Lima than is found in the modern cities of Argentina, Chile, or Uruguay. The viceregal court, so long the center of the best society of the continent, has left its imprint, as has also the Church, since here, in the person of the archbishop, was centered for many years the authority of the Catholic Church in the Southern Hemisphere. It was Lima, with its loyal patriotic population, that adhered to Spain and the Catholic king long after other Latin-American countries had followed the example of revolt set by Mexico and Argentina.

The Limeños are prouder of their Castilian inheritances than of growth in commerce and the shipping business. Most of the retail trade is in the hands of Frenchmen or other foreigners; the Englishmen and Germans, with some Americans, attend to the shipping, while Americans are largely owners and developers of mining and many industrial enterprises. Immigration, much needed in this land of opportunity, has not set in strongly as yet.

Courtesy abounds, as does enjoyment of the everyday pleasures of life, while world commerce and trade in general are left to foreigners, who are both more capable and much more adaptable to business activities. It is a commentary upon the commercial and industrial capabilities of the Peruvian Spaniard that virtually every important material enterprise of his country has been inaugurated and developed by foreign capital and foreign promoters.

There seems to be but little love for the rural districts on the part of the more cultured classes, Lima and the leading cities of Europe being far more attractive to them. Many Peruvians find the United States, especially New York, a pleasing place to visit, and in some cases to live in.

Fondness for dress and for horse-racing, with an occasional bullfight, and a great devotion to music and the fine arts, are general, and there is a significant literary coterie. Members of old Spanish families are inclined to keep somewhat apart, to have their pleasures among themselves, to intermarry, and to move in a restricted orbit, filled largely with the ancestrally elect.

The Peruvian men spend a large part of their time at their clubs and at public amusements, in which women have a very much smaller share than in the United States. There is, indeed, a semiseclusion practiced by the women remindful at times of the old days when Spain and Portugal were influenced by the customs of the North African Moors.

The influence of the medieval Catholic Church and monastery is more potently present in Peru than in any other large country south of Panama. The religion of the country is strongly Roman Catholic, and the devotion to the Church on the part of the women is particularly noticeable. Among the men, however, there is found a tendency to freethinking, if not to agnosticism, similar to that existing in other Latin-American countries of the present day.

As to the moral integrity and honesty in business of the Peruvians, there are varying opinions. There is a growing tendency for the men of the better class to engage in business affairs, in spite of the fact that this is somewhat *infra dig*. The more important Peruvian concerns are trustworthy, and while it is necessary, in Peru, as in the United States or any other country, for the foreign trader to look up the credit standing of his customer, there is little doubt that the Peruvian may be compared favorably with other Latin Americans in business matters.

In amiability and courtesy the Peruvians are hardly surpassed by any people. To fail in courteous gentlemanhood is to be *declassé* in this country, which has not lost traces of the old Spanish school of courtliness. As the English William of Wickham would say, "Manners maketh the man" in Peru. There is, moreover, a real sincerity in Peruvian politeness, and the North American business man, if he is successful, finds himself forgetting some of his Northern brusqueness and "do-it-now" practicality while he falls in line with the more leisurely and polite business manners of this nation.

The following words, uttered by a Peruvian gentleman, hold considerable truth :

You in the United States are a wonderful people, — wonderful in your organization and practical sense. We in Peru are people of feeling and emotion; we live from the heart. The ideal is to unite American practicality with Peruvian feeling; either one alone spells failure.

Like other Latin Americans, the Peruvian may not be the equal of the Northerner or the Englishman or the German in the facing and overcoming of business obstacles. No one can surpass the Peruvian in theoretical intelligence or in eagerness and enthusiasm in beginning a new venture, but too frequently he lacks the dogged perseverance of the Anglo-Saxon in carrying his undertakings, despite obstacles, to a successful finish.

Everyone takes life more easily in these equatorial latitudes than in more virile climates, the obligation of keeping appointments on time is far less strict, and there is no particular disgrace adhering to a man, young or old, who is "without a job."

In the matters of kindliness and attention to the amenities of daily intercourse, without which dollars and skyscrapers are alike inadequate to make the world a pleasant place in which to live, the Peruvian can teach us much. He is master of the fine art of living in harmony with his fellow men.

CITIES

Lima, the capital of the republic and its most important city as far as importing and exporting are concerned, has a population of more than 140,000. It is situated on the Rimac River and is 8 miles from Callao and 110 miles from the famous Cerro de Pasco mines. The city is the commercial center of the country and the headquarters of all the manufacturing plants in the vicinity. Wholesale jobbing firms send their representatives from Lima to canvass and solicit business in the interior, even to the remote towns of the Andes. Retail firms make direct importations, and foreign trading houses have their branches or agencies here.

Fig. 6. A group of business men. These men had much to do with giving Lima the Gran Hotel Bolívar, one of the finest hotels in South America. (Courtesy of the *Grace Log*)

Lima contains some of the oldest and best examples of Spanish architecture and church buildings, notably the old Spanish cathedral on the famous Plaza Mayor. The corner stone of this cathedral was laid by Pizarro, the Conqueror. In the neighborhood are many interesting suburbs and fashionable resorts.

In 1895 the pioneer electric-light plant came into existence in Lima in spite of much opposition due to Peruvian conservatism. The wires were considered a menace, and the public in general preferred other forms of illumination to this new and mysterious agent. After the company had struggled along for several years, one of Lima's far-seeing business men, Dr. Mariano Ignacio Prado y Ugarteche, became actively interested in the concern. He recognized the almost limitless source of cheap water power in the Rimac River, and, forming a syndicate, began an expansion which has been continuous. The result has been a highly satisfactory lighting capacity for the city, electric lines between Lima and Callao, the construction of large power plants, and service of high-class efficiency to suburban points. Many railway lines have been electrified. Dr. Prado and Señor Emilio Godoy were associates and pioneers in this electrical expansion which has meant so much to the capital and to the surrounding country of Peru.

All the power units of this enterprise and all the cars, with a few exceptions, are of American manufacture, while nearly all the accessories and supplies are from the United States. Today, with the increase of electric traction in Lima and vicinity, the New Yorker would feel quite at home during the rush hours, for the street-car conductors of Lima are said to be better " packers" than their brothers in the North.

Electricity is the universal artificial light in Lima, and even the poorest hut is usually possessed of at least one light. The increasing use of water, another innovation of the latter part of the nineteenth century, has added bathtubs in the homes, automatic electric pumps that lift the water to the roofs of the houses, and the attendant modern conveniences of an up-to-date city. Many of the small places of industry, like printing offices and woodworking shops, have installed electric power.

The use of electricity is rapidly extending to other cities and towns throughout the country.

Arequipa, the second city in Peru, has a population of about 50,000. Situated in the southern section at an altitude of 7750 feet, it has a delightful climate with a mean temperature of about 58 degrees Fahrenheit. It is located on the Chile River, about 100 miles from the port of Mollendo, and is reached by way of the Southern Railway. Arequipa is on the main line to La Paz (Bolivia), which is reached by way of Puno and Lake Titicaca. The city is the most important distributing point for the entire southern district of Peru, and important wholesale jobbing firms which import directly are located here. A large export trade is carried on in such products as alpaca, sheep's wool, and hides. The principal products, other than those mentioned, are cereals, cacao, rubber, gold, and silver. There are a number of local industries.

About Arequipa stand the famous Peruvian volcanoes Misti and Chachani, and in the distance the giant snow-covered mountain of Ampato and the still greater Coropuna, which, with a height estimated at over 22,000 feet, is a rival of the Bolivian Illampu and the Chilean Aconcagua. There are famous watering places in the neighborhood, as well as the present site of the Harvard University Observatory.

Arequipa was originally a rest-house station on the Inca track from Cuzco to the sea. Along this pathway the Incas maintained a service of swift Indian runners, who even carried up fresh fish from the sea to the monarch at Cuzco. Unlike Lima, Arequipa escaped the occupation by the Chilean army. Its people take great pride in its old families and ecclesiastical institutions.

Callao, the capital of the littoral province of Callao, has a population of about 50,000. It is located on the Bay of Callao and is the port for Lima, from which it is 8 miles distant. Callao is 1300 miles from the Panama Canal and 480 miles from Mollendo. It has a semitropical climate, and its principal products are sugar, cacao, sulphite of silver, and guano. There are a number of industries in the city, and in addition custom-house brokers and ship chandlers carry on business there.

The harbor of Callao is the safest on the Pacific coast of South America, and most of the foreign trade of Peru passes through this port. The chief exports are bars of copper, silver, and gold, and cotton. Furthermore, Callao is the only Peruvian port with modern docking facilities. At several of the other ports the long iron pier is used in landing cargo, which is taken from trains that come on the pier directly from the interior.

Cuzco, the ancient capital of the Incas, and now the capital of the department of Cuzco, lies at a height of 11,400 feet above sea level. It is 506 miles from Mollendo, on the Southern Railway, and its principal products are wool, hides, cacao, rum, rubber, sugar, and gold. Indians form the larger part of the population of 30,000 and furnish the chief market. The leading business houses are branches of those located in Lima. The city is visited by many travelers who are interested in the ruins of the Incas as well as those of an earlier civilization that are found here and in the vicinity. Cuzco has a famous cathedral, a university, and a notable plaza.

Trujillo. A good distributing business is carried on among the large sugar plantations in the vicinity of this city, which has a population of 22,000. Dealers import directly from this place, and certain of the Lima houses have branches here.

Ayacucho has a population of 20,000. It lies at an altitude of about 9000 feet and is a mining town, its principal products being gold, silver, copper, and cobalt. Silver filigree and pottery are made here. Ayacucho was the scene of the last struggle of the Spanish army against the allied Peruvian and Colombian armies under the Venezuelan, General Sucre.

Iquitos is a port of 20,000 inhabitants. It lies east of the Andes on the left bank of the Amazon and is the center for rubber, the chief article of export from here. The principal commercial communication of this port is with the eastern rather than with the Pacific side of the republic, for the overland trip from the west requires from seventeen to twenty-five days, according to the season. It is usually reached by way of Pará (Brazil), on the Amazon. Besides rubber, its products are ivory nuts, cotton, timber, balata, chicle, rice, cottonseed, live stock, and hides.

Cerro de Pasco, the capital of the department of Junin, has a population of 15,000. It is 110 miles from Lima and lies at an altitude of more than 14,000 feet above sea level. It is a famous mining district. The Cerro de Pasco Mining Company, conducted by a group of North Americans, carries on the principal business of the town through its large copper mines. These mines, the highest in the world, are worked at an elevation of over 12,000 feet. The altitude places a severe strain upon the foreigner, and care is taken to see that the hearts and lungs of all the workers are examined before they are allowed to engage in work at these mines.

Mollendo, one of the leading ports of Peru, is known far and wide as one of the most difficult landing ports in the world. It is the entrepôt for goods shipped into southern Peru and Bolivia, and is the starting point of the railway between the Pacific and Lake Titicaca and other inland regions. Its exports consist largely of alpaca wool and sheep's wool. It has a population of about 10,000.

Among the northern ports of Peru are **Paita** and **Talara,** located in the rapidly developing petroleum region. **Eten,** with a population of about 3000, and **Pimentel,** with a population of some 2000, are the ports through which the agricultural wealth of a considerable section is taken, especially such products as sugar, rice, tobacco, cotton, hides, honey, and coffee. The principal industry of Eten is the manufacture of Panama hats. **Salaverry,** 196 miles north of Callao, is the port for Trujillo, and is the one through which the products of the famous sugar district in the valley of Chicama are shipped. **Pacasmayo,** about 300 miles from Callao, is one of the chief ports of northern Peru, with exports of cotton, cattle, and hides. It is in the neighborhood of large sugar, rice, and cotton mills.

GOVERNMENT

Peru is a centralized republic, with a constitution that was revised in 1920. The country is divided into departments and provinces, which are further subdivided into districts and smaller divisions. The president is elected for a term of five years and is ineligible for immediate reëlection. Suffrage is given to each Peruvian male citizen over twenty-one if he is a master-employer, a taxpayer, a real-estate owner, or is able to read and write. The national Congress consists of the Senate and the Chamber of Deputies, and meets annually for a session of ninety days. In addition, there are three regional congresses, or legislatures, in the north, center, and south of the republic, which sit for thirty days annually; their enactments, transmitted to the executive power of the nation for enforcement, are subject to veto by the chief executive. There are also the usual departments of government, similar to those of the other Latin-American republics.

ARMY AND NAVY

The Peruvians are subject to military service, and the standing army approximates 10,000 officers and men. The navy consists of a number of cruisers, several submarines, and a flotilla of vessels used in the river service on the Amazon. There are both military and naval aviation schools, and the republic has received certain expert supervision from the United States in its military organization.

CURRENCY

The Peruvian currency is based upon the unit called the *libra*, or Peruvian pound, equivalent to the normal pound sterling, or $4.8665. A libra is divided into ten *soles*, and one sole is equal to a hundred *centavos*. The country is on a gold basis, and all calculations, financial or commercial, are made in soles or libras. Paper money has been in circulation since the World War.

EDUCATION

Education, especially higher education, is fairly well served, but there is a great need for primary schools and compulsory attendance throughout the rural and remote districts. The percentage of illiteracy is large, and probably less than half of the children of the republic attend school. American teachers have been present in Peru for some time, and the post of director-general of education has several times been occupied by an American educator appointed by the president of Peru.

In 1921 a new education law was put into effect, reorganizing the various branches of public instruction according to more modern methods. While there are some agricultural and vocational schools in addition to the regular primary and secondary schools, there is great need for more of them. They are needed especially in the mountainous districts for the training of the Indians. The famous University of San Marcos at Lima, founded in 1551, is the oldest seat of learning in the Western Hemisphere, and there are smaller universities at Arequipa, Cuzco, and Trujillo.

PRODUCTS AND INDUSTRIES

In economic as well as in industrial affairs Peru is coming to a point, in her centuries of rather slow development, where she is able to take advantage of her almost limitless resources.

During the period of the Inca régime, a great agricultural era, the Indians proved that land could be cultivated and cattle raised not only in the narrow valleys of the Sierra region but also on the high Andean table-lands. Many of the irrigation works of the Incas are still evident in Peru, and even now these furnish the best means of irrigating the desert lands.

In colonial times, by reason of the quest for and the development of its rich minerals, Peru came to be one of the leading mineral nations of the world, both as to output and as to natural resources. Early in the period of independence the great guano wealth of the Chincha Islands and the nitrate wealth of southern Peru were developed. Later, however, Peru lost much of her guano industry to her creditors and her nitrate provinces to Chile. Then began her present era of industrial development, together with a renewed cultivation of her agricultural and mineral riches. It is to these last developments that Peru owes her present status and progress; and it is upon these agricultural and mineral resources that she depends for her future prosperity.

AGRICULTURE

Sugar. The leading agricultural product of Peru is sugar, which is also an important item in her exports. The introduction of new machinery and of modern improvements in cultivation has marked the last decade, and Peru's annual output of sugar has reached more than 300,000 tons. Immediately after the war with Chile, in 1879, the value of sugar exports from Peru amounted to only $1,355,773, while in a recent year the value of Peruvian sugar reached a total of more than $70,000,000.

An excellent example of a modern Peruvian sugar mill is the Central Chicama mill of Cartavio, an establishment that compares favorably with any similar plant in the world, both as to modern equipment and as to general administration. Hacienda Cartavio is an estate of about 30,000 acres, of which 8500 are devoted to growing sugar cane, the remainder being used for other crops and for pasture. It is situated on the coast of Peru about 25 miles north of Salaverry. The estate is flat, with a slight slope toward the west, and modern agricultural machinery of all kinds is employed on it. The village contains about 2500 inhabitants and forms a complete community in itself, with the large sugar mill as a center. There are 975 buildings, including laborers' and employees' houses, warehouses, shops, two schools, a moving-picture theater, a church, and a hospital. There are 2000 horses, mules, and oxen in use, and a railroad furnishes transportation to the mill. The sugar cane of Hacienda Cartavio and that of the neighboring estate of Chiclin is ground here, the grinding continuing throughout the year except for a short period in March or April. The capacity of the mill is 2500 tons of cane per day, an amount which gives evidence of the possibilities for increased sugar production in Peru with the increasing use of modern equipment.

The sugar-cane-growing departments in the coast zone are La Libertad, Lima, Lambayeque, and Ancachs, while the Sierra region, as well as the Montaña, also produces sugar. Many of the large sugar haciendas employ thousands of workers. The yield of sugar cane per acre in Peru is more than double that in the state of Louisiana. Salaverry and Puerto Chicama are the chief sugar ports, while Trujillo is one of the chief centers of the industry. The three largest users of Peruvian sugar are Chile, the United Kingdom, and the United States.

Cotton, which is raised on the Peruvian seacoast in Piura and Ica, is another outstanding agricultural product. While in 1887 the Peruvians exported only about $300,000 worth of cotton, in a recent year this figure reached over $50,000,000. The modern cotton mills about Lima and other sections of the coast are turning out a product the quality of which promises much for the future of this industry. The cotton from Piura, especially, has a very high reputation in world markets; the fiber is long and similar to that of Egyptian cotton. Cotton-growing is conducted under irrigation, and over 150,000 acres of land are devoted to it.

The local textile factories use an average of over 5000 tons of cotton annually and have a total annual capacity of some 55,000,000 yards, — an amount not produced every year, however. One large cotton mill, situated on the Central Railway of Peru, about ten miles up the Rimac valley from Lima, has 730 looms and 15,000 spindles, with 450 operatives. The cotton used is known as "Peruvian smooth," which has a longer staple than American "middling." The largest cotton mill in Peru is the Inca mill, situated on the outskirts of Lima, which employs 600 operatives and has 850 looms and 24,000 spindles. In all there are now in operation in Peru ten cotton mills and five woolen mills (which consume much raw cotton). These are equipped largely with modern machinery and represent an investment of several million dollars.

Other agricultural products. The variety of Peru's agricultural resources is revealed not only in the products of its different climates (which range from the approximately temperate to the tropical) but in the manifold crops of the sunny valleys on the eastern slope of the Andes, where coffee, vegetable ivory, rice, wheat and alfalfa, sugar, cascarilla, and nearly all the products and fruits of the soil native to tropical regions may be found. Rice is also grown in the department of Libertad and two or three other coastal sections, about 70,000 acres being devoted to the cultivation of this product. Cacao is raised in the Andean valleys, while vineyards along the coast in Ica and Moquegua recently yielded a million-dollar crop. Coca, the plant from which medicinal cocaine is obtained, is an important product in the Montaña district, especially in the Cuzco valley, while tobacco, wheat, maize, and potatoes are largely produced.

LIVE-STOCK INDUSTRY

The hide industry is of growing importance, goat and kid skins being of particular value. Alpacas, sheep, and llamas, the wool-bearing animals of Peru, furnish an annual export of wool amounting to nearly $10,000,000 in value, of which alpaca wool constitutes about two thirds. In addition to the amount exported, much wool is used for manufacturing purposes within the country.

FOREST INDUSTRY

The production of rubber in the Amazon River district is of great commercial importance, and the development has been rapidly advancing in the past two decades. In 1887 the production was only 976,800 pounds, while in 1915 the amount reached was 6,600,000 pounds. In spite of the competition of plantation rubber from Java and Sumatra the Peruvians maintain faith in the future of their rubber zone because of its unlimited resources.

MINING

Petroleum, the principal mineral product of the country, is being exploited to a considerable extent in the coast district of Peru, particularly in the northern section. Other oil fields are being developed in other parts of the country. One of these fields is in the department of Puno, near the Bolivian boundary. Seven fields are in operation at the present time. In 1903 about 300,000 barrels of petroleum were produced in Peru; by 1923 the production had increased to nearly 6,000,000 barrels. A small refinery is located at Zorritos and a large refinery at Talara, which is the leading petroleum port of Peru. Fuel oil, gasoline, and naphtha are exported to other South American republics and to the United States.

FIG. 7. Weighing crude rubber at Putumaya, Peru, jungle station. The Peruvian Indians are the main dependence of the country for agricultural and mining labor. (Photograph by Ewing Galloway, New York)

Copper. The department of Junin, in which is located the well-known Cerro de Pasco copper industry, ranks highest as a producing section. It is here, where copper is found in the largest quantities, that North American enterprise has constructed one of the most complete mining plants in the world, with holdings that have been developed at the cost of millions of dollars.

In 1903 the production of Peruvian copper amounted to about 20,000,000 pounds, while in 1923 it had increased to more than 80,000,000 pounds.

Gold made Peru famous and was the chief means of attracting to its shores the early Spanish adventurers. Today Peru ranks twelfth among the gold-producing countries of the world and third among the countries of South America.

The most important formations of gold are found upon the eastern slopes of the Andes, and it is estimated that one auriferous deposit in this region contains more gold than has ever been found in California. The traveler in Peru will be told how these mines were at one time worked by the Incas, that the Inambari River and its tributaries are veritable gold pockets, and also that the mountain regions of the Sierra proper are rich in quartz lodes. The scale of Peru's wealth in the latter mineral is indicated by the fact that in the southern part of the country there is a group of quartz lodes, many of which cross a deep valley, ascend the slopes, and traverse a high plateau. The outcrop of these lodes is said to be from 2000 to 3000 feet above the lowest level of the valley, while the lodes extend downward to unknown depths. The great difficulty in the mining of gold is the lack of sufficient capital to install machinery and to afford proper transportation.

Silver is found throughout the Andean region of Peru, particularly upon the high plateaus and slopes of the eastern side of the mountains. Much silver is found in connection with the copper-mining in the Cerro de Pasco district, and it is often found associated with lead.

Vanadium. This is an important mineral product, in the production of which Peru holds the first place in the world. Most of the world's supply of vanadium comes from the Andean section of Peru. Almost all of this mineral exported by Peru goes to the United States, where it is used for a great variety of purposes, — for example, to give greater strength and ductility to steel, and in the manufacture of glassware and pottery, as well as in the preparation of dyes.

To the Vanadium Corporation of America credit must be given for successfully initiating the mining of this useful metal. The mines are located in the department of Junin, west of Cerro de Pasco on the eastern slope of the main range of the Andes, and are some 16,000 feet above sea level. A railroad has been installed for transportation, and this development promises an ever-enlarging future.

Other minerals. Beginnings are being made in the mining of bismuth, quicksilver, coal, zinc, sulphur, and such rare metals as tungsten and molybdenum.

Summary. The agricultural and mineral developments which have been discussed, while already large, await increased irrigation in the desert portions of Peru, improved means of transportation, and economic and industrial pioneers like those who have already done so much, who are willing to back their enterprises with capital, initiative, and constructive genius. The government of Peru is sufficiently stable at present to insure capital investment on a large scale, and the foreign firms already securely intrenched in this rich republic indicate the economic possibilities of the future.

EXPORTS AND IMPORTS

In 1924 the total foreign trade of Peru was valued at nearly $210,000,000, of which exports accounted for $122,000,000 and imports for $88,000,000. Exports to the United States were valued at about $41,000,000, and imports from that country at $34,000,000.

The leading articles of export in 1924 were cotton, petroleum and its products, sugar, and copper. Alpaca and sheep's wool, and gold and silver, were also important. The United Kingdom took more exports than any other country, with the United States ranking a close second.

More than one third of the Peruvian imports in 1924 came from the United States, while the United Kingdom furnished about one fifth of them. Foodstuffs, manufactures of iron and steel, and textiles were the principal articles imported.

TRANSPORTATION AND COMMUNICATION

The Peruvian railways have been preëminently responsible for the achievements that have been noted in the preceding pages. This country of almost unparalleled altitudes boasts about 2000 miles of railway, some of which is remarkable for its scenic beauty. The two important systems are the Central Railway of Peru, which mounts the Andes to 15,865 feet above the sea, and the Southern, which traverses the most historic region of South America and includes a boat service on Lake Titicaca, nearly three miles above sea level.

The Central Railway of Peru, called "the eighth wonder of the world," was planned and engineered, and its most difficult section built, by Henry Meiggs, an American engineer and soldier of fortune. The trip from Lima to Oroya, 138 miles from the Pacific Ocean, through the famous Galera Tunnel, where the line runs through Mount Meiggs at an altitude of 15,665 feet above sea level, must be taken in order to appreciate the stupendous engineering task by which this American engineer and promoter opened the lofty heights of the Cordilleras to railroad transportation and modern industry.

At Anticona, on the Morococha branch of this road, the railway ascends to a height of 15,865 feet above sea level, the highest point reached by any standard-gauge railway in the world. As the traveler descends into the town of Oroya, lying between the two Andean ranges at a height of more than 12,000 feet, the vistas presented in all directions are probably unsur-passed in variety and grandeur in any part of the globe. Here are fields of corn and vast stretches of sugar cane, tall palms and banana trees. One is reminded that in spite of these great altitudes he is still in the tropics, only 12 degrees south of the equator, when, after passing great regions of verdureless desert, he reaches sections where irrigation has been employed and the lands are rich with peaches, melons, alligator pears, custard apples, and all the fruits of the temperate and semitropical zone.

Much has been done for transportation in Peru since the Incas cut their great roads into the mountain sides and built terraces on the hills, sometimes twenty or thirty of them piled one above another, — undertakings that even now bear mute but significant witness to the patience and toil of this primitive people. Much still remains to be done, however, before the resources of Peru can be developed to anything like their capacity.

CHAPTER V

BOLIVIA, THE MOUNTAIN REPUBLIC

The immensity and complexity of this nature speak of the vast scale on which natural forces work, and of the immense spaces of time which their work has occupied. — JAMES BRYCE [1]

A LAND OF OPPORTUNITY

The Republic of Bolivia, more truly isolated than any other South American state, has in recent years attracted much attention because of the rich opportunities for investment within its borders. It is more truly an untouched land of opportunity than any other South American republic. Its wealth and its natural resources for possible future industries are untold. Its mountain fastnesses are filled with deposits of minerals, and its valleys, with their equatorial sunshine, contain almost every possibility for agriculture.

GEOGRAPHY

Much of the western part of Bolivia is a plateau which lies between two huge mountain chains and has an average altitude of 12,000 feet. The northern part of this plateau is the most populous and contains the chief cities of the republic. The southern part is largely desert and is sparsely populated.

In the Bolivian Andes east of the great plateau are to be found three of the highest mountain peaks in the Western Hemisphere. Here are Sorata (21,214 feet), Illimani (21,188 feet), and Sajama (21,050 feet).

The larger part of Bolivia lies east of the Andes and is a vast plain. In the north and northeast the highlands descend gradually to the plain, and between the spurs of the mountains

[1] James Bryce, South America, Observations and Impressions. By permission of The Macmillan Company, publishers.

are fertile valleys known as the Yungas, where most of Bolivia's agricultural products are grown. The northern part of the plains area is largely forest-covered and merges with the tropical forests of the Amazon. To the south and southeast are grassy pasture lands, part of the great Chaco country.

The slopes of the Andes overlooking the plains and known as the Montaña are forest-covered.

This weird country possesses sharp contrasts of climate as well as of vegetation. There is a vast difference in the altitude of the Montaña, the tropical eastern slopes of the country, and the summit of Sorata. The climate through this tremendous range of altitude may be divided, as it is in Mexico, into the tropical, temperate, and frigid zones, — the "tierra caliente," the "tierra templada," and the "tierra fria." The mean temperature of the lowland region is 74 degrees Fahrenheit, that of the plateau about 50 degrees Fahrenheit, while in the extreme altitudes are found regions of ice and snow. There are two seasons, the wet, or rainy, season, lasting from December to May, and the dry season, lasting from May to December. As in all the South American countries south of the equator, the seasons are the reverse of those in the United States. When it is summer in Bolivia, it is winter in the United States, and vice versa.

The proximity to the equator affords a warmth of sun which makes this region livable, although the nights are cold. In the great plateau the climate is healthful and invigorating for those who are sufficiently rugged to be untroubled by the rarefied atmosphere. People in ill health, or with weak hearts or lungs, find living in this part of Bolivia difficult. Pneumonia is more dangerous here than upon lower levels, since the rare atmosphere does not afford the patient sufficient oxygen. Only the Indians who are inured to this climate through many generations seem to be perfectly at home physically in these elevated regions. The Andean Indians have become adapted to this climate and altitude, and find it difficult to survive transplanting to the lower coastal regions.

The diversity of the climate makes possible the cultivation of a wide range of products, and the trader or traveler in La Paz sees llamas loaded with ice from the north coming into the city, to meet there mule trains loaded with oranges and other fruits from the southern and eastern borders of the country. It is estimated that 5000 mules travel daily between the Yungas and La Paz.

HISTORY

In 1535 Bolivia was invaded by Pizarro. He had already conquered the Inca empire and found the peaceful Indians of Bolivia comparatively easy to subdue. He placed the country in the administrative power of his brothers, Hernando and Gonzalo Pizarro. The discovery of the rich silver mines was followed in these early days by the advent of a horde of adventurers. In the year 1780 the Indians, led by Tupac Amaru, the last of the Inca chiefs, killed the Spanish authorities and drove many of the settlers out of the country. It was not until after a decade of fighting that the Indians were finally overcome and Tupac Amaru and all his family executed.

For two centuries after the Spanish conquest Bolivia was a part of Peru, and even today there are few, if any, differences between the characteristics of the country and people of Bolivia and those of the neighboring sections of Peru on the northwest. In 1776 the viceroyalty of Buenos Aires was created by the Spanish government, and there was assigned to it the supervision of all the River Plate countries. At the same time the Spaniards set up a separate administrative authority for the southeastern sections of what had formerly been the upper portion of Peru, locating its *audiencia* at Chuquisaca.

In 1809 the contest with Spain for independence began. At that time the inhabitants of La Paz deposed the Spanish authorities. Final independence was not achieved until 1825, when Simón Bolívar, called the George Washington of South America, assisted by General Sucre, led the Bolivians to their freedom from Spain. In honor of their deliverer the people took his name for their country. Bolivia was the first of the South American states to teach by example the fine art of liberty, and she is justly proud of that fact. In the first Act of Independence are the words, "Upper Peru was the altar on which the first blood was shed for liberty in the land where the last tyrant perished."

The triumphant leaders of the revolution decided to maintain this southern region as a political unit, separate from Peru, thus constituting a republic lying between Peru and Argentina. A constitution, drafted by Bolívar, was adopted with some amendments and was formally proclaimed on November 19, 1826, when General Sucre was elected the first Bolivian president. Although Bolivia has maintained her independence as a republic, a valuable section of her territory adjoining the Pacific was unfortunately lost to her in a war with Chile. The condition of the great inland state has been relieved somewhat in recent years, however, by the completion of three railways running to one Peruvian and two Chilean ports.

PEOPLE

Bolivia is one of the most sparsely populated of all the Latin-American states, having but a little over five persons to the square mile. The estimated population is not far from 2,800,000. Of this number about 50 per cent are Indians, while the pure white population is less than 20 per cent. The population of La Paz is about 107,000, but no other city or town of Bolivia can be credited with many more than 30,000 inhabitants.

In an estimate of the population above seven years of age, made in the year 1900, it was found that 564,000 persons were engaged in agriculture, 399,037 in industries, 55,521 in commerce, 49,647 in the liberal professions, 36,285 in domestic service, 12,625 in mining, and 3106 in artistic professions. The foreign population at this time numbered 7425, of whom 2072 were Peruvians. Although these figures have naturally increased, the general ratio remains about the same.

The Bolivian Indians. The Indians of this republic, the Aymarás, the Quichuas, and the Mojos, together with many minor tribes, are the mainstay as far as agriculture and labor in the mines are concerned. The Aymarás are the principal laborers in the Alto Plano. The Quichuas are also agriculturists, but their habits and customs are somewhat different from those of the other Indians. The Aymarás language is spoken by three fourths of the inhabitants of La Paz, making the Bolivian capital virtually an Indian city. La Paz contains a larger aboriginal population than any other city in the New World, with the possible exception of Asunción in Paraguay.

The Bolivian Indians are still half civilized and less than half Christianized. They prefer their own language to Spanish

and still indulge largely in their primeval nature worship. They are herders of the llamas and sheep, and cultivators of all the land that is under agriculture. From generation to generation the Bolivian Indians have lived on certain estates, and nothing would induce them to leave their familiar haunts. While they are not actually serfs, by habits and customs they are closely associated with their respective sections, in which they prefer to live and labor. Since there is no manufacturing to speak of in

FIG. 8. Cambas Indians, Chiriguano tribe, from southward of Santa Cruz, Bolivia. This country is sometimes called the Indian republic

Bolivia, agriculture and mining being the sole occupations, the Indians make up the entire laboring support of the country.

They usually live in small villages, having two important officers to govern them. The ilacata is the administrator of land; he supervises labor, takes receipts for the common land, and attends to the yearly division of the land to be cultivated. The alcalde combines the executive and judicial powers and is sometimes called the mayor. He is supposed to maintain order, settle disputes, and lead the fighting forces when fighting is necessary.

Although the Indian laborer is legally free and possesses a legal vote, he seldom accepts the opportunity of suffrage. Certain landowners exercise oppressive powers over labor, but such oppression is held in check by the possibility of an uprising among the Indians, who in recent years have possessed themselves of firearms and would be a formidable force if they could secure a strong leader to unite them against the landowners.

The Indians have little in the way of education, and they seem to be satisfied to take their recreation at fairs and festivals, in chewing the omnipresent coca leaf, and in the use of alcohol. They are suspicious of the white man and have good reason to be. They lack initiative but are excellent workers and good fighters under proper leadership. Their morals have remained substantially unchanged through the centuries, and they neither love nor hate the white man, but rather fear him. The white man in turn despises the Indians and in some cases fears them.

In Bolivia military service has been made compulsory for Indians between the ages of nineteen and twenty-one. German officers and instructors have been employed to drill them, and this combination of education and military exercise has been of marked benefit to the Indians of certain sections. They have been taught to obey and to read and write, and they have received a faint glimpse of modern civilization. It seems strange that a race of people upon whom the entire population of a country depends for its support should have been neglected educationally for so many years.

The cholos. The cholos, a mixed breed, are also an important element of the population of Bolivia. The name *cholo* properly means the offspring of a mestizo and an Indian, but the name is used quite generally to describe a peasant with a marked strain of Indian blood. In the department of La Paz the cholos compose 8 per cent of the population; and in Cochabamba, nearly 52 per cent. Much of the shopkeeping is done by their shrewd women, while the men act as superintendents of estates and as skilled laborers. The cholos are picturesque in their dress.

White people. Ranking above the Bolivian Indians and the cholos are the descendants of old Spanish-American families, many of whom are landlords, and a comparatively small foreign colony, composed of Germans, British, and Americans engaged in railroad, mining, and trade enterprises.

CITIES

La Paz, the metropolis of Bolivia, is the Bolivian seat of government, although Sucre is still the legal capital. It is the world's loftiest capital city, located 12,470 feet above sea level, an elevation at least 2000 feet higher than Quito and 5000 feet higher than Mexico City. Ranking next to La Paz in altitude is Lhasa, in Tibet, which is situated 11,830 feet above the sea.

The average annual temperature of La Paz is 50 degrees Fahrenheit, and the climate is bracing. Because of the lack of heating arrangements the people seek the sunshine for warmth and, as in certain other west-coast sections, they put on their wraps when going into the house or anywhere out of the actual sunshine.

La Paz is one of the picturesque cities of the world. The traveler's first glimpse of it, lying in a valley about 1500 feet deep, inclosed within vertical mountain walls and surrounded by snow-capped mountains, makes an unforgettable impression. Five rivers crossed by large bridges flow through the valley. An electric-car line built by an American takes the traveler down into the heart of the city, where there are a number of fine buildings, the legislative palace, post office, theater, hospitals, and several old and impressive-looking Spanish churches. The statues of Bolivian heroes are found in the public parks. There are fine old Spanish houses, many of which have been owned by former governors, and the galleries about the patios and the armorial bearings on the gateways remind one of Spain. Here in these lofty regions, if the patio is not directly in the sunshine, it is likely to fulfill the description of a certain traveler who defined this institution in a Spanish-American house as a "reservoir of chilled air." The city is equipped with electric lights and is rapidly taking on modern material improvements which do not detract from its charm.

Viscount Bryce, in his book "South America, Observations and Impressions,"[1] describes this picturesque city as follows:

Thus, though there is not much for the tourist to see or do, nor for the art student to admire, still La Paz is a picturesque place with a character so peculiar that it makes for itself a niche in the memory and stays there, as being unlike any other place. The strange irregularity of the steep, rough streets, with cliffs of brown earth standing up at the ends of them, the brawling torrent, the wild-looking Indians and their particolored dresses, the flocks of graceful llamas, with their long, curved necks and liquid, wondering eyes, the extraordinary situation of the city in this deep pit, deep but not dark, for the vertical sun blazes into it all day long; and above all, the magnificent snowy mass of Illimani towering into the sapphire blue sky with glaciers that seem to hang over the city, though they are forty miles away, its three pinnacles of snow turning to vivid rose under the departing sun, — all these together make La Paz a fascinating spot, one of those which flash vividly and quickly before the mind when you think of them.

La Paz is a railroad center for several important lines, the city being the pivot of the Bolivian railway system as well as the center of the commercial activity of the country. About 1000 miles of railway bring the people and produce to the central market places of this city. With three lines of railway connecting it with the Pacific Ocean on the west, with a new railway joining it with Buenos Aires and the Atlantic on the south, and the Madeira-Mamoré Railway, which taps the tropical resources of Bolivia on the Brazilian border, and will connect the country by rail and water with the Brazilian coast, La Paz is destined to become the "Mecca of the Andes."

Cochabamba, the second city of importance in Bolivia, has a population of about 30,000. It is situated in the lower regions of the country east of La Paz at an altitude of 8435 feet. The climate is agreeable, with an average temperature of 66 degrees Fahrenheit.

Lying in a fertile valley and possessing a half temperate and half semitropical climate, the region surrounding this city is

[1] James Bryce, South America, Observations and Impressions. By permission of The Macmillan Company, publishers.

rich in such agricultural products as corn, barley, and wheat. Immense plains in the neighborhood of this fertile valley are covered with large herds of cattle and with rich forests. Cochabamba is sometimes referred to as the granary of the republic. It is located about 275 miles from La Paz and 130 miles from Oruro, from which it is reached by a railway that was opened to traffic in 1917. Four trains a week enter Cochabamba, and the railway journeys in this section furnish some of the finest scenic attractions to be found in the whole of Latin America.

This city is the distributing center for eastern Bolivia and contains some large business houses and excellent buildings. An American school for boys is located here. Many of the firms doing business in Cochabamba import directly from the United States. The city is the home of several important German firms. There is a rich mining region here which, together with the other advantages of Cochabamba, promises a prosperous agricultural and commercial future for this locality.

Potosí has been known for many centuries, owing to its silver mines. It is still rich in silver, tin, tungsten, copper, and lead.

In the early part of the seventeenth century Potosí had five or six times its present population, which is about 30,000. The extreme altitude of the city — about 14,000 feet above sea level — is something of a handicap. The climate of Potosí is unique in that here four seasons may be experienced in a single day, the daily temperature varying from 9 to 59 degrees Fahrenheit.

Potosí was founded in 1540, and the remains of the Spanish settlements are still to be seen in the old dams, called *lagunas*, built by the Spaniards in 1621 to supply the city with water. The mint here was constructed in 1773 and cost over $1,000,000, and there are other notable and historic structures. The famous silver mountain is still being worked at Potosí. During the Spanish dominion, it is said, these mines produced silver to the value of more than $3,600,000,000.

In the department of Potosí is also the city or town of **Uyuni**, with 6000 people. This city is important because it is here that the railway from La Paz to Antofagasta, on the Pacific coast, is joined by the new railway which provides a through route from

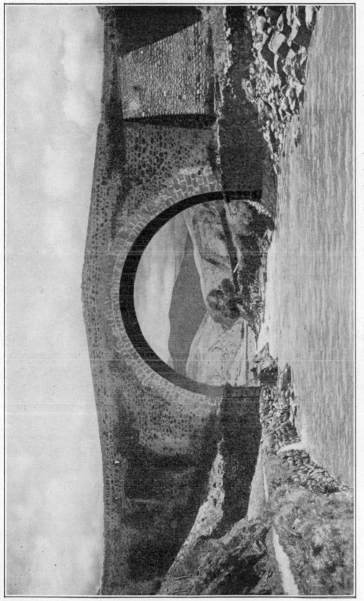

FIG. 9. Ancient bridge near Potosí, Bolivia, constructed by the Spaniards three centuries ago

central Bolivia to Buenos Aires. This road makes a railway connection across the continent from the River Plate to the Pacific, bringing La Paz within twenty-four hours of one ocean at Arica and eighty hours of the other ocean at Buenos Aires.

Oruro, with 31,360 inhabitants, is 127 miles south of La Paz. It has an altitude of 12,100 feet and a temperature averaging 50 degrees Fahrenheit. Oruro is the center of the railway system of Bolivia, the commercial center of the great tin-mining district, and the home of a number of firms doing direct import business. There are other business houses here which conduct their foreign trade through La Paz.

Oruro is another old and famous mining town, owing its foundation, in the year 1595, to the mines discovered in its vicinity. A school of mines is located here. A large proportion of the miners are foreigners, and much of the business is in the hands of Germans. The manual labor, as is the case throughout Bolivia, is done by Indians and cholos.

There are several important cities in the lower levels of the country. Of these, Santa Cruz, toward the east, in the rich agricultural region, has a population of about 25,000. It has a warm climate, the temperature averaging 80 degrees Fahrenheit. Santa Cruz carries on business through Puerto Suarez on the Paraguay River. Eventually, however, it will be connected with the Argentine border by a railway from Yacuiba. The products of this region are rubber, sugar, alcohol, and petroleum. There are a number of factories for the manufacture of chocolate, and also tanneries and sugar refineries.

Sucre, the legal capital of Bolivia, with 29,000 inhabitants, has had an interesting history. It is the seat of the national Supreme Court and Archbishopric. It has no railway connections, but has an automobile service to Potosí. Some direct trading is done with the United States. Sucre is not the only city that has been distinguished by being the capital of Bolivia. An Englishman is reported to have asked, "Where is really the capital of Bolivia?" A Bolivian answered this question by saying, "The capital of Bolivia is the back of the horse which the President rides." Sucre reminds one of a city of old Spain gradually being dressed in modern clothes.

GOVERNMENT

Bolivia has a representative form of government with administrative departments that are similar to those of the United States. In this centralized republic the president exercises wide and almost absolute authority. Suffrage is given to male citizens over twenty-one, with the exception of domestics. Voters must be able to read and write, they must have a certain fixed income, and their names must be registered.

The republic has eight departments and three territories.

ARMY

The law provides for a standing army of 4600 officers and men, military service being compulsory. There is a military college at La Paz. Considerable progress has been made in aviation, and a military aviation school has been established.

CURRENCY

Bolivia is on a gold basis. The *boliviano*, the unit of value, is equivalent in United States currency to $0.389; twelve and a half bolivianos are equivalent to one pound sterling. English and Peruvian pounds are legal tender in the country. Paper money is in use, as well as a few coins of small denominations.

EDUCATION

The progress of education in Bolivia is slow because of the difficulties presented by the wide range of altitudes and the long distances between districts. Only about 57,000 students are enrolled in the schools, including private schools and kindergartens. Some normal-school training is given, and professional and higher education is provided for in the University of La Paz, in the University of Sucre, and in the University of Cochabamba. The various faculties of these institutions cover the usual branches of university subjects. There is a mining school at Oruro, and certain commercial and industrial schools also exist. Coeducation has been adopted in nearly all the institutions, and students of merit are sent abroad at government expense, while foreign teachers are employed as supervisors, principals, and teachers of special branches, especially in physical and industrial training.

PRODUCTS AND INDUSTRIES

Bolivia finds its chief sources of wealth in minerals and in agriculture. The western Cordillera is especially rich in copper and silver, and the eastern section of the Cordilleras is notable for its gold and tin. It was from these eastern Andean regions that the Incas mined the golden treasures that attracted the Spaniards. It is estimated that Pizarro obtained from Atahualpa, the Inca chieftain, $15,000,000 worth of gold on a promise that the Inca's life would be spared. The promise was broken immediately after the gold was delivered. Old Spanish historical writers state that a far greater amount of gold was buried or sunk in the Andean lakes, and Peru and Bolivia have never been without their adventurers seeking this lost treasure.

Bolivian revenue is derived chiefly from customs duties upon such commodities as tin, silver, gold, tungsten, antimony, and other minerals, together with its resources in rubber export, patents, and stamps. A comparatively new tax has been placed upon the net profit of the mineral enterprises.

During the World War Bolivia achieved prosperity unparalleled in her history, owing to the great demand for her products, chiefly her metals. The world depression affected her as it did other countries, but returning prosperity is evidenced with the renewed demand for mineral production, which will probably give Bolivia a decided impetus during the coming decade.

MINING

Tin. One fourth of the world's total output of tin is produced in Bolivia, which stands next to the Malay Peninsula in the production of this metal. American capital has been invested to a considerable extent in the mines of Bolivia.

The area containing the principal tin and silver mines of the country extends from the Chacaltaya mine on the north to the

FIG. 10. One of the largest tin mines in the world is the Llallagua at Llallagua, Bolivia. (Courtesy of Duncan, Fox & Co., Inc.)

Chorolque on the south, a distance of about 350 miles. Within it are found such famous mines as the Llallagua, the Uncia, and, most wonderful of all, the Potosí. The greater part of this area lies in the eastern slope of the Cordilleras. The vast snow-covered peaks of this range rise to a height of 20,000 feet and are flanked by deep glacier-scored valleys, magnificent in scenery and rich in buried treasure. Descending by rugged trails from these vast heights, it is possible to reach the typical climate and rich vegetation of the tropics within four hours by travel on muleback.

Some two years ago an American firm became interested in tin deposits in the Quime District of the province of Inquisivi. A large area was acquired by purchase and denouncement, and work was vigorously pushed in order to test the deposits and prove their value. Here the ore bodies are at an altitude of from 15,000 to 17,000 feet. The veins occur in granite, and have been formed by replacement along its joints and fissures. The tin occurs as cassiterite (dioxide of tin) and is accompanied by a great variety of minerals, the most important of which are chlorite, tourmaline, pyrite, quartz, and sphalerite. The veins do not carry silver in commercial quantities. The climate in this section is severe, especially during the rainy season, which is the summer; but the precipitation during the winter months is negligible, and for this reason the snow does not remain long and the camps and workings are therefore easily accessible during the greater part of the year. An excellent road has been built from the railway station of Eucalyptus to the mines, a distance of about 70 miles.

The economic factors operating against the exploitation of tin in Bolivia are the necessarily heavy freight charges, the dependence upon the price of tin in the Straits Settlements, the export duty, and the fluctuation of Bolivian money.

Petroleum. Large concessions of petroleum have been secured by American firms in Bolivia, and negotiation of others is under way. According to the statistics obtained from the Bolivian consulate in New York, heavy machinery for the drilling of oil wells has been shipped to Bolivia in considerable quantities; all this activity was begun in the eastern part of the country.

An immense oil field is thought to exist on the eastern side of the republic, part of a field stretching from the vicinity of the Orinoco River to the Argentine Republic. While portions of this territory have already been prospected, there are still vast regions awaiting the explorer and the promoter.

Other minerals. Extensive deposits of common salt exist in the southern portion of Bolivia, and silver mines upon which the entire world was at one time dependent for silver coinage continue their output to such an extent that Bolivia is sometimes called "The Land of Ten Thousand Silver Mines."

From 1540 to 1750, a period of two hundred and ten years, the gold mines of Bolivia produced $2,100,000,000 worth of gold. From 1750 to the beginning of the nineteenth century the mines and placers in the provinces of Larecaja and Caupolican produced gold valued at $14,000,000, and from 1818 to 1868 the output was valued at $3,000,000. The value of the products of other mines and placers in the country from the middle of the eighteenth century to the latter part of the nineteenth century is estimated at $125,000,000. At present the annual gold production of Bolivia is valued at about $350,000.

Bolivia holds an important position among the countries producing bismuth. In Bolivia this product is combined with other metals, from which its separation is easy. It is found in the departments of La Paz and Potosí, the principal section being that of Tazna.

AGRICULTURE

Great as is the mineral wealth of Bolivia, the future of the country is also dependent upon the steady development of its agricultural and pastoral resources. It is from these sources that wealth accrues directly to the citizens of the country, while foreigners with foreign capital usually conduct the large mining enterprises, carrying away the wealth obtained therefrom to other lands.

Although agriculture is somewhat antiquated in Bolivia, there are upwards of 4,940,000 acres under cultivation. There is a large production of wheat, barley, beans, and potatoes for local consumption, while coffee and coca are exported to

Chile and to Argentina. Coffee and cacao are grown on the slopes near La Paz and Cochabamba, while coffee and numerous other tropical and semitropical products are successfully cultivated in the departments of El Beni and Santa Cruz.

FOREST INDUSTRY

Rubber is the most important product of Bolivia, with the exception of tin. In the value of its rubber exports, which amount to about $4,500,000 annually, Bolivia stands next to Brazil among the countries of South America.

An annual export tax regulates by law the exploitation of the rubber lands. These lands lie chiefly in the northwest, near the Peruvian boundary; in the east, in the province of Santa Cruz; and in the Acre and Beni territory. There are two varieties of rubber trees found in this district: the *caucho*, which is cut down in order to extract the sap, and the *hevea*, which is tapped for rubber. The trees in this region are tapped when from thirty to fifty years old, and are expected to yield for twenty years, after which they become useless.

LIVE-STOCK INDUSTRY

Large areas in Bolivia are suited to grazing, and the raising of live stock is an important industry. There are upwards of a million head of cattle, one and a half million head of sheep, one hundred thousand horses, fifty thousand mules, and hundreds of thousands of domestic fowls, goats, vicuñas, and llamas, called the "camels of the Andes." There are also three hundred thousand alpacas, the wool of which brings a high price in the world market.

EXPORTS AND IMPORTS

The chief exports of Bolivia are silver, tin, copper, antimony, bismuth, lead, gold, tungsten-bearing ores, rubber, hides, and wool. The chief imports are provisions, hardware, wines and spirits, lumber, cotton, linen and silk goods, ready-made clothing, agricultural implements, automobiles, chemicals, electrical machinery and supplies, explosives, and ammunition.

The exports from the United States to Bolivia follow generally the same lines as those to Ecuador, Peru, and Chile. Cotton textiles, machinery, construction materials, and various small manufactured articles make up the bulk of the export trade, while such foodstuffs as tea, lard, and canned goods are shipped in large quantities to the mining regions.

Figures from the consulate at La Paz show that exports from Bolivia to the United States declared at that consulate during 1923 amounted to $2,787,002 as compared with $6,090,030 in 1922. The decline in copper and tin exportations to the United States explains a considerable part of this reduction, the decline being due to cheaper refining in Europe. In 1923 Bolivia imported from the United States products to the value of about $3,000,000.

The other competitors for Bolivian trade are the United Kingdom, Germany, France, and Chile. There has been a decided decrease in both the export and the import trade of Bolivia since the years immediately following the World War.

TRANSPORTATION AND COMMUNICATION

Railways. Although Bolivia has no ports of its own, it is connected by railway with the Chilean ports of Antofagasta and Arica, and with the Peruvian port of Mollendo. La Paz has railway connections with all three of these ports.

The Antofagasta and Bolivia Railway is the longest of the lines to the Pacific coast ports, and perhaps the most picturesque, while the line from Arica to La Paz is the shortest. The route from Mollendo is part by railway, and part by a steamer trip on Lake Titicaca. The extension of the Antofagasta and Bolivia Railway to the Argentine border, where it joins the line connecting with Buenos Aires, has been completed only recently. This line will prove of great importance to Bolivia as an outlet to the Atlantic coast. Heretofore the Madeira-Mamoré Railway, which connects the Bolivian border on the north with steamer lines on the Madeira and Amazon rivers, has been the only direct means of communication with the Atlantic, and it has not been sufficient.

Waterways. In addition to its more than 1000 miles of railways, Bolivia possesses a network of navigable rivers. For over 1000 miles the Paraguay is navigable for steamers drawing from eight to ten feet. The Itenez is navigable for 1000 miles; the Beni for 1000 miles, for steamers of six-foot draft; while a dozen other rivers can be used by light-draft vessels for distances of 200 to 1000 miles. The total length of the navigable waterways in the country, including rivers and lakes, is estimated at 12,000 miles. All the rivers except the Desaguadero flow toward the Atlantic Ocean, in the general direction of the Amazon or the Paraguay.

Lake Titicaca, one of the largest lakes on the American continent and famous as the highest steam-navigated lake in the world, has an area of 4000 square miles and is situated about 12,500 feet above the sea. There is a regular line of steamers on this lake.

FUTURE TENDENCIES

The possibilities of Bolivia, born of the immense resources of the land, have hardly been fully discovered as yet. The open doors are many, and the opportunities for foreign capital in mining, agriculture, and pastoral industries are apparent. It should be realized, however, in considering the import trade of Bolivia, that the population of the country is small and the number of consumers of imported commodities still smaller.

The Bolivian Congress has passed a bill prohibiting, with certain exceptions, work on Sundays in factories, shops, commercial houses, and other business establishments. The country is adjusting itself to modern practices. There is desperate need of commercial and business training, and such schools as the Mercantile Institute of Santiago, Chile, which has opened a branch school in La Paz under the management of a Bolivian professor educated in Chile, are furnishing an example and fulfilling an important need.

Bolivia, the Mountain Republic, awaits immigration, modern pioneers, and leadership in industrial enterprises, in mining, and in railroad construction. There is also a need for the training of the Indians along industrial lines, since they make very satisfactory laborers. More capital is required for the large mining and transportation enterprises, as well as for a modern system of education adaptable to the diverse elements of the republic. This money must come from the outside, and a considerable portion of the recent large loans floated in the United States for Bolivia will be devoted especially to railroad and transportation developments. Because of these loans, taken by American investors, as well as by reason of mutual and reciprocal markets, the United States may legitimately expect to take a preëminent place in the commercial and industrial life of this country, which is so rich in natural resources.

CHAPTER VI

CHILE

The Chileans are the offspring of isolation. The ancestors of the present inhabitants of this narrow lane between the Andes and the Pacific had to hustle for what they got. When they did not fight man they fought nature. Only within the last forty years has nature revealed its riches to the Chileans. Hence only the fittest have survived in Chile. — EARL CHAPIN MAY [1]

GEOGRAPHY

Chile, sometimes called the "sliver" or "tape line" republic because of its shape, is mainly a long and narrow strip of country, averaging 87 miles in width, between two mountain ranges. It stretches along the Pacific Ocean for about 2700 miles, a distance greater than that represented by a line drawn from New York City to San Francisco, or from Sitka (Alaska) to the tip of Lower California.

Chile is the only west-coast republic lying entirely on the western slope of the Andes. Here the Andean range, with peaks in the north rising from 14,000 to more than 23,000 feet in height, and in the south from 5000 to 9000 feet, forms a bulwark on the east, while the Cordillera de la Costa range, from 2000 to 3000 feet in height, which runs along the Pacific very near the shore, shuts the country in from the sea on the west.

Throughout the extent of this country, with its long seaboard and high plateaus, may be found nearly every climatic condition. In the north the nitrate desert, composed of low, stony hills and barren, sterile regions, is rainless and therefore has no shrubs or vegetation of any kind. The Andes extract every drop of moisture from the trade winds that blow across from the east, and no rain has fallen in this region for many years. It is hot and dry here during the day, with occasional dust storms, and often there is frost at night.

[1] Earl Chapin May, 2000 Miles through Chile. The Century Co.

This region occupies the portion of Chile extending from 18 degrees south latitude, the boundary line between Peru and Chile, to the neighborhood of Coquimbo, at 30 degrees south latitude. Only a part of this section is profitable because of its nitrate deposits, the remainder being almost useless desert.

The central portion of Chile extends from Coquimbo to Puerto Montt, in 42 degrees south latitude. This region, which is over 600 miles in length, has a temperate and salubrious climate. The temperature ranges from 27 to 86 degrees Fahrenheit, influenced by both altitude and latitude. More or less moderate but regular rains occur, and there is an abundance of water, supplied by the melting snows of the mountains in the shape of streams and rivers, that can be used for irrigation purposes and water power. In this region are many fertile valleys, in which is grown almost every agricultural product known to exist. It has naturally become the most important and densely populated part of Chile.

From Puerto Montt to 54 degrees south latitude is another dreary stretch of territory, here composed of archipelagoes, wooded islands, and some wooded mountain territory on the mainland, instead of barren desert land as in the north. This region is visited by rain at all seasons; sometimes as much as 150 or 200 inches fall during the year, although the average amount is less. The prevailing winds, blowing southeast across the warm Pacific, bring much moisture, which is precipitated when they strike the western slopes of the mountains, thus causing weather conditions exactly the reverse of those existing in the northern part of Chile.

Chile resembles Egypt in that both countries have a narrow strip of arable country. It reminds one more, however, of the Pacific coast of the United States and Alaska taken in inverse order: the deserts; the fertile valleys, like the San Joaquin of California; and the forest-clad indented coast of Alaska, with its mountains and fiords, and its fog and rain.

Of Chile's total area of 290,000 square miles, woods and forests form 25 per cent, pastures $7\frac{1}{2}$ per cent, irrigable land 5 per cent, and arable land $12\frac{1}{2}$ per cent. Certain conditions, however, are favorable to the increased development of Chile in spite of the dearth of usable land. The soil in the central valley, said to be over 300 feet deep, is very fertile; the forest country to the south has been as yet only partially developed; and the resources of the northern provinces are almost incalculable.

HISTORY

Historically the development of Chile includes the story of the conquest of the Araucanian Indians by the *conquistadores*. The first attempt was made in 1535, not long after the founding of Lima, by Diego de Almagro, a lieutenant of Francisco Pizarro. Almagro was given the grant of a large section south of Peru and was sent with an army to take possession of it in the name of the king of Spain. Marching over the Bolivian plateau and through high mountain passes into Chile, he and his men met with great physical hardships and were attacked by fierce Araucanians; they were finally forced to retreat.

In 1549 Pizarro sent out a second expedition, commanded by his quartermaster Pedro de Valdivia, who went southward by sea and in February, 1541, landed at the mouth of the Rio Maipú, where he founded the city of Santiago. Pushing still farther south, he established other settlements at Concepción, Imperial, Villarica, and Valdivia, the last place being named for him. Valdivia was killed in 1553 by the Araucanians, who vigorously disputed every inch of progress made by the Europeans.

Trouble with the Indians continued until 1640, when the Spanish governor of Chile concluded a treaty with them in which the Biobio River was recognized as the boundary line between the possessions of the whites and the Indians. Thereafter a more friendly feeling prevailed, and about this time the Indians joined with the white men in a defensive warfare against the invasions of Dutch and English buccaneers.

On September 18, 1810, the Chileans deposed the Spanish authorities and created a provisional government. Spain resisted this stand, and troops were rushed into Chile from Peru, then the royalist stronghold. Through the aid of the Argentine patriot and soldier, General San Martín, the Spaniards were defeated at the battle of Maipú on April 5, 1818, and Chilean independence was made permanent. Thus ended the rule of Spain in Chile.

The first head of the Chilean nation was General O'Higgins, who had taken a foremost part in the Chilean war of independence. He was made supreme dictator, and on October 23, 1818, a constitution drafted by a committee appointed by him was formally adopted by the people.

The years between 1818 and the present time have registered many difficulties for Chile, but only one serious revolution. This occurred in 1890, when President Balmaceda quarreled with the Chilean legislature over the levying of taxes. When the navy supported Congress, however, Balmaceda was overcome. Since that time Chile has been almost wholly without revolution or serious menace to its internal government.

PEOPLE

The population of Chile is about 4,000,000, or 13 persons to the square mile. Of this total the Indians are estimated to number from 80,000 to 140,000, and the remainder of the population is white. As in Ecuador, few negroes are found in Chile.

Shut in by a barren desert on the north, by deep forests and the ocean to the south, and by towering mountains on either side, the Chilean race has been developing in a compact central region and is probably the most homogeneous, patriotic, and united people in South America.

The language of the country is Spanish, which is the prevailing medium used in business. The Chileans, like other Latin Americans, are good linguists, and many of the higher classes speak English, German, and French in addition to their native tongue.

Whites. The country is said to be ruled by old Spanish-Chilean families who have established themselves in Santiago, the capital, and are at the head of the conservative party of the country. There is as yet no great middle class save that composed of artisans and shopkeepers.

The migration to Chile, about two centuries ago, of people from northern Europe is the explanation of the presence of so many Teutonic and English types in Chile and of such names as O'Higgins, Edwards, MacKenna, Lispenberger, and Blumenthal. It is said that not more than a third of the students in the university at Santiago have parents both of whom are Chilean. The flourishing German settlements in the central and southern regions of Chile have had a decided influence upon the prosperity of that section of the country.

Rotos. The term *roto* is applied to the members of the poorer laboring class of Chile. The rotos are sturdy peasants who are half Indian and half white. They work in the nitrate fields and on the farms, and are the chief source of labor supply.

Indians. The greater part of the Chilean Indians are Araucanians, who are found in the southern section of the country. They are descendants of those Araucanians who were more famous than the Incas for their bravery and their resistance to the encroachments of the white men. They resemble Asiatic types in their short, sturdy stature and broad faces, and subsist for the most part by tilling the land. There are also tribes of Indians who live on the islands off the southern coast of Chile or along the mainland, and in the Strait of Magellan. As a rule the Indians do not live in settled communities of any size.

The Chilean Indians are diminishing in number year by year, becoming victims of tubercular diseases and alcoholism, both of which evils have spread among them from the whites. The government has appointed a protector of the Indians, and certain laws have been passed for their benefit, but these laws are not always successfully enforced. On the whole the Indians are good workers and would form a more valuable element of the population if they could be securely protected against the ravages of drink.

Chilean characteristics. Many of the aristocratic class are rich landholders or politicians, and take little part in the actual business and industrial life of the land. The landed aristocracy, resembling somewhat that of the feudal period in Europe, usually spend the summer on their estates and the rest of the year in Santiago, where they find a stimulating social atmosphere and an up-to-date society. They employ peasants as tenants or laborers to cultivate their lands. In spite of the strong tide of more liberal ideas that is setting in against the older ideas based on traditional and ecclesiastical influence, aristocratic and political prestige is still an important factor in Chilean life.

The Chileans are a social and pleasure-loving people. The horse races at Viña del Mar, an attractive residential suburb of Valparaiso, arouse tremendous interest throughout the country each year and are real social functions. The foreigner feels the charm of these people at once in such social centers as the famous Union Club of Santiago, where the gentry and politicians gather and where courtesy is as natural as it is delightful.

The laboring class, or rotos, of Chile are good "raw material," as most of them are intelligent. They are more or less volatile in temperament, however, and they need leadership. In the schools attended by both Chileans and Germans the teachers find the Chileans more alert and quicker of perception than the Germans, but the latter hold to their aims, while the Chilean temperament changes with the day. Someone has called the Chileans a "quicksilver" people "because they get over their political grudges so easily."

Throughout central and southern Chile the influence of northern European blood is seen in the traits of the people and the customs of the country. This holds true even in their sports, for the Spanish bullfight has no such hold in this country as in certain other parts of Latin America. Political life in Chile is more stable than in many other South American republics, — a fact due, in part at least, to the influence of this foreign racial strain.

The members of the upper class of Chile are unsurpassed both in intelligence and in ability. Chile has a promising future in business, and the Chileans, like the people of all young nations, give the impression of eager activity and the desire to be in touch with modern scientific and material advancement. Indications of this advancement are shown by the thriving university, the fine museum, and the zoölogical and botanical gardens in the capital city.

The Chilean religion recognized by the state is Roman Catholic, but other faiths are allowed. Although there is a general national loyalty to the Church, there is a tendency, as in other Spanish-American republics, toward agnosticism among the university students and certain of the governing classes. Adherence to the Church is stronger here than in certain other Latin-American states, however, and there is a Church party that exerts a decided influence upon politics.

In spite of modern tendencies it is still foreign capital and initiative that make possible and maintain most of the material developments in Chile. The hand of officialdom and ecclesiastical prestige is still heavy upon the land. In certain native schools where many of the youth of the better class are educated there remains the impression that the life of a "gentleman" is to be preferred to that of a man of business. As in most Spanish-American countries, education in the past has been one-sided, with the literary, legal, and political part of the curriculum overemphasized, at the expense of the practical industrial and scientific training, which is needed above all in an agricultural and mining country.

CITIES

Chile possesses cities and towns that are notable and vigorous for a country of its size. A knowledge of the character and business activities of these cities makes for a better understanding of the country.

In spite of the aridity and barrenness of the northern provinces, there are here several ports and flourishing towns, some of which have been the cause of considerable dispute between rival nations because of the rich products of the region.

Arica, with a population of 9000, is the northernmost important port of Chile. Its importance is due to a railway extending from this port to La Paz, Bolivia. It is a central distributing port for the province of Tacna, and a considerable volume of freight is handled for the interior of Bolivia. The principal exports are tin, copper, sulphur, nitrate, silver, tungsten, gold, wool, cotton, and sugar cane.

Iquique is the capital of the province of Tarapaca and the most important nitrate port in Chile; its population numbers 46,000. Situated 784 miles north of Valparaiso, it has a mild climate with an average temperature of 66 degrees Fahrenheit. This port, as well as Antofagasta, is served by practically all the west-coast steamship lines and also by the Grace Line and the Pacific Steam Navigation Company. In addition to nitrates, iodine and salt are important exports. Large nitrate plants are located in this vicinity, and many importing firms do business in Iquique. There are also iodine and silver deposits.

FIG. 11. Thirty thousand sacks of copper concentrates ready for shipment by a Grace steamer from Arica, Chile, to Tacoma, Washington, United States of America

Antofagasta, another important port of Chile, is associated with nitrate in the minds of all who know South America. It is connected with one of the richest mining regions of the continent by the railway that extends to La Paz (Bolivia), a distance of 719 miles; hence it is the chief entrepôt port for the products of that country. A Bolivian customhouse is located here.

This city, with its population of 65,000, is 575 miles from Valparaiso, and is a port of call for the principal west-coast steamship lines. Its leading exports are copper, iodine, nitrate, silver, and borax. Many foreign concerns have branch offices here, the United States being well represented among them. Antofagasta is often selected as the place for establishing an agency from which to canvass northern Chile and certain cities in Bolivia.

Coquimbo, which has a population of about 16,000, is a port lying midway between Antofagasta and Valparaiso. Its importance is due largely to the copper and iron mines in the vicinity, and copper mining and smelting are among the leading industries. Coquimbo is easily reached from Valparaiso by railway and by local steamers. It exports considerable quantities of native products, including wool, hides, and skins.

Valparaiso, with a population of about 200,000, is the second city in size in Chile and is the chief port of the country. It is also the largest port of the Pacific coast of the Americas south of San Francisco. The harbor is always filled with ocean steamers and sailing ships whose flags represent nearly every nation of the world. This harbor has been subject to violent northern gales, but extensive construction works for protecting shipping, handling cargo, and shielding the port are now nearing completion.

The city reminds one of a picturesque old Italian town, built as it is on a hillside with a narrow stretch of land at the water's edge, where the main shipping, banking, and business establishments are to be found. The upper town, about 200 feet above this section, on the hills, contains the residences of the wealthier classes. Communication between the upper and lower towns is by means of elevators or trolley cars.

Santiago, the capital city of Chile, is 116 miles from Valparaiso, 72 miles from San Antonio (the nearest seaport), and some 900 miles from Buenos Aires. Situated at an altitude of 1800 feet, it enjoys an excellent climate, with an average temperature of 60 degrees Fahrenheit.

This capital city has an atmosphere of modernity. There is here the pride of family and of race, the pride of accomplishment, and notably a pride in fighting abilities. The home life of the city, like that of the country at large, is patriarchal, families being large, and sons and daughters, aunts and cousins,

FIG. 12. Harbor scene at Valparaiso, Chile. This city is called "the Chicago of South America"

making such a wide circle of social life that the Chilean need not cultivate outside acquaintances for the sake of society unless he particularly desires to do so. In this respect the family life in Chile resembles that of the South in the United States in the days before the Civil War.

The city boasts many beautiful buildings and residences, as well as delightful parks and a remarkable avenue called the Alameda, or Avenida de las Delicias. The latter is a fine boulevard 325 feet wide, which traverses the city for a distance of over three miles. Its sides are lined with modern business houses and some of the finest residences. As the center of the political, cultural, and social life of the nation Santiago has no close competitor.

After Valparaiso, Santiago, with its population of over 500,000, is the most important market in Chile. Among its principal products are copper, silver, and all kinds of fruits. Here are found flour mills, foundries, machine shops, woodworking plants, tanneries, breweries, and shoe factories. In fact, nearly every kind of business is transacted in this city.

Santiago is located in the very center of the north-and-south railway systems of the country and also on the direct line of the Transandine Railway between Valparaiso and Buenos Aires. It is thus accessible from every part of Chile, and business houses canvass the entire republic from here. A United States ambassador and commercial attaché are located in Santiago, and there are a number of American and foreign banks, as well as wholesale importing establishments.

Los Andes is 87 miles from Santiago, at an altitude of 2675 feet. It is the terminus of the Transandine Railway and the place for railway connection between Santiago and Buenos Aires. Owing to its importance as a railway center, Los Andes is growing, and now has a population of 10,474. Its products are cereals, tobacco, wine, cattle, silver, and copper, and it has some fruit-preserving plants and tanneries.

Talca, a flourishing city 155 miles south of Santiago, is situated in a rich agricultural and wine-growing district. Its population numbers about 42,000. The city is well built, and modern in aspect.

Concepción, with about 70,000 inhabitants, is the capital of the province of the same name and is situated in the southern part of Chile on the Biobio River. It is 354 miles from Santiago.

For over three centuries Concepción was known as the frontier post against the Araucanians, and in colonial times it had considerable political and ecclesiastical influence. Today it is one of the most enterprising modern cities in the country, and the third city in importance. It has a mild climate, the average temperature being 56 degrees Fahrenheit, and the ample rainfall makes irrigation unnecessary. For 300 miles to the south stretches some of the best farming land in Chile. The city lies in the heart of a prosperous farming district and is therefore a distributing center for such products as wine, wheat, oats, barley, vegetables, fruits, and wool and hides.

Concepción promises to become one of the large manufacturing centers of Chile. Textile mills (among them a British cotton-cloth factory), tanneries, breweries, woodworking plants, and other manufacturing establishments are found here, and the coal-mining and copper-smelting industries are important.

Many of the Concepción merchants now import goods directly, instead of depending upon Valparaiso and Santiago as in the past. Certain of the large business houses maintain branches here.

Talcahuano, the port of Concepción, has nearly 50,000 people. It is 9 miles distant, at the mouth of the Biobio River, and is connected with Concepción by steam and electric railways. Here are the shipyards and naval training station of southern Chile. This port is also the seat of the whaling industry, the oil being refined at Concepción before it is shipped out.

Just south of Concepción and Talcahuano, in the Chilean coal region, are Coronel and Lota, which are important coaling ports, supplying coal to naval and merchant vessels. Although Chile is the principal coal-producing country of South America, it consumes more than it produces, and therefore has to import a considerable amount of coal as well as of fuel oil.

Valdivia, situated still farther south, is named for the famous *conquistador*. The city is Spanish only in name, however, since the population of some 25,000 is the development of an industrious German colony established about 1850. Agricultural and timber resources are largely responsible for its prosperity.

The city is inland on the Valdivia River a few miles from its outport, Corral, and is readily accessible by river. The government has expended many millions of dollars in dredging, thus enabling ships to pass through the channels and unload their products at Valdivia. The thriving industries of the city, which include shoe factories, tanneries, flour mills, and breweries, are mostly in the hands of men of German origin, and the Teutonic influence is much in evidence on every hand. Valdivia is said to be the cleanest city in Chile.

Punta Arenas, important for its cattle, wool, and fur industries, is situated on the Strait of Magellan and is the southernmost town of Chile. It is as far south of the equator as Sitka (Alaska) is north of it, and is more than 1000 miles farther south than the South African port of Cape Town.

Until the opening of the Panama Canal the Strait of Magellan offered the only water crossing in the entire length of the Americas. With the establishment, in the early sixties, of the first steamship lines between Valparaiso and Liverpool, Punta Arenas became a great repair and coaling station, developing into the most important commercial port between Valparaiso and Buenos Aires. The opening of the Panama Canal lessened its importance somewhat, but the port continues to thrive as a center for the industries of southernmost South America.

Though the winds blow constantly here, making it a dreary place in which to live, the city is nevertheless healthful. The climate is cool, the average temperature being 43 degrees Fahrenheit, and rain falls about 150 days in the year. The people, who number about 23,000, are representative of many nations; there are Chinese, Scotch, Italians, Spaniards, Indians, and Germans. The Scotch have been the most industrious and make the best shepherds, the life and type of country being not unlike that of their native land.

The rich grazing lands of this southern part of Chile, which also extend northward into Argentina, are covered with countless sheep, horses, and cattle. There are, indeed, millions of sheep on the mainland and on Tierra del Fuego and other islands. One of the largest sheep-farming companies of the world is located near Punta Arenas. This port is therefore the natural outlet for the products of the region, and is noted for its exports of wool, as well as of hides and tallow. These products are brought from the surrounding country on huge carts, although motor roads are now being built northward toward the Argentine Pampa.

Punta Arenas has also been an important fur market for many years. Seals, sea lions, and otters have been hunted and killed until the seal rookeries were finally destroyed, but there is still an abundance of fur-bearing animals.

There are coal deposits of some value in this vicinity, and an abundance of peat. There are also gold mines, but these are of little importance today.

Importing establishments and a number of banks are found here. Steamships sail fortnightly to northern west-coast ports, and there is also service to Buenos Aires. Communication with the northern world is also carried on by telegraph and by wireless.

GOVERNMENT

Chile is a centralized republic with legislative, executive, and judicial branches. The president is elected for five years by electors chosen by direct vote. He is not permitted to hold office for two consecutive terms, and may not leave the country during his term of office, or for one year after its expiration, except by the consent of Congress.

The twenty-three provinces of the country and their eighty-two subdivisions, or departments, are administered by *intendentes* and *gobernadores* appointed by the president. The Territory of Magallanes includes the southern mainland and the coastal islands.

Voters are required to own property and to be able to read and write, so that, with 25 per cent of the population illiterate and most of the laboring classes destitute of land, the government is left largely in the hands of the leading Chilean families. In 1923, however, the right to vote was extended to domestic servants.

Although the visitor in Chile will be told by the patriotic
Chileans that no socialists are to be found in the country, no one
can live here long without realizing that radicals of various
kinds are present and that socialism and labor troubles are to
be found at least in embryo. Undoubtedly Chile must grapple
with many of the social and labor problems with which the
United States and all other growing republics are forced to deal
sooner or later.

ARMY AND NAVY

Chile exacts obligatory military service, and a yearly call for
military activities is made upon all male citizens over twenty-
one years of age, keeping them on first reserve until they are
thirty. The active Chilean army in war strength is estimated
all the way from 200,000 to 300,000, and there is a standing
army of about 20,000 men. Previous to the World War the
army was trained by German officers, and the German military
system has been carefully copied.

The navy consists of about fifty vessels, including battleships,
destroyers, submarines, and torpedo boats. In time of war the
ships of the Compañia Sud-Americana, subsidized by the government, may be turned into auxiliary cruisers. The Chilean
navy is modeled on that of England, and the men have been
trained by British officers. The peace-time personnel is about
8000 men.

The navy has charge of the military administration of ports,
coast defenses, lighthouses, and the Hydrographic Bureau. At
Valparaiso is the Naval Academy, the School of Mechanics, a
naval hospital, and other establishments. Talcahuano has
two dry docks and a floating dock, and Arica, Punta Arenas,
and other ports have shipyards.

THE PRESS

Chile has a free press of excellent character, and there are
many newspapers and periodicals, one or two of the former
being among the oldest established in South America. The

newspaper *El Mercurio* of Valparaiso and Santiago is well known throughout Latin America and ranks with the best newspapers of Argentina and Brazil.

CURRENCY

The gold *peso* is worth $0.365 in United States currency. The paper peso is in general use and fluctuates considerably in value. Although Chilean currency is on a gold basis, gold is rarely used in commercial transactions. There are notes in multiples of the paper peso, a silver peso, and silver and copper coins representing various numbers of *centavos*.

EDUCATION

Education in Chile, especially for the middle and upper classes, is well provided for. There are two universities in Santiago : the University of Chile, which admits women, and the Catholic University. Both of these are equipped with the usual departments. There are also in the capital a number of normal and professional schools, as well as schools of other kinds. Education is free in the state schools and compulsory in the primary grades. There are two excellent schools, one for boys and the other for girls, managed by American Methodist missionaries, and here the sons and daughters of many prominent Chilean families are educated. The country is well provided with military, naval, and aviation schools, and with a number of industrial and vocational institutions. Students are sent abroad annually by the government for study in foreign institutions of learning, and an exchange of teachers with the United States was established in 1920.

PRODUCTS AND INDUSTRIES

Three sets of products and industries are native to Chile, and these are in line with the three distinct zones through which the long republic extends. In the Strait of Magellan region, in the southern section, the pastoral industries, especially sheep-raising, are developing rapidly, and certain mineral possibilities have been revealed. Timber and forest products are found here.

The central portion, which includes the central valley of Chile, is the agricultural area, where all the products of the temperate zone and many subtropical varieties grow in abundance. This section contains some of the most fertile and valuable lands in Latin America. In addition to the growing of grains, fruits, and vegetables, grape culture is very important here, and there are numerous vineyards as far south as Concepción. Wine-making is a prominent industry, and dairy farming is increasing in importance.

The northern zone comprises the nitrate and mineral section, where the most important industry of Chile is carried on. During the World War the revenue from the tax on the exports of nitrate alone was enormous, amounting to $30,000,000 in 1916, and brought great prosperity to the republic.

Manufacturing is increasing in Chile, and there are nearly 8000 factories in the country, representing a capital of approximately $224,000,000. Among the leading enterprises are food-producing industries, the leather industry, gas and electric plants, and factories for the manufacture of clothing. The ship-building industry is also worthy of note, and many other industries are important, as the manufacture of textiles, metals, beverages, and paper. More than twenty shoe factories are scattered through the various cities.

MINING

Nitrate. The nitrate deposits lie chiefly between Pisagua and Taltal, a distance of about 450 miles, in an elevated plateau between the coast range and the higher Andes. This plateau rises from 3600 to 13,000 feet above sea level, and is barren and without water.

The normal annual export of the nitrate fields is about 3,000,000 metric tons, and it is estimated that, at the present rate of consumption, the deposits are sufficient for at least two hundred years. In these fields are many short railways for carrying the nitrate to the coast towns for shipment after it has

FIG. 13. A trainload of *caliche* (soil-bearing nitrate) ready to leave the Chilean nitrate desert for the oficina where it will be crushed and boiled and made into pure sodium nitrate

been refined. A large amount of United States capital has gone into the nitrate industry, and the United States has been the best customer for Chilean nitrate since the World War, with the United Kingdom a close second.

The chief use of nitrate is as a fertilizer. It is utilized in the manufacture of gunpowder, however, and also in the production of nitric and sulphuric acid. Iodine, a by-product of nitrate, is a valuable export, and costs as much per ounce as saltpeter does per 100 pounds. Iodine is a limited product.

Copper. Copper, also found in the northern zone, is the second most important mineral product of Chile. One of the largest copper deposits in the world is situated at Chuquicamata. Of the 9000 acres of this claim 2000 are said to be mineralized, and the outcrop of copper is one and a half miles in length.

The copper industry has been largely developed by United States capital, but there are also copper mines owned and developed by French capital. The largest mines have modern dwellings, hospitals, and other up-to-date facilities for the comfort of their employees.

The copper exported annually from Chile is valued at more than $30,000,000, that exported in a recent year being valued at nearly $50,000,000. Most of the copper exported is in the form of ingots. The United States is the principal importer.

Coal. The coal fields of Chile are near the coast and extend from 36 degrees south latitude into the Magellanic lands. While Chilean coal has been known since the Spanish conquest, it was not mined commercially until 1840. Many of the veins are very near the sea, and some are even beneath it, while there are also veins in the interior. Among the most important fields are those at Coronel, Lota, Curanilahue, and Lebu. A large coal industry is carried on at Arauco by a British company which operates its own railways.

Of the 2,500,000 tons of coal consumed yearly by the country, 1,700,000 tons are mined in Chile. Coal is therefore not exported, and considerable quantities are imported from Great Britain, Australia, and the United States.

Gold and other minerals. Gold was mined in Chile to a considerable extent during the eighteenth century, and some gold is still found in connection with copper. Iron-ore deposits to the amount of 1,000,000,000 tons exist at Atacama and Coquimbo. Salt mines are an important resource, and among other minerals to be found in Chile are gypsum, manganese, and silver, the latter having contributed considerably to the country's wealth in other years. Chile furnishes about half of the world's supply of borax, and in a recent year 10,000 tons of sulphur were produced. Petroleum developments are small, although it is thought that this commodity exists in the extreme southern district and also on the northern part of the Bolivian frontier. Chile imports petroleum from the United States, Mexico, and Peru.

AGRICULTURE

The bulk of the agricultural products are grown in the central region of Chile, where, in the long, narrow central valley, are found most of the cultivated lands of the republic. Wheat occupies the greatest area, although only a small percentage of the 15,000,000 acres suitable for this crop is under cultivation. Other grains and forage crops are raised, among them corn and alfalfa; of the latter more than one crop is obtainable in a year. Agricultural machinery is increasingly employed, although on some of the *estancias* are still found farmers who plow with bullocks, using a crooked stick, as did their fathers.

The products of the vineyards of this region are very valuable, and vineyard land is worth all the way from $200 to $1000 per acre. The vineyards are usually owned by natives. Apples and other fruits and various kinds of vegetables are also grown here. Because of the abundance of the products of this region Chile is able to export a considerable amount.

LIVE-STOCK INDUSTRY

Stock-raising is carried on by British, Germans, and Chileans. Like the Argentinos and Brazilians, the Chileans are improving their herds by importing blooded cattle from Europe. Punta Arenas is the great cattle, sheep, and wool center. Frozen meat is an important export from here.

In connection with stock-raising development the leather industry is increasing, and in recent years tanning and the manufacture of leather goods have taken a high place among the manufacturing enterprises of the country; this industry has 10,000 employees and an invested capital of $21,000,000.

FOREST INDUSTRY

The forest area south of the Biobio River yields a large amount of timber, and the principal woods passing through the several thousand sawmills of this region are oak, Chilean mahogany, pine, ash, and laurel.

EXPORTS AND IMPORTS

In 1924 the exports of Chile were valued at $221,000,000, of which nitrates furnished slightly over half and copper about one fourth. Chilean exports to the United States in the same year were valued at $91,500,000. Important exports to the United States, besides nitrates and copper, are iron ore, iodine, and wool.

The imports for 1924 were valued at $132,500,000, of which textiles formed the chief item. Before the World War Great Britain and Germany were the leading Chilean importers, with the United States in the third place; but since the war the United States has risen to first place, with Great Britain a close second. Even before the war United States trade was gaining more rapidly in Chile than British or German trade, and the increased use of the Panama Canal and the new steamship lines between New York and Chile have greatly aided the commerce between the two countries.

TRANSPORTATION AND COMMUNICATION

Ports and waterways. The Chileans have always been excellent mariners, and their coast line, while not furnished with good natural harbors, is lined with ports, of which some fifteen are primary ports with customhouses. More than $100,000,000 has already been invested in the enlargement and development of Chilean ports, and there is still much to be done.

The west-coast route for steamers is now an accepted one, and familiar ports of call in Chile are Punta Arenas, Coronel, Valparaiso, Antofagasta, Iquique, and Arica. Certain routes also include the ports of Coquimbo and Talcahuano. Steamers of the Chilean Compañía Sud-America de Vapores skirt the entire west coast of South America, touching ports as far north as Panama. Through the Strait of Magellan ships connect with others bound for the United States or for England and other European countries. A Japanese line across the Pacific reaches Chilean ports.

In several European ports one may take passenger steamers direct to Valparaiso, although the quickest way to reach Chile from the east is by steamer to Buenos Aires and thence to Chile by the Transandine Railway. The eighteen-day trip by express steamers from New York to Valparaiso is revolutionizing trade and travel on the west coast. Many of the ships on this line furnish conveniences and luxuries similar to those of transatlantic travel.

Smaller ships are operated locally upon the navigable rivers of the southern portions of Chile. Among these rivers are the Maullin, navigable for small vessels for about 30 miles; the Bueno, navigable for about 50 miles; the Biobio, which is about 100 miles long and is navigable by flat-bottomed boats; and the Maule, navigable for small vessels for about 75 miles. There is service between the islands off the southern part of Chile and with the Juan Fernandez Islands, 400 miles to the west. Many of the lakes in the southern portion of the country are navigable for steamers and launches.

Railways. Like Peru, Chile has had to contend with many difficulties in railroad construction, but it makes a much better showing. Possessing only about half the area of its neighbor, Chile has some 6000 miles of railway against Peru's 2000 miles. About 65 per cent of the Chilean lines are owned by the government. Some 30,000 persons are employed on these roads, and of this number approximately 25,000 are employed on the government lines. The country contains the termini of three

international railway lines, two of which extend into Bolivia
and one into Argentina. Additional railway lines are under
construction.

The history of Chilean railways begins in the year 1849 and
is connected with the name of William Wheelwright, an American, the founder of the Pacific Steam Navigation Company.
The concession obtained by Wheelwright from the Chilean
government in 1849 was for a road fifty miles in length, extending from the port of Caldera to the mining town of Copiapó.
This road has the distinction of being the oldest railway in
Latin America, with the possible exception of the Demarara
Railway of British Guiana. It was built as a rival to transportation by oxcarts and pack animals, which had previously been
relied upon to carry the seekers of wealth of northern Europe
and the United States to their new treasure field and to bring
out the products of the region to the coast. This road was a
success and revolutionized the mining industry. Since that time
short railways have been constructed by the various nitrate
and copper companies, connecting their holdings with seaports.

The next line to be built in Chile was the state railway between Valparaiso and Santiago. Americans also had to do with
this early railway line. The surveys were made by Wheelwright
and Campbell, and the construction work was begun by S. W.
Greene of Rhode Island. In 1863 Henry Meiggs, the American
engineer connected with the Central Railway of Peru, completed this road. The construction entailed many knotty
problems because of the rugged section of country traversed.
Meiggs revealed not only his Yankee genius but also true
American sportsmanship by a contract into which he entered,
which stipulated that he would finish the road in three years
and would pay a fine of $10,000 per month for every additional
month required beyond that time. The contract also provided
that Meiggs be paid $10,000 per month for each month gained
in completing the contract. The American engineer employed
such energy in pushing the enterprise that, with his force of
60 engineers and 10,000 workmen, he gained more than a year
on his contract and incidentally a small fortune for himself.
The cost of this line was $11,300,000.

The trains of this railway, now a part of the Longitudinal Railway, carry American parlor cars, and the run to Santiago is made in three and one-half hours. The traffic of the road is enormous, resulting not only from the heavy shipping through Chile's first port, Valparaiso, but from local business, as well as from the rapidly developing mining, manufacturing, and agricultural enterprises of central and southern Chile.

The Longitudinal Railway, called the Central between Santiago and Valparaiso and between Santiago and Puerto Montt, is the great trunk line of the government system. When finished, this road and its branches will cover a distance of more than 3000 miles, stretching from Arica in the north to Puerto Montt in the south. The construction of the road is now progressing beyond Iquique. Connecting transversely with this long railway line are many branches, including lines to various ports on the west and branches to the east into the mountain section.

The railway connecting Arica with La Paz, a distance of 273 miles, is another government road, built with the coöperation of Bolivia. This road was opened for traffic in 1913.

Private lines include the Transandine Railway, which joins Valparaiso and Santiago with Mendoza and Buenos Aires in Argentina; the International Railway from Antofagasta to Oruro and La Paz in Bolivia; and a number of short railways for the transportation of nitrate and other mineral products, running from the west-coast ports to the interior.

The project of the Chilean government for the electrification of the section of railway uniting Santiago and Valparaiso by using the River Aconcagua as a source of power is an example of undertakings that are characteristic of future transportation development in Chile. The construction of a new transandine railway connecting Chile and Argentina 300 miles north of Santiago is planned. Such a railway will connect the nitrate fields of Chile with the agricultural sections of Argentina.

Telegraph and wireless service. In a recent year there were some 17,000 miles of telegraph lines and about 53,000 miles of telephone lines in Chile. The greater part of the telegraph lines are owned by the government, but the telephone lines are in private hands.

There is a chain of wireless stations along the coast from Punta Arenas to Arica, and stations have also been constructed on many of the islands off the coast.

CHILEAN RELATIONS WITH THE UNITED STATES

The United States has been associated with Chile in trade and also in social relations since the early part of the nineteenth century, when Chile declared her independence. In spite of occasional differences the two countries have been closely associated by reason of reciprocal markets and, since the World War, by a fairly convenient shipping situation. Chilean ports are reached from New York in eighteen or twenty days, and there is an ever-increasing tide of American business men, exporters, importers, and manufacturers going to investigate Chilean markets and to establish agencies and branch houses.

Because of its still largely undeveloped resources in minerals and agriculture, and in view of the fact that the Chileans are rapidly forging to the front in a vigorous and intelligent way in modern enterprises of every kind, this country offers an admirable field for the investment of capital and promises to become one of the greatest industrial states of Latin America. American capitalists have brought a new impetus to Chile's mining industry since the war and have helped the Chileans to establish new and valuable sources of wealth. In addition to investing large sums in mining, Americans have furnished and set up machinery and entire industrial plants for Chile. Moreover, Chilean loans have been readily absorbed in the United States since the war, and if it is true that "trade follows the loan," the commercial relations of the United States and Chile are certain to mean more and more in the future.

The close commercial relations between the United States and Chile have been greatly assisted by business organizations in the United States, composed of Chilean and American business men, while such organizations as the Chile-American Association in New York, under the leadership of Mr. Charles M. Pepper, have aided in bringing about a better geographical and commercial understanding.

CHAPTER VII

ARGENTINA, THE LANDED REPUBLIC

A country with an area of 1,153,418 square miles, — that is, equal to the United States east of the Mississippi, — about two thirds of which is suitable either for agriculture or for grazing, with a population of 8,500,000, largely homogeneous, — a country which has a foreign trade amounting to almost $2,000,000,000 annually, — is not, as a noted financial authority has pertinently declared, "a coming nation"; it is already here. — DR. GRAHAM H. STUART[1]

GENERAL DESCRIPTION

The characterization of Argentina is less difficult than is that of many of the South American and Central American republics, since there are in this country few Indians, few negroes, no distinct middle classes, and no religious-political parties to complicate generalizations.

The Argentino is devoted to material accomplishments, and his pleasures are associated chiefly with horses and horse-racing. The country is rich in live stock, and presents extraordinary opportunities for tillage. The absence of coal and also the lack of water power, except along the slopes of the southern Andes, has delayed manufacturing industries on a large scale. Industrial activities are connected chiefly with the land and grazing resources of the country, the products of which form the principal exports of the foreign markets. The sea has not attracted Argentine mariners or fishermen to any considerable extent.

In recent years immigrants have arrived in vast numbers from Italy, Spain, Germany, and France. With this immigration the country has received much-needed labor, together with certain tendencies toward anarchistic disturbances.

The land of Argentina, like that of Uruguay, is owned in large blocks by landed gentry, many of whom are heirs of the ancient Spanish stock. There are found also English, German,

[1] Graham H. Stuart, Latin America and the United States. The Century Co.

and Belgian landholders possessing large *estancias,* which are composed of vast tracts of treeless acres.

British capital has been largely responsible for the expansion of the railway system, while a considerable amount of American money is tied up in *frigoríficos* (frozen-meat plants) and other plants where beef and pork are prepared for the markets of the world.

The development of mineral resources has been confined chiefly to the production of petroleum in the government fields of Rivadavia. There are extensive deposits of gold, copper, tungsten, and coal in the Andean section, but they have not been mined for commercial uses. While Argentina imports the greater part of the petroleum products consumed, the progress being made upon the government fields promises to make this country an important exporter of petroleum within the next decade.

Among the manufacturing enterprises other than those industrial establishments for the packing of meats are flour mills, sugar refineries, breweries, sawmills, and factories for the production of wine, confectionery, butter, cheese, and quebracho extract. The boot and shoe manufactures have reached the exporting stage. There are many smaller establishments for the production of soap, candles, cement, glass, bricks, and leather.

The commercial position of the country is improving constantly, and the figures denoting trade with the United States reveal a large increase in both exports and imports. In the year 1924 the exports from Argentina to the United States and the imports from the United States to Argentina totaled more than $200,000,000.

One fifth of the people of Argentina dwell in Buenos Aires. The language of the country is Spanish, but considerable Italian is spoken in the larger cities. Few cities in the world give the impression of greater or more exuberant wealth and extravagance than does the capital of Argentina. The *Porteños* (people of the port), as the inhabitants of Buenos Aires are called, furnish the type and norm of the ambitions and ideals of the country.

In this republic the Latins of Europe are coming again to their own, and economic opportunity and prosperity connected with the land have awakened within them a new hope. Argentina, sometimes called "the United States of the Southern Hemisphere," resembles the Middle West of the United States of fifty years ago. There is a greater variety of climate, and the land, which is in large, feudal-like holdings, is given over more exclusively to herds and flocks than to agriculture on small farms, as was the case in agricultural North America in the last century. The possibilities, agriculturally speaking, are similar to those of North America.

Here is found a vigorous people whose great idea is progress, — progress beneath the ægis of the gods of gold, — a people proud of their accomplishments in a material way, who love pleasure as do the French, and who are keenly sensitive to the pride of civic idealism. The Argentinos are inheritors of a rich and beautiful land. Despite many vicissitudes they have been children of fortune. The civilization that they are working out is individualistic, having only slight ties with the old Spanish or Indian races and traditions; it is a mixture of Spanish, Basque, and Italian elements with those of other nations, the resulting amalgam being a distinct product of the new South American world. Many thousands of square miles of virgin lands form for Argentina her rich heritage and her open door.

GEOGRAPHY

Spatially Argentina is impressive, being the second largest country in Latin America. Its area of 1,153,418 square miles is about one third that of the United States. This area is approximately one and one-half times the extent of Mexico and about twenty times that of England.

Argentina has an Atlantic seaboard extending 1565 miles from the mouth of the Rio de la Plata to the bleak limits of Tierra del Fuego, and a western boundary of 3000 miles along the eastern edge of Chile, composed for the most part of the southern Andean mountain chain. The northern boundary is composed of parts of three countries, — Bolivia, Paraguay, and

Brazil. The Uruguay River for a distance of 625 miles forms part of Argentina's eastern water borders.

Argentina may be conveniently divided into four geographical regions: the Pampa, an extensive lowland area which lies west and southwest of Buenos Aires; the Andean region, extending south from Bolivia along the border of Chile; the Gran Chaco, lying in the northern part of Argentina and stretching into Bolivia and Paraguay; and Patagonia, geographically the southernmost bit of the country.

The word *pampa* is of Indian origin, from the Quichua language, and signifies a level, treeless plain, or savanna. It is a "great ocean of land." The meaning of this word in general coincides with the Spanish word *llano* or with the Russian word *steppe*. Flat and monotonous as the sea, the wide and undulating surface of the Pampa is broken only by the occasional *estancia*, about which the landholder, or *estanciero*, has planted a few eucalyptus or paraíso trees; or perhaps a desolate-looking ombu tree breaks the horizon. There is an extent of dead level country for a distance of nearly two thousand miles, and one can proceed for hundreds of miles without seeing a hill, or even a tree, on the horizon. For a vast expanse of featureless prairie the Pampa of Argentina has no competitor.

The grass of the Pampa, growing in tufts often seven and eight feet high, is the hard grass (*pastos duras*) which was brought from Spain by the early Spanish colonists, while other grasses were brought from England and other parts of the earth. Alfalfa, a fairly modern introduction, is common. The soft and agreeable climate is conducive to the heavy growth of this plant, which helps to make Argentina one of the best grazing countries of the world. The soil of this region is of a rich alluvial nature and contains all the possibilities for agriculture found in either Australia or the United States. The Pampa of Argentina is the great wheat country of South America and the prairie home of millions of cattle and sheep.

The Andean region forms the western border of the country. The mountains here are not the highest of the Andes, but they are for the most part lacking in vegetation. Mining is the chief interest, the land being too dry and mountainous for agriculture.

FIG. 14. Harvesting alfalfa in Argentina. A typical scene on the vast Argentine prairies

The Gran Chaco is a sparsely populated and little known region. It is peopled largely by Indian tribes. In the western part tropical agriculture is carried on, and in some places cattle are raised. The forests of the southern part yield quebracho wood and tannin in large quantities.

Patagonia was until recent years a wilderness inhabited only by Indians. Railways have been built through the region, and people have gone there to settle. Sheep-raising has become an important industry. By irrigating the soil it is possible to raise vegetables and fruits in the northern part of the region, where the summers are hot.

There are wide variations in the climate of Argentina, since this wedge-shaped country extends over 34 degrees of latitude, reaching from the torrid tropics in the extreme north almost to the antarctic regions. The greater part of the country lies in the temperate zone. The climate in the central portion is about like that in the state of Kansas; the northern portion has a heavier rainfall than occurs in the central west and the southern parts. Irrigation is needed in the western portion, where the land readily responds to the use of water.

The average annual temperature in the central coast region is 63 degrees Fahrenheit. January is the hottest month, the mean temperature being 77 degrees Fahrenheit. The temperature here rarely reaches the freezing point in winter, although there are occasional snows and hailstorms. Rainfall is abundant and is most frequent in summer and autumn. The city of Buenos Aires enjoys sea breezes during the day and land breezes at night, and there are occasional high winds.

In the central region of the country are found more variations of climate. The summers are hot, with light rainfall, the temperature often reaching over 100 degrees Fahrenheit. Frosts occur in the winter, and windstorms are more or less common.

The Andean regions are very hot during the day and cold at night, with little rain. The diurnal variation is sometimes as high as 68 degrees. The *pamperos* are cold southwest winds blowing from the Andes from June to November, while the hot winds, the *zondas,* blow from the north and northwest chiefly in September and October.

In Tierra del Fuego it is cold all the year, the maximum summer temperatures ranging from 46 to 48 degrees Fahrenheit, and the winter temperatures from 36 to 38 degrees.

The Argentine is greatly favored in climate as compared with its west-coast neighbors, there being few mountains and no barren wastes or deserts, as in northern Chile, and an absence of the dull, sunless days experienced on the western coast of Peru. Despite the wind and the lack of rainfall in certain regions, the climate of the country as a whole is exceedingly healthful.

HISTORY

The early history of Argentina reveals severe struggles prior to the notable date of July 9, 1816, when the Congress of Tucumán declared the Argentine provinces an independent republic.

Settlement of this land began four hundred years ago, and famous names are associated with the discovery and founding of the country. In 1516 Juan Diaz de Solis, with a party of Spaniards, discovered the mouth of the Rio de la Plata while seeking a southwest passage to the East Indies. After the death of Solis at the hands of the Indians in 1520, that far-famed Portuguese sailor, Ferdinand Magellan, engaged in the service of Charles V, also sailed into this vast estuary in his voyage around the world. Then came Sebastian Cabot, the Venetian, who had transferred his services from England. He arrived in 1527 and ascended the Paraguay and Paraná rivers for one thousand miles.

At about the time when Pizarro was founding Lima, in 1535, Pedro de Mendoza laid the foundation of the city of Buenos Aires (the city of good airs). Owing to famine and Indian attacks this first settlement failed to prosper, and in the year 1580 Juan de Garay rebuilt Mendoza's settlement, with more successful results. In 1776, the year so truly notable in the United States, Buenos Aires was made a viceroyalty, with jurisdiction over the present republics of Argentina, Paraguay, Bolivia, and Uruguay. This territory was engaged in many wars for the following twenty or thirty years. Attacks upon

Buenos Aires were made by the English, but finally, in 1810, the British forces were worsted and Buenos Aires in her self-reliant strength elected a provisional committee of patriots. In 1812 General Belgrano, at the head of an Argentine army, defeated the Spaniards at Tucumán, making way for the Congress of Tucumán, which in 1816 declared Argentina's independence.

The declaration of independence did not do away with wars in Argentina. During a considerable portion of the nineteenth century there was conflict both within and without the country. In this century occurred the wars with Paraguay and the war with Brazil over the *Banda Oriental*, the latter war resulting in the independence of Uruguay. Famous names came into prominence during these years of warfare. Among these were the names of General San Martín, who gave of his genius to help in the liberation of Chile; Bernado Rivadavia, the first president of the confederation following the surrender of the territory by Spain; and Juan Manuel de Rosas, who was the Argentine dictator from 1829 to 1853 under the titles of governor and captain-general. In 1861 General Mitre became president of the united provinces, with Buenos Aires as the capital, and from that time to the present the country has been rapidly assuming the rôle of an ordered and progressive state.

PEOPLE

A recent official estimate of population in Argentina is 9,500,000, or about 8.3 persons per square mile. The United States has approximately 35 people to the square mile. Of the population of Argentina about 1,800,000 reside in Buenos Aires, the capital. Approximately 90 per cent of the people of the country are found in 40 per cent of the total area.

It is estimated that the tremendous stretches of unoccupied and uncultivated land in Argentina are capable of nourishing and maintaining 200,000,000 people. One of the chief hindrances to the rapid filling of these vast domains by an industrial population is the old feudal condition of *latifundia*, which has turned hundreds of thousands of workers into temporary immigrants. Immigrants from Europe, failing to find the oppor-

tunity for securing land for a small farm, have formed the habit
of temporary residence in Argentina, returning to their homes
in Europe following the harvest periods. *Pampas 7 families cordul*
Pliny said that the creation of the enormous estates in Italy *2ach track*
eventually led to the downfall of Rome. Although attempts *750,00 a.*
have been made with some success to break up the large Argentine landholdings, which sometimes embrace a hundred thousand acres or more, the purchase of real estate is associated with
such long and tedious formalities and expense that the would-
be homesteader gets discouraged and decides to remain merely
a temporary immigrant. One of the chief hopes for remedying
this situation is the passing of the present generation of landholders and the dividing of their properties among their
numerous children.

Composition of the population. Immigration is a vital factor
in Argentina and is increasing from year to year. The population is chiefly of European and Latin origin. In the last fifty
years there have settled in the country over 2,000,000 Italians,
1,150,000 Spaniards, over 200,000 French, 70,000 Austro-
Hungarians, about 50,000 English, over 50,000 Germans, 30,000
Swiss, 21,000 Belgians, and of other nationalities sufficient to
make a grand total of about 4,000,000. The present immigration amounts to several hundred thousand persons a year.

The original racial stock of Argentina is Spanish, and Spanish
is the language of the country. The population is undergoing
processes of change and amalgamation, and it is as yet difficult
to determine the distinct features of the future Argentine type.
In Buenos Aires, which is a fairly good guide to the country
with respect to the character of its inhabitants, about half of
the Latin element is native to Argentina, less than a quarter is
Spanish or Basque, and more than a quarter is Italian. The
Italians come largely from northern Italy and engage more
readily in commercial activities than in the work of day laborers. Buenos Aires has approximately 800,000 foreign-born
among her inhabitants.

The fusion of the three leading types — Argentinos, Spaniards, and Italians — is made more readily here than in certain
other Latin-American states, where there are many negroes or

Indians. Assimilation is much more rapid here than in the city
of New York, for example, where there is less unity of language
and fewer elemental likenesses between the foreign and native
elements. The literary and artistic and, to a degree, the political
tendencies are similar among the Latin races. There is an
identity of religion, of general culture, and of language. The
Argentine statesman Carlos Pellegrini is quoted as saying :

Unity of language necessarily favors the process of fusion, and
explains the fact that the descendants of immigrants of different
grades, language, religion, habits, and traditions are able to fuse so
completely as to form a perfectly homogeneous population, one in
mind and in sentiment, thus constituting a new nationality, young,
vigorous, and strongly individual.

Characteristics. The character of the Argentine people is unlike that of the South Americans of the western coast and that
of the usual types of people found in colonial Spanish America.
The Argentino is less bound by tradition and is usually open-
minded, taking readily to all modern improvements. He
possesses a rampant optimism and a belief in himself and
his country. "Progress" is a great word with the people of
Argentina, and they resemble North Americans in their worship
of material accomplishment.

As soon as the traveler crossing the mountains from the west
coast arrives in Argentina he notices a different race and breed
of men. The trainmen are larger, and there is an air of independence and assurance reminding one of the United States
rather than of Latin America. The Argentinos, like the Americans, have seen miracles accomplished in their own land and in
their own time ; hence their buoyancy of spirit and their daunt-
less courage born of daring activities in the new country.
Although there are still many of the old families carrying along
the aristocratic Spanish culture, these are gradually disappearing, to make way for a new economic and industrial race,
interested in democracy and in the acquirement of wealth.
The Argentinos are Latin in racial strain, but they are no less
materialists than North Americans, adding to a strong idealism
a keen desire for superiority in the realm of trade and commerce.

Here in Argentina one is certain to find examples of self-made men similar to those in the United States. There is pointed out, for example, the career of one Pedro Luro, a Basque immigrant, who came to Argentina and obtained 100 square leagues (625,000 acres) of good land at a time when the government was glad to dispose of it at three and one-half cents an acre. He secured fifty Basque families to assist him with his grant of property, and several of these people became millionaires as a result. Today the land is valued at five hundred times what Luro paid for it. This Basque immigrant who landed at Buenos Aires in the year 1837, at the age of seventeen, with only a few shillings in his pocket, died a few years ago the owner of a million acres of land, half a million sheep, and a hundred thousand cattle.

This is not the usual accomplishment of the former colonial Spaniards, who considered work in connection with the land degrading and a thing to engage the attention only of slaves or people of the lower classes. The condemnation of labor is rapidly becoming a thing of the past in this land of opportunity, however. The hopeful, enthusiastic Argentinos of today, hospitable in the extreme, especially in the "Camp," are not unlike the inhabitants of our middle-western and northwestern states forty years ago. They have shaken off the chains of medievalism, they have disregarded many of the religious and social tenets found elsewhere in Latin America, and they are facing a future of rich material and commercial progress.

In his book "South of Panama"[1] E. A. Ross has described the Argentinos thus:

The ascendant element has come to misdoubt the very spiritual foundations of the old society as you find it still in half-colonial interior centers like Cordoba and Salta, — its disdain of labor, its indolence, its contempt for business, its reserve and personal pride, its social exclusiveness, its masculinism, its seclusion of women, its patriarchal customs, its clericalism, its spirit of authority and its hostility to the "gringo." Anything that has worked well in the advanced countries now obtains an attentive hearing in Argentina. Its policy of lay education, its democratic school system, its educa-

[1] E. A. Ross, South of Panama. The Century Co.

tion of girls, its normal schools, its reliance upon the woman elementary teacher, its cultivation of athletic sports, its boy scouts, its public libraries, its bacteriological laboratories, its experiment stations, its boards of health, its National Department of Agriculture, which spends half as much as the United States Department of Agriculture, — all these innovations witness to the willingness of Argentina to risk change of soul.

The destiny of Argentina is that of a white man's country, for not over 5 per cent of the people are of non-Caucasian blood, while in the United States 8 or 9 per cent are non-Caucasians. Racially the Argentinos are more European than any other nation in the Western Hemisphere, save possibly the Canadians. But while the language of the country is Spanish, the spirit and motive of the people is South American Argentine, which is another way of saying that it is dominated by that practical and economic urge belonging to the races who are called upon to subdue and develop a new agricultural country, building their institutions and society upon modern and material, rather than upon ancient and spiritual, bases.

The Argentine gaucho. Another class of Argentinos, now rapidly disappearing, is the *gaucho*, or South American cowboy. This picturesque and often quixotic character, with his love of adventure, romance, and the horse, will live after the next fifty years only in the songs and innumerable legends which have interwoven his life and acts with the Argentine Pampa. He, like the Indian before him, whom he drove out and superseded, is to be replaced by the modern and scientific agriculturist; but when the gaucho goes, he will take with him much of the simplicity of life and the romance of the plain. As the buccaneers made the Spanish Main a historic reality of abiding interest, so the gaucho has gathered to himself the local color of the Pampa. The Argentino's children's children will learn of the pioneering days of the earlier settlers through the tales of the adventurous exploits of the gaucho, his manner with the horses and with cattle, and his vanity, partly of Spanish and partly of Indian origin, since he was an inheritor of both blood strains. An excellent picture of this character, who has undoubtedly been a real factor both in the wars of independence and also in the land and cattle industries of Argentina, is found in the book "The Romance of the River Plate," [1] by W. H. Koebel, who quotes a contemporary description of the gaucho as follows:

The gaucho proper is a class — a race it may be called — by itself, and, like the Indian, is but very slowly modified. Within a radius of very many leagues extending from the chief cities of the Platine Republic, his occupation is now gone. Tillage and sheep-farming have driven him out, and he is retiring across the same ground over which the Indian has retired before him. There is a certain poetry or picturesqueness about the "race," as, in a different way, about the Moors of Castile, which almost makes one regret to see pass away a fellow who will sleep on his saddle at your doorsill, like a faithful dog; who endures heat or cold, hunger and thirst, without uttering a complaint; who rides five hundred miles on end at your bidding, sleeping in the open air, providing his food with the lasso, and disposing of it by the simple appliances of his knife, flint and steel, with bones or dried weeds as fuel; who would take the cows, neats, or horses of anyone but his "patron"; who perhaps might knock a man off his horse and cut his throat for his spurs and stirrups, if these took his fancy, but who, in his patron's service, could with perfect confidence be trusted with hundreds of pounds, to go as many leagues and purchase and bring in cattle; who moves with grace, speaks with courtesy, asks after all the family in detail, sends his compliments to the "patrona," or compliments her if he has the opportunity; who marks on the ground the different brands of horses or cattle of numerous owners, and traces stolen or strayed animals over thousands of leagues — such is my friend the gaucho. Yet even some of these come within the circle of civilization and industry, and become patient tenders of flocks. Still, as a class, the gaucho proper must pass away under modifying influences and altered conditions; and where these do not reach, the race, from that lack of domesticity which is fatal to propagation, must literally die out.

CITIES

Buenos Aires, the predominating Argentine city, has been called "a pretentious capital in a pastoral republic." The natives are always talking of its size and its superiority to all

[1] W. H. Koebel, The Romance of the River Plate. Hugh Ponsonby, London.

other South American cities. Such expressions as "the Paris of America," "the second largest Latin city in the world," "the largest city in the world south of the equator," and "the fourth city in size in the Western Hemisphere, only surpassed by New York, Chicago, and Philadelphia," are all indicative of the ambitions of the Argentinos and their pride in a really beautiful capital.

Lying on the right bank of the Rio de la Plata, at this point 28 miles wide, Buenos Aires is about 125 miles from Montevideo and 171 miles from the Atlantic Ocean. The city covers 82 square miles of territory, an area surpassing that of Paris, Berlin, Hamburg, or Vienna, though smaller than that of New York or London. The presence of 800,000 foreign-born people makes Buenos Aires one of the great cosmopolitan cities of the world.

The pride of the Argentinos in their capital has solid ground for existence. Anyone traveling for months among the cities and towns of the west-coast countries of South America (in the Andean sections, and in the rural parts of Ecuador, Peru, Bolivia, and Chile, where a traveler must still endure many privations) is wont to associate these countries with much that is ancient or medieval. The remains of the Inca civilization, the cathedrals of the colonial period and other buildings significant of days long since past, and the customs that are more Moorish than modern with regard to social questions, especially the treatment of women, confront the traveler throughout his west-coast journeys.

Buenos Aires breaks upon him like a veritable new world. There is a luxurious splendor about the city, with its shining boulevards, splendidly lighted and lined with imposing buildings. One finds here high-powered automobiles, first-class modern hotels equal to any found on the continent of Europe, an underground subway, 500 miles of street railways, impressive harbor facilities, including long lines of warehouses and docks, imposing government buildings, theaters, markets, and large parks.

The Argentinos are proud of what they justly call the most complete and up-to-date newspaper building on the continent, one of the largest banks in the world, and the Colon Theater, more expensive and elaborate than all its European rivals.

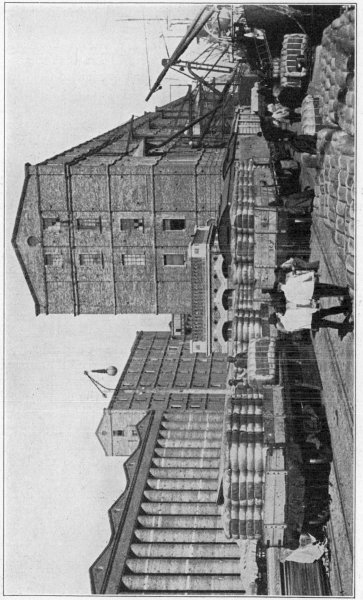

Fig. 15. Loading a cargo of American cotton goods on flat cars at Buenos Aires for shipment to cities and towns in the interior of Argentina. (Photograph by Burton Holmes from Ewing Galloway, New York)

They assert that the capital city has more millionaires in proportion to its population than has New York or any other world metropolis. One writer on Argentina has given a recent book the title "The Amazing Argentine." It would seem that some of the lust for gold and material wealth that dominated the early Spanish explorers and settlers has been revived in the ambitious accomplishments of their modern children. That which Charles Kingsley once said in another connection could be aptly applied to this Argentine city : "It looks gold, it smells of gold. . . . Yea, the very waves, as they ripple past us, sing of gold, gold, gold."

Yet this "city of good airs" is not merely a city of splendor ; it is a great business and commercial city. There is a system of stone docks and immense warehouses that leaves little to be desired in the interests of overseas trade. Extending for two miles along the Rio de la Plata is the main port where ocean steamers are received. Along these docks, with their thirty or more huge warehouses, are vast grain elevators, two dry docks, and every modern convenience and facility. The Latin-American love of lights is shown by the long line of over 800 electric lights that the *Porteños* have placed, a hundred feet apart, to illuminate the harbor entrance. The predominance of Buenos Aires in the Argentine, both as a port and as the capital city, is illustrated by the fact that 22,000,000 tons of cargo have entered this harbor in 64,000 ships in a single year. These ships have brought in 85 per cent of all the imports of the country and have taken out 50 per cent of its exports. The docks are modeled on the Liverpool system and are said to have cost more than $50,000,000. The business of the port has increased so rapidly that further port facilities are already needed and are being contemplated.

Nearly all the nations of Europe are interested in the banking, transportation, and commerce of the city. The British and the Germans are heavy investors and are reported to have $2,000,000,000 in various enterprises. The United States was the last country to enter the banking business in this field. Of the foreign interests represented here, those of England predominate.

The cosmopolitan character of the city is shown by the fact that there are daily papers published in Italian, German, and

Fig. 16. On the Pampa of Argentina vast numbers of beef cattle are raised. Here are some of the cattle penned in the great stockyards at Buenos Aires. (Photograph by Burton Holmes from Ewing Galloway, New York)

French, and there are also several English papers, in addition to the very complete Argentine press.

Buenos Aires has extensive steamer connections. Every month an average of about 200 ships enter and leave the port. There are weekly sailings in excellent passenger steamers to various parts of Europe and to the United States. More than fifty agencies represent steamship lines with regular or irregular sailings. The service between the United States and Buenos Aires has improved greatly since the World War, when high-grade passenger and freight lines were inaugurated between Buenos Aires and New York, making the voyage in less than twenty days.

In the region of Buenos Aires are large *frigoríficos* and slaughterhouses, in some of which several thousand head of cattle are killed daily. These establishments are settlements in themselves, comprising auction rooms, cattle yards, office buildings, and laboratories. Particular attention is given to the checking of any disease among the animals.

Buenos Aires is more or less of a center from which radiate railways extending to various parts of the republic and connecting with others in the neighboring states. The city is thus connected with Asunción, the capital of Paraguay; with Santiago, the capital of Chile; with Rio de Janeiro and Montevideo; and with lines reaching the frontier of Bolivia and even as far as La Paz. There are daily river steamers to Montevideo and a considerable coast and river service both north and south. The railways are as good as the country roads are atrocious.

One finds in the Argentine capital English, German, and American colonies composed largely of business men and those engaged in foreign trade. An American Chamber of Commerce connected with the United States Chamber of Commerce has rendered good service in raising the standard of commercial dealings between the two countries. There is also a French colony, whose members seem to give more attention to intellectual matters and pleasure than to business. The large American meat companies have been doing a considerable business for some time, and an increasing number of American business houses engaged in overseas trade are establishing branch houses in Buenos Aires. There is an increased stream of travel between the United States and Argentina following the better steamship service.

The other Argentine cities, while having a much smaller number of people, are growing in importance, since some of them, at least, occupy strategic positions for both foreign and domestic trade. This is particularly true of the ocean and river port cities.

Rosario, the second city of the republic, located in the province of Santa Fe on the bank of the Paraná River, is 189 miles from Buenos Aires. It has a population of about 250,000 people. Rosario has modern docks accessible to ocean steamers, and carries on an extensive business in the shipping of grain and other agricultural products. Situated as it is in the very midst of the grain district, this city surpasses Buenos Aires as a grain port. A considerable amount of sugar is also produced here. Several railways center at Rosario, affording direct communication with other provinces. As elsewhere throughout the republic, a Spanish-American civic pride is revealed in modern public-service improvements, fine buildings, banks, and well-paved streets.

Córdoba, known for its old and important university, was founded in 1583. It is located 432 miles from Buenos Aires and is the capital of the province of the same name. The principal products are wheat, maize, wood, linseed, hay, flour, cattle, hides, and marble, and the local industries include the manufacture of shoes, soap, candles, carriages, and furniture. There are also flour mills, foundries, marble works, tanneries, and paper mills here. Although the population of Córdoba is only about 140,000, the city is considered one of the most important for business agents outside of the capital. A large amount of flour is produced here, and much is shipped annually to Europe and elsewhere. The famous San Roque Dam is about twenty miles from the city; it is one of the best storage basins and electric-power stations in the world.

Córdoba is a center of culture. There are several unusually fine buildings in the city, among which is the national observatory. The mountains in the neighborhood are known as the "Argentine Switzerland."

La Plata, the capital of the province of Buenos Aires, and situated only 34 miles from the metropolis at the mouth of the Rio de la Plata, has a population estimated at 140,000. It is an important shipping port, having an up-to-date hydraulic equipment for handling freight. A progressive city with fine buildings, La Plata contains the university of the same name. It is easily reached from Buenos Aires.

Tucumán, with about 100,000 people, is the fifth city in population. It is situated 718 miles from Buenos Aires. Tucumán is the center of the country's sugar industry. Thirty-two of the forty-two sugar mills and refineries of the country are located in the province of Tucumán, of which this city is the capital. Tobacco is an important crop, and the lumber business also flourishes here. There are gold, silver, and copper mines in the vicinity. While the merchants deal principally with the Buenos Aires importers, considerable direct importing is carried on. A large surrounding country is supplied by wholesalers located in Tucumán.

Mendoza, said to be the most healthful town in the republic, is the capital of the province of the same name and is located in the foothills of the Andes, at an altitude of 2465 feet, and on the Transandine Railway, 651 miles from Buenos Aires and 252 miles from Santiago, Chile. It has a population of about 60,000 and is the center of a large grape-growing and wine-making industry.

Mendoza is the first large town that the traveler from the west coast sees after crossing the snowy Andes. It reminds him of California or of a patch of Italy, with its extensive vineyards, its wide orchards, and its fields of melons, peaches, apricots, and maize. The train glides through vast plantations of fruit trees, and the traveler is informed that Mendoza alone has more than 3000 acres of orchards like these, as well as 140,000 acres of irrigated land given over to the raising of grapes. Already the Mendoza fruit is finding its way into the markets of New York, and since it reaches the Northern markets in the off season for grapes, this export business is considered to have a bright future. Mendoza is the distributing point for western Argentina, and its commercial firms enjoy a good reputation.

Bahia Blanca is the most important city of southeastern Argentina. It is a commercial gateway and serves a vast hinterland of the Pampa. It also does a large export and import business. With a population of about 50,000, or 80,000 if the suburbs are added, this port city carries all kinds of stocks needed for the development of a new country. Exports such as wool, grain, and in fact all kinds of agricultural products promise to make it a city of rapidly increasing importance. The wide Pampa lies around Bahia Blanca, but the west and northwest have been opened for cultivation only within the past fifteen years. This pivotal center is being visited by commercial agents dealing in a wide variety of goods.

Santa Fe, with a population of about 60,000, is located some one hundred and four miles up the Paraná River from Rosario and is the center of a vast cattle, grain-growing, and quebracho district. A certain amount of trade is carried on with Paraguay, with which there are fair railway connections. Santa Fe has its chief mercantile relations with Buenos Aires and Rosario, although as with all the larger Argentine towns, there is some direct exporting and importing.

Other cities. Among the other Argentine cities smaller in population but of growing importance is **Salta,** on the great trade route connecting Jujuy and Tucumán with Chile and Bolivia. **Paraná,** the capital of the province of Entre Rios, on the Paraná River not far from Santa Fe, is a great cereal center, with a number of manufactories. **Jujuy,** a prosperous city on the direct line between Buenos Aires and Bolivia via La Quiaca, is easily reached from Salta. Its industries are agriculture and mining. **Mar del Plata,** two hundred and fifty miles south of Buenos Aires, is one of the most famous seaside resorts in South America. Its excellent situation on the Atlantic coast seems destined to make it a notable Argentine port.

GOVERNMENT

A new constitution of federal character was made in the city of Santa Fe on May 1, 1853, and this constitution, with a few slight amendments, is now in force in Argentina.

The form of government is based on that of the United States. In a message to the Congress of La Plata, on December 16, 1824, Governor Las Heras of Buenos Aires said:

We are under a large obligation toward the United States of North America. That republic, which, since its formation, has presided over the civilization of the new world, has solemnly recognized our independence. At the same time, it has made an appeal to our national honor by supposing us capable of struggling singlehanded with the power of Spain, but it has constituted itself guardian of the field of battle in order that no foreign power may interfere to give aid to our rival.

Again, on January 5, 1860, at a constitutional convention in Buenos Aires the influence of the United States Constitution was seen. In his report the chairman of the committee on constitutional amendments spoke as follows:

The committee has been guided in its recommendations by the provisions of a similar constitution, recognized as the most perfect, viz., that of the United States. The provisions of this constitution are most readily applicable to Argentine conditions, having served as a basis for the formation of the Argentine Confederation. . . . It would therefore be both presumptuous and a proof of ignorance were we to attempt any innovations in constitutional organization, thus ignoring the lessons of experience and the manifest truths accepted by the human conscience.

Argentina has fourteen provinces, corresponding to our states, each of which possesses a governor and a legislative assembly chosen by itself. There are also ten territories and the Federal District of Buenos Aires. While the president has certain rights of intervention in the affairs of every province, there is found, as in the United States at times, a certain lack of unity in the laws, each province going its own way in law-making. As in Brazil, the foreign trader is often sorely tried by the differing types of legislation affecting business. The doctrine of states' rights is no myth here, and often it is the smallest and most insignificant province that is most insistent upon the letter of its constitutional privileges. The provinces have equal voice in the Senate regardless of their population.

The national Congress consists of a Senate of thirty members (two from each province and two from the Federal District), who serve for nine years, one third retiring every three years, and a Chamber of Deputies, elected by direct popular vote, one for every 33,000 inhabitants, for a term of four years. Half of the Chamber is renewed every two years. The president and vice president, elected indirectly as in the United States, hold office for six years and are not eligible for an immediately succeeding term. The Argentinos guard against a dictatorship. The president, who must be an Argentino, receives a salary of 72,000 paper pesos ($31,600 in gold). He is the head of the army and navy, as is the president of the United States, chooses his ministers and the diplomatic representatives to other countries, and nominates judges.

There is a property qualification for a senator, who, moreover, must have resided in the country for six years. He must also have been a resident in his own province for at least two years before election. The government is based less on principles than on the leadership of particular individuals. The socialist deputies are seemingly on the increase. The Italian and Spanish immigrants, naturalized after two years' residence in the country, usually vote the socialist ticket. The first departure from the traditional custom of choosing the president from the governing, or aristocratic, class came in 1916, when the radical party elected as its representative for president Doctor Hipólito Irigoyen.

Male citizens of Argentina have voting rights at the age of eighteen years. The exercise of the franchise is obligatory for all native-born citizens, and for foreigners as well after a residence of two years. Citizenship is given at once to a man who marries an Argentine woman, and every child born in the country is counted as an Argentino. Among the laws of inheritance that are somewhat distinctive is the law that a father must leave four fifths of his property to his wife and his children; if there are no children, the husband must leave half of his property to his wife. An unmarried son must leave his parents two thirds of his property.

The government levies heavy duties on imported manufactured articles except upon such commodities as are supposed to benefit the country, — farm machinery, for example. Any person establishing a new industry, inventing something useful, contracting to build a railroad, establishing a colony, or becoming a teacher may receive citizenship immediately.

The religion of the republic is Roman Catholic, but the Argentinos in general, especially the men, are more or less indifferent to religion of any kind. No bar or hindrance is placed against any kind of religious faith.

ARMY AND NAVY

Service of a year is compulsory in the army or navy, and men between the ages of twenty and forty-five are subject to call. Every man must learn to shoot. The standing army consists of about 30,000 men, and effective mobilization is reckoned to be in the neighborhood of 500,000 men. Naturalized citizens are exempt from military service for ten years.

The navy has about seventy vessels of various kinds in its fleet. The battleships *Rivadavia* and *Moreno*, of 28,000 tons each, were built in the United States and are considered among the best sea fighters in the world. There are some 8500 men in the navy, including the reserves.

CURRENCY

The paper peso, equal to about 42 cents in United States currency, is the unit of value for commercial transactions and is used in paying ordinary bills and hotel accounts, in making purchases in shops, for carriage hire, and other purposes. There is a theoretical gold peso, which has a value of $0.965 in our money and is used in government reports unless specifically stated to the contrary.

EDUCATION

The system of education is similar to that of the United States, although in Argentina there is a slight fee for secondary education, and it is not compulsory. Primary-school education is compulsory. About 42 per cent of the children attend the primary school. This small attendance is due largely to the vast distances that must be traversed before school privileges can be enjoyed, and to the lack of proper transportation. There are the usual special schools for training in agriculture and in industrial, commercial, and technical subjects. There are five excellent national universities: Córdoba, the oldest, with three faculties; Buenos Aires, the largest, with six; La Plata, also with six; Tucumán, with four; and the new University of the Littoral, organized in 1920, with six.

There are many private schools with government supervision, carried on by foreigners, and forty-one private normal schools. There is a naval and military college, and physical drill and rifle-shooting are taught in the two highest classes of the secondary schools.

PRODUCTS AND INDUSTRIES

The success of Argentina is due to its pastoral and agricultural pursuits. Despite the large production of the land, only about one fourth of the area of the great Pampa which is suitable for crops is under cultivation. The total area of the country is about 740,000,000 acres, of which approximately one third may be cultivated and another third may be used for cattle-raising.

Argentina has furnished Great Britain with a large part of its food products, and has been one of the chief sources of raw materials for use in manufacturing in the United States. This country is the principal market for most of Argentina's raw materials such as wool, linseed, quebracho, and casein and other animal products. A large amount of Argentine wheat and flour is taken by Brazil, and in some years Brazil is second to England in the amount of foodstuffs purchased from Argentina.

The mining industry is overshadowed by the agricultural and grazing industries. Borate of lime, onyx, mica, tungsten, salt, and limestone are produced in quantities large enough for export. Gold, silver, copper, and petroleum are also produced.

The leading forest industry is the production of quebracho extract and the shipment of quebracho logs.

EXPORTS AND IMPORTS

The food products exported by Argentina are wheat, corn, oats, barley, frozen and chilled beef, mutton, lamb, cheese, and butter. The industrial products exported are linseed, hides and skins, wool, hair, tallow, casein, glue, and quebracho.

The principal imports of Argentina include manufactured products ready for use. Among these are textiles, iron and steel, railway cars and equipment, automobiles, carriages, structural iron, phonographs, motion-picture films, typewriters, and lumber. Other important imports are pharmaceutical products, paper, agricultural implements, mineral oils, tools, manufactures of wood, copper, zinc, and tin, paints, pottery and glassware, together with furniture and house fittings. With the exception of rice, coffee, and some sugar, Argentina does not import primary food products, although a considerable amount of elaborated food products and condiments are brought into the country.

Among the leading items which Argentina imports from the United States are agricultural implements, hardware, machinery, petroleum products, iron and steel products, cotton goods, automobiles, musical instruments, and photographic supplies. Shipments of automobiles, adding machines, tobacco, yellow pine, and agricultural implements have more than doubled in value in recent years.

The total trade of Argentina in both exports and imports has reached in each of several recent years a figure of approximately $1,500,000,000. In 1924 the export trade was valued at $981,000,000, and the import trade at $804,000,000.

TRANSPORTATION AND COMMUNICATION

Railways. The railways of the country are developed to a greater extent than in most of the other South American countries. The level surface of the land has facilitated railway construction. There are about 23,000 miles of railways in Argentina, 18,000 of which are in private hands; 4000 miles are owned by the government, 670 miles are of provincial owner-

Fig. 17. Grain elevators in the port of Buenos Aires

ship, and 600 miles are of industrial ownership. Great Britain is said to have $1,000,000,000 invested in Argentine railways, and France is also a large foreign investor.

There is a busy traffic about the capital city, five hundred passenger trains leaving Buenos Aires daily. The Central Argentine Railway, with a mileage of 3300, is said to have the finest railway station and terminal in South America. The freight station of the Buenos Aires Great Southern Railway, which serves the province of Buenos Aires mainly, has a capacity of 230,000 bags of grain and 2000 tons of other freight, and is one of the largest freight stations in South America.

Telegraph and wireless service. About one half of the telegraph system belongs to the government, and there is an agreement between the government lines and the privately owned lines for facilitating this service. The cable service is good and is in private hands for the most part, the company subscribing to the international conventions. Argentina was the first of the South American countries to adopt wireless telegraphy, and the Argentine navy has a complete installation of wireless on all its vessels.

COMPETITION FOR ARGENTINE TRADE

The World War made significant changes in the Argentine markets. Prior to the war Great Britain held the chief place in the import trade of Argentina, with Germany, the United States, France, and Italy following some distance behind. German trade disappeared during the war, and the United States became the first nation in overseas trade with Argentina, Great Britain taking second place. Immediately after the war the United States and Great Britain furnished two thirds of all the manufactured articles imported by Argentina.

Keen international competition for Argentina's trade was renewed and has been continued since the European conflict, with the result that Great Britain has now regained in this market the position which it held prior to 1914. Germany is steadily gaining ground, but the United States still holds second place. The Germans are buying heavily of Argentine wool, grains, quebracho, and hides, and are sending to Argentina an increasing number of manufactured articles such as hardware, machine tools, electrical supplies, kitchen utensils, toys, and school supplies. As a rule these articles are supplied to Argentina at a price cheaper than that of similar manufactures from the United States, the prices of some of the German goods being from one third to one half those of the American goods. The German goods are also reported to be much inferior in quality. German paper has undercut American paper in the matter of price, and large supplies of German chemicals and drugs are being shipped to Argentina. Germany has been handicapped, however, in the matter of shipment because of conditions in the Ruhr and because of her unsettled finances.

Other European countries, utilizing the advantage of depreciated exchange since the war, have been pushing their sales in Argentina. The chief countries making advances in trade here are France, Italy, Belgium, and Brazil. All these are contesting the right for fourth place in the Argentine markets. Belgium has been particularly successful in reaching these markets with her railroad equipment and other products of iron and steel. The matter of credits has been an important item in the advances made by European countries in Argentine commerce, especially in the cases of Germany and Belgium. The Belgian manufacturers have received large support from the banks and from their government in the financing of their sales abroad.

SUMMARY

All this vast achievement and opportunity of the new nation waits upon certain factors other than gold and exports and imports. John Ruskin once spoke of three guardian angels of a nation, — Conduct, Toil, and Thought. Argentina has a stable government, a rapidly growing foreign trade, and a boundless faith in everything Argentine; but, like the United States, it may well guard itself against materialism that makes no place for things of the spirit, and against a plutocracy that may be as evil in the end as the dictatorship which the country has already known. One of the professors in the University of Buenos Aires said: "My great aim is to rid my country of two of her arch foes, socialism and religion." It seems that socialism is growing and religion is fading. The friend of Argentina might wish that these tendencies were reversed. Yet it is not for other countries to prescribe the political or religious creeds for their sister nations. The Argentinos, intelligent, progressive, and not without political genius and good sense, must be trusted to add to their material riches that flowering of culture which has made memorable their mother countries, Spain and Italy.

The critics of Argentina often state that the country has not yet produced art or literature of any great importance. The republic is often pictured as unduly self-appreciative; yet it has flung its doors open to all European races, who are being urged to become Argentinos, it is not troubled with the menace of Asiatic labor, and its lack of the negro strain of blood has freed it from problems of race prejudice found in the United States. One of the chief handicaps of the country no doubt lies in that great middle space between the plutocracy and the working classes. The poor immigrant and even the salary-earning clerk find it difficult to rise. The cost of living is heavy throughout the country, and there are no such economic opportunities for poor farmers as the United States and Canada have offered for the last century. Yet there are evident tendencies toward the gradual breaking up of the vast estates that the landed classes will be unable to resist. The race now in formation possesses traditions in language and culture that will undoubtedly appear in the next fifty years in the flowering of those traits and talents having to do with the cultural side of the people.

To quote the words of Sir John Foster Fraser [1]:

But it is an amazing country, nevertheless. For ages it has been lying in the womb of Time. It has just been born, and its growth is one of the wonders of the world. Its inhabitants are quickly adapting themselves to modern needs. The revolutionary days are of the past. It has millions of acres under the power of man; it has many millions more awaiting population. It is crying out for population. And great steamers from Spain and Italy are driving southward over

[1] John Foster Fraser, The Amazing Argentine. Cassell and Company, Ltd.

the line of the equator carrying what Argentina needs. She receives nearly three hundred thousand new arrivals annually, and within a couple of years most of them become Argentine citizens.

Despite the space given by certain writers on South America to the attitude of the Argentinos toward the United States, and their suspicion of the Monroe Doctrine, these two great republics, having so much in common in their political constitution, are being bound together more closely every year. Large loans are bringing the countries together financially; foreign trade is increasing rapidly because of mutual markets and better steamship service; and a much better understanding is being brought about by the ever-enlarging tides of travel both north and south. Particularly is it true that the problems of these two countries, as far as cultural industries are concerned, are more nearly identical than is the case between the United States and any other South American republic.

CHAPTER VIII

URUGUAY

Democratic equality in manners is combined with a high sense of personal dignity, an immense hopefulness, an impulsive readiness to try all experiments, a national consciousness none the less intense because it already rejoices over the triumphs it is going to achieve. — JAMES BRYCE [1]

THE "LITTLE BELGIUM OF THE NEW WORLD"

Those who are accustomed to associate bigness with success, and to disparage small countries simply because they are limited in area, would give Uruguay, the "little Belgium of the New World," scant treatment in the study of Latin-American republics and their actual and potential markets. That this would be a grave mistake is evident to those who contrast the economic and commercial status of the cities and towns of the *Banda Oriental*, or "east bank" (the name sometimes given to Uruguay because of its position to the east of the Uruguay River) with that of the cities and towns of Argentina on the opposite side of the river.

GEOGRAPHY

Uruguay is the smallest of the South American republics. Its area of about 72,000 square miles is greater, however, than the combined area of the New England States, although it has a population only one fifth as large.

This republic contains the best pasture lands in all South America. Its grassy plains are almost unbroken by mountains, save in the extreme north, where are found some comparatively low ranges separated by wide and fertile valleys. There is no extensive unexplored hinterland here as in Brazil and Venezuela,

[1] James Bryce, South America, Observations and Impressions. The Macmillan Company.

and there are no deserts or inaccessible altitudes as in Peru and Bolivia. Practically the whole area of Uruguay is available for tillage or pasturage, and the name "garden country" is often given to it. Its cereal and pastoral products have gone far toward establishing the world-wide reputation of the Rio de la Plata markets.

The fact that Uruguay is favorably situated in the temperate zone on the Atlantic coast and has prevailing southeast coast winds accounts for its equable and delightful climate. The vegetation and general conditions for agriculture are similar to those found in the central and southern portions of the United States. The winters are like those of Florida, and the summers like those of Pennsylvania; hence Uruguay is sought by wealthy Argentinos and Brazilians throughout the year as a pleasure and vacation resort. The average annual temperature is 62.5 degrees Fahrenheit, and the rainfall is moderate and distributed through the year.

HISTORY

The early history of Uruguay was stormy, and there have been frequent political contests that have taken the form of revolutions, not without bloodshed. With the coming of the twentieth century these internal disturbances have become less frequent.

In 1515 Juan Diaz de Solis discovered the Rio de la Plata and, landing in what is now Uruguay, took possession of the lands in the name of the Spanish crown. Solis and his party were soon attacked and killed, however, by the savage Charrúas, the tribe of Indians who occupied the country at that time. Although there were various attempts at exploration and settlement by Spanish and Portuguese during the century following, it was not until 1624, when the Jesuits came, that permanent settlements were made. For two hundred years the possession of the country was contested by Spain and Portugal, and in 1777 it was finally ceded to Spain.

On May 18, 1811, the Uruguayans gained their independence under the leadership of the Uruguayan General José Gervasio

Artigas. The Brazilians soon laid claim to the country, however, and there were more conflicts until 1825, when the Uruguayans again declared themselves independent and promulgated a constitution on July 18, 1830. The first president was General Fructuoso Rivera, and the second president, General Manuel Oribe, was elected in March, 1835. War broke out between the adherents of these two generals, and the partisans, lining up with Oribe, who rode a white horse, or Rivera, who rode a bay horse, formed the famous Uruguayan parties, the Blancos and the Colorados, or the Whites and the Reds, which still exist. The Blancos in time became for the most part the country party, upholding the Church, while the Colorados formed the urban and anticlerical party. These parties are now practically hereditary, since the principles have not changed greatly in many years. Since 1864 the Colorados have been in power.

PEOPLE

Composition of the population. Of Uruguay's population of about 1,500,000 only one fifth is of foreign birth. No other country in South America possesses such a truly homogeneous white population. As in Argentina, both Indians and negroes are few in number.

The racial stock of the *Fluvenses*, or river folk, as the Uruguayans call themselves, has been largely Spanish (with little intermixture of Indian blood) until recent years, when there has been considerable immigration from Italy in addition to that from Spain. The standard of the population is high, for immigration in Uruguay is carefully restricted and there is no general or wholesale acceptance of foreigners.

The Uruguayan viewpoint with regard to immigration has been expressed by former President Viera thus:

To be sure we want immigration here, but we want additional population of the right kind. Uruguay does not possess facilities and resources for manufacturing because of her lack of coal, wood, and iron. The republic has, on the other hand, tremendous resources for the raising of live stock and also for agricultural development. It is necessary to have our recruits chosen with a view to the kind of work which the nation needs. We do not require the vast influx of laboring population which Argentina and the United States have been receiving, since the time is not ripe for them, and, furthermore, they would find little congenial to their abilities in Uruguay.

Uruguayan characteristics. Modest in manners and possessing a natural courtesy that prosperity has not spoiled, the Uruguayans have a distinctive quality of culture which makes a pleasant change from the culture based on the too often artificial and overmaterialized products of modern civilization found in both South and North America. They are impulsive and energetic, sincere and lovable, and dependable in business.

A decided Latin strain in the character of the Uruguayans is revealed in their political and social relations. They have a pronounced love of theory and a penchant for the new and progressive, while at the same time they often lack a proportionate love of action and practical achievement. They are enthusiastic idealists, but, like the people in many another Latin-American country, they do not always establish the proper relation between principle and practice.

There is no state church, and although the prevailing religious faith is Roman Catholic, a liberal spirit of tolerance for all religious beliefs exists. It is significant that Uruguay is the only Latin-American republic that is openly anticlerical, although in many of the other republics the power of the Church over the more progressive men is slight.

The reign of conservatism in all social relations is as distinct in Uruguay as in other Latin-American countries. The home is central in the affairs of the Uruguayan, and the mother, as the central figure of the home, is the constructive and controlling force in the family life; she is rarely found engaging in the outside activities which are common to women living in northern countries.

In spite of the progressiveness of all the political leaders, atavistic and conservative customs, reminders of Moorish heritage, are evident in the inviolable social conventions of the country, according to which the sexes are carefully separated

until marriage, and in the old Spanish-Moorish house, which
still presents a forbidding exterior, with its balconies and closed
shutters and its open patios, which are very cold and cheerless
when the weather is cold or rainy.

In contrast to the town-bred Uruguayans, who are natural-
born politicians and have strong partisan leanings, the rural
population of the *Campana*, as the Pampa is styled here, often
remind one of the eighteenth rather than the twentieth century.
The wide *Campana* has so long been an independent pastoral
country, where conditions of life are dominated by the live-stock
situation, that the coming of certain evidences of modernity
long in use in the cities has been slow here, for the people are
inclined to scout the value of ways of life different from those
familiar to their fathers.

No Uruguayan type is more interesting than the gaucho, or
plainsman. Not so dashing as the gaucho of a generation ago,
he is, nevertheless, sufficiently picturesque, with his love of
out-of-doors, his breeziness, and his recklessness and fighting
qualities. His life is largely associated with the care of stock,
and riding is second nature to him.

The Uruguayan gaucho is taller than the Argentine gaucho.
He wears a varicolored poncho, and often a sombrero, carries a
knife in his belt and a revolver in his holster, and frequently has
silver decorations for his saddle and spurs. His work and recreations resemble those of the Mexicans. He is highly patriotic and
is fond of relating the exploits of the gauchos when they fought
under the national hero, Artigas, and helped to free Uruguay.

CITIES

Montevideo. Montevideo, the capital of Uruguay, is by far the
largest and most important city of the republic, with its population of about 400,000 and its excellent position at the mouth
of the Rio de la Plata. The greater part of the city is situated on
a peninsula swept by ocean winds, and the climate is extremely
healthful. The harbor is on the west, and on the ocean side are
fine beaches, which are becoming more and more popular resorts
for visitors from neighboring states.

Fig. 18. At the docks of Montevideo, Uruguay. This city is one of the important ports of call on the east coast of South America for steamers

From the Cerro, a conical hill 500 feet in height, on the south-western side of the bay, the entire city and its environs may be seen. In his book "The Purple Land"[1] W. H. Hudson, the late writer and naturalist, has described this view as follows:

Whichever way I turn, I see before me one of the fairest habitations God has made for man: great plains smiling with everlasting spring; ancient woods; swift, beautiful rivers; ranges of blue hills stretching away to the dim horizon. And beyond those fair slopes, how many leagues of pleasant wilderness are sleeping in the sunshine, where the wild flowers waste their sweetness and no plough turns the fruitful soil, where deer and ostrich roam fearless of the hunter, where over all bends a blue sky without a cloud to stain its exquisite beauty? And the people dwelling in yon city, — the key to a continent, — they are the possessors of it all.

Founded in 1726, Montevideo had a population of 70,000 in 1879. Now it has nearly six times as many inhabitants, and soon its population will be half a million. The city is modern in all its appointments except for the old Town Hall, which dates from colonial days. Many of the buildings are of French or Italian architecture, and there are picturesque bungalows and flat-roofed houses of varied colors. There is a theater where is heard much of the best artistic talent of Europe and the United States, a fine university, botanical gardens, an athenæum notable for its scientific and literary sessions, schools, hospitals, an Avenida two and a half miles in length, and parks overflowing with roses, wisteria, and bougainvillea, and having many fine trees. Although Montevideo is a thriving and prosperous city, it is not so ostentatiously wealthy as Buenos Aires and has far less of the hustle and bustle characteristic of the great city only 125 miles away. The people give the impression of having more time to enjoy life.

Three fourths of the foreign trade of the country passes through Montevideo, the chief products going out from this port being meats and meat extracts, hides, and wool. Since the expenditure of between $25,000,000 and $30,000,000 on the

[1] By permission, from "The Purple Land," by W. H. Hudson. Published by E. P. Dutton & Company.

harbor to provide good docking facilities for large ocean-going craft the city has made rapid advances and is destined to become one of the large commercial and maritime cities of the world. There is now an air mail and passenger service between Montevideo and Buenos Aires.

Paysandú, the second city of Uruguay in commercial importance, is far smaller than Montevideo, having a population of about 25,000. It is the last port of call for ocean-going vessels on the Uruguay River. Situated in an agricultural and pastoral district, Paysandú is naturally the center of the meat-packing and frozen-meat industry and has some factories for curing meat. It has modern facilities, like street cars, electric lights, and telephones. **Fray Bentos** is south of Paysandú and has similar industries. It is a thriving center for the preparation of beef extract and has some 12,000 inhabitants.

Salto, north of Paysandú on the Uruguay River, is the third important city, and adds fruit-growing to its pastoral activities. It has a population of about 30,000.

Artigas, a town on the Brazilian border with a population of about 9000, is better known for its timber than for its cattle and grazing activities, although the latter are important.

Mercedes, on a branch of the Rio Negro, has a population estimated at between 15,000 and 30,000 and is noted for its agricultural and live-stock industries. There are a number of smaller cities and towns engaged largely in work connected with the beef industry.

Colonia, across the Rio de la Plata from Buenos Aires, is a town of 15,000 people. It may one day be the eastern terminus of a tunnel beneath the river.

GOVERNMENT

Uruguay's constitution, which in its revised form was put into effect in 1919, provides for a more centralized government than does the Constitution of the United States. Executive power is divided between the president and a National Council of Administration composed of nine members, with a similar number of alternates. The president is elected by the people for a term of four years, and the National Council for six years. The president can appoint certain of the members of his cabinet, while the others are appointed by the National Council.

The legislative branch of the government consists of two houses: the Senate, with nineteen members, and the Chamber of Representatives, where the number of members is in proportion to the population. There is no vice president, and the Senate is the judge of the election of the president as well as of the members of the National Council.

Congress elects the members of the Supreme Court, who in turn elect members of the other courts.

The right to vote is accorded to all citizens, natural or legal, who are eighteen years of age and whose names are inscribed in the civil register. In 1921 suffrage was granted to women.

In its governmental affairs Uruguay approaches the ideal of a highly advanced independent state more closely than any other Latin-American country. Legislation of recent years includes laws establishing minimum wages and regulating working hours, and also laws prohibiting bullfights and cockfights. The authority of the Church over matters of government has been almost entirely abolished, and there is a distinct trend toward state socialism and government ownership.

ARMY AND NAVY

Uruguay has a small standing army of about 10,000 and a National Guard with a total strength of approximately 100,000. Service in the former is optional, but it is compulsory in the latter for men between the ages of seventeen and forty-five. There are three classes of service in the National Guard, ranging from a division organized for immediate service with the standing army to a division for garrison service in its own districts.

The navy consists of a training vessel, a light cruiser, a torpedo gunboat, and several smaller vessels.

CURRENCY

Although Uruguay has no gold coin of its own, the country is on a gold basis. The Uruguayan *peso*, or dollar, is equivalent in gold, in normal times, to $1.034 in United States currency. Almost any gold coin is legal tender here, and there is an easy exchange from Uruguayan paper into gold.

EDUCATION

Uruguay has a good school system. Primary-school attendance is required, and there is reported to be one public school to every thousand people in the country. Secondary-school instruction is given in the various departments. In Montevideo and several other cities there are normal schools. The University of Montevideo, with its agricultural, engineering, law, and other departments, is also in the capital city, as are the military, naval, and naval-aviation schools. Several agricultural and trade schools are maintained in Uruguay.

PRODUCTS AND INDUSTRIES

Uruguay is, first of all, and always has been, a pastoral country. At least 95 per cent of its exports are composed of live stock and related products. Of its 46,000,000 acres over 40,000,000 are devoted to the live-stock industry, while only about 2,000,000 acres are used for agricultural purposes, and 1,700,000 acres for forestry. The remainder of the country is practically unproductive.

LIVE-STOCK INDUSTRY

With its wide, unbroken spaces of well-watered lands lying in the temperate or subtropical zones, Uruguay has every advantage for the raising of live stock. It is estimated that there are in the country 11,500,000 sheep, 8,000,000 cattle, 500,000 horses, and a lesser number of swine, mules, and goats.

The Uruguayans, like the Argentinos, take great pride in the improvement of their herds, and scientific cattle-raising is in progress. Various breeds, such as the Durham, Hereford, Devon, Aberdeen, and Angus, have been introduced from England, and it is not uncommon for an estancia owner to pay thousands of dollars for an imported bull. Swiss, Dutch, Flemish, and Norman stock is also imported for breeding purposes in the dairy industry. Great care is taken in the breeding of sheep, and the best Merinos are brought from Spain, Rambouillets from France, and Southdowns from England.

Meat is naturally one of the leading products of the live-stock industry, and there are a considerable number of establishments in Uruguay for salting and freezing meats and preserving their extracts. Meat-packing in this country dates back to 1786. Frozen and chilled beef, as well as mutton, is exported in large quantities, and meat extracts, canned meats, and by-products of the meat industry are also important.

Wool is one of the most valuable products of the country, and great care is taken that the wool raised shall be of excellent quality. Sheepskins and cattle hides also rank high in value.

Dairying is an industry of growing importance, and milk, butter, and cheese are produced in a number of the southern provinces both for home consumption and for export.

AGRICULTURE

The average size of a Uruguayan farm is about 250 acres, although the majority of farms are considerably smaller than this. That agriculture has a comparatively small place in Uruguay is largely due to the fact that so much of the land is in large holdings. The estancias, or cattle ranches, are on a huge scale, a single estancia sometimes including from 40,000 to 60,000 acres. An attempt has been made to reduce these vast holdings and form small farms, with the intention of increasing agricultural activities and enlarging the population. With all of Uruguay eminently adapted to agriculture, such a condition is to be desired; but it is not easily brought about in a country where, as in Argentina, the large landowner is also something of a politician and quite awake to his own opportunities for conserving his property and profits.

Most of the agricultural products are raised in the southern provinces. Wheat occupies the largest acreage, with corn next in order and oats third. Linseed is important, and some barley, birdseed, and rye are also raised. These products are exported to some extent, but their value is still considerably less than that of live-stock products, although it has increased in the last few years.

OTHER INDUSTRIES

Uruguay has many mineral deposits, but comparatively little has been done to develop them. There are several gold mines and also deposits of copper, manganese, and petroleum. Recently deposits of coal have been discovered that give promise of future wealth.

There are seal fisheries on islands off the coast of Uruguay, and the flesh of these animals is used in making lubricating grease and various kinds of polishes. Nutria fur is another valuable product.

EXPORTS AND IMPORTS

The exports and imports of Uruguay are similar to those of Argentina, although they are on a much smaller scale. In 1925 the total foreign trade of the country was valued at approximately $200,000,000, of which exports furnished $102,000,000 and imports $98,000,000.

Meat and meat products are the most valuable exports of Uruguay, as might be expected. Of this class of exports frozen and chilled beef are the chief items, although jerked beef, canned meats, frozen mutton, beef extract, and the many by-products of the meat industry are also important. Wool is the second export in value, and hides and skins, taken as a whole, the third. Linseed, wheat, and oats, the leading agricultural exports, rank far below the live-stock exports in value. Among the minor exports are sand and paving stones, heron plumes (or aigrettes), and ostrich feathers.

Petroleum products, coal, cotton and silk goods, food products such as sugar and potatoes, and automobiles are among the principal imports of Uruguay.

In 1925 approximately 24 per cent of the exports of Uruguay went to the United Kingdom, while about 12 per cent, valued at $12,000,000, were sent to the United States. Germany, France, Belgium, and Argentina also took a considerable share. In the same year the United States was the principal source of Uruguayan imports, furnishing some 26 per cent, while the United Kingdom ranked second with 19 per cent. Germany and Argentina ranked next, each furnishing about 10 per cent.

TRANSPORTATION AND COMMUNICATION

Railways. The railways of Uruguay radiate from Montevideo, touching most of the larger towns. They touch the Brazilian border at three points, at two of which they connect with Brazilian lines. One can go from Montevideo to Rio de Janeiro by rail, and a British company is now planning to establish airplane service between these two cities and Recife (Pernambuco).

Uruguay boasts only some 1650 miles of standard-gauge (4 feet, $8\frac{1}{2}$ inches) railway, but this mileage is greater than that of many other Latin-American republics when the size of the country is considered. About 90 per cent of the railways are owned and controlled by the British, the remainder being owned by the Uruguayan government. The Central Uruguay Railroad is the main road, operating 980 miles of track on its main branches.

Montevideo is the natural railway center of the country as well as the chief port. There are large warehouses here and modern facilities of unusual excellence for unloading and loading vessels. Large vessels can come up to some of the docks at all times, including low tide, and thus connect with the railways. Passengers and freight are carried by a port railway.

Roads. People traveling in the interior of Uruguay are often surprised to find that so little has been done to provide good roads. This backwardness is not to be accounted for because of lack of good material for road construction, for paving stone of excellent quality is to be had, but rather because of the conservatism of the people in the rural districts, discussed elsewhere in this chapter. There is no doubt that good roads will be built in the future, however, if Uruguay continues slowly, but surely, to carry forward its sturdy spirit of progress.

Telegraph and wireless service. There are some five thousand miles of telegraph lines in the republic, part of which are operated by the government and the other part by private companies. Uruguay has a telephone system and direct cable communication with the United States and Europe. Wireless equipment is practically compulsory for all steamers calling at Uruguayan ports, and there is a large wireless station near Montevideo, as well as stations at Rivera, Lobos Island, and several other places.

ECONOMIC CONDITIONS

The economic growth of the country is tempered by the fact that about 5000 men own 80 per cent of all the land, and 100 individual owners claim approximately an equal percentage of the capital employed in business enterprises not financed by foreign capital. It is estimated that in this country foreigners own 40 per cent of the land and the business capital, and, as is the case in many other Latin-American republics, a large portion of the annual earnings goes out of the country to foreign stockholders and proprietors. The country urgently requires a more equable division of land into small farms, and more and better roads for the transportation of crops and merchandise. When these conditions are brought about, a larger working population will be necessary. At present, although it is claimed that there are 1000 manufacturing concerns in the republic, a careful investigation discloses that these are small and as a rule provide only for local needs.

Considering all the handicaps of this small but animated state, one must give the Uruguayans credit for being both good bankers and good business men. With comparatively little capital of its own, Uruguay has in the past depended largely on Europe for its financing. More recently the republic has placed successful loans in the United States. The shifting of some of its credits from Europe to the United States has tended to strengthen Uruguay's economic condition, especially at a time when the financial turmoil of the countries of Europe is reflected in the sections dependent upon them for credits.

The country's excellent financial record has been summarized as follows by a member of the National City Bank of New York, a branch of which is situated in Montevideo:

Under the most trying conditions, when the Argentine and Brazil did not hesitate to reduce their foreign debts by methods which are commonly familiar, and when Uruguay had equal or greater provocation to follow their example, the Oriental Republic arranged for a settlement of its liabilities in full, succeeding at the same time in keeping its currency uniformly on a gold basis.

Since Uruguay is rich in cattle products, which are shipped to many countries, its exports under favorable conditions more than offset its imports, the balance of trade being met by service payments of the government's foreign indebtedness, together with the transfer of dividends on foreign investments. This means that occasionally gold must be shipped. Revenues from importations represent from 50 per cent to 55 per cent of the value of imports, and nearly 65 per cent of all revenues. For example, the government revenues for imports worth $1,000,000 are $600,000. If conditions arise here or in other countries that result in a loss of $1,000,000 in imports, the government treasury is drained of this $600,000. It is not strange, therefore, that one hears it said among bankers that "a pistol shot in the Balkans means a failure in the River Plate," and that this condition is a cause of much solicitude to Uruguayan bankers and business men in a period like the one attending the World War. Such conditions will be remedied sooner or later, when means of livelihood are provided for a greatly enlarged population, so that the country may become more nearly self-supporting.

CHAPTER IX

PARAGUAY

The epoch of the Conquistadores was an epoch of illusions, of *ignes fatui*, and in no part of South America did these illusions cast a more potent spell over the conquerors than it did over the iron-hearted adventurers in the vast territory so long known as the Province of La Plata. — J. A. ZAHM [1]

GEOGRAPHY

Paraguay, like Bolivia, is an inland republic, lying about four hundred miles from the Atlantic Ocean. The country has the advantage over Bolivia, however, because of its connection with the coast by the famous Paraná River. This river, with Brazil, forms the eastern boundary of the country. Other long, navigable rivers run through the interior and along the southern and western boundaries.

Paraguay has an area of 196,000 square miles. The settled portion is somewhat larger than the state of Missouri and is in many ways similar in character. The eastern section is traversed from north to south by broad, irregular belts of highlands, and resembles a vast plateau, averaging about 2000 feet in height, which is a continuation of the large interior plateau of Brazil. There are vast and almost impenetrable forests sloping down toward the Paraná on the east; to the west of the Paraguay River, which divides the country almost in halves, lies El Gran Chaco, a huge, grassy plain interspersed with swamps and forests.

Paraguay proper lies east of the Paraguay River. Here the country is beautifully rolling, affording fine pastures and wheat fields, the crops of which can be easily transported by means of the waterways. The low mountains are covered with forests which not only add to the beauty of the country but supply many of its chief products.

[1] J. A. Zahm, Through South America's Southland. D. Appleton and Company, New York.

181

Philologists have given us various derivations of the name *Chaco*. Some state that it signifies a hunting ground, while others contend that it means a swamp, since there are large *bañados* (marshes) making up a considerable part of its area. The Chaco extends from the marshes of Santiago del Estero, in Argentina, to the llanos of the Chiquitos in Bolivia, and from the Paraguay River to the mountain ranges of Tucumán and Santa Cruz de la Sierra. In the western section of this extensive plain there is excellent pasturage for cattle, while the mountain slopes are covered with forests. This land is associated with warlike tribes of Indians who have shown special hostility toward the European conquerors of South America. Among the fiercest of these tribes are the Tobas, who are famous for their cruelties and fighting qualities and have been a menace to intruders.

Paraguay has a hot climate, but as a rule a healthful one. The northern third of the country is within the tropics, and the southern two thirds is within the temperate zone. The average summer temperature is 81 degrees Fahrenheit, and the average winter temperature is 63 degrees. Frequent sudden changes in temperature occur, a shift of winds often bringing torrential rains with a drop in temperature. There is no special rainy season, although the rains are heavier and more frequent in September and October than at any other time. In the temperate section of Paraguay the climate is so equable that the country has sometimes been styled "the sanatorium." There are two seasons, summer lasting from October to March, and winter from April to September. April is the most temperate month in Paraguay.

The climate and soil of Paraguay are favorable to extensive agricultural development, the subtropical region being well suited to the cultivation of such articles as indigo, sugar cane, tobacco, and cotton, while the undulating grassy plains are excellent for flocks and herds. The extensive river systems furnish an unlimited water supply.

The republic never experiences snowfall. It is a land of wonderful prairies, trees, flowers, and sunshine, destined to become an important Mecca for travelers as well as a rich agricultural and grazing country.

HISTORY

The early history of Paraguay is closely connected with the history of the Rio de la Plata and its tributaries. In the early part of the sixteenth century a party of Spanish explorers headed by Juan Diaz de Solis sailed up the Plata for a short distance, but was attacked by the Charrúa Indians. Several of the party were massacred, and the remainder set sail again for Spain. In 1520 Magellan also entered the mouth of the Plata but made no attempt at exploration.

The first actual attempt to explore what is now Paraguay was made by Sebastian Cabot in 1527. Cabot set sail from Spain for the Moluccas by way of the Strait of Magellan, but was forced to change his course, and, finding himself at the mouth of the Plata, known as the River of Solis, he decided to explore it. He made his way up the Paraná and then back to its junction with the Paraguay and up the latter stream. Here he learned through Indian messengers that a second European expedition was proceeding up the Paraná, so he turned back and met an exploring party headed by Diego Garcia, who had accompanied Juan Diaz de Solis on his fated trip and had now come back for further exploration. Cabot soon persuaded Diego Garcia to return to Spain and leave him in full possession of the newly discovered territory. After waiting many months for promised help, Cabot also decided to return to Spain and get the necessary assistance. He never came back to the Plata region.

On Cabot's journey up the Paraná and Paraguay rivers he was given silver plates and ornaments by the natives, and, concluding that the region adjacent to the big river was rich in silver, he changed the name of the Rio Solis to Rio de la Plata (Silver River).

Cabot was followed by Don Pedro de Mendoza, a gallant Spaniard, in the exploration of this region. Mendoza had orders from the Spanish monarch to communicate with the land of the Incas. He sailed up the estuary of the Plata, landing at the present site of Buenos Aires, where he founded a township.

The actual settlement of what is now Paraguay began in 1536, when Juan de Ayolas, second in command of Mendoza's expedition, pushed up the Paraguay River in search of more congenial headquarters and founded a settlement on the present site of Asunción.

Alvar Núñez Cabeza de Vaca, a Spaniard, famous for his explorations in North America, became one of the first governors of the province of Paraguay, which at first included all the country drained by the Rio de la Plata.

In 1608, at the invitation of one of the early governors of the province, Jesuit missionaries came to Paraguay. They founded schools and missions, and treated the Indians with such kindness that they were soon able to form what became practically an independent state. This existed until 1769, when the Jesuits were expelled from the Spanish colonies in America by King Charles III because of the power they had taken to themselves.

In 1811 Paraguay separated itself from Spain and set up as an independent republic. For a few years the new republic was governed by a junta composed of four officials, but in 1814 José Gaspar Rodriguez de Francia became dictator, and for nearly thirty years he ruled the country in a most despotic manner. In 1844 Carlos Antonio Lopez became constitutional president of Paraguay. During his rule of eighteen years, intercourse with other nations was begun, the commerce of the country became of considerable value, roads were laid out, and many reforms were instituted; but at his death in 1862 Lopez was fast becoming a dictator of the worst type. He named as his successor his eldest son, Francisco Solano Lopez, who lost no time in asserting his power. His chief aim was directed toward building up the army. He provoked the War of the Triple Alliance, in which the army of Paraguay was obliged to fight the forces of Uruguay, Brazil, and Argentina. The war began in 1865 and lasted until Lopez was killed in 1870. The greater part of the male population was sacrificed during those five terrible years, many of the women and children starved to death, and the country was absolutely denuded of everything necessary for the work of reconstruction. Besides all this, Paraguay's territorial cessions at the end of the war amounted to some 56,000 square miles.

The Paraguay of today was built up from the wreck of 1870, and its slow development is accounted for by the scarcity of man power and the bankrupt condition of the country at that time.

PEOPLE

The population of Paraguay is over 800,000, an average of five people per square mile. In the year 1917 the population was estimated at 1,000,000. One finds here the result of the terrific destruction caused by the Paraguayan tyrants. Dawson states that when Lopez was dethroned, Paraguay's population had decreased from "1,300,000 to a little over 200,000, only about 29,000 men, and 90,000 children under fifteen years of age."

The population, exclusive of from 50,000 to 100,000 untamed and savage Indians inhabiting the Gran Chaco, is a mixture of Guaraní (Indian) and European blood. Many of the Indians inhabiting the land were more civilized even in the days of the Spanish conquerors than those found elsewhere, and intermarriage with these Indians began earlier. Nearly all Paraguayans, therefore, have some Indian blood in their veins.

Because of the instability of the government and the isolation of the country, attempts at immigration have usually failed.

While the language of Paraguay, like that of all the other Spanish-American republics, is Spanish, the various Indian tribes have many dialects. Father Dobrizhoffer, after eighteen years spent among the Paraguayan Indians, stated that the Europeans have great difficulty in understanding the members of these tribes, since they "hiss with their tongues, snore with their nostrils, grind with their teeth, and gurgle with their throats, so that you seem to hear the sound of ducks quacking in the pond rather than men talking." He found these Indians without any word in their vocabulary that signified "God" or "divinity." These "rude children of the Pampa and the Great Chaco," making up as they do a large part of the population of Paraguay, still furnish a real problem for the republic, and one not easily solved.

CITIES

Asunción, the capital of Paraguay, with a population estimated at from 90,000 to 100,000, is located on the east bank of the Paraguay River about 935 miles from Buenos Aires by railway and 1000 miles from the ocean. This is by far the largest city in the republic, and is the seat of all the financial, business, and social life.

Besides being one of the oldest cities on our hemisphere, Asunción was long one of the chief centers of civilization and more important for a time than Buenos Aires or Montevideo. The approach to Asunción from these cities was originally by way of the Paraná River, requiring a journey of five or more days; but now an all-rail route brings the traveler to the city in about fifty hours.

Asunción is laid out in rectangles according to the Spanish style, with here and there a park or plaza. Many of the streets are well paved, and electric-car lines serve all parts of the city, even the outlying districts. Everywhere women are seen doing all kinds of labor, — a condition reminiscent of the disastrous effects of war.

The average temperature here is about 72 degrees Fahrenheit. The chief industries are sugar-refining, tanning, and distilling. An American minister, consul, and vice consul are located in Asunción.

About 10 per cent of the total population of the republic is found in this city, and this proportion represents about 25 per cent of the total buying capacity of the country. The Argentinos, Spaniards, and Italians form the most important elements in the foreign population of the city. There are numerous important wholesale dealers here, and many retail firms make direct importations. The interior of the country is usually supplied with merchandise from Asunción, and business agencies should be located here.

Concepción, with a population of about 15,000, is the commercial center of the northern part of the republic, being the distributing center for the towns located on both sides of the Paraguayan-Brazilian border. The city is located on the east

Fig. 19. Customhouse and wharf at Asunción, Paraguay. (Courtesy of the Pan-American Union)

bank of the Paraguay River, one and a half days' sail by steamer north from Asunción. There is a biweekly boat service between these two cities.

Concepción is chiefly concerned with the cattle-raising and yerba-maté-growing industries. It is also the business port for the distribution of quebracho wood from towns along the river. Outside of Asunción, Concepción is of greater interest to commercial travelers than any other city in Paraguay.

Among the other cities is **Villa Rica,** the second city in size in Paraguay, with a population of 26,000. It is in the midst of a rich agricultural region. **Encarnación** is an important commercial city at the terminus of the Paraguay Central Railway. It is the port of entry for the rail traffic between Paraguay and Argentina.

GOVERNMENT

The present constitution of Paraguay was drawn up in 1870. Like the constitutions of most Latin-American countries it is patterned somewhat after the Constitution of the United States; it provides for a republican form of government with legislative, judicial, and executive branches.

The executive power is vested in a president, who is assisted by a ministry of five members. The president and a vice president each serve for a four-year term. They are chosen by an electoral system similar to that of the United States. The president may be reëlected only after an interval of eight years.

The legislative branch of the government consists of a Congress composed of a Senate and a Chamber of Deputies, all members of which are elected by popular vote. Senators are elected for six years on a basis of one to every 12,000 inhabitants. Deputies are elected for four years on a basis of one to every 6000 inhabitants. Congress is in session annually between April first and August thirty-first. A Permanent Committee of Congress sits during the recess between the regular sessions.

A Supreme Court of three justices heads the judicial department of the government. There are also courts of appeal, courts of first instance, and justices of the peace.

The right to vote is given to all male citizens over eighteen years of age, but it is only in recent years that the people of Paraguay have taken much interest in political affairs.

ARMY AND NAVY

The national army of Paraguay usually consists of about 2500 men trained according to German principles. A National Guard consisting of citizens between the ages of twenty and thirty-five is liable to military service.

A few converted merchant vessels armed with modern guns are a faint semblance of a navy.

CURRENCY

The gold *peso* is the unit of money, the basis for which is the Argentine peso valued at $0.965 United States gold. The paper peso is the currency at present, and in normal times it takes fifteen paper pesos to equal the value of one gold peso. There are in circulation, in addition to the paper, subsidiary coins of 20, 10, and 5 *centavos*. The gold unit is employed in most reports of financial transactions. The paper peso is used as commercial currency. The gold and silver coins of Argentina have been recognized as legal currency in Paraguay.

EDUCATION

Primary education in Paraguay is free and compulsory. Attempts are being made to push education even into the most remote sections of the republic. Special attention is given to the teaching of agriculture in the rural schools.

There are six normal schools in Paraguay for the training of teachers, a military aviation school, and various schools that give training in painting, music, and industrial subjects. The National University at Asunción, in addition to the usual departments, has schools of pharmacy and of obstetrics, and a school for notaries.

The government of Paraguay has granted scholarships for study in foreign countries, and some students have gone to Europe and the United States for technical training at their own expense.

PRODUCTS AND INDUSTRIES

AGRICULTURE

Paraguay is at the present time, and will doubtless remain for many years, an agricultural and stock-raising country. Owing to inadequate means of transportation, agriculture has not been highly developed as yet, and great quantities of food-stuffs must be imported every year. Nevertheless Paraguay exports yerba maté, oranges, tobacco, sugar, and other products which are grown in her fertile soil.

Tobacco. Among the agricultural products tobacco is the most important from a commercial standpoint. It makes up a large part of the agricultural exports of the country. Tobacco is grown over a large part of Paraguay, but is produced best in the region east of Asunción, where the soil is particularly adapted to its growth.

Modern methods of cultivating and curing the tobacco are still the exception rather than the rule, but recent years have seen great improvement in the quality of tobacco produced. In the manufacture of cigars and cigarettes in Paraguay imported tobacco is mixed with the home-grown product.

Sugar. The sugar industry is one of the most promising in Paraguay. Both the soil and the climate of the country are adapted to the growth of sugar cane. The area of production is still very small, but with the coming of capital to modernize methods of cultivation and manufacturing the acreage of sugar cane is sure to increase.

Oranges. Paraguay is particularly well suited to the cultivation of oranges. Orange trees grow wild in nearly all parts of the country. The seeds were introduced and planted by the Jesuits at an early date. Large orchards of oranges have been planted which produce fruit of excellent flavor. Owing to an expensive system of marketing and to the poor care given to the orchards the growing of oranges has not proved profitable.

Oil of petit-grain, extracted from the leaves of a native orange tree, is being produced on a considerable scale. It is used in the manufacture of perfume and flavoring extracts.

Live-Stock Industry

Wherever there is an open area of land to serve as a pasture, cattle are found; but the Chaco holds greater possibilities as a cattle-raising region than any other part of Paraguay. Little care is given to many of the herds, and a large number of the cattle are a degenerated type of the old creole stock which dates back for centuries. Efforts are being made to improve the native stock by introducing pure-bred cattle such as Durhams and Herefords. The investment of American and European capital has done much to raise the standards of cattle-breeding and to establish meat-curing plants and canning industries. Preserved meats and jerked beef rank high among the exports of Paraguay. They are sent largely to Cuba, Brazil, and Spain. Hides are a valuable export to Europe.

Forest Industry

A large part of Paraguay is heavily forested, and lumber camps have sprung up on the edges of the forested areas in regions convenient to the large rivers or to the railway.

Quebracho. Hard woods, especially the famous quebracho, are found in the Chaco. The word *quebracho* means "ax breaker" and is suggestive of the hardness of the wood. Quebracho is used for railway ties and for the manufacture of furniture. All parts of the tree yield an extract rich in tannic acid. Thousands of tons of the extract are produced annually, and it is imported into the United States and other countries for tanning purposes. Railway lines have been extended into the forests, and steamers make their way up the rivers emptying into the Paraná, to receive the wood or the extract as it comes out of the forest.

Yerba maté. The forests of Paraguay yield millions of pounds of maté annually. This is made from the dried leaves of the yerba tree, which grows wild in large tracts in the eastern and northern parts of the republic. Yerba maté (or herva maté, as the plant is called in Brazilian Portuguese) was known to the Guaraní and used by them as a drink long before the advent of the Spaniards. Their name for it was coá guazú, meaning "big, or splendid, weed." The Indians originally gathered the leaves from the wild trees in the forest, but the Jesuits replenished the trees by cultivating and transplanting.

The method of preparation of the maté is somewhat primitive. The leaves or branches are gathered and piled in a heap and smoked. Then they are ready to be reduced to powder. There are extensive maté factories in southern Brazil, and the increasing use of this beverage will in turn increase the production by modern methods of cultivation.

There are said to be at least 10,000,000 drinkers of maté in South America, and the supply is not always equal to the demand. About half the annual production of approximately 18,000,000 pounds is exported. Of the European countries France is the larger user of yerba maté, followed by Germany, Italy, Spain, and Portugal. The product is sent also to England, Chile, Argentina, Uruguay, Brazil, and in small quantities to the United States.

MANUFACTURING

Manufacturing in Paraguay is confined largely to the industries that have developed as a result of the raw materials produced in the republic. These industries consist chiefly of meat-packing, sugar-refining, and the preparation of quebracho extract. A few products, such as shoes, cigarettes, furniture, matches, vegetable oils, and soap, are made on a small scale for home consumption. Lace is made by Paraguayan women in their homes. The latter industry may become an important one.

EXPORTS AND IMPORTS

The foreign commerce of Paraguay consists largely of the exchange of raw materials for manufactured goods. It is less than that of any other country of South America, averaging in a recent ten-year period about $18,500,000 annually, which was divided in most years quite evenly between imports and exports.

The exports consist of forest products (mainly yerba and quebracho extract), animal products, and agricultural products, of which tobacco is by far the most valuable. Argentina, the United States, Uruguay, and Italy take the bulk of the exports. A considerable part of the exports into Argentina represent goods for reëxportation.

Textiles, foodstuffs, and machinery and hardware make up about three fourths of the value of all Paraguayan imports. Manufacturing has been so little developed in the country that manufactured goods occupy an important place in Paraguay's imports. Argentina, the United Kingdom, the United States, Brazil, and Germany supply Paraguay with three fourths of its imports. A large part of the manufactured goods credited as imports from Argentina were originally exported from the United States or Europe.

TRANSPORTATION AND COMMUNICATION

Waterways. Transportation in Paraguay depends largely on the rivers. The Paraguay River is the principal commercial thoroughfare of the republic. Regular lines of boats ascend this river to Asunción from Buenos Aires. During high water 1000-ton vessels ascend as far as Corumbá, Brazil, a distance of 1800 miles; and throughout the entire year smaller steamers go as far as Cuyabá, Brazil.

The Paraná River, although navigable for ocean vessels to Rosario in Argentina, and for small steamers to Guaira Falls in Brazil, is of much less importance to Paraguay than is the Paraguay River.

Railways. Only one railway of importance enters Paraguay. This is the Paraguay Central, one of the oldest railways in South America, extending from Asunción to Encarnación, a distance of 232 miles. There are other shorter roads of minor importance, most of which operate to the forests, bringing the quebracho logs to the lumber mills and extract plants.

Telegraph and wireless service. There are nearly 1000 miles of telegraph lines in Paraguay. Wireless stations have been erected at Asunción, Encarnación, Concepción, and Paraguari. Connections are made at Buenos Aires with cable lines to the United States and Europe.

THE FUTURE OF PARAGUAY

While Paraguay is at the present time the least important commercially of all the South American republics, its natural resources and favorable climate promise well for the time when capital, increased transportation facilities, and the immigration of white people shall bring prosperity and growth to a most unfortunate land.

CHAPTER X

BRAZIL, THE LEVIATHAN REPUBLIC

Read, mark, learn and inwardly digest, and treat with the contemptuous scorn it merits, any attempt to discredit such a country as Brazil. — J. C. OAKENFULL

GEOGRAPHY

Americus Vespucius, in speaking of the Southern Hemisphere, called it "a new world: — a new fourth part of the globe." The major part of the western half of the Southern Hemisphere is made up of Brazil, which may be called the Leviathan Republic. This country has a gigantic area of 3,276,358 square miles (an area greater than that of the United States without Alaska) and a coast line on the Atlantic Ocean approximating 5000 miles in length. Undoubtedly the very size of Brazil, with its enormous natural resources, is bound to determine its destiny, which is important to the whole world. One need only consider the extent of this republic's territory, and its present and potential industries, to realize why the British, the Dutch, the French, the Spanish, and the Portuguese were all vigorously engaged, at various times, in the attempt to own and control this country.

This prodigious republic exceeds in size all other countries, with the exception of Russia, China, Great Britain and her colonies, and the United States, if with the latter Alaska and the Pacific possessions are included. Through its colossal area flows the largest river in the world, the Amazon, which has a length of 3900 miles, a hundred of its two hundred branches being navigable. The sweep of Brazilian lands extends through both temperate and tropical zones, and rolls from valley and table-land to green mountain summits, the loftiest peaks of which are 10,000 feet above the sea level. Brazil is perhaps the only country in the world that still possesses hundreds of thousands of square miles of unoccupied territory, much of it utterly unexplored; thousands of square miles of forest which have never yet resounded to the feet of civilized man; and regions as extensive as half of Europe, in which the deposits of iron, manganese, and minerals of almost every description await the coming of a world's need.

The Brazilians themselves are scarcely aware of the riches in this great country. Those who have penetrated the fastnesses of the Amazon region report that they have found many areas of rich savanna country, with rolling hills and woods and fertile soils, — lands seemingly intended by nature to be the future grazing and agricultural land par excellence of all the world.

Brazil differs from other great areas in that there are no deserts throughout the sweep of lands (from north to south covering 29 degrees of latitude, and in the wide stretches east and west over 39 degrees of longitude), and in its extreme wealth of unused land and river territory, the fertility of which only waits for transportation development in some cases, and in others for the explorer and colonizer.

Northward and westward from the long coast line of Brazil, where the chief habitations of the country began, the course of empire is gradually taking its way into the heart of this massive land. The mining, railway, and timber colonizers and prospectors are already edging northward through Rio Grande do Sul, Santa Catharina, Paraná, and São Paulo, forcing their modern enterprises into the enormous interior states of Matto Grosso and Goyaz, which comprise a fourth of all Brazil. One day in their pioneering march they will reach the almost immeasurable state of Amazonas, the giant of the Brazilian states, and here they will join with the rubber and sugar pioneers moving westward and southward by river and railway from the Amazon and Belem (Pará). Within a few generations great inland cities will undoubtedly mark the passage of the Amazonian forest; there will, perhaps, be a Brazilian Chicago in the virgin heart of South America, or, seated in her queenly strength halfway between the southern oceans, a new and vaster Rio de Janeiro, whose scepter of unequaled position and preëminence will be over all the Brazils. It is significant that the Federal

constitution of the twenty autonomous United States of Brazil
ordains that the future capital of the republic shall be built in
the interior central districts.

The great central plateau of Brazil covers about half of the
republic and lies from 1600 to 3200 feet above sea level. This
highland region, with its rich resources, extends from the foothills of the Andes on the west to the coastal mountains along
the eastern border, and from the Amazon valley to the low-
lying plains in the south. The coastal mountains possess few
high peaks, the highest not exceeding 10,000 feet, and between
these mountains and the sea, in the states of Ceará and Maranhão in the north and in the state of Rio Grande do Sul in the
south, is found a rather wide coastal plain; elsewhere this plain
is very narrow, and in fact it hardly exists in the other regions
between the mountains and the sea, especially in the case of
Rio de Janeiro and Santos.

Almost all of Brazil yields products of value. In the most
northerly frontiers, however, near the borders of Guiana, and
along the northern coast between the mouth of the Amazon
and Cape Saint Roque, there are more or less barren and stony
tracts where protracted droughts are common. There are few
settlements in this section. The great central section of the
east, consisting largely of table-land, is rich in possibilities of
tropical crops and fruits, and of mining. It is a fairly healthful
region, with great forests, and is a feasible country for white
men. One of its present disadvantages is the lack of white labor
and the inefficiency of the black labor.

Passing south, one finds a vast country in a temperate zone,
which includes the states of São Paulo, Paraná, Santa Catharina, and Rio Grande do Sul. This section is well suited to the
American or European, and, in addition to vast tracts excellent
for grazing, there are opportunities for raising cereal products
of all kinds, for the lumber business, and for a variety of manufacturing enterprises which are gradually being developed. In
a general way one may say that the eastern section is a land of
cotton, cacao, sugar, and the various products of the tropics,
while the southern region is the land of coffee, cattle, general
agriculture, and the beginnings of manufacturing industries.

The vast western and northwestern parts of the country, most of which is still unexplored, have future economic and industrial possibilities, for here are wide, rolling plains; selvas, lying back from the Amazon, suitable for grazing; huge rubber forests still practically untouched; and, when conditions for civilized living are procured, opportunities for the raising of nearly all the other tropical products that are native to Brazil. The portion of Brazil adjoining Bolivia — a vast, undulating country partially grassy and partially covered with woods — will be available for either cultivation or ranching as soon as the world's markets are brought within range by suitable transportation.

"Taking Brazil as a whole," writes Viscount Bryce, "no great country in the world owned by a European race possesses so large a proportion of land available for the support of human life and productive industry." [1]

In climate as well as in vast areas of land and water Brazil holds in reserve for itself a great career. The country probably surpasses every other land with respect to the diversity of its climate. No product or type of cultivation, in all the range of the torrid and temperate zones, is alien to its possibilities. A considerable portion of Brazil possesses a climate modified from tropical extremes by numerous high table-lands and mountain chains, as well as by an unusually extensive hydrographic system. In the inland elevated regions the climate is less humid, growing constantly drier as one journeys inland from the coast. In the Amazon basin the average temperature for the year is about 80 degrees Fahrenheit, the changes being between 65 degrees and 95 degrees. The rainy season in this section is between November and March, and there is also some rain between August and October. In the coastal section the annual temperature is somewhat lower than on the Amazon, and in Rio Grande do Sul the thermometer registers from 20 degrees to 80 degrees.

In the regions of the Brazilian plateau the climate varies, the mean temperature being 68 degrees, with an occasional frost. As a rule there are warm days and cool nights in the plateau

[1] James Bryce, South America, Observations and Impressions. By permission of The Macmillan Company, publishers.

region, and heavy rains from January to May. On the table-lands of southern Brazil a temperate climate exists, with much rain and occasional frost, but never any snow.

The health condition of the inhabited parts of the country is good, and particular attention is given to sanitary conditions in large cities. Yellow fever, which once infested cities of the southern and eastern coast, has been entirely stamped out. But in the Amazon Valley there are malarial regions, especially in the upper sections of the river territory, and the country still awaits such health pioneers as have already thoroughly reno-vated the residential coastal regions.

HISTORY

The people of this vast republic are proud of the title "the Brazilians," and they are not more devoted to Portugal, their motherland, than are the Spanish-American republics to Spain. It is nevertheless true that the Portuguese had a considerable part in the making of Brazilian history even up to the fall of the empire in the year 1889. The early history of the Brazilian colonization resembled that of the Spanish-American colonies, the country being ruled by a series of medieval seamen, gran-dees, and priests, whose aim seemed to be rather to enrich themselves and fill the royal coffers of Lisbon than to develop the country.

The discovery of Brazil is generally attributed by the Brazil-ians to Pedro Alvares Cabral, a Portuguese sailor, who, on one tropical April day in 1500, with a small squadron of thirteen ships, dropped anchor in the harbor at Porto Seguro, immedi-ately south of Bahia, the first Brazilian capital. He is said to have taken possession of the land in the name of the king of Portugal and to have named the country Terra de Santa Cruz, or Land of the Holy Cross. It seems to be a matter of historic fact, however, that Vincent Yañez Pinzon, an associate of Columbus and commander of the *Niña* in the admiral's first voyage in 1492, was the real discoverer of the region now known as Brazil. It is recorded that this Spanish explorer sailed for two months along the coast of South America, from Cape São

Augustin to the island of Trinidad. He visited the mouth of
the Amazon, thinking it to be a large fresh-water sea. But the
convention of Tordesillas awarded the Land of the Holy Cross
to Portugal, thus diminishing the value of Pinzon's discovery.
The name "Brazil" was derived from the Brazil dyewood, a
product which this country produced in abundance.

The influence of Portugal. There is no doubt that Portugal
exerted upon her new-world child, now grown to larger stature
than the mother country itself, a far-reaching influence in the
maintenance of the aristocratic and old-family ideals still held
by the upper classes in Brazil. Excepting Peru, perhaps no
Latin-American republic is so jealous of a royal lineage with
nobility of blood and chivalric ancestry. In Brazil, as in Peru,
the racial idealism of the past has been less diluted by outside
immigration, and the direct descent from royal and imperial
sources is traceable in the aristocratic language and culture.

In the early days of conquest and settlement Brazil was more
fortunate than Peru and the rest of western South America, not
only in the class of Portuguese assisting in the founding and
development of the new colonies, but also in the privilege of
contact with European ideas from more than one nationality.
While soldiers of fortune, freebooters, and a class of buccaneers
in whose program plunder and bloodshed seemed to be the
object as well as the means of their search for gold were ex-
ploiting western Spanish America, Brazil was ruled for more
than three centuries by Portuguese grandees of the mother
country (governor-generals of some prominence) and also by
the Dutch, who ruled for thirty years in northern Brazil.
Certain sections, also, were under the sovereignty of the French.

The Jesuits. The Jesuits gave to Brazil certain ideas of
humanitarian and cultural civilization. There probably never
existed more astute and intelligent, though politically minded,
clerics than these. The Portuguese nobles and grandees, while
ruling their large jurisdictions autocratically, were under greater
restraint from the crown than were those Spanish mariners left
on the bleak and distant shores of the Pacific to work their
plundering way almost unhindered by any laws of God or man.
During the early period of colonization one of the most in-

fluential Jesuits in Brazil was Father Nobrega. This priest was
a contemporary of St. Francis Xavier, and a follower of the
latter in his disinterested exertions in behalf of his fellows. In
contrast to his work was that of the priest-adventurers following
in Pizarro's train, who held a fiery cross over the land of the
Incas as scathing and consuming as was the blood-stained
sword of the Spanish chieftains.

Early colonists. At the beginning of the sixteenth century a
great tide of emigration from Portugal set in toward Brazil. It
looked at one time as though Lisbon and other Portuguese cities
would be depopulated. Times were hard in the mother country,
laws were severe, the Church had been shorn of much of its
power, and the king was all supreme. The new and fabled
country across the seas, offering greater riches and more freedom
than did the mother country, attracted this maritime people,
and the result was inevitable. Many of the hardiest and best
sons, of Iberian, Celtic, and Saracen blood, entered the lists of
pioneers in the new Portuguese world.

The first three hundred years of Brazilian colonization was a
vexed and checkered period. All Europe was jealous and
coveted the country. The Indians were hostile; the French
formed settlements in northern Brazil with the Dutch; and
the Spanish, taking advantage of the apathy of the Portuguese
court, which often disregarded the future of its colony, settled
on the banks of the Paraguay River.

The Portuguese king, João III, established his famous
captaincies, giving to fifteen of his grandees, who had distinguished themselves by service to the crown, land grants of
150 miles of seacoast with an unlimited depth of interior area.
They were given the unusual privilege, if it could be called such,
of occupying, pacifying, and developing their feudal holdings at
their own cost, — probably the most economical scheme of
colonization ever devised. The scheme did not work well,
however, since the nobles became petty kings and abused their
privileges. Governor-generals were then appointed to watch
and control the nobles, who were stripped of their plenipo-
tentiary powers, possessing their lands as fiefs. During these
centuries slaves were imported from Africa for labor; Brazil's

enormous riches in gold and precious stones were discovered;
the sugar mills and the coffee berry arrived; and Durand de
Villegaignon, a native of Provence and a Knight of Malta,
made his attempt to plant a colony of French Huguenots on an
island in the Bay of Rio de Janeiro, the first Protestant colony
of the New World.

Brazil under monarchical rule. The decisive destiny of Brazil
as an independent state was directly affected by the French
Revolution, the principles of which reached Brazil by way of
the mother country. Napoleon, the imperial ruler of France at
the beginning of the nineteenth century, demanded that Portugal give assent to the Continental system, which meant that
she must break with her old ally, England. The prince regent,
John VI, found himself in a desperate dilemma between the
two great powers of the era. With Napoleon marching on
Lisbon, and with Sir Sidney Smith and the British fleet block-
ading the mouth of the Tagus, the monarch of Portugal was
given two choices by the English ambassador: either to surrender the Portuguese fleet to England or, together with the
entire royal family, to be conducted by the British squadron
to the coasts of Brazil. On November 29, 1807, the Portuguese
ruler accepted the latter alternative, and, with the treasure and
archives of the Portuguese crown and a host of court followers,
sailed for Brazil to begin the first reign in person of a king in
the new American world.

The early days of the Portuguese prince's rule gave much
hope to the new country. He enforced the adoption of a *carta
regia* which opened wide the gates of world commerce to Brazil,
— a great step in the emancipation and development of this
colony. He also brought to the country the first printing press
and the royal library of 60,000 volumes, which he opened to
the free use of the public.

This period was described as follows in "The Brazilians and
their Country":[1]

New academies of Fine Arts and Medicine sprang into being almost
full-grown; new diplomatic embassies from England and France

[1] Clayton Sedgwick Cooper, The Brazilians and their Country. Frederick A
Stokes Company.

arrived; new buildings were erected; fashions from Europe began to change the provincial aspect of social customs; better communications with the interior parts of the country were accomplished; and the entire face of the Brazilian land underwent a sudden change. It was only a few years after these transformations that Brazil was raised to the rank of a kingdom, forming an integral part of the United Kingdom of Portugal; and when the Prince Regent was crowned Dom John VI in the palace square of the nation's Capital, the very palms that rustled their tropical heads above the sun-stained roofs of Rio seemed no less beneficent and peaceful than was the happy aspiration that breathed across all the Brazils.

It was not long, however, before antagonistic and diverse ambitions and ideas began to clash. Imperialism and democracy have never mixed well in the New World. For thirteen years the king struggled in vain with his 20,000 or more adventurers, with their monarchical ideas, whom he had brought with him from the old country. He tried in every way to appease the Brazilians, making knights of business men, traders, and coffee merchants, thus turning many a good merchant into a bad politician. France and the English North American colonies, as well as neighboring Spanish-American provinces, engaging in successful revolutionary struggles for their freedom, exerted an influence upon the Brazilian issue. In 1817 there was a revolt in Pernambuco, where the spirit of self-respect and excellence in colonizing was notable. A corrupt court aggravated the people. A revolution in Portugal in 1821 was simultaneous with one in Brazil, and King John VI was obliged to confer upon his twenty-three-year-old son Dom Pedro I, prince royal, the office of "Regent and Lieutenant to his Majesty in the Kingdom of Brazil." The Portuguese monarch, with his royal family and nobility, left Brazil for Portugal on April 24, 1821.

The new prince, Dom Pedro I, was a decisive factor in opening the revolutionary movement which, some seventy years later, resulted in a republic. The Independence Day of Brazil, September 7, 1822, was declared by the young ruler, who, though recalled to the mother country, refused to go, and took his stand decisively for Brazil, remaining to be called "the Washington of Brazil." The proclamation speech of independence of this youthful ruler, who really began the expressed democracy of the Brazilian nation, is worthy of a place among the great historic pronouncements of the New World.

Let no other shout issue from your lips but "Union!" Let no other word be reiterated from the Amazon to La Plata but "Independence"; let all our provinces be strongly chained in unanimity not to be broken by any force; let our prejudices be banished, substituting in their place the love of the public good — Brazilians! Friends! let us unite ourselves; I am your companion, I am your defender; let us obtain as the only reward of all our toils the honour, glory, and prosperity of Brazil; for the accomplishment of which I shall always be at your front in the most dangerous places! Permit me to convince you that your felicity depends on mine. It is my glory to rule an upright, reliant, and free people. Give me the example of your virtues and of your union, and be assured that I shall be worthy of you.[1]

Portugal, sending a large force of soldiers from Europe, endeavored in vain to resist the claims of the young independents, and within three years from the declaration of Brazilian liberty on the plains of Ypiranga, Lisbon acknowledged an independent Brazil. Dom Pedro I ruled for ten years, and in this time unity and a new self-respect came to the people. At first immensely popular, Dom Pedro became involved in political troubles, and through these, together with the financial stringency of the country and the connection that he maintained with Portugal, his influence waned. During his reign occurred the Cisplatina War, by which Brazil lost Uruguay, and the revolt on the part of Pernambuco presaged the emperor's downfall.

The imperial constitution, given by the emperor and ratified by the people on March 25, 1824, was probably more liberal than any other established by a South American people up to that time. It provided for a government "monarchical, hereditary, constitutional, and representative." The religion of the country was to be Roman Catholic, but all other religions were to be tolerated. The constitution made provision for judicial public proceedings, the right of habeas corpus, and trial by

[1] Clayton Sedgwick Cooper, The Brazilians and their Country. Frederick A. Stokes Company.

jury. It provided that the senators and representatives of the General Assembly should be chosen by electors, as is the president of the United States, while the provincial legislators were to be chosen by universal suffrage. The presidents of the provinces were to be appointed by the emperor, but the press was free and there was no color proscription. The constitution, as far as many of its tenets are concerned, is still in existence in Brazil today, and the democratic elements of the country are in line with the free spirit of this instrument, the monarchical characteristics being now eliminated.

The republic formed. With the downfall of the first emperor his son, Dom Pedro II, was acclaimed ruler in the year 1831, and for fifty-eight years his intelligent and benign sway was a most important factor in the making of modern Brazil. In 1889 the country became a republic through a bloodless revolution, and the old emperor, who had been one of the notable personages of his generation, and who, as a descendant of the European houses of the Braganzas, the Bourbons, and the Hapsburgs, had brought to the new country certain valuable inheritances of culture and chivalric dignity, departed for Portugal.

Thus Brazil passed through four distinct periods in leading up to the present republic. There was the long colonial era of exploration, settlement, long-distance officialdom, and conflicts with other powers looking covetously upon the riches of this giant land; then the brief reign of the Portuguese king, John VI, with his title-loving adventurers; then that notable and historic decade when Dom Pedro I, Brazil's first emperor and the country's liberator, united the scattered fragments of a dissentient people in a constitutional union of freedom and equable laws; and, finally, the cultured régime of Dom Pedro II, whose memory is still revered throughout the Brazils.

The long rule of the last emperor marked a historic period for this country. Steam navigation was inaugurated for all Brazil; the Paraguayan war was fought, in which the bravery and patriotism of the country were placed on permanent record; the period was darkened by the horrors of slavery and lightened by its abolition in 1888; and industry and trade, no longer "noosed and haltered," ran ahead. This era was the dawning of a new order in Brazil, the last great American nation to join the sisterhood of Western republican states.

First presidents. The Republic of Brazil came into being on November 15, 1889. There was a military dictatorship by Marshal da Fonseca, and in February, 1891, a new constitution was established, and another soldier, Marshal Floriano Peixoto, became the head of the government. There followed some disorder, owing to the emancipation of the slaves in 1888. A revolution beginning in 1892 in Rio Grande do Sul continued for three years, the Federal government being called upon to restore order, while the fleet sided with the revolutionists. Marshal Peixoto was a notable factor in the crisis, and the army finally saved the situation.

The first civil president was Dr. Prudente de Moraes, who, taking office in 1894, put an end to the civil strife with which the republic had been torn, and began the work of reconstruction and national development along modern lines. In his administration, through the good offices of the United States as arbiter, the limits between Argentina and Brazil, after a dispute of one hundred years or more, were fixed in favor of Brazil.

In 1898 Dr. Campos Salles, a Paulista, became president. It was to his credit that he helped to establish the financial position of the country, which at this time was going through dark days. In 1902 Rodriguez Alves, another Paulista, became president. His administration was marked by new railway construction and the rebuilding of the city of Rio de Janeiro.

Brazil and Brazilian products were brought vividly to the attention of the United States in 1904 at the St. Louis Exposition. The magnificent White Palace, which served as a home for the fine examples of Brazilian products, was transferred to Rio de Janeiro and rebuilt on a site fronting Guanabara Bay, in the midst of gardens and promenades. This distinctive structure of marble and granite was called the Monroe Palace, in honor of the Monroe Doctrine. It was made noteworthy early in its life by becoming a meeting-place for the third Pan-American Congress, which was attended by eighty representatives of twenty nations.

Dr. Affonso Penna became president of Brazil in 1906. He died June 14, 1909, after a short illness. In the election that followed, in 1910, two strong candidates, Marshal Hermes da Fonseca and Dr. Ruy Barbosa, each waged a fierce campaign. While the marshal (who was the nephew of the early Brazilian dictator, the fiery Deodoro da Fonseca) was declared president, the other candidate and his followers claimed, and still claim, the success of their election.

Among the splendid names of modern republican Brazilians that of Baron Rio Branco stands out notably. His political acumen and his humanity made him one of the great prime ministers of modern times. Dr. Ruy Barbosa, in his scholarship and eloquence as well as in his public service to Brazil, is to the southern republic what Daniel Webster was to our own early history. Dr. José Carlos Rodrigues has been called the Charles Dana of Brazil, since he was the founder and, for almost a generation, the publisher of one of the best newspapers in the Western Hemisphere, the *Jornal do Comercio*. The position of Judge Amaro Cavalcanti, who has acted as mayor of Rio de Janeiro and for many years took a leading part in the making of the government, is a reminder of the distinguished place which Joseph Choate occupied so long in the United States. Here, as throughout Latin America, the personality of the individual official leader is quite as important as are principles and platforms in forming public opinion. The man who leads is more important than party doctrines.

PEOPLE

The population of Brazil, while larger than that of any other Latin-American country (being 30,635,000 according to the census of 1920), is far short of what the country could easily support. If the population of Brazil were as dense as that of Belgium at the beginning of the World War, this country would contain more human beings than there are at present on the entire face of the earth. It is conservatively estimated that the present Brazilian population of 30,000,000 could be increased eightfold in view of the resources of the republic.

The late Moreau Gottschalk, formerly American Consul-
General at Rio de Janeiro, stated the situation to the author
thus:

We need men, — labor, labor, labor, — that is the cry of all these
sparsely populated South Americas. Immigration should be encouraged, but this can only be done if you find the class of immigrants who will not assume the strut of conquerors; and to make
them come you must give them roads, — good roads, — not foreign-
concession railroads, but cheap and good highways and waterways,
so that every little farmer may learn that a crop is worth growing,
because he can carry it somewhere and sell it. The lack of roads here
is the crying evil. Make your small man prosperous and he will gain
self-respect; then he will demand for his children the public-school
education which he himself has lacked. Functionarism, the great
curse of administration here as in other countries of Latin America,
would be largely done away if you could encourage thrift and self-
respect in the governed. I till my field and want to sell my crops
unhindered, and I want my son not to be a pensioner on the State but
to inherit my field and by thrift to increase it. If this were the prevailing spirit the horde of functionaries would fall away. The easy
and free communication between the interior and the coast, and
between the several states, seems to be the remedy for much of
the evil.

The result of four centuries of racial fusion in Brazil is a wide
range and variety of population. There are in the country
several distinct populations, possessing their own characteristics, activities, and traditions. In one section the Portuguese
stock is comparatively pure, while in another it is variously
mixed with negro and Indian strains. It is said that about three
hundred high-class Portuguese families were brought to Brazil
by the king of Portugal, and the present civilization of the
country is undoubtedly tinctured with the standard of this
inheritance. The Brazilian will tell you with pride that the
best blood of the old country was brought here, and he is proud
of his aristocratic ancestry.

Brazil is a Latin republic in the sense that the people show
the traits of the Latin rather than the more practical features
of the Anglo-Saxon. The republic was built, in part at least,
upon imperial sympathies, influenced deeply by the heritage of

Moorish civilization which affected the Iberian Peninsula for centuries. The climate and the presence of many negroes in the tropical section have had their influence in shaping the people.

Brazil is sparsely settled, averaging only about nine persons to the square mile as contrasted with thirty-four to the square mile in the United States. Foreign immigration into Brazil did not begin in any considerable measure until the early part of the nineteenth century, since Portugal did not permit foreign immigration into the country, and populated the region entirely from her territories. Today one finds many nationalities represented here. There are many French people and strong French influences in Rio de Janeiro ; there are large German colonies in southern Brazil ; traces of the Dutch and early English settlements are plainly seen in the north along the coast ; while Italians, Poles, Hollanders, and the stock of other nations are found in large numbers in the southern coffee and lumber sections. The fundamental white structure of the population is formed by the Portuguese, and the Portuguese language is the language of the people, though the upper classes speak French to a considerable extent. The Brazilians do not care for the use of Spanish in their country, and those ill-informed merchants who send to Brazil catalogues in either English or Spanish invariably leave a poor impression, in addition to their failure to make sales. Brazil has far less prejudice as to color than have the other South American or North American countries. It is estimated that there are nearly 8,000,000 inhabitants of mixed white and negro blood, about 4,000,000 negroes, and 4,000,000 Indians.

Racial mixtures. The traits of this people are understood only by the student of ethnology. The present racial mixtures arise from the mingling of Portuguese, negroes, Brazilian Indians, and a dozen or more European and North American races. In the sixteenth century the Portuguese settlers intermarried with the Indians. Negroes from Africa were introduced for labor in 1583. There was a great amount of intermarriage, and the result of four centuries of this triple fusion of races has been such a wide variety of people that it is necessary to state the section of country when speaking of the characteristics of the

Brazilian. The type which is now in the making, especially between the Amazon estuary and Rio de Janeiro, is perhaps the most numerous and distinctive type in Brazil. It reveals one of the most remarkable race competitions in existence — Indo-Aryan, American Indian, and African negro. There is no color distinction, and there is a greater freedom from race prejudice than is found in any other part of the world where white men mix with men of color.

The evolutionary progress of the Brazilian of the future is quite certain to reveal the characteristics of the fiery, passionate spirit of the Indian, the idle and affectionate disposition of the African negro, overlaid with the traits of the Portuguese, — aristocratic, intelligent, and always courteous, — the whole mixture being rich in emotional qualities. The Brazilian is intuitive, imaginative, and romantic, and possesses an active and expansive temperament with a touch of sadness and reserve. He loves the tragic drama and the lyric opera; he is tropically tempered, and his feelings lie near the surface. He is devoted to his children, and the home life in Brazil is a distinctive characteristic of the civilization. The wife is accustomed to the semiseclusion common to most Latin-American women, and is primarily a home-keeper, spending her time with her children. The education of Brazilian girls is inclined to be dilettante, including music, painting, and languages, while every Brazilian boy of the better class has strong leanings toward law and politics. Only in comparatively recent times has the urge of trade and industry attracted in any large measure the youth of Brazil.

It is only fair to say that the distinctive and traditional traits of the Brazilians have been greatly influenced during and since the World War by their closer contact with the business and industrial sections of the United States, by the increased personal visitation due to better steamship facilities between the two countries, by the interchange of students, and particularly by renewed admiration for North Americans, induced by large investments of North American capital in Brazil and by the fact that large Brazilian bond issues have been readily absorbed by North American investors.

The Brazilian Indian. A class of the Brazilian population which is destined to have a part in the civilization of this great country is the Brazilian Indian. Unlike the Indians of North America, the Brazilian Indians are increasing in numbers and are gradually being taught the use of farm implements and trained to engage in service in connection with the telegraph lines in the interior, while some of them have become useful workers in the rubber regions.

It has been demonstrated by Dr. Roquette Pinto that since 1872 the Indians have greatly increased in number, while the negro and half-breed population of the country has been diminishing. In 1872, according to the investigation by the members of the National Museum of the Federal capital, the proportion of Indians to the whole population was 7 per cent; in 1890 it was 12 per cent; and in 1912 it had become 13 per cent. It is estimated that the proportion of Indians at the end of the next century will be 17 per cent, thus controverting the idea that the red man is a fading quantity, at least in Brazil.

The character of the Brazilian Indians is somewhat distinctive. They resemble the North American Indians in their superstitions, and they are far less inclined to advance in the arts of peace and organized communities than were the industrious and agricultural Incas of the Peruvian Andes. The Brazilian Indians, as far as physical appearance is concerned, belong in general to two types: one is the short, stout Indian, with a flat nose, yellowish complexion, and slightly oblique eyes, reminding one of the Mongolian races; the other is more like the Caucasian, with a tall, thin, straight body, a ruddy skin, an aquiline nose, and expressive eyes. That these Indians are still in a barbarous and uncivilized state in certain parts of Brazil has been tragically proved to various lumber companies many of whose laborers have been shot through the body with the long Indian arrow, the chief weapon of defense of the Brazilian red men.

Colonel Mariano de Silva Rondon, the Indian's friend for twenty-five years or more, has labored to tame these red men and to mitigate their hereditary hatred and suspicion of the white men. He has tried to make this large and growing population ready for useful labor and citizenship. In 1910 the government decreed the rights of citizenship to the Indians, and agencies were set in motion for their development. In fact, there is in Brazil an awakened conscience in regard to the emancipation and training of this part of the population, influenced, in part at least, by the desperate need of workers in the tropical Amazonian region, where the white man is unfitted to the climate and to living conditions. It is also to be remembered that Indian blood runs in the veins of many of the Brazilians, who are usually proud to state their *Caboclo* inheritances.

Colonization. If all the Brazilian Indians were today capable of doing their part in the development of this huge country, there would still be need of large populations to develop and even to explore the fastnesses of the sequestered central and northern regions. The government has shown itself eager to encourage immigration and colonization, and already there are large numbers of Europeans located in various parts of the republic, in some cases forming considerable communities.

The first attempt at colonization, other than by Portuguese, was made in 1818-1819 by King John VI of Portugal. Two German villages were started by him in Bahia, and a Swiss village was established in Novo Friburgo in the state of Rio de Janeiro. In the year 1851 the Emperor Dom Pedro II started an important colonization project by inviting a number of Germans, who founded colonies at Blumenau and at Joinville in the state of Santa Catharina. These German settlements flourished, and today they remind the traveler of a new Germany in language, customs, and industries.

The Brazilian Colonization Department of Agriculture, Industry, and Commerce states that 116,150 German immigrants reached Brazil between the years 1820 and 1912 inclusive. These German immigrants were outnumbered, however, according to the government figures, by the Italians, who came in this same period to the number of 1,327,808; by the Portuguese, who had sent 883,351; and also by the Spanish, whose immigration since 1820 had amounted to 412,438. Following the Germans down the list were the Russians, with 92,413; the

Austrians, with 75,774; the Turks and Arabs, of whom 39,286 arrived; the French, with 25,748; the English, with 16,396; while in this period of ninety-two years immigrants in fewer numbers consisted of Swiss, Swedish, Japanese, Belgians, a comparatively small number of Americans, and a variety of other nationalities. It is thus seen that Brazil is a veritable racial melting-pot and is destined to become more so.

The proportion of the foreign population to the inhabitants born in Brazil is about 8 per cent; in the United States the proportion is about 13 per cent; while in Argentina the foreign element reaches 30 per cent. The largest percentage of foreigners in Brazil is in the Federal District and in São Paulo, where the Italian settlers alone are said to number 800,000 and are largely engaged on the coffee estates. There are 80,000 or more Poles, Austrians, and Russians in the state of Paraná, and two thirds of all the Germans are to be found in the southern states of São Paulo, Paraná, Santa Catharina, and Rio Grande do Sul.

The government gives every assistance to immigration, and among the inducements that have been offered to newcomers over twelve and under sixty years of age are the following:

Free passage on transatlantic liners from port of shipment in Europe or America to Brazil; free landing for families and baggage, and accommodation at the hostel especially devoted to that object; free transportation to the colonial site selected by the immigrant, and accommodation there for the first few days; sale at long credit of a plot of land properly divided and marked out, with one portion of it cleared and prepared for preliminary cultivation, and a house erected with the necessary accommodations; gratuitous supply of implements, seeds, animals, and transport vehicles; optional employment, paid by wage or by the piece, on works in their own settlement for the purpose of assisting those who have no means of subsistence; gratuitous medical assistance; free elementary instruction for children; and facilities for reception and despatch of postal and telegraphic correspondence.

There are no exacting conditions of any kind regarding religion, and among the colonists are found not only Roman Catholics but many Protestants, as well as Jews, Mohammedans, Positivists, and members of many other faiths. The colonists' earnings are quite secure, and all the privileges of citizenship, rights of property, safety of person, and legal and police protection belonging to any Brazilian are granted.

Characteristics of the Brazilian people. Turning to the general traits of the Brazilians, one must remark at the beginning that generalizations concerning a people inhabiting a country other than one's own are attended with some difficulty. One may find oneself in the position of the Englishman who cabled from New York City to some of his friends in London, "It is a pleasant day in the United States." Yet in order to understand the men and women of this republic one must obtain some idea of their outstanding characteristics and reactions, their traditions, their temperament, and the tendency of their present-day ideals.

In order to discover what the Brazilians, as well as certain foreign residents of the country, thought as to the dominant traits of these people, we asked a wide circle of people, "What is a Brazilian?" The answers were substantially as follows:

The Brazilian is a person born in Brazil, no matter what may have been the nationality of his parents.

A man of effusive friendliness.

If of the upper classes, a cosmopolitan who often prefers Paris to Rio de Janeiro.

A product of mixed marriages and races.

A good business man when engaged in business for himself; not so reliable as a worker for a corporation or for the government.

Generous to a fault if he likes you; prefers to do business on the basis of favor and friendship.

Religion nominally Catholic, sometimes Positivist; more often rather indifferent to religion.

Lacking in industrial initiative on a large scale, generally willing to let foreigners undertake and carry on the big enterprises requiring capital, patience, and high business efficiency.

Always a fine dresser, a good linguist, and not a bad fellow.

Without exception fond of the opposite sex.

A man loving mildness and having a horror of violence; always the soul of courtesy, but theoretical rather than practical.

An inordinate lover of gambling and politics.[1]

[1] Clayton Sedgwick Cooper, The Brazilians and their Country. Frederick A. Stokes Company.

The foreigner doing business in Brazil will very soon perceive that the Brazilian places his pleasure before business to a greater degree than does the North American. This penchant for recreation is revealed in the numerous holidays, festivals, saint's days, and annual carnivals, some of which interrupt business for nearly a week at a time. On such occasions the entire population seems to flock to the cities and towns, to the main avenues and plazas, with a zest for enjoyment characteristic of a people inhabiting a land of boundless resources which yields rich rewards to those who exert themselves even slightly.

The kind-heartedness of these people is clearly apparent. A roster of the charitable institutions, hospitals, and asylums, and the ever-ready open hand to the poor and unfortunate, are evidences of this trait, which is further emphasized by the generous manner in which Brazilians adopt children regardless of the fact that their homes may be full already of their own progeny. This trait will also be echoed by the foreigner who has had a taste of Brazilian hospitality either at the big *fazendas* in the country or in one of the spacious city homes.

As to the tendency to "delay and postpone," showing a lack of appreciation of time taken so seriously by the Northerner, an American official says:

We must of necessity work slowly here; officials are slow to reply, there is an interminable amount of red tape and ceremony, and the man who is in a hurry and unable to restrain his rushing habits had best not come to Brazil.

The reply quite generally received in answer to the insistent importunities of the nervous, impatient, and do-it-now American is: "Paciencia; amanhã" or "Espera um pouco, senhor!" ("Patience; tomorrow." "Wait a little, sir!")

There is a dislike of change and a conservatism inherited from the Portuguese ancestry. The ancient legend is often heard in Brazil of how Adam, struck with homesickness, requested leave to revisit the world of his former estate. Permission was granted and an angel was commissioned to conduct him. On wings of love the patriarch hastened to his native earth, but so changed and so strange all seemed to him that he did not feel at home anywhere until he came to Portugal. "Ah, now," exclaimed he, "set me down; everything here is just as I left it."

Undoubtedly the tropical climate of a large section of Brazil is in part responsible for the intermittent energy and aversion to the effort; for change, while the Oriental strain of blood inherited from the Moors, who for centuries deeply influenced both Spain and Portugal, has left its imprint. One finds among the people of Brazil a consciousness of an ancient social hierarchy that has been almost completely lost in Argentina, where the craving for modern wealth and individual accomplishment and independence is more generally in evidence. The Brazilian is quick to inform you, if he is a member of the aristocratic class, that he is the son of an old civilization, — Portuguese, — and in his opinion the Brazilians come from a sounder stock than do the majority of Spanish-Americans.

The Brazilian is patriotic when it comes to being a citizen of his own state; he seems to be less sensitive to patriotism for his country as a whole. This fact may be attributed to the wide differences in climate and ways of life in the various sections, separated by great areas, many of which are isolated from one another because of the absence of intimate transportation facilities. The link binding the entire country together is the Portuguese language, together with an individualistic culture, derived largely from Portugal, and a strong national tradition. Until recently this tradition has been allowed to grow by the very isolation of the country, caused by the infrequency of mails, expensive cable tolls, and the difficulty of maintaining world contacts.

The country, like many another Latin-American state, is official-ridden, and there are large pension lists. A considerable amount of graft is present, and the characteristics of the politicians are not unlike those found in many of the large cities of America half a century ago, and which are not yet eliminated from our own republic. The Brazilians have always been able to secure loans from Europe and, more recently, from the United States. Their country is so tremendous and diverse in its productivity, so unlimited in its undeveloped and even undiscovered wealth, that the people have the habit of taking hard times with a smile and believing that the morrow will be golden. Is there not always the customs revenue, and is there not always a boom in some Brazilian commodity, — gold, dye-woods, cotton, diamonds, rubber, coffee, live-stock products, or minerals?

CITIES AND STATES

NORTH AND CENTRAL BRAZIL

Northern and central Brazil comprises about 80 per cent of the total area of the republic and contains about half of the population.

AMAZONAS, the largest state of Brazil, lies in the north-western part of the republic. It has an area of about 730,000 square miles and is nearly equal in extent to the combined states of Idaho, Montana, Nevada, Colorado, California, Oregon, and Washington. In this vast territory the estimated population is only 363,000, or about one person to every two square miles.

Amazonas is one of the four inland states of Brazil. Its main resources consist of its forests of rubber, and the population tends to decrease when there is a falling off in the rubber trade. There are also vast quantities of timber, medicinal and oil-bearing fruits and plants, gums of all sorts, sarsaparilla, Brazil nuts, and cacao, together with mineral riches which have never been fully explored.

Manáos, the capital of Amazonas, with a population estimated at 70,000, is situated on the northern bank of the Rio Negro, about seven miles from its confluence with the Amazon. Manáos is 4150 miles from New York, 3204 miles from Rio de Janeiro, and 925 miles from Belem (Pará). It is the most important inland port on the Amazon and contains a number of business houses doing direct exporting, in addition to agencies established here for the upper Amazon. There is easy access to Iquitos (Peru) from this place, and the city is a distributing and collecting center for the various activities which take place on the rivers Madeira, Negro, Purús, Juruá, and Aquiry (Acre).

Manáos is reached by steamer from Belem (Pará), the journey upstream taking four days. It is the chief wilderness city of Brazil, but possesses, nevertheless, many modern advantages such as port works, electrically equipped warehouses, expensive public buildings, schools, and good sanitation.

ALAGOAS, a triangular state, has a population of nearly a million. It is located on the Atlantic seaboard immediately south of Recife (Pernambuco) and has 137 miles of coast line and a large amount of coastwise trade.

Maceió, its capital and chief port, is distant 120 miles from Recife by sea and 220 miles by rail. It has a population of 70,000. A considerable export and import trade is carried on in this place. The export trade is heavy in sugar, cotton, tobacco, rice, mandioca, hides and skins, lumber, castor beans, maize, and oil cake. There are a number of large cotton mills here, and the country roundabout contains rich deposits of minerals. The beginnings of a cattle industry are also to be found here.

BAHIA is one of the most important states in Brazil as well as one of the largest. It has an area of about 165,000 square miles and 625 miles of coast line. Bahia is one of the largest cacao-producing areas in the world and raises as much tobacco as does Cuba. The state is also famous for its oranges and pineapples, and for its whale fisheries. It is the source of an important supply of monazite sand and of carbonados (black diamonds), diamonds, and manganese. Monazite sand contains thorium, which is used in the manufacture of incandescent mantles. Other important products of the state are sugar, coffee, lumber, hides and skins, and cotton.

There are more than 1000 miles of railroad in Bahia, and some river navigation. The São Francisco River has a length of 850 miles in this state.

The city of São Salvador (Bahia), the capital, was formerly the capital of all the Brazils. It is now the third city of the republic and has a population of about 325,000. The bay of Todos os Santos, upon which São Salvador is situated, is 25 miles wide, with a width of 3 miles at the entrance, making the city an unusually fine port. Transatlantic liners and steamers from

FIG. 20. A view of São Salvador, the ancient capital of Brazil, now the third city of the republic. More than a thousand large steamers enter this port annually. (Photograph by Burton Holmes from Ewing Galloway, New York)

North America make São Salvador a regular port of call. It is estimated that over 1000 large steamers, with a tonnage of 2,300,000, enter the port annually.

São Salvador contains approximately 100 industrial establishments of different kinds, having a combined capital of $20,000,000. The manufacture of cotton, tobacco, and jute, and the refining of sugar are the leading industries. The city has several hundred sugar mills.

CEARÁ, a state with an area of about 40,000 square miles, a coast line of 436 miles, and a population of about 1,300,000, is especially noteworthy for its large pastoral industry. There are about 2,000,000 cattle in the state.

The chief products of the state include cotton, sugar, sheepskins, goatskins, carnauba wax, valuable woods, and a certain amount of cultivated rubber. The droughts of Ceará have been a menace to the state, driving a large part of the inhabitants to the Amazonian rubber forests for labor during certain months of the year.

Fortaleza (Ceará), the capital and chief port, has some 78,000 inhabitants. It has water communication by various steamship lines to the coastal ports of the republic, and there is considerable direct importation from a rich hinterland, a large trade being carried on with the state of Pernambuco.

GOYAZ, the fourth state of Brazil in size, with an area of 288,000 square miles, is one of the four inland states of the country. It has an estimated population of about 512,000, including many Indians whose number is more or less difficult to obtain. Agriculture and stock-raising are the chief industries, and the mineral wealth is very great. Diamonds and rock crystal are produced, and gold is found in many streams.

The city of **Goyaz,** the capital of the state, has about 20,000 inhabitants. It is located some 1500 feet above sea level and is handicapped by poor communication, there being almost no roads of any consequence in the entire state outside of the cities.

MARANHÃO, with the Atlantic Ocean as its northern boundary, has an area of approximately 177,000 square miles, 140 miles of coast line, and an estimated population of over 875,000.

Its chief products are cotton, hides and skins, and oil nuts. As in many other states of northern Brazil, the cattle industry flourishes here. There are rich forests and some important forest products, such as rubber. There are also rich mines of copper and iron.

São Luiz (Maranhão), the capital city, has a population of about 53,000 and is an excellent, well-sheltered port. A large export and import trade is carried on, the principal products being cotton, sugar, balsam, rubber, hides and skins, and grain. There is also considerable cotton spinning and weaving here. The city has communication by river and railway with towns in the interior, and numerous importers are located here.

MATTO GROSSO, the second state in extent in Brazil, has a vast area of approximately 530,000 square miles, while its population is only about 275,000. Matto Grosso is a pastoral state, and its chief prosperity lies in its herds of cattle and in its forest products. The name of the state signifies "thick forests," and rubber trees and fine timber grow here in abundance. Maté is produced, and the agricultural possibilities, though undeveloped, are enormous. Diamonds and auriferous sands are found here.

The state as a whole has never been fully explored. The chief need is for railways and country roads, which are comparatively rare in this large territory, the chief communication being by water. Less time would be required to travel from Rio de Janeiro to Paris than to the inland city of Corumbá, the river port of Matto Grosso, through which that part of the state maintains its communication with the outside world.

Cuyabá, the capital of Matto Grosso, has a population of 20,000. The temperature here ranges between 106 degrees and 39 degrees Fahrenheit. Cuyabá is an important and rapidly developing distributing center.

Corumbá, another trade-distributing city of this state, has about 10,000 inhabitants. It is situated on the Paraguay River, which is 1000 feet wide at this point and 6 feet deep at the docks at low water. This port is only two hours distant from Puerto Suarez (Bolivia), and river steamers visit Corumbá from Montevideo, 1800 miles away.

PARÁ, the state which is sometimes called the "New California of South America," is notable for the fact that its capital city of Belem (Pará), with 236,000 inhabitants, is situated at the mouth of the Amazon and has thus become the great rubber port of Brazil. The island of Marajó, situated about six hours from the capital city, possesses large herds of cattle, and the future possibilities for the increase of the cattle-raising industry are hopeful. There are upwards of 2,000,000 head of cattle in the state as a whole.

Dr. Ruy Barbosa, Brazil's famous statesman, speaks of Pará, the state which stands sentinel, key in hand, to the most extensive and potentially rich river valley in the world, in the following words:

If in our country there were no other lands than that of Pará, we might still consider its wealth with pride, and celebrate its fame before all who might be tempted to question its sterling properties. . . . Indeed, the splendid future of our country may be said to be guaranteed by the superior advantages which nature has dispensed to this magnificent State of Pará.

The city of **Belem** is the receiving center and also the distributing center for northern Brazil and a vast interior country. The Amazonian rubber crop has been the main source of the city's commerce, but there is an increasing and diversified export trade in Brazil nuts, cacao, and hides and skins. There are also valuable woods, mahogany and cedar for building purposes being especially abundant.

Belem is the first port of call for ships coming from the United States, and many business houses canvass all northern Brazil, and even eastern Bolivia, from this point. A thousand or more steamers call at the port yearly. Water communication is possible to almost every part of Brazil, affording cheap transportation for the chief exports.

The city has a mean temperature of about 80 degrees Fahrenheit. There are expensive harbor works, attractive streets, plazas, and buildings here.

PERNAMBUCO, with a population of nearly 2,000,000, is a growing and important state in northern Brazil. It has a coast line of 112 miles on the Atlantic, and an area equal to that of the state of New York. The main products are cotton and sugar, raw cotton being exported sometimes to the value of $5,000,000 a year. Cattle and dairying are important here, and, like Pará, its port is a regular port of call for ocean steamers.

Recife (Pernambuco), the capital city, has a population of 250,000. The imports through this port surpass those of any other Brazilian city except Rio de Janeiro. Recife is the most easterly port of South America and the terminus for four railway lines. Its location is strategic for business transactions in a large territory adjacent to it, and direct importing and exporting is carried on by numerous concerns. The city reveals evidences of Dutch occupation in its orderliness and its architecture. An American Chamber of Commerce and a branch of the National City Bank of New York are located here.

Among the other states of northern and central Brazil are PARAHYBA, with an area of about 29,000 square miles and a population of 600,000, the capital city of which, Parahyba, has a population of 52,000; PIAUHY, with an area of 116,000 square miles and a population of 600,000; and RIO GRANDE DO NORTE, with an area of about 22,000 square miles and a population of approximately 537,000. Natal, the capital city of the latter state, has a population of 30,000 people. It is the port nearest to Europe and one of the best in northern Brazil. It is utilized by the Brazilian government as a naval depot, and a large import and export business is carried on. SERGIPE, the smallest of the Brazilian states, has an area of a little over 15,000 square miles and a population of 535,000. The capital city is Aracajú, with 35,000 people.

All these states have similar climates and products. Agricultural resources such as cotton and sugar predominate, although coffee, tobacco, and cereals are cultivated and the pastoral industry and forest industries contribute to the support of the country.

ACRE TERRITORY, on the far western side of Brazil, with an area of about 60,000 square miles and a population of some 100,000, is the Federal government's great rubber asset, while its woods and medicinal plants are noteworthy.

Thus northern and central Brazil reaches from a tropical littoral across great mountain ridges and over wooded and fertile plateaus into steaming jungle and rubber lands. It is cut by mighty rivers which afford every possibility for hydroelectric development and also furnish unusual means for transportation; it is traversed only here and there by railways. The section is almost unlimited in future possibilities for agriculture, mining, and forestry, and is slowly but surely advancing in modern development.

SOUTH BRAZIL

In many respects the southern part of this leviathan country has thus far been a more progressive and practically important division than the less developed northern section of the country. This has been due largely to the constantly increasing importance of the coffee industry, and, more recently, to grazing. On the other hand, the production of rubber, the leading resource of northern Brazil, has been falling off in late years, owing to the lack of modern facilities for cultivating it, as well as to the competition of other markets.

SÃO PAULO. The state of São Paulo constitutes the central area of coffee cultivation. It is largely because of this fact that São Paulo has become one of the richest and most influential of the Brazilian states. About the size of Arizona, with an area of 112,278 square miles, this state has a population of about 4,600,000. It is the leader in agriculture, producing more than 60 per cent of the world's coffee and raising large quantities of cotton, sugar, tobacco, and cereals. Its manufacturing industries are of growing importance, being second only to those of Rio de Janeiro, while it is notable for its mineral riches, its progressive stock-raising activities, its railway service, and its educational advantages.

The wealth of this state is estimated at $1,100,000,000 in agriculture, $500,000,000 in manufactures, and $170,000,000 in railways, together with a miscellaneous wealth of $2,230,000,000. One cause of the serious disturbances in Brazil during the year 1924 was the fact that the state of São Paulo, yielding 65 per cent of the revenue ceded yearly by the Brazilian Union to the

Federal government, claimed that the apportionment of the privileges and money to this state was not in proportion to the revenue which it gave to the government.

With a healthful climate, agreeable all the year round, with excellent railway service both north and south, with an equipment of modern agricultural improvements and up-to-date electric light and power systems, and with a well-organized colonization plan, the Paulistas claim with some reason that theirs is the leading state in Brazil.

The city of **São Paulo,** the capital, which has a population of about 650,000, is one of the most flourishing and modern business cities in Latin America. Its stability and material wealth are evidenced in a practical way by the large loans that have been floated in the United States by this municipality since the World War.

The population of the city is 42 per cent foreign. The majority of the population is white, with some mixed blood, but there are relatively few negroes. There are many thousands of Italian subjects and of Brazilians of Italian blood in the state; there are also many Germans, English, French, Spaniards, and Portuguese, with a few Americans.

São Paulo, situated at an altitude of 2500 feet, is 304 miles from Rio de Janeiro and 50 miles from Santos, its chief port, with which it is connected by an excellent railway running from the plateau down to the seacoast. Among the industries of São Paulo are cotton spinning and weaving mills, foundries, and furniture, shoe, and match factories; there are also important flour mills, jute mills, a glass factory, and hosiery mills.

Numerous wholesale jobbing houses have representatives here who canvass the wide territory, and a large amount of business is transacted. A branch of the National City Bank of New York is located in the city, as are large and important banks representing both native and European capital, and there is an American Chamber of Commerce.

Santos, with a population of over one hundred thousand, is situated in the eastern part of the state and is famous as the greatest coffee-shipping port in the world. The climate here is subtropical. The city has a busy commercial atmosphere, and it handles a very large volume of import and export trade. A branch of the National City Bank of New York and an American Chamber of Commerce are located here, and the port has up-to-date arrangements for carrying on extensive merchandising and commercial undertakings for overseas trade.

RIO DE JANEIRO, the state containing the Federal District of Brazil, as well as the capital of the country, has also its own capital in **Nictheroy,** with a population of 86,000. In addition it has the summer capital, **Petropolis,** which lies about 2500 feet above sea level and has a population of 30,000.

The agricultural products of the state, especially coffee and sugar, are important, while mineral and forest products are among the other resources. Rio de Janeiro competes with the state of São Paulo in manufacturing industries. The city of Rio de Janeiro has a beautiful harbor, and there are a number of excellent smaller ports in the state.

Rio de Janeiro. The Federal District of Brazil contains the capital of the country, Rio de Janeiro, the commercial life of which is advanced by the exceptional harbor afforded by Guanabara Bay. Every advantage of nature combines with modern improvements in docks and warehouses to make this great city one of the most remarkable seaports in the world. With a population of 1,157,000, it is the seat of the Federal government of Brazil and the distributing center of the states of Rio de Janeiro, Minas Geraes, and other states of southern and eastern Brazil. Branch houses of many foreign business firms whose representatives canvass nearly the whole country are located here. There is a flourishing American Chamber of Commerce and also branches of the American Foreign Banking Corporation and the National City Bank of New York. The city is also a banking center for Canada and for other countries carrying on export and import business in this large republic.

Rio de Janeiro is well served by direct steamship lines to both the United States and Europe. It is distant 4775 nautical miles from New York, first-class passenger and freight steamers making the voyage in from eleven to sixteen days; it is 304 miles from São Paulo, 738 miles from São Salvador, and 1297 miles from Buenos Aires.

Fig. 21. Rio de Janeiro, Brazil, most enchanting of cities, with the ancient Carioca Aqueduct in the foreground.
(Courtesy of the Pan-American Union)

Among its industries are textile, jute, and flour mills, sugar refineries, shipbuilding yards, and slaughtering and meat-packing plants. An American ambassador, a consul-general and vice consul, and a commercial attaché, together with mercantile agencies of R. G. Dun & Co., assist greatly in the conduct of business between Brazil and the United States.

Rio de Janeiro has been suitably called "the City of Enchantment." As a city of beauty, culture, and charm it has few equals. Its broad, well-lighted avenues, its beautiful public buildings, its libraries, its magnificent Opera House, its Academy of Fine Arts, its modern clubs, its notable tramway, telephone, and electric-light service, and its general up-to-date character make it a worthy capital of the largest republic of the Western Hemisphere. Here are found many of the old aristocratic and wealthy Portuguese-Brazilian families who wield a strong influence throughout the entire country, both in social and in economic power.

MINAS GERAES. This state, the name of which means "general mines," is the Brazilian home of gold, diamonds, and other minerals, and is potentially capable of producing cereals, tropical fruits, cotton, and tobacco. Cattle, hides, and rubber are also among the exports of the state, which has an area of 220,000 square miles and a population of nearly 6,000,000. A large part of Minas Geraes lies on the elevated plateau that rises abruptly from the sea to form the wide table-lands of Brazil. Here are famous mineral springs, where a successful business in the bottling of medicinal waters is carried on.

The mineral wealth of Minas Geraes attracted adventurers as early as the seventeenth century. It was in its famous diamond mines that some of the richest gems of the earth have been found, and the state is also the home of the black diamond. Two of the principal gold-mining companies here are promoted by British capital, and one of them has been operating in the state since 1830. Manganese ore has been exported from Minas Geraes to the United States in considerable quantities, and the state is also connected with the interesting and important development of monazite sand.

In spite of the fact that Minas Geraes has the largest population of all the Brazilian states, it is notable for containing no cities of great size, no seaport, and no large industry. The population is characteristically rural, and life flows along here with the slow and contented rhythm to which it was set hundreds of years ago.

Bello Horizonte, the capital of the state, has a population of 55,000 and is important for its gold, manganese, and iron, its cotton and textile mills, and its mineral waters. Many merchants here depend upon the importers of Rio de Janeiro, although some import directly.

Espirito Santo, with an area of about 17,000 square miles and a population of 479,000, is a small commonwealth northeast of the state of Rio de Janeiro, upon which it depends largely for its import and export trade.

Victoria, the capital of the state, with a population of 20,000, is located on the southwest shore of the island on Espirito Santo Bay. This city promises to be the center of Brazil's manganese trade, handling this export product from the states of Minas Geraes and Espirito Santo. A considerable distributing business in such products as coffee, cacao, tobacco, timber, sugar, rice, manioc, beans, flour, corn, and hides and skins is carried on with the surrounding country.

Extreme Southern Brazil

The extreme southern part of Brazil, which is now experiencing a great awakening, contains the states of Paraná, Santa Catharina, and Rio Grande do Sul. Here is the great cattle country of Brazil and a country rich in timber and diverse agricultural possibilities. The section lies largely in the temperate zone, has fairly good service, both by railway and by port, for its exports and imports, and is populated in many of its cities by energetic and progressive Germans, Italians, and Brazilians. It is a section similar to what the great Middle West of the United States was fifty years ago, and is capable of much the same type of agricultural and industrial development. There is no richer promise in any part of South America than that found on these rolling prairies of southern Brazil, at present given up largely to grazing, but soon to be the scene of the cultivation of all kinds of cereals and, in the lowlands, of certain subtropical products.

PARANÁ. The state of Paraná has a dozen rapidly advancing cities and towns near the seacoast, graceful pine forests in the higher sections (which promise great possibilities for the lumber industry, and at present form a considerable export), and an unexplored interior. In this state are also located what are probably the best wheat lands of Brazil. There are nearly 700,000 people here, of whom many are Germans, and there is an immediate need of a larger population.

Curitibá, the capital of the state, has a population of 80,000. It is about 70 miles from the port of Paranaguá and is situated on a plateau at an altitude of over 3000 feet. The climate here is temperate, with an average temperature of 65 degrees Fahrenheit.

Curitibá is the principal center of the maté (Paraguay tea) industry, there being over seventy-five mills in the vicinity of the city. The great timber resources of the interior add to the wealth of Curitibá, and in addition to maté the principal products are coffee, sugar cane, bananas, and dairy products.

SANTA CATHARINA. This state has products similar to those of the state of Paraná, including cattle and dairy products, and is second in the production of maté. Certain coal mines are being exploited in the state, but as yet Brazil has not given evidence of being a great coal country, since, because of its good port facilities, it has been able to import coal more cheaply than it could mine it under difficult transportation conditions. With an equable climate and a fertile soil, Santa Catharina is capable of great agricultural progress. At least 20 per cent of the entire population are German colonists. The trade of the town of Joinville, with a population of 8000, is almost wholly in German hands.

Florianopolis (Desterro), the capital of the state, with a population of 40,000, is situated on an island immediately south of Santa Catharina. It is one of the best ports south of Santos and is connected with Rio de Janeiro by a number of steamship lines. The Brazil Railway has been developing the excellent old port of São Francisco, on the northern coast of the state, as a large railway terminus and shipping port.

RIO GRANDE DO SUL, the southernmost Brazilian state, with its area of 91,000 square miles, is equal in size to the states of Indiana and Illinois combined. It has a population of more than 2,000,000. This state is adjacent to the northern borders of Uruguay and is separated by the Uruguay River from Argentina on the west and, in part, from the state of Santa Catharina on the north. Its chief resources lie in cattle-raising, and its 10,000,000 head of cattle are said to be the best in Brazil.

Of all the coming states of southern Brazil, Rio Grande do Sul gives perhaps the richest promise for the future. Here is a vast horse-ranching and cattle-ranching land, — an almost boundless stretch of rolling plains, capable under proper cultivation of producing well-nigh every product of the temperate zone. Situated well out of the tropics, the state possesses well-defined seasons, — a healthful and often cold winter and a dry, hot summer. Large streams of colonists from Europe have come into this great free and favored land of the pioneer. The gaucho, with his flowing robes and distinctive habits, is found here, while men of the plains and farmers mix with foreign colonists on the streets of the cities and towns. Among the chief products of the state, in addition to cattle and other live stock, are wheat, oats, cotton, rice, sugar cane, tobacco, and corn, with a wide variety of minerals. There are many industrial establishments, including several textile mills.

Porto Alegre, the capital of Rio Grande do Sul, has a population of 200,000 and is the most important commercial center of southern Brazil. A large amount of direct importing business is carried on in this locality, and the city is canvassed by nearly all foreign travelers, for many merchants here prefer to deal directly with the United States and foreign countries, and there is a reluctance to work through subagents of Rio de Janeiro houses. The leading industry of the district is cattle-raising for the export of beef and by-products. Manufacturing industries include lard refineries, sawmills, jerked-beef plants, breweries, tanneries, and woolen mills. The population of Porto Alegre is cosmopolitan, one fourth of the inhabitants being of German descent.

Rio Grande do Sul, the southernmost and chief port of this state, with a population of 50,000, is located 180 miles north of Montevideo by sea and 1000 miles south of Rio de Janeiro. There is a large refrigerating plant here, and the port is a distributing point of considerable importance.

These southern cities are favored, as are few of the cities of Brazil, with adequate railway and water transportation. They have received the large streams of immigration flowing to Brazil in the past quarter of a century. Their present progress is due to modern methods of utilizing the great herds of cattle, and to adequate transportation facilities. Foreign capital is coming in and is being invested in timber lands and large refrigerating plants. The Brazil Railway has been an agent of great value in penetrating nearly every important section of this extreme southern portion of Brazil. The future is bright in material promise.

GOVERNMENT

The government of Brazil is that of a federalized republic, with the constitution modeled on the Constitution of the United States, although the states are much more loosely federated than are those of the northern republic. This independence of the states, which extends even to fixing export taxes, levying tax duties, and dealing with other state matters directly affecting commerce, has brought about and continued many inconveniences to trade.

There are twenty states, a Federal District, and the territory of Acre. Each state has its own administrative body, some of the states having one house of legislation and others having two, with a governor or president as chief executive. All male citizens over twenty-one have the right of suffrage, with the exception of illiterates, soldiers, beggars, and members of monastic orders subject to vows of obedience.

The Federal government, or what is known in Brazil as the Union, has control of the Federal army and navy and of all monetary questions, and is supposed to fix and apply the customs duties on the imports of foreign merchandise. The postal service is also managed by the Federal government. With the acquirement from Bolivia of the territory of Acre, which is one of the chief rubber-producing regions, the Union has increased in dignity and authority, since the revenues from Acre have not only paid off in three years the indemnity promised to Bolivia, but continue to form a valuable addition to the governmental budget.

According to the views of many prominent Brazilians there is in Brazil a need of federalizing. An official in the capital describes the electoral condition as follows:

It is curious to note that the Federal Government at each election falls into the hands of a President and a group of his friends who invariably represent one state in the Union, rather than a party with a platform. To-day we are governed by Mineiros (Minas Geraes men). Before that it was Paulistas (São Paulo men), and so on. Under the Empire it was a government of Cabinets which fluctuated and changed while the Sovereign remained fixed.

There is a widespread indifference among the people in regard to voting, and the old Brazilian families, who live apart and form the influential ruling classes, have not been sympathetic toward the forming of new political parties, faithful to a set of principles. The constitution contains an article providing for the settlement of international disputes by arbitration; and while the country has engaged in numerous wars, the trend of public sentiment is undoubtedly toward peace. Brazil, in common with certain other South American republics, is experiencing, and will continue for some time to experience, the truth of the statement of Viscount Bryce that "the conducting of government by the will of the majority is the most complicated of all human undertakings."

ARMY AND NAVY

In time of peace the Brazilian army consists of some 40,000 men. Every citizen between the ages of twenty-one and forty-four is subject to military service. Those men between the ages of twenty-one and thirty compose the "first line" of defense and must serve for several months each year; while those between thirty and forty-four compose the "second line" and the National Guard. The latter class generally serves four weeks annually. Military aviation is becoming increasingly important. There is a military aviation school at Rio de Janeiro.

The Brazilian navy consists of a variety of vessels, some of them of the most modern types. There are three naval arsenals, one of which is located at Rio de Janeiro. A naval aviation school is also situated here.

CURRENCY

The money question in Brazil is intricate, the unit being one thousandth instead of one hundredth, as is usual. The gold *milreis* (1000 *reis*) is equivalent to $0.546 in United States currency, but the exchange varies widely. A *conto* is 1000 milreis (written 1,000$000). Paper milreis form the ordinary currency of the country, having a nominal value of $0.3244, which fluctuates considerably. Silver milreis, and multiples and fractions thereof, are also in circulation.

An act has recently been passed by Congress which is intended to put the currency of Brazil on a gold basis with the *cruzeiro* instead of the *milreis* as the standard.

The exchange of American funds into Brazilian currency should be made by application to the banks or express companies. It is advisable to consult several banks in order to obtain the most favorable rate.

EDUCATION

While higher-grade schools are well provided for, the extension through the states of a system of compulsory education for the lower-grade schools is greatly needed. Many of the states cannot afford to inaugurate such education at present. Along with the improvement of this condition the country should have good roads constructed in the widely separated rural districts, for without these the work of education, like business, is difficult of accomplishment. The percentage of illiteracy is high at the present time.

PRODUCTS AND INDUSTRIES

The products of the field, the forests, and the mines are the great sources of wealth in Brazil. The chief agricultural crop is coffee, corn is second in importance, while cotton ranks third. Cacao, sugar, beans, rice, nuts, tobacco, potatoes, wheat, manioc, and a number of other products are important.

The live-stock industry is a considerable and rapidly developing source of wealth, and there are many companies in existence for the raising of cattle, the operating of packing houses, and the exporting of both refrigerated and preserved meats as well as hides and wool.

Among the minerals in which Brazil is rich are diamonds, gold, and manganese. The diamond district of Diamantina has become famous. Iron-ore deposits are large, and some coal and copper are mined.

AGRICULTURE

Coffee. Brazilian coffee represents about 80 per cent of the world's crop. The extent of the area in Brazil capable of coffee production is almost unknown. This product furnishes the chief buying power of the republic. The practical task has been to limit overproduction in order to keep up coffee prices. "The Brazilian berry," says Charles M. Pepper, "is the world-dominating factor in coffee production."

The coffee plant was introduced into Brazil in the eighteenth century, receiving its name from the city of Kaffa in Abyssinia, where the coffee tree is thought to have originated. The coffee industry began in the states of Rio de Janeiro and Minas Geraes, Rio being the chief overseas shipping port. São Paulo, with its elevated plateau, rich soil, and well-watered land, was found later to be better adapted to the growth of coffee, and it is now the leading coffee region of the country, with the city of Santos as the preëminent coffee port. Brazil furnishes approximately 12,000,000 sacks (a sack equals 132.76 pounds) of coffee annually for export, and of this amount about 10,000,000 sacks pass through Santos.

The economic value of the coffee business in the state of São Paulo is shown by the fact that a *fazenda*, or plantation, of 50,000 trees in good condition is worth upwards of $25,000. These 50,000 trees, properly cultivated, will produce 240,000 pounds of coffee yearly. Crops of vegetables of different kinds are sometimes grown between the coffee trees.

Brazil possesses more than 1,400,000,000 coffee trees, which occupy 4,500,000 acres in this enormous republic. The state of São Paulo owns 2,000,000 acres of the total, the investments in this area being considerably more than $500,000,000. The Brazilian coffee crop is harvested in May and June, each tree yielding four pounds or more of coffee.

The workmen on the Paulista coffee estates are chiefly Italians, although there are a goodly number of negroes and an even larger number of the so-called *caboclos*, the racial type resulting from the mixture of Indian and Portuguese blood. The workmen on the coffee estates are given houses by the proprietor of the estate, and are satisfactorily paid. A day laborer not a member of one of the families employed on the estate receives about 62 cents a day as his wages. A German employed in one of the hulling factories was said to receive a house and $26 a month; his son, a lad of sixteen, received $15 a month.

There is a government bureau, where the colonist or employee may enter complaint against ill-treatment. Such cases of complaint are comparatively rare, however, and the democratic spirit which has swept over Brazil since the days of the royalists has reached all ranks of society.

Opportunity for foreign investments in coffee estates is good, but it is difficult for a foreigner to compete with the Brazilians, who are owners of these large coffee-producing lands and are experienced in growing and exporting, as well as in the actual business of raising coffee. Certain foreigners have been eminently successful in coffee-producing in Brazil, however, notably the Englishmen who own and operate the Dumont estates. It

© E. M. Newman from Publishers' Photo Service

Fig. 22. Drying coffee beans on the sunny coffee floors of Santos, Brazil. Santos is the greatest coffee port of the world

is commonly stated in Brazil that the greatest single owner of coffee trees in the world is Francisco Schmidt, who came to Brazil as a poor German immigrant and has since become the possessor of many millions of coffee trees.

The yearly outlay in keeping up coffee plantations is considerable, for the regular upkeep of each tree costs on the average 10 cents per year. As there are many *fazendieros* who own more than 1,000,000 trees, the yearly outlay is no small item. On a smaller plantation, containing, for example, 250,000 trees and requiring at least fifty families as residents on the property, one owner was reported to have made a profit of about $50,000. This result, however, was due to several generations of careful coffee culture on the part of families who had made this business a specialty. The tyro from any part of the world will find competition with the old Brazilian families very formidable in the matter of large-scale coffee-growing.

On many of these coffee estates today one finds the owners interested in large herds of cattle, kept because the land needs constant fertilizing. Even the Argentine breeder would be satisfied with the up-to-date stables and modern appliances for the scientific raising of cattle on some of these coffee estates, although the raising of cattle is only a side issue with the Brazilian *fazendieros*.

Cacao. Another important Brazilian product is cacao, which comes largely from the district about São Salvador. Half of the output of this crop goes to the United States. The supply of cacao keeps fairly even with the world's demand.

Cotton. This is an outstanding product of the country. It is grown in most of the states along the coast from the Amazon to São Paulo. Pernambuco has led in the production of cotton, and until the comparatively recent expansion of the textile industry in the country, which has absorbed most of the domestic crop, cotton has formed one of the chief exports.

Sugar. Among other important products is sugar cane, which has been cultivated in Brazil from early times. In most years the United Kingdom takes approximately half of the sugar exported.

Tobacco. Tobacco-raising has its center in the state of Bahia, where the largest amount is produced, although nearly every

state raises some tobacco. The soil of Bahia is similar to that
of Cuba. A large part of the Brazilian tobacco has been exported to Germany, and the export value of this crop has
reached $7,000,000 a year.

LIVE-STOCK INDUSTRY

The growth of the grazing and live-stock industry in Brazil,
particularly in the southern part of the country, has been coincident with the awakening of southern Brazil, where the temperate climate and the boundless stretches of rolling plains and the
numerous streams make the conditions for grazing almost
ideal. Large numbers of European colonists have taken up
farm lands here somewhat as did our homesteaders in the
United States half a century ago. Indeed, southern Brazil is
our Far West of the last generation, the gaucho with his con-
summate skill with horses and cattle taking the place of our
Western cowboy.

The following paragraphs are quoted from "The Brazilians
and their Country." [1]

The towns and cities are filled with farmers, colonists, and sun-
browned cattle men, buying their provisions, their musical instruments, and their gay saddlery. The stations are surrounded as the
trains arrive with wagonloads of passengers and produce, and with
motley crowds; great bunches of horses saddled and tied in rows —
all speaking plainly of the status and character of the civilisation.
Until recently these hill prairies have been the uncontested home of
the cattle ranges, and even to-day the trains startle great herds with
wide, heavy horns and powerful shoulders, which gallop away in
fright at the sharp whistle of the engine.

Over all this animal world is the sway of the race of gauchos, or
cowboys, the Brazilian horsemen living in the saddle, many of them
still unlettered, and breathing the air of their ruder ancestry. Along
the prairie stretches there are now growing up everywhere the homes
of colonists, and agricultural progress and the inception of great
modern beef industries are becoming known. There is a sense in
which the pastoral life and the modern land and industrial progress,

[1] Clayton Sedgwick Cooper, The Brazilians and their Country. Frederick A.
Stokes Company.

growing up side by side, have richer possibilities in Rio Grande do Sul than in any section of which we know. Seldom save in rural France has agriculture flourished alongside of stock raising. The cattle lands have been the rule first and these have made way, as in Argentina, for the plough of the farmer. This great State, however, promises to provide the example of agricultural and cattle enterprise developing hand in hand.

The states of Goyaz and Minas Geraes, as well as certain sections in the extreme north, are also becoming stock-raising centers, while the large state of Matto Grosso promises to become one of the most important cattle regions of the world. The establishment of many large companies for the raising of cattle and the operating of packing houses and frozen-meat plants are signs of the times in southern Brazil. The export of meats, both refrigerated and preserved, as well as of hides, wool, and leather, is constantly increasing.

Forest Industry

The forest area of Brazil is estimated at 1,500,000 square miles, the Amazonian rubber region alone covering 1,000,000 square miles, half of which lies in Brazil. The lumber industry, while still in its infancy, has reached an export business amounting to upwards of $6,000,000 a year.

Among the different kinds of trees in Brazil are rubber trees, those which furnish gums and resins; hard woods, those, such as quebracho, which supply tannin; the Paraná pine, often spoken of as the candelabra tree. Of the latter there are said to be 800,000,000 in the state of Paraná alone.

A forest product of growing importance is carnauba wax, which is not unlike beeswax. It is secured from the under coating of the leaves of the carnauba palm. This tree is found in the states of northern Brazil. There are said to be some 15,000,000 carnauba palms in Rio Grande do Norte and in Ceará. The wax is used in the manufacture of shoe-blacking, and when mixed with beeswax and fat makes excellent candles.

Lumber. A visit to the Brazilian sawmills gives the impression of the possibility of a great lumber industry in this country.

For example, the Southern Brazil Lumber and Colonization Company at Tres Barros, under the general control of the Brazil Railway, is conducted by American lumbermen and utilizes high-grade modern machinery. A colony of four hundred men and their families has sprung up around this lumber plant. Many Americans are in responsible positions, and the remaining body of workmen is composed of Brazilians, Italians, Poles, Germans, and Hollanders. Some 45,000 acres of pine forests are being worked by this company, and the mills cut 110,000 feet of lumber daily, this being at the rate of a log a minute. Some of these massive pine logs weigh not less than two and a half tons each.

In reply to a question as to the opportunity for Americans in the Brazilian lumber business the manager of this plant replied:

There are openings for good men who know the lumber business, and there are opportunities, as in other lines in Brazil for men with capital and brains who are not of the get-rich-quick variety. This business does not offer much inducement for the American workman or colonist who is absolutely without money. These would hardly be happy here, while the European from Italy or Poland or Germany is more nearly adapted to the early stages of development in these lumber and colonisation sections.

Rubber. The forest product of Brazil which has been of most importance commercially is rubber, which has usually stood next to coffee in value among all the products of the country. But in recent years Brazilian rubber has found the scientifically raised rubber of the Eastern plantations a close competitor. Brazil has produced, in the past, a yearly output of 39,000 tons of rubber, — about 25 per cent of the world's supply. The Eastern plantations have been producing somewhat more than 125,000 tons yearly, and in the last ten years they have increased their production of cultivated rubber more than 250 per cent.

The Brazilian species of standard rubber is called *Hevea brasiliensis*, — the "wild" rubber trees found in the Amazon territory in well-nigh unlimited quantity. The future development of this industry demands scientific methods of cultivation, proper conditions for labor, and the elimination of unhealthful conditions. Brazilian rubber has been found superior in quality to any other rubber in the world, and the industry here is quite certain to have a brighter future.

The United States has been Brazil's best customer in the rubber business, being followed by the United Kingdom, Germany, and France. Certain government restrictions handicap the market, however, and there is also need of some systematic policy by which rubber may be manufactured throughout the whole year.

Maté. Another important forest industry is the harvesting and preparing of the leaves of the maté tree. Herva maté is grown largely in the states of Paraná, Santa Catharina, and Rio Grande do Sul. The product is manufactured in a scientific way, and, in addition to the considerable amount used for home consumption, large quantities are exported to Argentina, Uruguay, and Chile. In a recent year Brazil exported about 90,000 tons of herva maté. There is a small but growing market for this beverage in the United States.

MINING

There are large iron-ore deposits in the state of Minas Geraes, but as yet they are little developed. A few gold mines are regularly worked, as well as the far-famed diamond mines. The production of monazite is significant. Manganese ore from the states of Minas Geraes and Bahia is exported in amounts varying from 150,000 to 450,000 tons annually, of which the United States takes by far the larger part.

A low grade of coal is found in small quantities in the southern states, but for the smelting of the iron ore it is necessary to import coking coal or coke.

MANUFACTURING

Brazil has been in the midst of an industrial advance, with governmental assistance in the development of national coal mines, hydroelectric power, and iron and steel industries. Of late years there has been greatly increased activity in the textile industry in the states of Minas Geraes and São Paulo. Domestic manufactures are increasing in prosperity each year, and there are numerous factories for the production of such articles as boots and shoes, textiles, tobacco, beverages, salt, and pharmaceutical products. There are a large number of factories and manufacturing plants in the country, many of them doing local business on a small scale.

EXPORTS AND IMPORTS

Exports in 1924 reached $422,708,315, and the imports for 1924 amounted to $305,203,172. This gave Brazil a favorable balance of trade amounting to approximately $117,500,000. This balance of trade is affected from year to year, however, by valorization coffee shipped on government account for sale in consuming markets.

An approximate idea of the standing of the various countries in the import trade with Brazil is indicated by the following percentages for 1924, when the United States sent 24 per cent of Brazil's imports; the United Kingdom, 23 per cent; Argentina, 12 per cent; Germany, 12 per cent; France, 6 per cent; Belgium and Italy, each 3½ per cent.

Of the imports the largest values were those of such products as wheat, oil, coal, manufactures, jute, cotton, wool, cement, chemicals, tin plate, and vegetable extracts. Among the chief manufactures imported into Brazil were engines, railway cars, automobiles, tools and hardware, iron and steel products, paper, arms and ammunition, earthenware, porcelain, cotton piece goods, woolen goods, sewing machines, glass, preserves, and extracts and beverages.

The principal cities receiving imports are Rio de Janeiro, Santos, Recife, Rio Grande do Sul, São Salvador, Belem, Fortaleza, and Porto Alegre.

In the amount of exports received from Brazil the United States has led in recent years, taking nearly one half in 1924, while the countries next in order were France, Italy, the Netherlands, Germany, Argentina, the United Kingdom,

Belgium, Uruguay, and Sweden. The principal exports were coffee, hides, oil seeds, cacao, chilled meat, herva maté, rubber, tobacco, and cotton.

TRANSPORTATION AND COMMUNICATION

Need of shipping facilities. The chief problem in the export and import trade of Brazil is that of transportation. With the recently enlarged shipping facilities between the United States and Brazil, the opportunities for trade between the two republics have been greatly increased. An important element in trade competition is distance. In this respect the United States has a distinct advantage over many European countries. The distance between New York and Rio de Janeiro is 4775 nautical miles, a shorter distance than that between the capital of Brazil and any one of the following European ports with which the Brazilians have traded. Liverpool is 5160 miles from Rio de Janeiro, Bordeaux 4895 miles, Hamburg 5519 miles, Barcelona 4808 miles, Genoa approximately the same distance as Barcelona, and Southampton 5034 miles. The advantage of frequent sailings is, of course, another factor in trade competition, for these lessen the interest charges, require a smaller investment for a larger turnover of commodities, and reduce the risk of losses.

Foreign commerce with Brazil requires also reciprocity of products. It not only involves securing a market for American goods in Brazil, but it also means affording a market for Brazilian goods in the United States. Commerce does not signify merely selling to Latin America; it also means buying from Latin America. The steamship lines must have cargoes both ways in order to make money and continue in the business, and it is only as the requirements of both export and import trade are considered together, and as inextricably related, that permanent trade results.

Atlantic Ocean communication. Speaking of European steamers as the advance harbingers of trade, Mr. William Lowry, former manager of the United States and Brazil Steamship Lines in Rio de Janeiro, had this to say:

The superior passenger accommodation of these European steamers as well as their more rapid voyages, induced the heads of European firms to offer to their passengers, as relaxation from a luxurious sea voyage, an investigation of the commercial possibilities of the countries with which they had business relations. Such commercial possibilities began to be exhaustively developed as a result of personal investigation — the homely adage that "seeing is believing" was verified. Mutual needs and the national idiosyncrasies of the foreigner became better understood by the man who really counted, and as a result of this understanding, a degree of commercial confidence was reached which it will be impossible to develop between the merchants of the United States and those of Brazil until like shipping conditions make parallel results possible.

It is significant that since this statement was made, in 1917, new steamers of first quality have brought the ports of Brazil nearer to the United States and have furnished passenger and freight accommodations quite equal to those presented by European steamship service. It is now possible to go from New York to Rio de Janeiro in thirteen days, and to continue the voyage, if desired, on the same boat to the ports of Santos, Montevideo, and Buenos Aires. The fare from New York to Rio de Janeiro is about $300.

There are steamers two or three times a week from Rio de Janeiro to Europe. The time consumed between Brazil and Lisbon is from eleven to sixteen days. Italian and Spanish vessels sail to Barcelona and beyond via the Strait of Gibraltar. In addition certain freight steamers from both the United States and Europe sail at irregular intervals down the eastern coast of South America, through the Strait of Magellan, and up to Valparaiso, Chile, stopping at many of the smaller ports not included in the schedule of the large combination passenger and freight boats.

There are many coasting steamers along the entire 5000 miles of Brazilian coast line and up the Amazon River. Among the Brazilian ports reached by these intercoastal carriers are Manáos, Belem, São Luiz, Parnahyba, Fortaleza, Natal, Cabadello, Recife, Maceió, Aracajú, São Salvador, Victoria, Rio de Janeiro, Santos, Paranaguá, São Francisco, Itajahy,

Florianopolis, Rio Grande do Sul, Pelotas, and Porto Alegre. Coasting vessels are necessary to reach most of the above-mentioned ports, with the exception of the larger cities and the towns on the Amazon and Paraguay rivers, where foreign service is available.

It should be noted in trading with Brazil that the time required for getting from one section of the country to another is an important factor. The voyage from Rio de Janeiro to Belem by certain steamers, for example, takes as long as a voyage from Rio to London. Three weeks is often required to go from Manáos on the Amazon to Rio Grande do Sul. There are no adequate transportation facilities in Brazil outside the southern portion of the country. In the past, inland trade and transportation have depended greatly upon the rivers, and the main points in Brazil are not as yet entirely connected by railways.

The coastwise shipping of the republic is carried on by a dozen or more lines of Brazilian boats. A trimonthly freight and passenger service is also carried on with New York by this line. It is in accordance with Brazilian law that coastal navigation for the transport of merchandise is possible only in duly registered Brazilian vessels. With rare exceptions foreign ships are prohibited from engaging in coastwise trade, but permission to transport passengers from one port of the republic to another is given to foreign vessels. Ships intended for navigation to and from the Amazon Valley are exempt from import duties, and river and internal navigation is permitted to all nations by the laws of Brazil.

Inland waterways. Relative to inland transportation and the unique Brazilian waterways the following paragraph is quoted from "The Brazilians and their Country." [1]

There are few countries where water transportation is more intimately and vitally connected with the growth of trade. The thousands of miles of shore line pierced by extraordinary harbour facilities, with new port works being constructed at great cost along modern lines; the exceptional opportunities for commerce along the numerous rivers — the Amazon River and its tributaries alone furnishing

[1] Clayton Sedgwick Cooper, The Brazilians and their Country. Frederick A. Stokes Company.

a network of water ways forty thousand miles in extent — all call for ships. The spirit of the old Portuguese navigators is still in the veins of their Brazilian descendants, who have been in the forefront of national commercial navigation. Their ports were made wherever possible, as the only means of communication for many, many years in Colonial days, between the widely scattered settlements, was by sea. In short the ports were the centers of colonies and have since become the capitals of states. In front the sea, immediately behind usually forest-covered mountain ranges, and inland vast plateaus and the fertile Matta or the sweeping wastes of the Sertão. The rivers were the railroads, and they seemed to run everywhere.

The area of the Amazon River valley is estimated at 2,000,000 square miles. Although much of this lies outside of Brazil, the main course of the great river, as well as that of its numerous tributaries, is in Brazilian territory. The valley of the vast river of central Brazil, the Paraguay, shared by several states, is also enormous, and its hundreds of square miles of water meadows form some of the finest grazing land of the country.

Southern Brazil seems to be almost independent of roads by reason of its many rivers. The Uruguay and the Paraná receive the contributions of a cluster of Brazilian streams. Such tributaries of the Paraná as the Paranahyba, the Tieté, the Rio Grande, and the Pardo would stand out as notable in any country that was not so richly blessed with large navigable streams. A full list of Brazilian rivers, with a story of the events that have taken place along their banks, would in itself make a history of the country. Many of the streams have short and tumultuous currents, possible only to the Indian with his canoe, while others wind through upland valleys and pierce mountain gorges on their journeys to the sea. Most of the latter are served by lines of steamers, which in some cases are still the only means of communication that vast sections of Brazil have with the outside world. There are more than 120 river steamers plying on the Amazon and its tributaries.

Railways. The building of Brazilian railways has been no easy task. It would seem as though 20,000 miles of railway were a small allotment for a country covering more than 3,000,000 square miles, especially in contrast to the United States, which possesses more than 250,000 miles of railway for a smaller area. The configuration of the country, however, as well as the fact that the greater portion of Brazil is still a vast unexplored wilderness, would offer some explanation. The formidable Brazilian coastal barrier of mountains, stretching along almost the entire water front and separating the Atlantic coast and the chief cities from the elevated plateaus of the interior, has made railroading extremely difficult. The best of engineering skill has been required to construct roads through the narrow passes of the mountains, and sometimes, as in the case of the road from Paranaguá to São Paulo, along the precipitous sides of these mountain ranges. The first large railway tunnel (2445 yards in length) built in Brazil took seven years to build, and resulted in the bankruptcy of the Central Railroad of Brazil.

Because of the vastness of the country, railroading at first followed the lines of least resistance, mainly between the coastal towns. This resulted in a series of short, disconnected lines of road bearing little relation to one another and lacking in co-ordination. Brazil has lacked railway geniuses to knit together her lines in transcontinental and affiliated systems.

The foreign concessionaries to whom Brazil farmed out the privileges of railway construction at a prescribed price per kilometer evidently centered their thought upon the number of kilometers they could build, rather than upon the need of the railway in the particular section in question, and upon the co-ordinating of systems. The result is that on certain roads, especially in southern Brazil, it is difficult to discover in what general direction one is going, so multitudinous are the curves. One short railway, for instance, which was built by early foreign pioneers and covered 98 kilometers between its starting point and its destination, was reconstructed not long ago by an American engineer so that it covered 43 kilometers. In the beginning of Brazilian transportation development the following railway maxim, once stated by an expert railway man, was evidently overlooked: "You are operating a railroad at all times; you are building a road but once."

There are federal, private, and state railroads in Brazil. Other roads have been built by corporations under a guaranty of interest on the capital invested, while still others have been built without a guaranty but in return for grants of land or other inducements.

The two states of São Paulo and Minas Geraes contain about one third of the total population of Brazil, and they also possess within their confines nearly half the entire railway mileage of the country. In the north some success is being achieved in knitting together the various short railways leading from the seaports and radiating inland, and a continuous railway 1967 miles in length connects Rio de Janeiro with Montevideo. Frequent attempts have been made to connect Brazilian roads with the railways of Bolivia in order to form a transcontinental line, and undoubtedly this project will be brought to fruition sooner or later. A republic, however, having over 10,000 miles of navigable waterways open to river steamers and ocean-going vessels, with 20,000 miles of additional waterways navigable for light-draft and flat-bottomed boats, and with most of these river transportation systems in the interior, has been slow to undertake the highly expensive operation of railroading in its inland and sparsely settled areas.

It is significant that the Brazilians have doubled their railway mileage since 1900, and that agricultural development and immigration have followed these new roads into some of the most productive sections of the republic. By reason of such railway pioneering and the resulting intercommunication and exchange brought about by these transportation benefactors, business and trade of many kinds have been reanimated, and many of the old, easy-going commercial ways, inherited from the days of the empire, have been exchanged for new and vigorous methods of the twentieth century. Since the future of Brazil in trade is largely dependent upon the extent of its transportation facilities both by sea and by land, and since the republic is aroused to this fact and offers opportunities for foreign capital and leadership in the building of new roads, important developments along these lines may be expected during the coming twenty-five years.

Telegraph and wireless service. Brazil is fairly well supplied with telegraph and telephone systems; the telephone system especially is steadily increasing its area of service. In the cities of Rio de Janeiro and São Paulo the Rio de Janeiro Light and Power Company, a corporation promoted largely by Canadian capital but administered by Americans and Brazilians, has been of untold service in producing modern facilities. Wireless service is particularly advantageous to Brazil in communicating with remote regions, and a number of stations afford direct communication with the United States, covering a range of 4000 miles.

Aviation. Airplane transportation is developing, especially along the coast. There is a Brazilian law providing for two aviation lines between Rio de Janeiro and Porto Alegre. One route, carried out by hydroplane and directed by the Ministry of Marine, is to follow the coast, while the other follows the inner side of the Coast Range and is carried on by airplanes under the direction of the War Department. There are also many private aviation interests in the country, while military and naval aviation, for which there are schools at Rio de Janeiro, is progressing rapidly.

CHAPTER XI

VENEZUELA

To retain ... trade with Venezuela and to increase it, the keynote should be an intensive cultivation of the personal relation with Venezuelan business men; better attention to the commercial possibilities and industrial enterprises that need only capital, ingenuity, and ability; and a close and detailed study of the potentialities of the country. Study of the merchandise needs and requirements and attention to the details of exporting are absolutely essential. Americans who display an interest in Venezuela will be met more than halfway by Venezuelan business men.

P. L. Bell [1]

THE COUNTRY'S HANDICAPS

Venezuela has several serious handicaps to its development, among them its sparse population and its poor facilities for transportation. Like Colombia, this country has scarcely begun to develop its prodigious natural resources, many of which still remain inaccessible or undiscovered because of the difficulties involved in exploration and exploitation. Political disturbances have been frequent, and until very recent years the term "republic" has been highly flattering when applied to Venezuela.

GEOGRAPHY

Located on the extreme northern border of South America, with a coast line of 2000 miles on the Caribbean Sea, Venezuela claims nearly 400,000 square miles of territory. This is an area equal to the combined areas of California, Nevada, and Arizona.

Venezuela, Colombia, and the Guianas, the north-coast countries of South America, are closely related geographically and, taken as a whole, may be divided into four zones.

The Andean section extends from the Pacific coast of Colombia into northeastern Colombia and northern Venezuela, and includes the coast ranges along the Caribbean in the latter

[1] P. L. Bell, Venezuela: Commercial and Industrial Handbook. Department of Commerce.

country. The elevations in this section are varied. Some of the peaks are more than 13,000 feet in height, while along the coast of Venezuela the altitudes are considerably lower.

The Andean range extending farthest north in Colombia separates two coastal-plain regions. In Venezuela the coastal-plain region consists of the rich alluvial district bordering Lake Maracaibo and the Gulf of Venezuela.

Lying north of the Orinoco are the great plains known as the llanos. These plains stretch from the delta of the Orinoco in the east to western Colombia, a distance of approximately 600 miles, and from the Orinoco River to the Caribbean or the ranges bordering it. The llanos are destined to become a great cattle-raising region.

To the south and east of the Orinoco River is the region known as the Guiana Highlands, which extends westward into Venezuela from the Guianas, forming a natural boundary between the two countries and Brazil. Most of this section is a plateau 1000 feet or more in height (the highest point being Mt. Roraima in the southeastern corner of Venezuela); it is largely unexplored.

Venezuela has a large number of rivers, many of which are navigable. The Orinoco is by far the greatest of these and one of the largest in South America. It is 1500 miles in length and has a basin area of 300,000 square miles. Lake Maracaibo is the largest of the lakes of the country, which number more than two hundred.

Venezuela lies wholly in the tropical zone; but because of the variety of altitudes found within its area, it has three climatic zones. The tropical zone includes the coastal region, the llanos, and a large part of the Guiana Highlands. Those portions of Venezuela with elevations of from 2000 to 7000 feet have a temperate climate. In this zone are the famous coffee plantations on the lower slopes of the Coast Range in the north. The cold zone includes the higher mountain regions, with altitudes above 7000 feet, where the climate is cold and damp and where few people are found.

The amount of rainfall received varies as greatly as does the climate, and for much the same reason, — the varied topography of the country. Most parts of Venezuela have two distinct seasons, a wet season and a dry season. On the llanos the wet season lasts from April until November, and during this time the vast, grassy plains are partially covered with water. The rainfall is especially heavy on the Orinoco delta and in the Guiana section, and much of the vegetation here is of the dense tropical type.

HISTORY

Venezuela was sighted by Columbus on August 1, 1498, during his third voyage. Cumaná, a town on the coast founded in 1520, is said to be the oldest European settlement in this hemisphere. There were attempts at exploration by various Spanish adventurers, but it was some fifty years before Spain gained a real foothold in the country. This was due partly to the fact that when the land was discovered it was inhabited by tribes of some of the most warlike and savage Indians to be found in the Americas; among these were the Caribs and Teques.

Following the early settlements came a century and a half of almost constant conflict between the Indians and the Spaniards, as well as fighting and political quarrels among the Spaniards themselves. In addition a harassing warfare was carried on by British, French, and Dutch buccaneers over the entire Caribbean region.

During the last half of the eighteenth century Venezuela was under a captain-general. By 1800 a movement for independence had started, and uprisings of varying seriousness continued until 1819, when the Venezuelans, under Simón Bolívar, defeated the royalist forces. Venezuela then joined with the viceroyalty of New Granada, and a few years later with Ecuador, in forming the republic of Colombia, but this union was dissolved in 1830, when Venezuela declared itself independent.

Disorder still continued, however, and for the next forty years one government rapidly followed another as the result of conflicts of political forces and the revolutions that attended them. In 1870 Guzmán Blanco became president, and for twenty years he ruled as dictator, either in office or as the power behind the nominal officials. The country came nearer to

prosperity during this period than ever before, giving evidence
of the fact that the word "republic" does not always imply
successful government, and that in the earlier stages of development of nations a strong and wise dictator has proved to be
at times the best possible governing force.

From the year 1892 internal trouble and international disputes again took the stage. Political adventurers were plentiful.
Among the men who played the part of dictator under the nominal title of "president" was Cipriano Castro, who seized the
republic in 1900 and almost immediately plunged it into a civil
war lasting two years. He was also eminently successful in
embroiling his country in international disputes with European
nations, especially Great Britain, Germany, and Italy, and also
with the United States. The European nations to whom Venezuela owed money demanded payment by the use of force. The
United States government objected, considering such a proceeding to be contrary to the Monroe Doctrine. In the midst of the
conflict Castro fled to Europe, and Juan Vicente Gómez, one of
Castro's former lieutenants, became president. Gómez was
more tractable and amenable to reason regarding Venezuela's
debts, and partial settlement was consummated with the various foreign governments. In the years that followed, Gómez,
while ruling the country with very much the same irresponsi-
bility as to internal affairs as did his predecessors, was careful
to preserve peaceful relations with other countries.

The attachment of the educated classes to politics rather than
to progressive plans for the development of the country's resources is not unusual in the Latin-American republics. Until
Venezuela has a better government, more foreign capital, and
an increased population through immigration, it must struggle
along with a more or less belated civilization.

PEOPLE

The population of Venezuela has been estimated to be from
2,400,000 to 3,000,000, with an average density of about 7 inhabitants to the square mile. The Indian, white, and negro
races are largely intermixed, and, with the exception of the old

Spanish families, and Indian tribes in the northwest and the far southwest, pure racial strains are comparatively rare.

The people of mixed race compose about 70 per cent of the total population. Most of them receive small wages and are very poor. Immigrants are needed to aid in the development of the resources of the country, but they have not come in large numbers. There are about 25,000 Europeans in Venezuela, the majority of whom are engaged in trade in the larger cities. Germany, Italy, France, and Spain are the principal countries represented. There are some Americans here, and in the chief cities several business houses of the United States have offices.

The white people, who form about 10 per cent of the population, are the wealthy and governing class. The Venezuelans are known for their hospitality and their intense national pride.

CITIES

Caracas, the capital of the republic and the main commercial city of the central portion of the country, has a population of more than 90,000. Situated over 3000 feet above sea level in the valley of the Guaire River, Caracas is one of the most picturesquely beautiful cities of Latin America. Although in the tropical zone, it enjoys springlike weather by reason of its lofty situation, and its average temperature is about 68 degrees Fahrenheit. The city has notable buildings and beautiful drives, and an atmosphere of flourishing business.

A railway twenty-three miles in length, running through picturesque country, connects Caracas with the port of La Guaira. The principal products of the capital city are coffee, cacao, tobacco, sugar, and hides. There are textile mills here, a cement factory, a match factory, tanneries, and establishments for the manufacture of commodities such as glass, shoes, soap, candles, and paper.

The city is the most important financial center of the country, as well as a commercial center, and here are located the chief branches of many lines of business and industry, some of which maintain similar branches in other cities. From here commercial salesmen start out to visit all parts of the country.

La Guaira, the chief port of entry of Venezuela, has a population of about 14,000. There are few industries here, but nearly all the exports and imports of the central part of the republic pass through this port. The principal exports are coffee, cacao, and hides.

Valencia has a population of about 30,000; it is the center of culture and social life of the country. Around the city is a well-developed agricultural district, the products of which are very similar to those of Caracas. Cattle-raising is an important industry here. Valencia is the most important manufacturing city in Venezuela and has several cotton mills and a number of soap factories, besides other industries.

Puerto Cabello, with a population of about 20,000, is situated about 34 miles north of Valencia, and is connected with that city by rail. Its importance as the third port of Venezuela is due to its excellent harbor. A number of steamship lines touch this port, which has a large coastwise traffic, and several of the leading business houses of Caracas have branches here. The famous Caganange marble quarries, of which the marble is similar to that of Carrara, Italy, are in the vicinity. Other industries are corn-milling, the manufacture of cotton cloth, and cigarette-making. Foreign salesmen visit Puerto Cabello in connection with their visits to Valencia.

Maracaibo, the second city of the republic in size, has a population of about 50,000. It is 572 miles from Caracas. With the possible exception of Ciudad Bolívar, Maracaibo is the hottest of the larger cities of Venezuela, the average maximum temperature being 95 degrees Fahrenheit and the average mean temperature being 82.4 degrees. Malaria is prevalent here.

Although the second port of the country, the export trade of Maracaibo exceeds that of any other Venezuelan port. Many large wholesale importing and exporting firms are located here, and a considerable trade is carried on with the surrounding country and with eastern Colombia via the Zulia River. The district of which Maracaibo is the center is the most important region of the country in the production of coffee and sugar, and both of these products are exported in large quantities. Cacao is another valuable product. Petroleum production is becoming

FIG. 23. Farm products are brought in from the rural districts by pack mules to this market in Caracas, Venezuela.

increasingly important with the development of fields in this district. An airplane service between Maracaibo and the oil fields has recently been started.

Ciudad Bolívar has a population of about 20,000. Situated on the right bank of the Orinoco, 230 miles from the Atlantic Ocean, it is the center of the steamer trade of the river and is an outlet for much of the trade of the interior. Products are even sent here from the Colombian border by way of the Apure and Arauca rivers, tributaries of the Orinoco.

The city has a large floating population of about 6000 men who are engaged in the gathering of rubber and in other forest-product industries. One of the busiest periods at Ciudad Bolívar is that just before the rainy season of April and May, when the balata and rubber gatherers are fitted out with supplies for their work in the interior.

The leading products of Ciudad Bolívar are gold and silver, tobacco, sugar, coffee, and woods. Among its industries are cattle-raising and the manufacture of cigars. The city is included in the itineraries of salesmen from foreign countries.

Other Venezuelan cities of some note are **Barquisimeto** and **San Cristóbal.** Barquisimeto, a very old city, has a population of about 24,000. It is the commercial center for the region of the northern Andes and has a number of commercial houses of importance, all of which make direct importations. Among its products are coffee, cacao, sugar, and copper. The making of fiber goods is one of the leading industries. San Cristóbal, with a population of approximately 20,000, is well situated with relation to traffic from the western llanos to the Maracaibo district or to Colombia, and is an important trade center.

GOVERNMENT

Venezuela has a federal, representative form of government, the twenty states of the republic being autonomous in their internal affairs and the Federal government having limited powers only. Congress consists of a Senate, composed of forty members, two from each state, and a Chamber of Deputies, the membership of which depends on the population. The president is elected by Congress for a term of seven years. He appoints his cabinet of seven ministers, each of whom is in charge of a department, such as that of Interior Relations, and these ministers are responsible to him alone.

ARMY AND NAVY

Since 1919 military service has been compulsory, with certain exceptions, for all male citizens, who must serve two years in the army or navy and are considered members of the reserve forces until they are forty-five years of age. There is a military school at Caracas and also a school of military aviation.

Several cruisers, a number of gunboats, and some auxiliary craft constitute the navy, the chief use of which is for the protection of the long coast line of the country.

CURRENCY

Venezuela has gold, silver, and nickel coins of varying denominations, all based on the *bolivar* as the monetary unit. The latter is worth $0.193 in United States currency.

EDUCATION

Public education is controlled by the Federal government, but there are also schools provided by the states and municipalities and by private agencies. Primary education is free, and attendance is compulsory between the ages of seven and fourteen. Secondary education is also free, and there are a number of normal schools with courses for elementary and high-school teachers. The Central University of Venezuela at Caracas and the University of the Andes at Mérida are the chief sources of higher education. There are commercial schools in Caracas, Maracaibo, Ciudad Bolívar, and other cities; there are also schools for industrial arts and fine arts, and others giving special training in various subjects.

PRODUCTS AND INDUSTRIES

Venezuela is primarily an agricultural country, although its mineral reserves are considerable. A greatly increased population and expenditure of capital are necessary, however, before all the resources of the country can be developed to their fullest extent.

AGRICULTURE

Coffee forms one of the main resources of the country, the exports of this product amounting to 50 per cent of the total foreign shipment. The United States is a large importer of Venezuelan coffee.

Coffee is grown in the temperate regions from 1500 to 2000 feet above sea level. The Coast Range and the districts around Maracaibo, San Cristóbal, and Mérida are the principal producing regions. The various coffee estates are estimated to cover an area of 450,000 acres and to contain 260,000,000 trees.

Cacao ranks near to coffee in value as an agricultural export. It comes from a tree indigenous to the country, which grows best on the mountain sides of northern and northeastern Venezuela, although it is found in other parts of the country. By far the largest part of the cacao crop goes to the United States.

Other agricultural products. Sugar is produced in the Lake Maracaibo district, and also near Caracas and Valencia. In recent years the exports of sugar have increased. Cotton is grown in some parts of northern Venezuela, but most of it is used in the mills of Caracas and Valencia. The country also produces a certain amount of tobacco, corn, wheat, and vegetables, all of which are used in domestic markets.

LIVE-STOCK INDUSTRY

The wide, grassy llanos provide excellent lands for the raising of live stock, and there are many square miles of plateau south of the Orinoco that are well adapted to grazing; yet it is estimated that at present there are not more than 3,000,000 head of cattle in the country. This is due largely to the climatic extremes of the llanos region, which range from drought to flood conditions. With improved means of protection against these conditions and with sufficient transportation facilities to the coast, where modern refrigerating plants have been established (notably at Puerto Cabello and at Barrancas, near the mouth of the Orinoco), this industry promises to be one of the most important of its kind in all Latin America. Cattle hides, goatskins and deerskins, and beef cattle are now exported, but there is an opportunity for increasing the production of all these. Coöperation on the part of the government is needed instead of the tendency to interfere with business that has characterized the past history of the industry.

FOREST INDUSTRY

Nearly one half of the total area of Venezuela is covered with forests, which yield various kinds of hard woods, such as lignum vitæ, and dyewoods. Of the latter class the divi-divi tree is especially important, for its fruit is an excellent and cheap source of tannin. Balata gum and rubber are found in the regions south of the Orinoco. The exports of balata are the most valuable of the products of this class. Balata is used in making belts for machinery, and for many other purposes.

MINING

Petroleum. In connection with asphalt deposits in the vicinity of Lake Maracaibo, petroleum has been found, while the delta of the Orinoco River and the islands adjacent to the coast show promise of large oil production, although these regions have not been developed to nearly the same extent as the Lake Maracaibo region. There has been considerable activity on the part of foreign capital in the oil industry, and the increase of production of Venezuelan petroleum from 69,000 tons in 1920 to an estimated output of more than 1,400,000 tons in 1924 is an indication of a promising future. Much of the petroleum produced in Venezuela is sent to Curaçao and Trinidad for refining.

Asphalt. The largest known asphalt deposit in the world is the Bermudez asphalt lake in northeastern Venezuela, which has an area of 1000 acres. This lake is tending to rival the famous "pitch lake" of Trinidad in commercial importance. It is about ten times as large as the Trinidad lake, but is not so deep. Asphalt is also found near Guanta, in the same part of the country, as well as on the shore of Lake Maracaibo. This product is used not only for paving and road-making, for roofing, and as a waterproofing material, as well as in the composition of varnishes, but it is also in great demand for the covering of electric cables, for inner linings of cold-storage plants, for calking seams of wooden vessels, for buffers, and in the composition of shoe blacking. The market for this material throughout the world is enlarging.

Gold is found in every state of the republic, although the only mines being worked at the present time are in the extreme eastern part of Venezuela, in the vicinity of the Yuruary River. One gold mine in this district yielded 540,672 tons of crushed gold ore, valued at $25,000,000, between the years 1871 and 1890. Nearly all the gold exported is sent to the United States.

Other minerals. Venezuela, like Colombia, possesses mineral wealth as yet undiscovered and unexplored. Coal, copper and iron ore, and silver are all mined, but there are many unexploited deposits of all these minerals. Pearls and mother-of-pearl are found in the vicinity of Margarita Island, off the northern coast of Venezuela. The pearl fisheries are controlled by the government. Other islands have rich deposits of phosphate rock.

Venezuela, also, has diamonds and other precious stones, but these are not exported in large quantities, owing to the fact that the sections containing these minerals are as yet too remote and inaccessible. The development of transportation facilities in Venezuela will do much for the mineral industry.

EXPORTS AND IMPORTS

The chief exports from Venezuela in 1923, in order of value, were coffee, crude petroleum, cacao, balata, and sugar. Coffee was by far the most important of these, its shipments being valued at $13,230,000, while those of petroleum, the second export, were valued at more than $5,000,000. Other minerals exported were gold and asphalt, and hides and skins and cattle were the leading exports of the live-stock industry.

The Netherlands (including the island of Curaçao and Dutch Guiana) and the United States are the leading importers of Venezuelan products. In 1923 these two countries took nearly half the exports of the republic, which were valued at $30,000,000. The value of exports to the United States was more than $8,000,000.

Cotton cloth, machinery, metal goods, and wheat flour were the principal imports of Venezuela in 1923. The United Kingdom supplied the greater part of the cloth; the United States, of the machinery and wheat flour; and Germany, of the metal goods. Other products imported were automobiles, drugs and medicines, paper, and rice. Of the total imports, valued at $29,000,000, the United States supplied products valued at $14,000,000, the United Kingdom ranking next with imports valued at $7,000,000.

TRANSPORTATION AND COMMUNICATION

Waterways. Venezuela, together with Colombia and the Guianas, is more dependent upon its waterways for transportation than are many of the other Latin-American countries, for its railway mileage is small as compared with its size. The republic is fortunate, however, in its natural waterways.

There are in Venezuela at least seventy rivers that can be used by boats of shallow draft, the navigable parts of these rivers making a total of 6000 miles. The Orinoco (the third largest river in South America) and its tributaries provide 4000 miles of waterways, some of which can be used by sea-going craft, and the rest by smaller boats. Steamers can ascend this river as far as San Fernando de Apure. Other navigable rivers are the Meta, the Portuguesa, and the Escalante.

Lake Maracaibo, which has a circumference of 370 miles and an area of 8000 square miles, is entirely navigable. A strait from eight to ten miles in width provides a passage to the

lake from the Caribbean Sea, which is deep enough to permit
the entrance of vessels of as much as 5000 tons.

The coast of Venezuela is rich in good harbors. In addition
to the three larger inlets of the Caribbean there are fifty bays
and thirty-two ports of varying size. There is direct steamship
service from New York to La Guaira; also, it is possible to go
from New York and New Orleans by steamer to Colon, Panama,
and thence by steamer to La Guaira. Certain United States and
European steamship lines call at Puerto Cabello, other lines
reach Maracaibo and other Venezuelan ports, while steamers
from New York go up the Orinoco River to Ciudad Bolívar.
It is possible also to go to Trinidad and from there by river
steamer across the Gulf of Cara, making stops along the Orinoco.

Railways. The mountainous character of Venezuela makes
railroad building an expensive and difficult proceeding, and
there are only some 650 miles of railway in the country. The
longest railway is the one built by Germans from Caracas to
Valencia. In the course of its 111 miles there are 86 tunnels and
212 bridges, the road often coming out of a tunnel onto a bridge
and immediately entering another tunnel. In past years, when
revolutions have been in progress, some of these bridges have
been blown up and some of the tunnels blocked.

The road from La Guaira to Caracas, built by the British, is
only 23 miles in length, but in this short distance the road
ascends to an altitude of more than 3000 feet, and it is said that
there are not fifty feet of straight track in one stretch in its
entire extent. This road, which has a very heavy traffic,
is now being electrified. On the 33-mile railway line from
Valencia to Puerto Cabello, also owned by the British, a rack-
and-pinion supplementary track is required to ascend some of
the grades.

A number of other railway lines establishing connections with
agricultural or mining centers are in operation. Plans for the
construction of several additional railways and highways have
been made. In some cases work has already been started on
these new developments.

Electric street railways are found in Caracas and in the other
larger cities of Venezuela.

FIG. 24. A donkey pack train, followed by Indian drivers, descending a mountain trail in Venezuela. The donkeys are loaded with cacao beans. (Photograph by Publishers' Photo Service)

Roads. Cart roads and pack trails, although poor and inadequate, are of great importance. The policy of the government in recent years has been to encourage the building of new roads and to repair the old ones. Roads suitable for automobiles now connect Caracas, Valencia, and other large cities with the districts in their immediate vicinity, and eventually a system of highways will cross the country from east to west.

Telegraph and wireless service. There are more than 6000 miles of telegraph lines in Venezuela, and telephone service is supplied in the most densely populated districts.

Caracas, La Guaira, San Cristóbal, Ciudad Bolívar, Puerto Cabello, and Maracaibo all have wireless stations.

ECONOMIC PROGRESS

Like all the northern Caribbean states, Venezuela has few domestic industries. Its chief manufactured products are cigars, cigarettes, boots and shoes, cotton goods, matches, and glassware, all of which are utilized locally. There are some tanning factories that produce leather of good quality, and several sawmills and lumber factories that work on native wood. In all these undertakings there is evident a lack of progressiveness as well as a need of foreign capital to extend the range of manufacturing industries. Even the bags for sacking coffee and cacao are imported from foreign countries.

In spite of the lack of transportation facilities, Venezuela's showing in foreign trade is more creditable, comparatively speaking, than that of its neighbor, Colombia. The United States has been taking an increasing share of both the export and import trade of Venezuela. When we realize, however, that only about 10 per cent of the population of the country are consumers of imported goods (with the exception of textiles), we can readily understand that larger trade and firmer markets depend upon the advance of education, the increase of transportation facilities, and the greater interest of Venezuela in foreign capital and immigration. Venezuela has large resources, natural and industrial, but most of these are yet to be exploited.

CHAPTER XII

COLOMBIA

GEOGRAPHY

Colombia, "the Keystone State of South America," has not yet lived up to its great possibilities. Lying along the Caribbean Sea for 641 miles and having a Pacific coast line of 468 miles, it is the only South American republic whose borders touch both oceans. Its area of about 440,000 square miles is some ten times the size of the state of New York and larger than the combined areas of France, Germany, the Netherlands, Belgium, and Switzerland.

The western part of the country is traversed from north to south by three mountain chains, — the western, central, and eastern Cordilleras. Of these the central Cordillera has the loftiest peaks, Mt. Tolima, the highest peak in Colombia, rising to a height of over 18,000 feet. In the mountains and plateaus of this Andean region live the greater part of the Colombians, for here the climate is more healthful than in any other section of the country. The capital city, Bogotá, is situated more than 8000 feet above sea level. Communication with this city and with other parts of Colombia has necessarily been greatly limited. The Magdalena River, which is navigable for a considerable part of its length, and a number of its tributaries are the chief means of communication with the interior.

In the northern part of the country is the coastal plain, where, in the parts cleared of tropical forest, are raised sugar cane and cacao. To the east and southeast of the mountain region are the great plains of the Orinoco and Amazon basins, covering more than half of the country. The northern part of these plains is a continuation of the Venezuelan llanos, and the southern part consists for the most part of jungle forest. Little is known about the jungle region because of the difficulties in the

267

way of exploration, and the lack of transportation facilities has prevented the development of the llanos.

The climate of Colombia, like its topography, is varied, and ranges from the tropical heat of the coastal and interior plains to the cold of the lofty elevations of the mountains. Bogotá, although lying near the equator, has a cool and salubrious climate throughout the year. Its annual mean temperature is 57 degrees Fahrenheit, while the mean temperature of Cartagena, on the low Caribbean plain, is 80 degrees.

The rainfall is excessive in the lowlands of the coast and the interior, and in certain sections the rainfall is almost continuous; but the llanos are drier. In the northern part of the country there is a wet season and a dry season, each lasting, with variations, some six months. Nearer the equator there are two wet seasons and two dry seasons each year.

HISTORY

The history of Colombia dates from the fourth and last voyage of Columbus, who, after discovering Cape Gracias á Dios on September 14, 1502, sailed along the coast of what is now Colombia for a considerable distance. He made no attempt to found a settlement at that time.

In 1508 Alonzo de Ojeda was granted land lying east of the Darien River and called it the Province of Urada. He established himself firmly along the coast, but not without continuous battles with the Indians, especially those of the old Chibcha kingdom. The Chibchas, who lived in the high plateau country, were highly civilized aboriginal Indians resembling the Incas of Peru. It was not until 1536 that these tribes were subdued by Jimenez de Quesada and friendly relations were established. Quesada founded his capital at Bogotá, near the site of the Chibcha capital, and from there explored the country.

This new Spanish territory was called New Granada and was a province of the viceroyalty of Lima until 1718, when a viceroy, with headquarters at Bogotá, was placed in charge of an area consisting of New Granada, Ecuador, and Venezuela. In 1810 the people of Bogotá deposed the viceroy then in power and began a long war against Spain. Under the guidance of Simón Bolívar the viceroyalty of New Granada united with Venezuela in 1819, and later with Ecuador also, forming the great Colombian republic. This union was dissolved in 1830, and in 1831 New Granada adopted the title of Republic of New Granada. Subsequently this title was changed to Granadine Confederation, then to United States of Colombia, and finally to Republic of Colombia. At this time a republican form of government was adopted, which has existed since then.

PEOPLE

The population of Colombia is about 6,000,000. According to a recent census 50 per cent of this number is composed of mestizos (people of white and Indian blood); 18 per cent, of whites; 18 per cent, of Indians; and 14 per cent, of negroes and negro intermixtures. Most of the negroes are found in the coast towns. There are not many Europeans in Colombia, although the country has been in contact with Europe for four centuries.

Spanish is the language commonly in use, save among certain of the Indian tribes, where primitive dialects are still heard. The people of the cultured class claim the distinction of using the Spanish language in its purest form.

The standard of life among the people as a whole is comparatively low. The tropical climate of parts of Colombia and the ease of securing subsistence in such regions are not conducive to the expenditure of energy, and the inaccessibility of much of the country has greatly hindered its development and consequently the welfare of the people. Conditions have improved notably in recent years, however, and the increasing contact of the country with the outside world since the completion of the Panama Canal is having a valuable influence.

CITIES

Bogotá, the capital of Colombia, is situated on an elevated plain of the eastern Cordillera and has a population of about 160,000. The climate here is springlike, with heavy rains from March to May and frequent rains from September to November.

The city possesses notable public buildings, including schools, the National Theater, and the National Library. It is a center of culture and art and is the winter home of many wealthy people. Electric lights, telephones, and a street railway system are among the evidences of modernity here.

The products are coffee, wheat, and other grains to be found in the temperate and subtropical zones, and stock-raising is important in this region. Among the local industries are the manufacture of chocolate, cigarettes, shoes, and soap, and there are flour, cotton, and woolen mills.

Bogotá is the center of trade and commercial activity for the central and eastern table-lands. This region is the most extensive and populous commercial section of the country. Trade is handicapped, however, by the difficulties of transportation. Much of the produce has to be brought into Bogotá by pack mules and oxen. The Magdalena River is the main artery of commerce, but freight rates are high and goods are sometimes delayed for months because of transportation conditions on the river.

Foreign concerns that expect to canvass this region properly establish agencies at Bogotá. The credit standing of many of the firms of this part of the country is high, and they carry on a considerable wholesale as well as retail business.

Bogotá is reached from Barranquilla, 745 miles distant, by a combined rail and water route. Recently an airplane service has been inaugurated between Barranquilla and Girardot, a river port 75 miles by railway from the capital, thus reducing the journey, which by river and train consumes from seven to ten days, to between one and two days.

Medellín, the capital of the department of Antioquia, is situated nearly 5000 feet above sea level. It is the second city of Colombia in population, having about 80,000 inhabitants, and is one of the most prosperous cities in the republic. The people of Antioquia are the descendants of the Basques of northern Spain who emigrated to Colombia in colonial times. These people are thought by many to have a strong Jewish strain. The purity of the race has been preserved, as well as the industrious habits, and the communities of this department are particularly progressive.

The department of Antioquia contains a large number of towns of 10,000 or more inhabitants, but the territory for which Medellín is the commercial center contains some 2,000,000 people. The city is therefore an important distributing center, especially for coffee, and is the leading industrial city of Colombia. Cotton and woolen goods are manufactured here, also Panama hats, cigars, and cigarettes.

Medellín is reached by a railway line from Porto Berrio on the Magdalena River. Between Cisneros and Santiago this line is broken by the Quiebra Mountains, and the connection is made by an automobile service between the two places. It is expected that these railheads will be connected in the future by a tunnel through the mountains.

Barranquilla, with a population of about 65,000, is situated on the western bank of the Magdalena River seven miles from its mouth. It is one of the best-known cities of Colombia and is at the head of the river-steamer service. Although inaccessible to ocean-going vessels because of sand bars at the mouth of the river, it is joined by a railway to Puerto Colombia, its port, seventeen miles distant. Barranquilla is the principal port of shipment for goods destined for the interior, as well as for outbound products, and it is estimated that approximately 60 per cent of the country's trade passes through this port. The principal exports here are coffee, hides, and gold. A project is under way to deepen the river so that larger vessels can proceed directly to this port.

The principal products of Barranquilla are coffee, tobacco, cotton, and timber, and there are a considerable number of local industries. Less than 10 per cent of the population are pure whites. The business element is composed of a mixture of nationalities, and one finds here Colombians, Italians, Syrians, Germans, and a few Englishmen and Americans. Most of the traders are Syrians, but the number of native Colombians in business circles is increasing.

A general importing business is carried on by the Barranquilla merchants, and a wide variety of merchandise is handled, cotton textiles being the principal line. Each importer has his own group of clients in the interior, from whom he purchases hides, cacao, tobacco, and other exportable products, supplying his clients in return with a varied stock of general merchandise. Here, as in the Amazonian section of Brazil, the client's account runs from one crop season to the next, the coffee-harvest season in June, for example, being the buying and settlement period.

Barranquilla and the port of Cartagena are rivals for the trade of the interior west of the Magdalena River, but Barranquilla easily outstrips Cartagena, having about three times as much trade.

Cartagena, which has a population of over 50,000, is an important Caribbean seaport 62 miles southwest of Barranquilla. Its chief exports are coffee, hides, platinum, and gold. It was at one time the principal seaport of Spanish America and has fascinating historical associations. The city supplies a large territory, chief among its products being coffee, cacao, ivory nuts, balsam, rubber, and cedar and other woods. The largest sugar mill in the country is located near this city.

The business men of Cartagena are capable and progressive, and at present modern buildings are being erected and modern offices opened. Commercial activities are handled by a number of large houses. Several private bankers are established here, who buy export material for their own account in the interior through well-established agencies and branches. The Syrians are able competitors of the older Colombian firms, and there is hardly a town in the interior without a Syrian merchant. These people specialize in cotton piece goods, and the larger Syrian firms import general merchandise.

Manizales, situated at an altitude of 7000 feet, lies at the junction of two well-traveled routes over the central Cordillera. It is 155 miles northwest of Bogotá and has a population of about 43,000. The climate here is delightful, the average temperature being 60 degrees Fahrenheit.

The principal products of Manizales are coffee, cacao, gold, and silver, and its industries are chiefly agricultural. The city commands the wide agricultural region in the Cauca valley. The business houses are strong and well-established and have an excellent reputation for meeting all obligations promptly.

FIG. 25. Colombia's chief means of transportation in the interior is by its rivers. This is a Magdalena River steamer at Barranquilla, Colombia. (Photograph by Publishers' Photo Service)

Cali is located 3400 feet above sea level on the west bank of the Cali River near its junction with the Cauca. It has a population of about 46,000. Lying at a point where many mountain roads converge, it is thus an important center of trade. The Pacific Railway connects this city with the Pacific port of Buenaventura, thus enhancing its importance, and lines are being extended southward and northward from Cali.

Coffee and hides are among the chief products, and a number of Americans are to be found here who have been successful in the coffee and sugar business. While many of the buildings of the city are of the Spanish colonial type, modern buildings are being constructed in the business district. Because of its location in the heart of the Cauca valley and its railway and road connections, Cali is destined to become one of the important and progressive cities of the country.

The city of **Buenaventura,** three hundred and forty-eight miles south of the city of Panama, is situated on an island in Buenaventura Bay, near the mouth of the Dagua River. It is the most important port on the Pacific coast of Colombia, being the entrepôt port for the rich Cauca valley, and is a port of call for steamers of a number of lines. Ships are obliged to anchor about half a mile from the shore, but a new pier is being built. The principal products exported from this port are coffee, platinum, gold dust, hides, and Panama hats.

Buenaventura has been notorious for years as a wet and unhealthful port. Back of the city lies a semi-jungle, malarial and forbidding, which extends to the foot of the Coast Range, and the precipitation here is heavy, rain falling nearly every day. Such a region is not a desirable habitation for white men, and it is not surprising that of Buenaventura's estimated population of 5000 some 90 per cent are negroes.

Tumaco, the southernmost port of Colombia, serves the southern part of the country. It has steamer connections with Buenaventura and with Panama, but is greatly handicapped by its lack of railway communication with the interior. It has some 15,000 inhabitants.

GOVERNMENT

The government of Colombia is of the unitary republican form, with legislative, executive, and judicial branches, according to the constitution adopted August 4, 1886. The general divisions are similar to those of the United States.

The president is elected for a term of four years and cannot succeed himself for the term immediately following. He is assisted by a cabinet of eight members, each of whom acts as the head of a department. Congress consists of a Senate and a House of Representatives. A unique feature in connection with this part of the government is the election of two alternate senators and two alternate representatives to fill the place of each member of Congress if for any reason he is unable to serve. A senator must be a native Colombian, must be thirty years of age or more, and must have an annual income of at least $1200. The membership of both the Senate and the House is based on the population, one senator being elected for every 120,000 inhabitants, and one representative for every 50,000. The length of a senator's term is four years, and of a representative's term three years. The Supreme Court is composed of nine members elected by Congress, who serve for five years, and there are various minor courts.

All male Colombians of twenty-one years of age or more who are engaged in some profession, art, or trade, or have a lawful occupation, are considered citizens and are allowed to vote.

ARMY

The army of Colombia consists of approximately 6000 men in time of peace, the president having the power to increase this quota as may be required. Colombia is composed of three zones for military purposes, and the army is divided accordingly, each zone having one division. Military service is compulsory. There is a military academy at Bogotá and also a school of aviation.

Colombia has no navy, although plans have been discussed for establishing a naval academy and a marine department.

CURRENCY

The monetary unit is the gold *peso*, equivalent to approximately $0.973. The multiple of the gold dollar is the English pound. The subsidiary coins are of silver and nickel, the former in denominations of 50, 20, and 10 *centavos*, and the latter of 5, 2, and 1 centavos. The paper peso, which represents the gold peso, is the ordinary medium of exchange. This unit of currency fluctuates greatly in value and is affected by the stability of the government. Business transactions are customarily in American dollars or English pounds.

EDUCATION

Primary education is free, but not compulsory, for children between the ages of seven and fifteen years, and there are more than 5000 primary schools, with an enrollment of nearly 350,000. The national government has charge of secondary education, although schools are also maintained by various public and private organizations. There is a normal school in each department and a number of industrial and technical schools throughout the country. An example of modern education in Colombia is found in the Gymnasio Moderno, a private school in Bogotá, where the most progressive educational methods are followed.

Among the notable institutions for higher education is the National University, located at Bogotá. Connected with it are schools of fine arts, medicine, engineering, and other branches. At Cartagena is the University of Bolívar; and the University of Antioquia, the Women's University (founded in 1919), and the School of Mines are all at Medellín. Colombia has made excellent progress in education in the past decade, but a large percentage of the population is still classed as illiterate.

PRODUCTS AND INDUSTRIES

AGRICULTURE

Certain agricultural experts have estimated that about one third of Colombia is adapted to cultivation, some 35 per cent of this area now being devoted to coffee-growing. In the eastern

section the country is exceptionally swampy, and much of the
territory is unexplored, while the mountain lands at elevations
of more than 10,000 feet are difficult to cultivate. On the other
hand, the lower plateaus and coast lands are capable of very
great productive development.

Coffee is the chief of Colombia's agricultural exports, the
value of the coffee shipments out of the country amounting to

FIG. 26. Loading coffee on dugouts at Girardot, Colombia, to be floated
down this small stream to the steamboats on the Magdalena River. The
coffee is from one of the plantations of B. Fischer & Co., an American
concern. (Photograph by Ewing Galloway, New York)

more than two thirds of the value of all exports. The principal
coffee-growing districts are in the central Cordillera and the
eastern Cordillera, for the coffee grows best at altitudes varying
from 2000 to 6000 feet above sea level. Colombian coffee is
noted for its quality. Barranquilla and Cartagena are the chief
coffee-exporting ports, although much coffee is sent out through
the Pacific port of Buenaventura and the Venezuelan port of
Maracaibo.

Bananas, which are grown in the coastal lowlands, have become an important product in Colombia in recent years. The

improvements in the transportation facilities for foreign trade
have led to increased banana exports, and in the future Colombia should realize greater wealth from her banana industry. The
Santa Marta district is the most famous banana-growing section, and Santa Marta is the leading port for the export of
this fruit.

Other agricultural products. Tropical products are more numerous and varied on the Atlantic coast than on the Pacific coast
because of the lighter rainfall. Here and in the lower valleys of
the interior are found sugar cane, cotton, cacao, tobacco, and
tropical fruits and vegetables. In the higher valleys of the interior, wheat, barley, and other cereals are cultivated. On the
Pacific coast bananas and corn are raised to some extent.

LIVE-STOCK INDUSTRY

The cattle industry has great possibilities if it is properly developed. Recent estimates of the number of cattle in the country range from 4,000,000 to 8,000,000 head. The coastal lands
are used most largely for cattle-raising at the present time, but
the llanos in eastern Colombia and the valleys of the Cauca and
other rivers provide excellent grazing lands. As in the case of
the other industries of Colombia, improved means of transportation can do much for the live-stock industry. There are
already a number of modern packing-houses in the country.
Cattle hides are the leading export of this industry.

FOREST INDUSTRY

Colombia is rich in its forest resources, but here too the
lack of transportation facilities prevents extensive development.
Rubber and tagua nuts are the chief forest products of the
Pacific coast region and of the Magdalena River valley. An
enormous amount of wealth is stored up in the timber of the
Colombian forests, but, aside from small exports of mahogany,
cabinet woods, and dyewoods, these resources will be little developed without further exploration in the eastern part of the
country and additional means of exit in all sections.

PEOPLE

The population of Nicaragua is about 638,000, or approximately 13 inhabitants per square mile. It is composed largely of Indians and negroes and mixtures of the two races with white blood. The proportion of pure white blood is about 10 per cent, and Indian blood predominates in the population as a whole. At least 75 per cent of the people, including the larger proportion of those of Spanish blood, live in the Pacific section. The eastern, or Caribbean, section is inhabited principally by Mosquito and Zambo Indians, but negroes from the West Indies also live here. There are some Americans in this section, most of whom are connected with the banana industry, and there are a number of English in the neighborhood of San Juan del Norte.

Community of interest between these different sections is difficult because of the continental divide and the extensive forest areas which separate the coffee-growing and cacao-growing regions of the Pacific coast from the low-lying tropical Caribbean coast. Communication between these two sections is usually made by way of Costa Rica, and the small freight shipments between the two coasts usually go by way of Panama.

The language of the country is Spanish, but among the Indian population there is a diversity of dialects. On the eastern coast there is a fairly wide knowledge of English.

CITIES

Nicaragua has two important ports. **Corinto,** with the small population of some 3500, is the chief port of the republic on the Pacific coast. About 65 per cent of the foreign commerce of Nicaragua passes through this port, which is connected with the interior by the Pacific Railway of Nicaragua. The principal export is coffee. On the Atlantic, or Caribbean, coast the principal port, and also the principal city, is **Bluefields,** which has a population of somewhat more than 7000; it is best reached direct from New Orleans. It is a distributing point for the banana, gold, and timber sections, being of special importance in the banana trade. The main products in addition to bananas, gold, and timber are rubber, cacao, coconuts, hides, and tortoise shell. There are some important concerns here, engaged in general outfitting and in wholesale and retail business.

Managua, the capital of the republic, with a population estimated at 40,000, is situated on the southern shore of Lake Managua. It is on the Pacific Railway and is an important distributing point where a number of wholesale firms are located. The city is a growing one, with substantial buildings and fine parks, and its chief products are coffee, cacao, cattle, sugar, corn, and cabinet woods and dyewoods.

Leon, with an estimated population of 38,000, is on the Pacific Railway 52 miles northwest of Managua. It is located in a rich agricultural district and is one of the most important distributing centers in the republic. A number of wholesale houses are located here, and the city is an important place for commercial agents to visit. Leon was formerly the capital of Nicaragua.

Granada, situated on the shore of Lake Nicaragua, with a population variously estimated at from 20,000 to 30,000, is one of the largest and richest cities of the country. Coffee, sugar, cacao, and fruit are among the principal products, and a large business is transacted here in connection with the products of the cattle, mining, lumber, and balsam districts on the other side of the lake. Certain retailers here carry on direct importations.

Matagalpa, which has a population of about 16,000, is situated in the mountain district approximately halfway between the Pacific and Caribbean coasts and serves a widely scattered area of commercial production. It is a base of supplies for timbermen and gold-miners, and produces washed coffee of the finest quality in the country. Before the war this coffee was exported to Europe, but more recently it has been shipped to San Francisco. Matagalpa has no water or rail connections, but must be reached by motor car, muleback, or horseback from Leon.

San Juan del Sur is a cable station situated on the Pacific coast not far from the border of Costa Rica. It is a regular port of call and was the point chosen for the western exit of the Nicaraguan canal as it was planned at one time.

Among a number of other Nicaraguan towns having populations ranging from 5000 to 17,000 are **Jinotega, Masaya,** and **Chinandega.** In the latter place is located the largest sugar mill in Central America.

GOVERNMENT

According to the constitution which went into effect in 1912 Nicaragua has a Congress composed of two chambers, one consisting of forty deputies and the other of thirteen senators. Senators and deputies are elected by vote of the people, the departments of Nicaragua being divided into electoral districts. The annual meetings of Congress are at Managua.

The executive power is exercised by the president and the vice president, both of whom must be natives of Nicaragua and over thirty years of age ; they are elected by direct popular vote. The terms of these two officers are four years, and the president cannot succeed himself. The departments represented in the president's cabinet are those of Foreign Relations, Government and Police, Public Instruction, Treasury and Public Credit, War and Marine, *Fomento* (Promotion), and Justice and Public Works.

All citizens over twenty-one years of age are entitled to vote, and, in addition, those over eighteen who are married or can read and write.

ARMY AND NAVY

There is an active army consisting of some 2500 men and a reserve of about 36,000. Military service is compulsory for at least one year. Eight small steamboats carrying guns constitute the entire naval equipment of the republic. They have for their chief work the prevention of smuggling.

CURRENCY

Nicaragua has a gold standard, and the unit of currency is the *cordoba,* which is divided into 100 *centavos.* The cordoba is equivalent in value to our dollar. Silver and copper coins representing fractional parts of the cordoba are in circulation.

EDUCATION

The government is particularly interested in spreading public instruction among the large number of illiterate Indians. Reorganization of the school system has been undertaken according to the study made by an American educational expert. Primary education, comprising six grades, is free and compulsory for children between the ages of five and fourteen years, and there is an attendance of more than 30,000 pupils at present. Large districts where elementary instruction is limited still exist, and education at best is of a more or less primitive character.

Secondary education is provided by institutes for boys, which, although privately managed, are supervised to some extent by the government. Secondary and normal instruction for girls is given in the Girls' Normal School at Managua, and there is also a normal school for men. There are professional schools at Managua, Granada, and Leon, and the National School of Agriculture is at Chinandega.

PRODUCTS AND INDUSTRIES

Bananas are the chief agricultural products of the eastern coast, although coconuts and other tropical fruits are grown here. Coffee of excellent quality, the most important crop of Nicaragua, grows best on the mountain slopes. The western part of the republic is best suited to the cultivation of sugar, cacao, and cotton. The sugar-growing industry and its by-products, rum and alcohol, are worth more than $3,000,000 annually to the republic. Corn, rice, and beans are grown for domestic consumption, and cattle are extensively raised.

Nicaragua is not so heavily forested as are some of the other Central American countries. Nevertheless, cabinet woods and some dyewoods are important items in the export trade of the country. Some rubber is produced from gums and resins, and there is a variety of medicinal plants.

The gold deposits of Nicaragua have contributed largely to the wealth of the republic. Many adventurers and explorers have followed the rivers and crossed the mountains of Nicaragua in search of this most precious metal. Of the 500 mines registered in the Nicaraguan Bureau of Statistics, 494 are producers of gold. Gold-mining is especially important in the eastern section. There are silver and copper mines and stone quarries scattered over the country. Nicaragua's mineral wealth has not been fully exploited as yet, but both American and English companies already have large mining interests here.

EXPORTS AND IMPORTS

Coffee is the most important export of Nicaragua. In 1924 the shipments of this product were valued at more than $7,000,000. Bananas, having an export value of nearly $2,000,000, ranked next in the same year. The United States and France are the leading consumers of the former product, and the entire banana export crop goes to the United States. Exports of cabinet woods and sugar were each valued at more than $1,000,000 in 1924. Among the other exports were gold and silver (all of which was sent to the United States), hides and skins, and cotton. The total value of the exports of the republic in 1924 was $13,000,000, of which exports to the United States amounted to $7,500,000.

Cotton goods; iron and steel manufactures; foodstuffs such as wheat flour, vegetable products, rice, and meat and dairy products; and chemicals, drugs, and medicines were the leading imports of Nicaragua in 1924. The United States furnished three fourths of all the imports in that year, which were valued at nearly $9,000,000.

TRANSPORTATION AND COMMUNICATION

Waterways. The San Juan River, which connects Lake Nicaragua with the Atlantic Ocean, is 140 miles long. It is navigable for 120 miles of this distance, and a regular steamship service is maintained from San Juan del Norte at its mouth to Granada on Lake Nicaragua. The Bluefields River is navigable from the port of Bluefields to the city of Rama, a distance of about 65 miles.

The longest river in Nicaragua is the Coco, or Segovia, which rises on the eastern side of the cordillera and flows for a distance

of 300 miles through mountain passes, wide plains, and picturesque valleys, finally emptying into the Caribbean. For much
of its length it forms part of the boundary between Nicaragua
and Honduras. This river is navigable for 240 miles, although
light-draft vessels can be used only for the first 110 miles.
Probably no other river in Latin America has so many different names in the various parts of its course.

Railways. With the exception of the twenty miles of private
railways on the Atlantic coast near the Rio Grande, the Pacific
Railway of Nicaragua is the only railway operating in the republic. This railway is situated in the western section and with
its various branches has a length of about 160 miles. Among the
chief cities which it connects are Corinto, Chinandega, Leon,
Managua, Masaya, Granada, and Diriamba. The road is owned
by the republic and was at one time accepted as an integral part
of the prospected "New York-Buenos Aires System," this part
extending from Corinto to Granada. The project of a railway
between the Atlantic and Pacific coasts, a distance of about
200 miles, has received considerable promotion.

Telegraph and wireless service. The telegraph and telephone
lines of Nicaragua are owned by the government. There are
more than 100 telegraph offices in the country, and the cable
office at San Juan del Sur keeps Nicaragua in close touch with
the United States and other foreign countries. Wireless telegraph stations have been contracted for by the government
at Managua, Granada, San Carlos, San Juan del Norte (Grey-
town), and Castillo. There is wireless communication by means
of a private station at Bluefields.

NICARAGUA AND THE UNITED STATES

The political career of this republic has been one of wars,
anarchy, and tyrants. Few of the Central American republics
have had so troubled a political history. Between the years
1900 and 1910 there were sixteen revolutions in Nicaragua.
From 1894 to 1910 the presidency was held by José Santos
Zelaya, who kept the country constantly stirred up by his
aggressive policies. The selling of concessions, the terrorizing of

the press, and the irregular taxation of imports and exports were the rule during his régime. As a result of his desire to form a Central American federation, war ensued with Honduras and Salvador, and peace was restored, in 1907, only through the intervention of the United States and Mexico.

Because of a revolt against him, and because of the attitude of the United States toward the execution of two of its citizens, Zelaya was forced, in 1910, to resign. Revolts against his successors continued, however, and in 1912 the foreign minister of the Nicaraguan government confessed his inability to protect foreigners and their property, and in the following words asked the United States to act:

My government desires that the government of the United States guarantee with its forces security for property of American citizens in Nicaragua, and that they extend this protection to all the inhabitants of the republic.

In response to this request 2000 marines were landed. After the suppression of the revolution the marines, except for 100 men who remained as a legation guard until August, 1925, were withdrawn.

Another revolt against the government caused the landing of more United States forces at Bluefields. It was at this time also that the administration found itself in worse financial straits than usual. Various financial arrangements and treaties were made then and later with the United States, and in 1914 a treaty was concluded whereby the United States paid $3,000,000 for the exclusive right to construct a transisthmian canal via the San Juan River and Lake Nicaragua.

At present certain responsibilities of supervision in Nicaragua are exercised by a commission of three members, one of whom is named by the Nicaraguan government, one by the United States government, and the third by the Secretary of State of the United States. The need of a strong government and a carefully enacted financial policy is imperative, although the will to install such a government seems to be lacking in the country, and the intervention of other governments cannot be continued indefinitely.

HONDURAS

GEOGRAPHY

Honduras, formerly a province of the captain-generalcy of Guatemala, derived its name from the Spanish word meaning "depths." It was so called because the explorers of the early days found difficulty in anchoring off its coast.

The third in size of the Central American republics, Honduras has an area of more than 46,000 square miles, or about 3000 square miles less than that of New York State. On the southwest the country has 60 miles of coast line on the Gulf of Fonseca, and mountain chains separate it from the Republic of Salvador. The Gulf of Honduras forms the northern boundary, while the River Coco, sometimes called Segovia, or Wanks, which is the longest, if not the largest, river in Central America, constitutes, for the greater part of its length, fully half of the boundary on the south between Honduras and Nicaragua. On the west Honduras has Guatemala and Salvador as neighbors.

The country is mountainous and has a great diversity of surface and of elevation. Such a country, with its broad and fertile valleys, its wide and elevated plains, and its mountains, many of them terraced to their summits, furnishes almost every variety of climate and soil, and of products ranging from oranges and pineapples in the valleys to peaches and pears on the table-lands.

There is as great a variety of climate as of products and soil. The plateaus and uplands are healthful and fertile, while the climate of the lowlands on the coast is generally torrid, although modified by trade winds and rainfall. In the vicinity of the capital city Tegucigalpa the average temperature is 74 degrees Fahrenheit.

The wet and dry seasons are clearly marked. On the Pacific coast the rainy season begins in May and ends in November, while on the Atlantic coast the rainy season lasts from March or April to November.

HISTORY

Historically the Republic of Honduras is one of the most interesting of the Central American states. It was during his fourth voyage that Columbus discovered Bonacca Island, lying north of Honduras, from which he could see the high mountains of the mainland. Proceeding from the island, on August 14, 1502, he stepped foot on the American continent for the first time at what is now called Cape Honduras, and immediately took possession of the country in behalf of the crown of Spain. Subsequently Columbus sailed along the shore eastward and southward, encountering many dangers, and after many delays and vicissitudes he arrived at the extreme eastern point of the present republic of Honduras, naming it Cape Gracias á Dios (Cape Thanks to God).

Twenty years later Hernando Cortez undertook an expedition into Honduras, after having conquered the empire of Montezuma. Accounts had reached him of the populous countries to the south, and he entered upon a campaign that for length and hardships stands unprecedented in the history of all his martial adventures. Cortez spent two long years of struggle and brave fighting in a vast and unbroken wilderness, finally reaching the point where Columbus first landed.

In these early years of the Americas, Honduras was notable for its development. As early as 1540, more than sixty years before Jamestown was founded in Virginia, and nearly one hundred years before Hudson entered New York harbor, Honduras possessed large and flourishing cities. The history of the Spanish conquest and rule was practically identical with that of the other Spanish-American colonies. It included the exploitation of the aborigines and the arbitrary domination of Spanish governors who were interested not so much in colonizing as in plundering the country and enslaving the natives.

Like the other Central American countries, Honduras was a part of the captain-generalcy of Guatemala until 1821, when the countries declared their independence, and later was a member of the Central American federation. Honduras withdrew from that union in 1839, and soon after there began a long series of conflicts through which the country made repeated attempts to form a federation at various times with Salvador, Nicaragua, and Guatemala. Insurrections in the interests of various presidential candidates took place from time to time, with frequent bloodshed.

The recent history of Honduras is also one of struggle and internal dissension. This republic was repeatedly made the arena in which the Nicaraguan tyrant Zelaya staged his so-called "international" plots. Zelaya was bitterly opposed by Manuel Bonilla, who became president of Honduras in 1903 and again in 1911. Bonilla died in 1913, but internal war has not ceased, and more than once United States marines have been landed to protect American property.

PEOPLE

According to the latest estimate, the population of Honduras is 673,408, or about 15 people to the square mile. The great part of the population is composed of people of mixed Spanish and Indian blood, most of whom live in the Pacific section. On the northern coast is a large negro population. The sambos are a mixed race of Indians and negroes (a disappearing racial mixture in Latin America) and are to be found in a small coastal section above Cape Gracias á Dios. There are several thousand people of European birth in Honduras, many of whom are Germans engaged in overseas trade and Americans interested in the banana industry.

The Indian tribes of eastern Honduras have accepted in part the Catholic religion while still maintaining their superstitions, and are for the most part industrious cultivators of the soil. It is said that fully 100,000 of the Indians of this section are un-civilized. Along the Atlantic coast there are still evidences of the Caribs, a vigorous race descended from the Caribs of St. Vincent, one of the Windward Islands. The Caribs having a mixture of negro blood are called black Caribs. These na-tives are engaged in mahogany-cutting on the coast.

The population on the northern coast near the ports of Tru-jillo, Ceiba, and Tela, engaged largely in the banana industry, is unique in its heterogeneous racial composition. Back from the coast the people are chiefly Indians, with a small mixture of Spanish blood; the coastal banana plantations, run by American capital, have American overseers; the Turks control the dry-goods business, and other commercial activities are carried on by Frenchmen, Spaniards, and Italians. The workers on the docks and plantations are mainly Jamaican negroes, some of them Caribs. The Bay Islands off the coast are controlled by Great Britain, and English is spoken here, while a mixture of white races makes up the population of the island of Utila.

CITIES

Tegucigalpa, the capital of the republic, has a population of 40,000 and is the most important city of Honduras. Located in the central southern part of the republic at an altitude of over 3000 feet, this city is the center of the most populous section, in which the people are chiefly engaged in mining and agriculture. The principal wholesale business of the interior is carried on from Tegucigalpa, and this city should receive visits from commercial agents who canvass Central America. Trips from the Pacific coast are made by automobile, and a road which will put the capital in communication with the northern coast is in course of construction. Agencies for the interior of the republic are established here.

Ceiba, with a population of about 10,000, is one of the most important ports of the country. The city is the terminus of a railway which runs through a rich banana country, and it is the center of a flourishing wholesale and retail business. The climate here is tropical, and the chief products are rubber, hides, oranges, coconuts, and bananas. Bananas and coffee are the chief exports.

Santa Rosa, with a population of about 10,000, is the third largest city of Honduras and the largest in the western part of the republic. It is situated at an altitude of 3400 feet and is the center of a rich coffee and tobacco district. Gold, silver, and copper mines are found in the vicinity, and cattle-raising activities are carried on.

San Pedro, located in the fertile and extensive Sula valley, on the National Railway of Honduras, is an important distributing point for the interior of northern and western Honduras. It has a population of 8000 and is a flourishing business center. Only American money passes here, the silver currency in use in the interior being of no value.

Gracias, a town of about 6600 inhabitants in the western part of Honduras, is reached from San Pedro. It is the capital of the department of Gracias, which borders on Guatemala and Salvador, and is one of the most interesting sections of Central America. The atmosphere, products, and general conditions of this part of the country are described in interesting detail by E. G. Squire as follows:

On the north are many beautiful valleys, among them that of Colon, celebrated for its ancient monuments. Among its mountains is found the Quetozal, the royal sacred bird of the aborigines. Peaches, apples, and plums flourish here, and the blackberry is indigenous among the hills. The vegetable products, actual and possible, exhaust the list of the tropics and the temperate zone. Wheat, barley, rye, and the potato grow on the mountains, while sugar cane, indigo, cotton, coffee, cacao, oranges, and plantains flourish in the valleys. Pine covers the hills, and there is much mahogany, cedar and grenadilla, also Brazil wood for dyeing and manufacturing. Copal balsam and liquid ambar are among the common gums, while the tobacco has a wide and deserved celebrity. Gold and silver mines are numerous and rich, although but little worked. Bituminous coal, in beds from eight to ten feet in thickness, is found in the plain of Sensenti, and asbestos, sinnabar, and platinum in various localities. Opals are frequent, principally in the Brindique, where as many as sixteen mines have been "denounced" in a year. Amethysts also have been found.

Among the other cities of importance are Comayagua, the old capital of Honduras, and Choluteca, Juticalpa, and Santa Barbara. All have similar agricultural and mining activities.

On the northern coast Puerto Cortés, Puerto Castilla, Tela, and Trujillo are important ports, in addition to Ceiba, while on the southern coast Amapala, on Tigre Island in the Gulf of Fonseca, is the only Pacific port. The harbor of this port has deep water in front, allowing ships of ordinary size to lie near the shore. Tigre Island was the favorite resort of pirates in the buccaneering days, and it was here that Drake established a depot for certain of his expeditions. This same adventurer selected Puerto Cortés as an entrepôt port of New Spain during his expedition into Honduras, and for more than two centuries this port was the principal one of the coast, the settlement being removed to Omoa, a few miles to the southwest, in the time of the buccaneers.

GOVERNMENT

The government of Honduras is republican in form and is based on a constitution proclaimed in 1924. The chief executive is a president elected for four years, who is assisted by a cabinet of six ministers appointed by the president and responsible to Congress. The latter consists of one body, a Chamber of Deputies, which is composed of forty-three members, elected for four years on the basis of the population.

As to the manner in which the government has worked, particularly regarding its financial record, Chester Lloyd Jones, in his book "Caribbean Interests of the United States," [1] says:

Nowhere, the world over, can a worse record be found of the manipulation of public loans for private profit. Like Nicaragua, the country has been in financial straits practically since the beginning of its separate existence. . . . Insufficient revenues and frequent revolutions induced repeated resort to foreign loans on which practically no interest has ever been paid.

The external debt of the country in 1923, including the interest that has accrued since 1872, was approximately $135,000,000, — an almost impossible load for the country at present.

ARMY AND NAVY

There are about three thousand men in the standing army, and military service is compulsory for all citizens of twenty-one or over. Honduras has no real navy.

[1] Chester Lloyd Jones, Caribbean Interests of the United States. D. Appleton and Company, New York.

CURRENCY

While Honduras is nominally on a silver basis, with the silver *peso* and fractional coins of silver and copper as units, there is comparatively little of the national silver currency in circulation, since most of the silver has been exported from the country. At present the currency consists almost entirely of American paper money.

EDUCATION

Education is free and is compulsory for children between the ages of seven and fifteen. The percentage of illiteracy is high, however, since it is difficult to enforce the attendance law. Secondary schools, located at Tegucigalpa, Santa Barbara, Comayagua, and Juticalpa, have a five-year course, and there are several normal schools in the republic. A number of private institutions also provide secondary instruction. At Tegucigalpa is the national university, a school of arts and crafts, and a military school, and at Comayagua there is a law school.

PRODUCTS AND INDUSTRIES

Honduras is the leading banana-producing country of Central America, and the cultivation and export of the fruit is its main industry. While this industry is largely confined to the northeastern coast, the possibilities for its extension throughout the country are excellent. Puerto Castilla, Tela, Puerto Cortés, Ceiba, and Trujillo are the chief banana-exporting ports.

Sugar production is centered on the northern coast in the vicinity of Ceiba. Honduras is not an important producer of this staple, owing chiefly to world market conditions and to transportation and labor problems; but soil conditions are excellent for the growing of sugar, and the future possibilities of this crop are great.

Coffee is not so important in Honduras as in the other Central American countries. It is raised to a limited degree throughout the republic, except in the coastal plain, but the greater part is raised on the Pacific slope. The bulk of the coffee exports are shipped through the port of Amapala.

Coconuts are grown on the northern lowlands, and tobacco is an especially important crop just west of the banana zone. Beans, corn, and other vegetables are raised for domestic consumption only. The growing of henequen has been started, aided by a government subsidy.

Cattle are raised throughout the republic, for the country is well adapted to this industry. Its development is hindered, however, by the lack of adequate transportation facilities.

Mahogany was formerly a leading export of Honduras, but most of the accessible forests have been exhausted, and further exploitation will be necessary to develop the forest resources of this country.

Honduras is rich in minerals, which are found in nearly every department, but much of its wealth is still unexploited. Silver, gold, lead, copper, iron, zinc, nickel, and lignite are found, but of these only silver and gold are important for purposes of export.

Exports and Imports

In 1923 the exports of Honduras were valued at $10,000,000, and the imports at $14,000,000. Bananas were by far the most important article of export. Sugar, coconuts and oranges, and coffee were other agricultural products exported. Silver was the chief mineral export, and the live-stock industry was represented by exports of cattle hides and deerskins. Cotton textiles were the chief item in the import trade, with iron and steel manufactures next. As would be expected, the greater part of this trade consisted of manufactured goods and food products, although such imports as lumber and mineral oils were important.

In 1923 the United States took approximately 90 per cent of the exports of Honduras and supplied 85 per cent of the imports. Of the other countries engaged in trade with Honduras, Great Britain and Germany ranked next to the United States.

Transportation and Communication

Waterways and harbors. Honduras has numerous rivers and excellent harbors. The Pacific port of Amapala is a notable example of the latter, while along the entire northern coast there are bays and indentations suggesting large possibilities for the development of commerce in the future.

Railways. Most of the present railway mileage of Honduras is in the Caribbean coast region, where fruit-growing is so important. Of the six railway systems in existence at the present time, only one, the National Railway, is owned by the government; the others are owned by the companies having fruit and sugar lands. The National Railway extends from Puerto Cortés to Potrerillos, but plans have been made for further construction. It is planned to extend this railway eventually to the port of Amapala. The privately owned railways are being considerably extended.

Roads. Since the railways are for the most part concentrated on the northern coast, much of the transportation in Honduras has to be carried on by mules or oxcarts. An interoceanic automobile road from San Lorenzo, on the Pacific coast, through the capital, to Potrerillos is partially completed, and other roads are being built. The government is working to increase the mileage of good roads, but as yet mule trails are the chief type of road outside of cities and towns.

Telegraph and wireless service. In a recent year Honduras had 279 telegraph offices and 4662 miles of telegraph lines operated by the government. There were also nearly 900 miles of telephone lines. Several wireless stations are located on the northern coast.

BRITISH HONDURAS

GEOGRAPHY

This British possession is situated on the eastern shore of the Yucatan Peninsula, fronting the Gulf of Honduras. With its area of approximately 8600 square miles it is only slightly larger than Wales.

The coast of British Honduras is approached through coral reefs which present considerable danger and difficulties to shipping. For some miles inland from the coast much of the region is swampy, covered with mangoes and tropical jungle. Farther inland there are forests of red pine, broad savannas, and then ridges that rise to a height of about 4000 feet in the Cockscomb Mountains of southern British Honduras. Many small rivers, having their sources in the highlands and mountains, flow into the Gulf of Honduras. Behind the Cockscomb Range there is a succession of valleys and hills, containing open grassy lands, where the climate is excellent for cattle-grazing.

The climate in general is hot and damp, and in the main would be called subtropical. The annual rainfall averages $81\frac{1}{2}$ inches, although almost twice as much as this amount falls in some places. The prevailing easterly trade winds temper the atmosphere, and the highest and lowest temperatures are 98 degrees and 50 degrees respectively.

History

During the seventeenth century British Honduras, then styled "Her Majesty's Settlement in the Bay of Honduras," became a resort for English logwood cutters. Many of these Englishmen had been engaged in buccaneering in the West Indies, and with the decline of piracy had turned to this district, rich in dyewoods, as a profitable field for exploitation. The early name of this possession, Belize, is said to have come from the French word *balise*, meaning "a beacon," since at one time there was doubtless some signal or light raised here as a guide to freebooters.

There were many contests between the British and the Spanish over the privileges of cutting logwood, for Spain claimed this coastal strip, although she had never colonized it, and numerous treaties were drawn up between the two nations whereby the rights of each were prescribed. Matters were finally completely adjusted between Great Britain and Spain in 1836, when Great Britain acquired a clear title to British Honduras. When the Clayton-Bulwer treaty was drawn up between the United States and Great Britain, in 1850, British Honduras was excepted when both powers bound themselves not to occupy or colonize any part of Central America.

The present boundaries of British Honduras were defined by the conventions of 1859 and 1893 between Great Britain and Guatemala as follows: "Commencing at the mouth of the river

Sarstoon in the Bay of Honduras, ascending that river to the rapids of Gracias á Dios, then turning to the right in a straight line to Garbutt's Rapids, the river Belize, and thence due north to the Mexican frontier."

PEOPLE

The population of British Honduras is slightly more than 45,000, or about 5 inhabitants per square mile. There are no aboriginal tribes in the country, but there are still many Caribs, who are descendants of wanderers from the West Indian islands. A large part of the population is composed of negroes who were originally introduced as slaves. Through the intermixture of Indians and Europeans a hybrid race has arisen.

Most of the people are engaged in cutting mahogany and dye-wood and in fishing, although a few cultivate the soil. A scanty white population is engaged in commerce and in the work of the sugar plantations. The official language is English, but some Spanish is spoken in the interior and along the borders of Mexico and Guatemala.

CITIES

Belize, the capital and most important town of the colony, is located at the mouth of the river Belize on both banks. It has a population of about 13,000, which is doubled during the Christmas holidays by the coming of the mahogany cutters. The chief products are bananas, coconuts, grapefruit, and hard wood.

Belize is 860 nautical miles from New Orleans and is reached from this city, from New York, or from Puerto Barrios in Guatemala, by steamship service. An important business in both wholesale and retail lines is carried on here, and importing firms do a good trade in general merchandise.

GOVERNMENT

The government is in the hands of a governor sent from England and of two councils, one executive, the other legislative. There are the usual judicial establishments, a hospital, an asylum, and an agricultural institution for gathering and distributing information.

CURRENCY

United States money is the standard currency and circulates interchangeably with that of the colony. The British sovereign is legal tender for $4.86 and the half-sovereign for $2.43. There is a paper currency and silver and bronze coins are in circulation.

EDUCATION

Almost all the schools are denominational, and none are aided by the government. In a recent year there were sixty-five primary schools and five schools with secondary departments in the colony.

PRODUCTS AND INDUSTRIES

The most valuable product of British Honduras is its woods, chief of which is mahogany. Cedar, rosewood, and logwood are among the other woods found here, and the cutting of all these, especially of mahogany, forms the principal industry of the colony. Chicle, which comes from the sapodilla tree and is used in making chewing gum, is another valuable product.

Bananas and coconuts are grown, in addition to the other fruits common to tropical Central American countries, and the cultivation of these crops affords opportunities for much greater development. There are sugar plantations here, several varieties of cotton are grown, and sarsaparilla and vanilla are found in the interior of the country.

Among the hills are found indications of gold, silver, and coal deposits, but these have been but little developed.

EXPORTS AND IMPORTS

The greater part of the export and import trade of British Honduras is with the United States. About two thirds of the exports go to this country, which supplies more than half the imports. In 1923 the products sent to the United States were valued at $2,227,000, and those sent from here to British Honduras were valued at $1,860,000. Great Britain ranks next to the United States both as an exporter and as an importer.

The remainder of the export trade is divided between the Bahamas, Mexico, and Nicaragua, while Mexico, Canada, Guatemala, Honduras, and British India are the other sources of imports.

Woods, especially mahogany, and chicle are the leading exports, and the coconut and banana exports are also of some importance. The chief imports consist of foodstuffs and manufactured articles.

TRANSPORTATION AND COMMUNICATION

Waterways and railways. The chief highway from the coast to the western and southwestern parts of British Honduras is the Belize River, which is navigable for light-draft motor and cargo boats for a distance of more than 100 miles. Aside from several very short lines used for carrying bananas and for logging, there is only one short railway in the colony. This line is owned by the government. Traveling representatives of business houses often canvass the various towns north and south of Belize in schooners or motor boats, which work up and down the coast.

Telegraph and wireless service. Through a wireless telegraph station at Belize there is communication with New Orleans and Jamaica. There are telegraph and telephone lines in the colony, and cable communication with Belize from all points in the United States is possible.

SALVADOR

GEOGRAPHY

Salvador, the smallest but most densely populated of all the Central American republics, is bounded on the northwest by Guatemala, on the north and east by Honduras, on the southeast by the Gulf of Fonseca, and on the south by the Pacific Ocean. It has an area of 13,176 square miles, and its Pacific coast line is 160 miles long.

Salvador consists mainly of a plateau, lying 2000 feet or more above sea level, which is crossed by two mountain chains. This plateau is broken by a large number of volcanic cones, and the country has been more than once visited by destructive earth-quakes. There is a narrow seaboard of low alluvial plain. The principal river of Salvador is the Rio Lempa, which is a considerable stream even in the dry season. It has a rapid current and is navigable for about two thirds of its course.

The lowlands of Salvador have a tropical climate, while the climate in the higher altitudes is temperate and agreeable. On the whole the climate is healthful. The summer season, which is wet, lasts from May to November, and the dry winter season lasts from November to April.

HISTORY

Salvador received its name from Pedro Alvarado, a lieutenant of Cortez, who conquered it for Spain in 1525. At that time he found it a rich and prosperous country. As a part of the captain-generalcy of Guatemala, Salvador took part in the Central American movement for independence in the early part of the nineteenth century, and in 1821 joined the Central American federation. After the separation of the federation from Iturbide's empire, Salvador shared in the unsettled conditions of this union until 1839, and in 1841 it formally declared its independence. From that time to the present, revolutions and internal dissension due to presidential elections and other causes have been frequent; but the republic has been without serious wars, and its financial standing has been much better than that of certain of the other Central American states.

PEOPLE

The population of Salvador is approximately 1,500,000, or nearly 100 inhabitants per square mile. The mestizo strain of mixed Spanish and Indian blood predominates. Pure whites are comparatively few, but there are a considerable number of Indians.

Salvador is said to be the only republic in Central America having a middle class.

CITIES

San Salvador, the capital of the republic, with a population of about 80,000, is situated at an altitude of over 2000 feet. It is the city of greatest commercial importance. Wholesale houses here represent practically all branches of trade, and there are many business agencies in the city.

The prosperity of San Salvador, as well as that of the republic, is governed largely by the condition of the coffee market. The principal products are coffee, rice, sugar, tobacco, balsam, hides, and beans. Among the manufacturing industries here are those of cotton goods, soap, and cigarettes.

Acajutla is the principal port of the republic. Most of its trade consists of exports, however, the chief item of which is coffee. **La Libertad** is the second port. Its chief products are grain, coffee, cattle, sugar, rice, and indigo. The population of both these ports is small.

Other cities carrying on a considerable trade are **Santa Ana,** which has a population of about 60,000 and is an important business point, having products including cigars, textiles, coffee, sugar, and cattle; **San Miguel,** with a population of approximately 30,000; and **La Union,** on the Gulf of Fonseca, the only protected port of any consequence in the country, with a population of 6000.

GOVERNMENT

Salvador is governed under a constitution the present form of which was adopted in 1886. The president and vice president are elected for a term of four years. The president is assisted by a cabinet of four members, each of whom has charge of a governmental department. The legislative power is vested in a Congress consisting of forty-two deputies, three for each department. Suffrage is not only universal for citizens over eighteen years of age, but it is compulsory.

ARMY

Salvador has maintained a considerable army for its size, as a defense against the possible encroachments of Guatemala, which would naturally like to extend its Pacific coast line. The army may be divided into three parts: forces that are available at any time; forces that may be brought into service on short notice; and reserve forces. In all there are nearly 80,000 men available.

CURRENCY

The currency of Salvador is on a gold basis. The monetary unit is the *colon*, worth $0.50 in United States currency. Silver and nickel coins are issued in various denominations of the colon, and paper bank notes are also issued.

United States gold, silver, and nickel coins are legal tender in the republic, but the use of silver and nickel coins in making payments is limited to a certain percentage of the payment, while the use of gold coins is unlimited.

EDUCATION

The government of Salvador takes a keen interest in education. It has made increasing efforts to improve its schools and adjust their courses to the needs of the citizens. Primary education is free and compulsory, and there are a fair number of secondary schools which offer a five-year curriculum. There are two normal colleges, one for boys and the other for girls, and normal training is given in some of the secondary schools. The National University, with its faculties of medicine, law, engineering, and others, is at San Salvador, and the National School of Finance and Commerce, the National Agricultural Institute, and several other schools providing technical instruction are also located here.

PRODUCTS AND INDUSTRIES

Coffee is the most valuable crop of Salvador and the leading export as well. The coffee of Salvador is of excellent quality. In a recent year there were approximately 100,000,000 coffee trees in the country. Corn, the crop which ranks next in value, covers the largest acreage. Sugar cane, rice, beans, and tobacco are other agricultural crops, the cultivation of cotton is increasing, and henequen is also grown.

Lumber, balsam, and indigo are the chief forest products of the country. The "Balsam Coast" of Salvador is famous, for the tree from which balsam is obtained does not grow naturally anywhere else in the world. The so-called Peruvian balsam has always come from Salvador. During the period of Spanish rule, when products from the South American and Central American coasts were shipped across the Isthmus of Panama, the origin of the products often became confused, and hence the name "Peruvian" has clung to the balsam.

Cattle are raised in Salvador, and hides are exported. Gold, silver, copper, lead, and some iron and mercury are found in the republic.

EXPORTS AND IMPORTS

Salvador's coffee, which accounts for nearly 80 per cent of the total export values, is sent to the United States and to countries of Europe. Sugar is also an important export, and exports of cotton and cottonseed have advanced rapidly in the past few years. Among the other exports are balsam, indigo, henequen, cattle hides, and gold and silver. All the gold and silver is sent to the United States. In 1923 the total export trade was valued at $17,000,000, of which about one third was taken by the United States.

Cotton goods is by far the leading import of Salvador. Other important imports, however, are wheat flour, iron manufactures and machinery, leather, bags for coffee and sugar, chemicals and drugs, and lard. In 1923 the United States furnished more than 60 per cent of Salvador's imports, which were valued at nearly $9,000,000.

TRANSPORTATION AND COMMUNICATION

Railways. Salvador has fairly good railway service. The line of the International Railways of Central America, which enters the country at La Union, now connects that port with San Salvador and is being extended. Eventually it will reach the Guatemalan frontier. A railway connects the port of Acajutla with San Salvador and with Santa Ana, and there is a short electric line between the capital and Santa Tecla. The total railway mileage in a recent year was 253 miles.

Waterways. Commercially speaking, Salvador is handicapped by its lack of good harbors. At both of the chief ports goods have to be handled by lighters.

The republic has numerous rivers, but these are navigable only for small boats. The Rio Lempa, the principal river, is a considerable stream even in the dry season. It has a rapid current and is navigable for about two thirds of its course.

Roads. The roads of this republic are better than those of many of the other countries of Latin America. An increasing number of roads are adapted for motor traffic. There is much travel by carts or mules.

Telegraph and wireless service. There are over 2400 miles of telegraph lines in Salvador, and about 2800 telephones. A wireless station is operated at San Salvador.

GUATEMALA

GEOGRAPHY

The republic of Guatemala, the most northerly of the Central American states, is situated immediately south of Mexico. British Honduras and the Gulf of Honduras lie to the east, while to the south and southeast Guatemala is bounded by the Pacific Ocean, Salvador, and Honduras. With an area of 48,290 square miles, the republic is about the size of Louisiana. Its Pacific coast line is 200 miles in length, and its Caribbean coast line 70 miles.

Like the other countries of Central America, Guatemala is traversed from north to south by a chain of mountains which form a series of high plateaus, healthful and fertile, with picturesque and delightful valleys through which several rivers flow.

The climate is varied, being tropical on the coast, with heavy rainfall, while in the interior, in and around Guatemala City, where the altitude is about 5000 feet, the climate is like spring in the temperate zone. At the important city of Quezaltenango, lying over 7000 feet above sea level, the weather is cold. In the interior the rainy season lasts from May to October and the dry season is from November to April. The hottest months are April and May and the coldest are December and January.

History

Guatemala was formerly a part of the captain-generalcy of the same name. From 1821 to 1839 the history of Guatemala followed closely that of the other Central American states in their successful revolt against Spain, their union with and then withdrawal from the Mexican empire of Iturbide, and their formation of the Central American federation. In 1839 the State of Guatemala was formed. This name was changed to the Republic of Guatemala in 1847.

Attempts to form another federation were made at various times by certain of the Central American countries. Among these was the attempt made in 1850 by Honduras, Salvador, and Nicaragua, who tried to force Guatemala into a union with them. The three countries were defeated, however. It was soon after this, in 1854, that Rafael Carrera, who had held office as president since 1840, was elected president for life. He tended to establish a dictatorship, a characteristic of most of the later Guatemalan presidents. During his rule, however, which ended with his death in 1865, he acted in concert with the clerical party, in power at the time, and maintained friendly relations with the European governments.

General Cerna was Carrera's successor. He was deposed in 1871, when the liberal party began to have increasing influence. The next president, General Justo Rufino Barrios, was a member of this party, and under him severe measures were taken against the Jesuits and members of the clerical party. Cities were opened to foreign commerce, and an alliance was formed with Salvador for offense and defense. Barrios's ambitious desire for federation with the rest of Central America led him to declare himself the head of the five states. War with Nicaragua, Costa Rica, and Salvador resulted, and Barrios was killed in battle in 1885. The new president, General Barillas, made peace the next year.

Since then Guatemala has not been without internal strife. A revolt in 1905 against President Cabrera, who held office from 1898 until 1920 and was known as an "efficient tyrant," caused President Roosevelt and President Diaz to intervene.

PEOPLE

The population of Guatemala is about 2,100,000, or approximately 42 inhabitants to the square mile. The most densely settled areas are on the Pacific slope. Some 75 per cent of the population is composed of Indians or native inhabitants of Guatemala, there are about 60,000 pure whites, and the remainder are of mixed blood. Europeans are not numerous.

CITIES

Guatemala City, the capital of the republic, is situated in the southern portion of the country on a fertile plateau, nearly 5000 feet above sea level, surrounded by ravines. It has a population of about 120,000 and is the chief city of Guatemala. It is a thoroughly modern city with well-paved streets and excellent public buildings. Important wholesale and retail houses are located here, and there is an important turnover of goods from this point. Transportation is furnished by the International Railways line. Coffee is the chief product, but grains and cattle and hides are also important. The city has a Chamber of Commerce and good banking arrangements, and an American minister, consul, and vice consul are stationed here.

From a scenic point of view Guatemala City is unique, and with its accessibility by both steamer and railway it is destined to become one of the favorite tourist resorts of Latin America.

Quezaltenango, the capital of the department of the same name, is located about 120 miles west of Guatemala City, at an altitude of 7351 feet. It has a population of approximately 30,000 and is the second largest city of the republic.

Quezaltenango has an excellent climate. Its principal products are wheat, coffee, cacao, and sugar cane. Among its industries are textile mills, tanneries, cigar factories, breweries, and flour mills. The city serves a territory of some size, and certain business houses of Guatemala City have branches here.

Puerto Barrios, a small city of about 2000 inhabitants, is situated on the Atlantic side of Guatemala and is the chief port of the country. A North American fruit company maintains a large office here and has many plantations in the adjacent territory. The principal products of the city are bananas, coffee, mahogany, and sugar. This port is 964 nautical miles from New Orleans.

Coban is about 100 miles north of Guatemala City in the midst of a rich coffee-producing region. It has a population of about 30,000 and is a strong German center. This city is a distributing point for an extensive region in the central portion of the republic, and there are trails and water lines from this point into various parts of the interior.

Other important cities of Guatemala are **Totonicapan,** with a population of 28,000; **Antigua,** famous for its ruins and historical associations, with 10,000 inhabitants; **Escuintla,** with a population of 13,000; and **Retalhuleu,** with a population of 7000. The latter place contains the only inland customhouse besides the one at Guatemala City. Through it pass nearly all the goods from the entire western coast. **Champerico** is the Pacific port of the country. It has less trade than Puerto Barrios, and only 1500 people; but it is important. Coffee is the chief export.

GOVERNMENT

Guatemala, while ostensibly a republic, has been ruled in a manner quite inconsistent with its constitutional form of government, the country having been without free speech or a free press. In spite of such handicaps, however, there has been great material progress, labor receiving its wages and capital being secure from forced loans to the government.

The president is elected for a term of four years, and there is no vice president. To assist the president there is a cabinet of seven secretaries and a council of state of sixteen members. The legislative branch of the government consists of the National Assembly, a body having one chamber.

The political divisions of Guatemala include 23 departments. The 10 cities, 22 towns, 304 townships, and 2000 hamlets in the republic are law-abiding and progressive, as a rule. Means of communication and signs of modernity are increasing throughout the country.

ARMY

Guatemala has a standing army of 5200 men in time of peace. Military service is compulsory for men between the ages of eighteen and fifty.

CURRENCY

The unit of currency is the paper *peso*, based upon the silver peso; none of the latter are in circulation, however. Nickel and copper coins of varying denominations are used. The American dollar is legal tender here.

EDUCATION

The educational facilities of Guatemala are incomplete, as in most of the other Central American republics. In addition to primary-school courses, which are free and compulsory, secondary-school courses are offered in a number of *Institutos Nacionales*. Besides the government schools there are private schools for both boys and girls. The National University is at Guatemala City, and other schools, such as a normal school, an art school, and an aviation school, are found there.

PRODUCTS AND INDUSTRIES

Coffee is the most important crop of Guatemala. The chief coffee districts are along the Pacific slope as far south as Guatemala City and in the region around Coban. Guatemalan coffee is of especially fine quality. Sugar cane, another important crop, is also grown on the Pacific slope. Both brown and white sugar are produced. Corn forms the main sustenance of the people, and the acreage devoted to its production is greater than that used for coffee. Bananas are becoming increasingly important. The United Fruit Company owns large plantations on the Atlantic coast in the vicinity of Puerto Barrios. Other agricultural products raised in the country include wheat, rice, beans, potatoes, cacao, and tobacco. Cotton-growing is encouraged by the government.

Chicle and lumber are the principal forest products. Mahogany and cedar are the woods most important in the commerce of the republic. The Atlantic coast region is favorable to rubber cultivation.

Cattle are raised on the high plateaus, and cattle hides are the leading export product of the live-stock industry.

Little mining is carried on in Guatemala, and comparatively little is known about the mineral resources of the country. Silver, gold, lead, and copper are among the minerals found here.

EXPORTS AND IMPORTS

Coffee accounts for approximately three fourths of the total value of exports from Guatemala. The bulk of it is sent to the United States and European countries. Bananas, all of which are shipped to the United States, rank next. Other exports of importance are sugar, timber, chicle, and cattle hides. In 1925 the United States took exports valued at about $14,726,000, the total export trade of Guatemala amounting to $29,662,000. Germany and the United Kingdom were the other leading importers of Guatemalan products.

The import trade of the republic was valued at $23,394,000 in 1925. Cotton goods and food products were the leading items, and iron manufactures, paper, machinery, linen, hemp, jute, and leather were also of importance. The United States led in the value of commodities sent to Guatemala, furnishing them to the amount of $13,852,000. The other countries sending imports in large amounts were the United Kingdom, Germany, and Mexico.

TRANSPORTATION AND COMMUNICATION

Steamship lines and waterways. Guatemala is well served by several steamship lines. The United Fruit Company provides service from New York and New Orleans, and there are a num-

ber of other lines from New York. Service from San Francisco
is provided by the Pacific Mail Steamship Company.

Several of the rivers of the republic are navigable for a part
of their lengths, but for small craft only.

Railways. The chief railway system in Guatemala is operated
by the International Railways of Central America; this company is subsidized by the government. The Atlantic Division
of this system connects the Atlantic port of Puerto Barrios with
the Pacific port of San José. Several industrial lines are operated. There are now about 500 miles of railway in the republic.

Roads. Apart from the railways, the greater part of the traffic
is carried on by mules. There are few good roads in the country.

Telegraph and wireless service. There are some 5000 miles of
telegraph lines in Guatemala, and a telephone system. Both of
these systems are owned by the government. Direct cable communication with San Francisco is to be had. There is a wireless
station at Guatemala City.

CHAPTER XV

MEXICO

Let us face the Mexican trade problem as it is, with its vast potentialities balanced, as they actually are, by the sinister elements of ignorance, bitter poverty and racial conservatism. Let us see the problem while we see the golden goal. For this problem is no mere issue of beating the British or the Germans to a thriving market. It is an issue of bringing into being the purchasing power of a populous nation, which is bowed down to-day by the horrors of revolution, of unthinking radicalism, of national degeneracy. He who shall solve that problem will win the trade of Mexico when she has trade. — WALLACE THOMPSON [1]

MEXICO LITTLE KNOWN

Among all the republics of Latin America, Mexico, our nearest neighbor and one of the largest of these Latin-American states, is perhaps the least known. Unfortunately the principal occasions upon which Mexico has been brought to the attention of North Americans have been those in which trouble has arisen between the two countries, or when revolution or other disturbance has brought Mexico into view.

GEOGRAPHY

Mexico, with an area of 767,198 square miles, which includes the islands along its coast, together with Lower California, forms the fourth largest American republic.

Like many of the South American countries, Mexico could be justly called a mountain republic. Two great mountain systems traverse the entire length of the country, and between them are located extensive plateaus, varying in altitude, together with many fertile valleys. There are about forty Mexican cities located at an altitude above 4000 feet. Mexico City is situated in the historic valley of Anahuac and is 7875 feet above the level of the sea.

[1] Wallace Thompson, Trading with Mexico. Dodd, Mead & Company.

Mexico is supplied with lofty mountains, among the more important peaks being Popocatepetl, 17,782 feet; Orizaba, 18,242 feet; Iztaccihuatl, 16,960 feet; Nevada de Toluca, 14,950; and Colima, 14,970 feet above sea level.

The length of Mexico carries it into both the temperate and the torrid zone, affording a diversified climate and making possible the cultivation and growth of a wide range of agricultural products. The usual crops of the tropical, semitropical, and temperate zones may be found within a radius of three hundred miles. The lofty altitudes of the plateaus temper the extreme heat, while along the littoral and the lowlands of the southern section, on both sides of the country, the heat is extreme.

Because of the extreme differences in elevation in Mexico there are three distinct zones of climate. The *tierra caliente*, or hot land, extends inland from sea level at the Gulf of Mexico to an altitude of 3000 feet on the adjoining mountain slopes. The average annual temperature of this region is between 80 degrees and 88 degrees Fahrenheit. Sea breezes moderate the heat at night. The summer rainy season lasts from June to November.

The *tierra templada* extends from 3000 to 5000 feet above sea level and has a temperate-zone climate averaging between 73 and 77 degrees Fahrenheit. The temperature rarely varies in this zone more than 6 or 8 degrees during the year. Some of the mountain slopes and part of the great plateau are included in the *tierra templada*.

The *tierra fria*, or cold region, has a height of 7000 feet and upward above sea level. The greater part of the central plateau is located in this zone, and the average annual temperature is between 59 degrees and 62 degrees Fahrenheit.

Traders and travelers should note the rainy and dry seasons in Mexico, for traveling during the rainy season, particularly in the mountainous or remote districts, is often impossible. The rainy season, generally speaking, begins in the middle of May and lasts to the middle of October, the rainfall being heavy and of almost daily occurrence. Mexico City, however, is favored with only one or two months of heavy rains during the rainy season. The dry season lasts during the remainder of the year, with very little rain falling in this period.

For a place of habitation or for travelers and traders, Mexico furnishes exceptional natural beauty, and the important cities and business centers are so located that foreigners coming from temperate climates suffer little or no inconvenience.

HISTORY

As an introduction to the historical study of this country we know of no better proceeding than to read Prescott's "Conquest of Mexico," in which the long, troublous, and adventurous story of the almost superhuman deeds of the Spaniard Cortez and his followers, fighting with the Aztecs to gain control of the country, are fascinatingly told.

Cortez landed at Vera Cruz in 1519, subdued various Indian tribes one by one, and was finally granted an interview with Montezuma, who was emperor of Mexico when Cortez landed. Following their ancient customs, Montezuma, in inviting Cortez for an interview, sent with his messengers priceless gifts of gold and jewels, which added to the inordinate ambition of the Spaniards to capture and control a country whose wealth in their minds exceeded the dreams of avarice.

In the battles that followed Montezuma was killed, and his nephew Cuauhtemoc ruled in his stead as emperor. There followed massacre after massacre, and thousands of Aztecs were killed. The almost unbelievable bravery that Cortez and his followers displayed made the superstitious natives believe that they were fighting against gods rather than men. After years of fighting Cortez overcame the Indians, was made ruler, and the Aztecs became his slaves.

The misrule of Mexico. For nearly three hundred years, following the rule of Cortez, Spain misruled Mexico. There was a long succession of viceroys, royal governors, audiencias, and administrative councilors, appointed by the king of Spain. In these three centuries between the conquest and independence, Spanish grandees ruled in a lordly manner over feudal states sometimes as large as Spanish provinces. Fabulous sums were spent in rearing vast cathedrals and churches. The Inquisition extended its baleful activities across the plains of Anahuac, and

Spanish galleons sailed from the shores of the New World with the golden treasure of the Mexican mines which were to enrich the treasuries of the Spanish king. It was a period of plunder and piracy. The Spanish Main was swept by pirates, coast cities were sacked, and the shadow of medieval barbarism lay across a good part of the newly discovered Western world. In the words of L. S. Hasbrouck, "Three hundred years of Spanish ambition, magnificence, and indolence, planted on the ruins of the Aztecs' civilization and basking in the sunshine of the New World: there we have the history of Mexico under viceroys."

The coming of independence. Then, in 1810, Hidalgo, humble priest of Dolores and called by the Mexicans "father of his country," rang out the tocsin from his parish church, crying to his followers, "Viva Mexico!" It was the beginning of thirteen years of struggle, after which the Spanish yoke was thrown off and Mexico became a republic. It was on July 21, 1822, that there occurred in the great cathedral in the City of Mexico the solemn and imposing ceremony connected with the anointing and crowning of Iturbide, who had been able to finish successfully the fight begun by Hidalgo. Iturbide and his wife were crowned emperor and empress of Mexico; but the empire was only short-lived, since the patriots of the revolution had been fighting not for autocracy but for freedom. Antonio Lopez de Santa Anna was the young general who was selected to head the forces against the newly made emperor, and on the sixth of the next December, 1822, Iturbide awoke to find himself an emperor without an empire. Santa Anna had been proclaimed president, and Mexico was a republic.

The rule of Diaz. Mexico, quite as much as any other Latin-American republic, made a record for revolutions and bloodshed in the early half of the nineteenth century, until Juarez, in 1857, gave to the country the laws of reform that marked the beginning of good government. Porfirio Diaz, about whose personality clustered some of the most successful and magnificent days of Mexico, ruled the country for over thirty years, bringing the nation into a respectable position among other states; and, although he was a stern dictator, he maintained

the semblance of republican government. Diaz ruled from 1877
to 1880, and from 1884 to 1911.

General Diaz has been described by Edith O'Shaughnessy as
follows:

About General Diaz hung visibly much of the magnificence of his
destiny. Romance clothed his past, and there were potentialities of
splendor about his future. He was the fabled, fancy-stirring, "man
on horseback"; the type of man that every government of Europe
openly inveighs against and secretly desires in this year of 1920;
the savior, who, like all coming to save, performs his task above and
beyond the crowd, which later, after salvation is accomplished,
resents his disdain and forgets his benefits.[1]

The days following the rule of Diaz in Mexico marked a
procession of rulers over a tragi-comic "democracy," — an experiment with an unripe republic, missing the methods of pater-
nalism and the firm hand of Diaz. Nevertheless this notable
man had given, during his long reign over the Mexican people
whom he understood so well, things that have remained.

Mexico, "the treasure house of the world," could open her
doors again in safety, enjoying her own riches a hundredfold,
and contributing to the wealth of other nations. Vast facilities
for transportation were inaugurated during Don Porfirio's
dictatorship, over twenty thousand miles of railways were constructed, running the length of the country, and the ports of
Vera Cruz, Puerto Mexico (Coatzacoalcos), Salina Cruz, and
Manzanillo were entirely remodeled. Mexico City owes both its
beauty and its health to President Diaz, and the valley its
health if not its beauty. The admirable work of draining the
valley, dreamed of and planned under the viceroys, was finally
carried out by him. The city, which was always flooded at the
rainy season, was also most unhealthful during the long, dry
months. Diaz had sewers constructed and the streets paved and
kept clean, and pure drinking-water was brought from the springs
of Xochimilco. Hospitals, asylums, schools, and new governmental buildings were generously constructed, and throughout
the length and breadth of the land like reminders of a dictator-

[1] From "Intimate Pages of Mexican History," by Edith O'Shaughnessy. Copy-
right, 1920, by George H. Doran Company, publishers.

ship still exist, resembling little the defaced buildings, the empty schools and asylums, the looted churches, the destroyed railways, flooded mines, and untilled lands of his successors.

Confused government. Between the years of 1861 and 1868 Mexico's form of government was changed ten times, and over fifty persons succeeded each other as presidents, dictators, or emperors. From the year 1911, when Diaz closed his rule over Mexico, the country has been plagued by many attempts at revolution, by military usurpation, and confused government. Stable business life has not yet arrived in Mexico, and the safety of property is not fully assured. The wealth of natural resources as well as the intelligence of the comparatively small upper class of Spanish Americans, who were called upon to conduct the affairs of the country, would seem to prophesy that sooner or later this unfortunate country will become one of the influential forces, not simply of Latin America but of the entire world.

PEOPLE

According to the 1921 census the population of Mexico is approximately 15,000,000, or about 20 persons per square mile. The inhabitants are chiefly mestizos (a mixture of Indian blood with that of Spaniards and their descendants), with a large number of uneducated Indians. There are considerable numbers of Europeans, and among the foreigners the Spaniards predominate. The important business enterprises are largely in the hands of foreigners. There are a considerable number of negroes living about the coastal regions, and there are many mixtures of races among the lower classes. It is authoritatively stated that 7000 families out of a population of 15,000,000 own and control the entire land surface of Mexico.

Land monopoly. The country has never been a land of homesteaders, and the Spanish régime of nonproductive and often destructive exploitation reached its zenith in Mexico, leaving a dark trail of ignorance, indolence, and inconsequential agricultural cultivation in its wake. Much of the Mexican problem consists of land problems inherited for centuries. Cortez, the imperious Spanish conqueror, parceled out the major part of the country to his followers, while the remainder was given by the Spanish crown to its favorites.

There are many descendants of these original settlers still occupying these lands. Two estates in Mexico are cited by Nevin O. Winter in illustration of this land monopoly. The estate of General Terrazes in Chihuahua is large enough to make a commonwealth equal in size to the combined areas of Massachusetts and Rhode Island, with a farm of a million acres in addition. Another estate, that of the Zuloaga family, is a huge hacienda thirty-five miles wide, nearly a hundred miles long, including about two million acres. The proprietors still occupy these vast domains, living a patriarchal life with thousands of peons attached to their possessions. One Mexican hacienda is said to control an army of 20,000 peons. When one realizes the enormous territory controlled by such landholders, who are extremely jealous of their ancestral prerogatives, one can judge of the difficult conditions confronting the country in the way of intensive agriculture.

Immigration. Immigration from foreign countries has always been at a minimum in Mexico, and the non-Spanish-speaking whites of the country are few in number; these, mostly English, Americans, and Germans, did not go to Mexico for the sake of making homes for themselves and their families, but rather to exploit the natural resources of the country, often at the expense of the native inhabitants.

The general ignorance of the majority of the population, also an inherited handicap from the policy, or lack of policy, of Spanish rule, is amazing. At the close of the Spanish régime 95 per cent of the people in Mexico constituted a menacing mass sunk in profound ignorance. When slavery was abolished, the majority of the lower class of the population were made peons, and these still constitute from 70 to 80 per cent of the entire population, and form one of the greatest problems of the country. These peons, however, are not without possibility of development. Diaz himself possessed one eighth of peon blood, while Juarez was a full-blooded Indian. Throughout Mexico, as in most other belated countries, the power of tradition and the aristocratic landholder class constitute two forces inimical

FIG. 29. A view of a large coffee plantation in the state of Oaxaca, Mexico. (Courtesy of Mexican Chamber of Commerce of the United States, Inc.)

to progress, and only time and strong rulers with settled government can bring about the necessary advance.

In the large cities and towns of Mexico only about 10 per cent of the population is of European descent, the remaining 90 per cent being composed of 15 per cent Indian and 75 per cent mixed races, or mestizos. This population presents many differing racial characteristics, the mestizos themselves being anything but a homogeneous division.

Naturally this diversity in type of civilization presents almost insuperable difficulties from the point of view of government administration. The administrators of this land are confronted with the problem of discovering a formula suitable to the fifteenth-century type of Indian, to the eighteenth-century type of mixed races, to the nineteenth-century type of educated mestizos, and to the twentieth-century section of foreigners and Mexicans of aristocratic and undoubted culture. No single remedy is more efficacious in the solution of the problems of Mexico than education, than which no instrument of civilization has been more neglected by the entire range of rulers, from the *conquistadores* to the present time. The extension of foreign commerce in any country depends upon the advance of the arts of civilization in that country. For example, as soon as education and modern civilized modes of living are extended to the large masses of Indians and mixed races in Mexico, there will be a great increase in the imports of merchandise, clothing, household furnishings, agricultural appliances, and other products that naturally belong to a progressive modern régime.

The economic questions, and especially the agrarian economic questions, are vitally important here. An equalization of taxes is imperatively needed. Small landholders have been crowded out because of the fact that large estates pay only about 10 per cent of the taxes levied by the law, the large landholders being able to misrepresent the value of their property. The small landholder, meanwhile, is obliged to pay the entire tax because he lacks the political influence to secure reductions and concessions.

The peons, moreover, have been kept in a state resembling slavery, because their wages are too small to cover their expenses, and the practice has grown up, on the part of the estate owner, of advancing money to the peons as a loan in lieu of future wages. These debts, transferred from father to son, have kept the children of the land in a subdued and resigned condition, legally bound to their farms and living the life of serfdom under those who control both the land and the government.

CITIES

Among the chief cities of Mexico the following are of commercial importance.

Mexico City, the capital of the country, with a population of about 635,000, is situated 1221 miles south of El Paso, Texas, on a table-land 7875 feet above sea level. The city is very pleasant as to climate, with the exception of some disagreeable days in midwinter. The average temperature is 60 degrees Fahrenheit.

Mexico City is the largest and most important commercial and industrial center of the country, and the leading wholesale importing houses, specializing in almost every line of product, are located here. Industrially the city is advancing, and there are a considerable number of manufactories. Among the latter are establishments for the manufacture of cigars and cigarettes, pottery, shoes, gold and silver articles, leather goods, cotton goods, and newsprint paper.

The accessibility of Mexico City from all directions makes it the logical point for the establishment of general agencies for the republic. Commercial agents usually canvass the entire country from Mexico City as a center.

Guadalajara, the second city in importance in the republic, with a population of 120,000, is the capital of the state of Jalisco and is in the center of a rich agricultural district. Among the industries are textile mills and breweries, flour mills, tanneries, foundries, and establishments for the manufacture of hosiery, shoes, matches, candles, soap, and brick.

The city is a center for mining supplies, and there are here many wholesale houses whose agents canvass a wide territory. A number of the retail establishments import directly, as do the wholesale firms. Guadalajara is easily reached from Mexico City, 381 miles away, and is usually visited by all salesmen interested in Mexican markets. It is a city where subagencies are frequently established.

Monterrey is an important and beautiful city, the largest in northeastern Mexico, with a population of 85,000. It is an important railway center, second in tonnage to Mexico City. Its modern, progressive, and businesslike character has given it the title of "the Chicago of Mexico."

Among its industries are smelting works, textile mills, locomotive and machine shops, and steel works.

There is a large American colony here, and its wholesale and retail firms make direct importations. Monterrey is frequently made the headquarters for commercial agents working in the northeastern division of the republic. The city has a Chamber of Commerce, up-to-date electric trolley service, and the largest steel works of the country.

Puebla, with a population of 125,000, is the textile center of Mexico. There are about forty cotton mills in and around the city. Puebla lies at an altitude of about 7000 feet and has a temperate climate. It is an important commercial center, and manufactures, in addition to textiles, glassware and tiling.

Tampico is the chief commercial city of northeastern Mexico and the leading port of the republic. It is situated on the Gulf of Mexico, 470 nautical miles from Galveston, Texas. The city has a variable climate, ranging from 97 degrees Fahrenheit in summer to 45 degrees in winter. There are located here, as in most of the leading Mexican cities, American consular offices, and there is also here an American Chamber of Commerce. Tampico is a terminus of two branches of the National Railway, the one leading to Monterrey and the border towns of Texas, and the other to San Luis Potosi and across a rich tropical section to the west of Tampico.

The maritime traffic from Tampico has surpassed that of Vera Cruz, which formerly was Mexico's chief port. It is the center of a large oil field and in 1925 exported more than 90,000,000 barrels of petroleum. It is the entrepôt for eastern and central Mexico, and its strategic position from the point of view of its railway and port facilities has made it a natural center for the establishment of commercial agencies for northern Mexico.

Vera Cruz, with its excellent harbor sheltered by a sea wall, located on the Gulf of Mexico, is a port of entry for the greater part of southern Mexico. The population is about 40,000. Here are factories and mills for the manufacture of flour, soap, candles, chocolate, and cigars.

The port facilities embrace six wharves, and ships of many lines call here. The Mexican Central Railway, the Interoceanic Railway, the Vera Cruz and Isthmus Railway, and the Alvarado Railway connect Vera Cruz with the interior of the country, making it the business center for the entire southern region.

San Luis Potosi, capital of the state of the same name, with a population of 70,000, is an important commercial and mining center. It is accessible by rail from all parts of the republic, and it is a notable distributing point for hardware, agricultural and mining implements and machinery, and automobiles and accessories.

In addition to the cities already mentioned the following commercial centers are vitally associated with Mexican markets, and nearly all of them contain sizable wholesale and retail firms engaged in exporting and importing activities.

Merida, the capital of the state of Yucatan, is chiefly dependent upon the export of sisal; **Chihuahua,** capital of the state of the same name, is the most important city of north-central Mexico and is a base of supply for a rich mining and agricultural country; **Aguas Calientes,** lying 6280 feet above sea level, is an important agricultural center and the site of shops of the National Railway.

The city of **Orizaba,** in the state of Vera Cruz, is located midway between the "hot country" and the plateau, and is noteworthy because it contains the largest cotton mills in Mexico. **Saltillo,** located in the vicinity of the famous Mazapil Copper Company, is easily reached from Monterrey and is a flourishing commercial city with textile mills and other industries.

Other Mexican cities of note are **Guanajuato, Morelia, Torreon, Colima,** and **Queretaro.**

GOVERNMENT

Since the end of the Diaz administration, in the year 1911, the government of Mexico has been characterized by turbulence and instability. Many Americans, together with other foreigners, suffered severe losses of property during the period of the World War, and our dealings with Mexico for the past six or eight years have been fraught with more or less misunderstanding. The present form of government is that of a republic like the United States, the president and vice president being elected for six-year terms. So much power and influence, however, are wielded by individual leaders — politicians, landowners, and soldiers of fortune — that the government has taken on a sectional rather than a national nature. The administration has frequently been threatened with insurrection or revolution. Elections have been more or less a farce, defeated candidates having the unfortunate habit of appealing to arms instead of submitting to the result of the elections.

The complexity of the political problem in Mexico is considerable, but no one wishing to do business here can afford to be uninformed concerning the political tendencies. Indeed, the main obstacle in the way of opening Mexico for world trade lies in the instability and uncertainty of the country's political affairs.

The constitutional system of government began about the year 1857 and has been nominally enforced since that date, although, as a matter of fact, General Diaz abandoned the constitution and followed a dictatorial policy. He made the appointments to office, and little or no attention was paid to elections, Congress, the supreme court, or local legislatures. There was no earnest attempt to educate the Mexicans, the lower classes particularly, in the provisions of the constitutional administration. The liberties of the republic were enjoyed only by the wealthier citizens of the country, or by foreigners who had sufficient influence to demand their rights from the president or from the supreme court.

In 1917 a new constitution was adopted, similar to that of the United States and other federal republics. This constitution instituted the distribution of large estates, — a project which has resulted disastrously, as the estates have been ill cared for and practically deserted, or else the river-bank settlements have cut off the water supply of the estates which lie in back of them and have rendered them unfit for agriculture or even for grazing. Another important economic edict has declared that all natural resources, minerals, gases, and so on belong to the government, and that property rights involving these and the waterways of the government can be assigned by the state only, and likewise withdrawn at will by the government. This has created an unstable position financially, especially for foreign investors, and has led to complications with other governments.

The Constitutional party of the country is fostering education and leveling the barriers between upper and lower classes. Its members advocate economic and agrarian reforms, a redivision of large estates, equalization of taxation, and in some cases the reëstablishment of the *ejidos,* or communal land systems.

The political problem in Mexico has been so all-important to the people as to absorb almost the entire public attention of the upper classes at the expense of the social and economic problems.

Francisco I. Madero was supported in his revolution against Diaz by the rural classes, who believed that the revolution would bring in certain agrarian reforms and better the condition of the masses. The method or policy by which this must be brought about was not clearly formulated, and when General Diaz retired in order to stop the revolution, the power of Madero's movement was arrested and reaction occurred in favor of the old régime. About this time the Catholic party arose and cast its influence in favor of the reactionaries. De la Barra, in his interim administration, showed disloyalty both to Madero and to the revolution itself, and tried to attain political leadership.

Madero came into power in November, 1911, and was forced to accept the followers of Diaz in his cabinet, being caught between the reactionary and revolutionary forces with little power to institute reforms. The army left by General Diaz was not in sympathy with revolution or with Madero, and the uprising at

Mexico City in 1913 gave General Huerta the opportunity to make himself the head of the reactionary forces. The uprising of Felix Diaz and the attitude of the foreign residents and the diplomatic corps gave to Huerta his opening, and Madero and Suárez were arrested and compelled to hand in their resignations. Huerta was indorsed as president of his country, Madero and Pino Suárez were assassinated as an expeditious way of getting rid of enemies of the new administration, and the dictatorial policy of General Diaz was continued. In fact, Huerta outdid Diaz in the rigor of some of his policies, while he lacked the caliber and greatness of nature and judgment of Mexico's most famous dictator.

The revolution that began at the end of the régime of General Diaz now resumed its whole force against Huerta, the reactionary leader, and even increased its fury in the remembrance of the revolting circumstances surrounding the downfall of Madero. The Carranza movement seemed possessed with the one purpose of avenging the death of Madero and putting back into office the officials appointed by him. The present government has a far wider purpose than this, namely the reform of social and physical conditions and the revising of the Mexican constitution in order that its provisions may fit more nearly the needs of the population.

Although the present condition of Mexico is comparatively peaceful, and new life is evident in its markets, there is always present with those representing foreign capital the fear of revolution, and with the Mexican government the sense of being unable to protect its inhabitants and their commercial interests. Until there is a stable government, assuring safety to life and property, the largest possibilities of business advance in Mexico cannot be realized.

CURRENCY

The money basis of Mexico is a gold-exchange standard, the *peso* having a value in American money of $0.4939 (in 1925). Many of the banking connections in the United States and Europe were disrupted because of the World War, and particularly in view of the unsettled political conditions existing in

Mexico during these war years. Gold is the usual medium of exchange, and the government peso is not generally trusted. A limited amount of commercial paper is in use.

ARMY AND NAVY

Mexico has a standing army of about 50,000 men, of whom 3000 are officers. Every citizen is compelled to serve in the active army or in the National Guard. There are a military college and training schools for officers. The navy is so small as to be unimportant.

EDUCATION

Mexico has been famous in educational annals in the Western Hemisphere for having a university, the University of Mexico, organized prior to the first North American college. This university dates back to 1553. A school of surgery, a college of mining, and a botanical garden were opened in Mexico in the eighteenth century and gave Mexico City a wide reputation for learning.

The present educational system in Mexico is hardly worthy of its ancient beginnings. While in the large cities there are fairly good school systems, in the rural districts, and in fact throughout the greater portion of the outlying sections of the country, schools are conspicuously absent, and the woeful ignorance of the people reveals one of the greatest present needs of the country; however, the need is realized, and a campaign against illiteracy is in progress.

The language commonly spoken and used in the schools in the Mexican cities is Spanish, though English and French are used interchangeably by many members of the higher classes. In the transaction of business the knowledge and ready use of Spanish is indispensable.

PRODUCTS AND INDUSTRIES

The troubled political life of Mexico has often concealed the fact that in potential resources and commercial possibilities this country is destined to be one of the great leaders of the earth.

There is enormous wealth in mines of silver, copper, gold, lead, antimony, and zinc. Mexico is especially rich in petroleum and in agricultural products. Its wide domains furnish exceptional opportunities for cattle-raising. The mountainous character of the country and the presence of many small but powerful rivers afford unlimited opportunities for the development of water power.

AGRICULTURE

It has been estimated that only about 5 per cent of Mexican land can be cultivated by modern methods because of the mountainous and broken character of a large portion of the country. Primitive land cultivation is possible throughout the greater part of the country, however. A system of extensive irrigation would open many sections having a fertile soil but requiring water for its cultivation. The wide variety of climate, altitude, and rainfall permits the agricultural development of a wide range of products, including nearly everything from tropical fruits to grains and fruits of the temperate zones.

The farming section is for the most part in the central and north-central parts of the republic. Corn, beans, and wheat are the chief domestic food products, and these are grown almost everywhere throughout the land. Barley, sugar, and potatoes are also produced. Among the chief commercial crops, henequen ranks first, followed by cotton and coffee.

Agriculture has been handicapped by the uncertainty of the tenure of land and growing crops, which are subject to expropriation under the agrarian law.

LIVE-STOCK INDUSTRY

There has been a considerable decline in the live-stock industry in Mexico of late, owing to the revolutionary conditions in the country. For example, while in the year 1902 the number of cattle reported in Mexico was 5,142,454, in the year 1923 this number had been reduced to 1,750,305. There have been some attempts at restocking, but the lack of capital and the uncertainty of land tenure works against enormous ranches and large herds.

FIG. 30. Sisal (henequen) drying field at Merida, Yucatan, Mexico. The fiber is spread on wires to be cured in the sun after the pulp is stripped from it by machinery. (Courtesy of Pan-American Union)

FOREST INDUSTRY

The northern sections of Mexico contain large forests of pine, white cedar, and mahogany, while in the south are found valuable dyewoods and cabinet woods. More than two hundred lumber factories are scattered throughout the country, producing doors, moldings, and flooring, from native timber.

MINING

Next to agriculture, mining is Mexico's oldest and most important industry. It is estimated that over $700,000,000 is invested in mining operations in this country, and that of this amount $500,000,000 is American money, $90,000,000 English, $10,000,000 French, and $30,000,000 Mexican.

The mines of Mexico are found from the northern border of the country to the Isthmus of Tehuantepec, and they follow generally the western and eastern mountain ranges, as well as the cross ridges of the great central plateau.

It is a characteristic of Mexican ores that most of the deposits are mixtures of silver, lead, gold, and other metals. For this reason many of the lead and copper mines can operate at a profit even with high production costs, since, along with lead and copper, silver and gold and other rare minerals are found. The year 1923 saw a marked increase in mining activities in Mexico, in spite of the revolutionary outbreak in December of that year, the mineral production of the country in 1923 increasing greatly over the record of the previous year.

There are vast deposits of coal in Mexico, but through lack of proper development the country has been dependent upon Europe and the United States for upwards of 5,000,000 tons of coal annually, producing itself only about 1,000,000 tons.

Petroleum. The existence of oil in Mexico was known even as far back as the time of the Aztecs, who are reported to have used petroleum oozing from the soil of Tampico in the ceremonies of their temple. The use of Mexican oil for commercial purposes began about 1900. Among the pioneers in developing this industry was an American from San Francisco, who began to exploit the oil regions around Tampico in that year, after having organized an oil company.

Other companies were formed by both American and English capital, and in the year 1907 Mexico was producing 1,000,000 barrels of oil a year; in 1912, 16,000,000 barrels; in 1913, 26,000,000 barrels; and in 1925, 115,000,000 barrels. Of the latter amount 96,000,000 barrels were exported. Mexico possesses some of the most prolific oil wells in the world. The well known as Protero del Llano, No. 4, near Tampico, produced 120,000 barrels a day for more than three months. New zones of production are constantly being explored and opened. Mexico ranks next to the United States in total production of petroleum.

The Tampico-Tuxpan oil region alone covers five million acres. There are many other regions where oil is known to exist, but where the possibilities are as yet unknown. The oil fields of the United States cover a combined area of 8,300,000 acres. Within the coming generation Mexico's oil fields will be called upon for a like great production that may prove a greater source of wealth to the country than all its mines of gold and silver taken together.

Unfortunately this great industry is at the mercy of Mexican government caprice and pays upwards of $50,000,000 a year in taxes to the Mexican government, and the holdings of foreign investors are not at all secure.

MANUFACTURING INDUSTRIES

Mexico's manufactories are of considerable variety; among them are cotton mills, woolen mills, paper mills, flour mills, sugar refineries, breweries, and cigarette, leather, hat, furniture, and match factories. The manufacture of textiles is by far the most important. The economic depression of 1923 retarded the work in industrial plants because of labor troubles and the difficulty of getting raw materials and of distributing the finished products. An evidence of the labor disturbances was the taking over of the plants of the Tampico Light and Power Company by the laborers in the early part of the year 1924.

IMPORTS AND EXPORTS

It is significant that probably four fifths of the people of Mexico take little from the foreign market except food. The majority wear no shoes but native sandals, clothes different from those usually found in civilized countries, and homemade hats, and they therefore buy few luxuries made abroad. The real foreign market is thus limited to about three million people who constitute the buying class.

In the year 1925 the foreign trade of Mexico amounted to about $530,000,000, of which $340,000,000 were exports and $190,000,000 imports. Of the total exports 75 per cent by value went to the United States. The remainder went largely to the United Kingdom, Germany, Cuba, France, and Argentina. The United States furnished more than 70 per cent of the imports in 1925, and was followed by Germany, the United Kingdom, France, Spain, and Switzerland.

The foreign trade of Mexico in 1925 showed an increase of about 15 per cent over that of 1924; this was due largely to the increase in exports of animals and animal products, gasoline, henequen, copper, lead, zinc, coffee, and rubber. Increased shipments of mineral products in recent years indicate the development of the petroleum industry, though there was a considerable decrease in the export of crude petroleum in 1925.

The imports of Mexico include a wide variety of articles, among which should be noted meat and dairy products, cotton and cotton cloth, automobiles and tires, shoes, cottonseed oil, flour, petroleum products, and lumber.

American products have had a fairly good market in Mexico for many years in spite of the internal disturbances in that country. The natural resources of Mexico are so great, and the industrial potentialities of the people so real, that export and import business revives readily after the more or less frequent revolutionary conditions. A period of normal and healthy commercial activity would be greatly hastened by the elimination of the uncertainty as to tenure of farm lands and industrial property, a definite and permanent tax policy, and reasonable wage scales and labor regulations.

TRANSPORTATION AND COMMUNICATION

Railways. Transportation facilities in Mexico are not entirely satisfactory. There are about 13,000 miles of railway in operation, of which 8500 miles are under the control of the National Railway system and the remainder are owned mostly by private companies. A few miles are controlled by states and municipalities. The National Railway connects the Atlantic and Pacific coasts of Mexico and the Texas and Guatemala borders. Poor transportation facilities into the interior of Mexico have forced many of the large mining and oil companies to build their own railways and to buy their own railway equipment.

Steamship lines. Many lines of steamships, starting from Europe and from the ports of the United States on both the Atlantic and the Pacific side, as well as from the Gulf ports, connect Mexico with the outer world. The Pacific Mail Steamship Line, running between New York and San Francisco via the Panama Canal, calls at one or more Pacific ports, while there is a direct steamship line from San Francisco, and one from Canada, running to Mexican ports on the Pacific side. Every two weeks a steamship line from Japan sends ships to the western ports of Mexico, and these ships proceed down the western coast of South America, touching important ports and calling, on the homeward voyage, at Hawaii and Hongkong. Tampico and Vera Cruz on the Gulf of Mexico are the most important ports of the country.

Roads. In Mexico, as in most Latin-American countries, there is a great need of good roads and country highways between city and rural districts.

Telegraph and wireless service. Mexico is fairly well supplied with telegraph and telephone lines, and there are several wireless stations.

FOREIGN CONCESSIONS IN MEXICO

The concessions of foreigners in Mexico have reached an unprecedented figure. According to estimates from the State Department Consular and Trade Reports, Americans own in Mexico

$1,570,770,000 of the total national wealth, which amounts to upwards of $3,000,000,000. The English own $321,302,800, the French $143,446,000, while Mexican citizens own $793,187,242. All other nationalities together own $118,535,380. Thus only a little more than 30 per cent of the entire wealth of Mexico is in the hands of the Mexicans themselves.

These concessions and the rights of foreign business are generally governed largely by privilege rather than by rights. The constitution of 1917 was promulgated seemingly in the spirit of "Mexico for the Mexicans," and the difficulties placed in the path of foreigners attempting to do business are considerable.

Mr. Wallace Thompson, in his book entitled "Trading with Mexico," [1] says:

The laws against their [foreigners] holding land are drastic and final in their import; no foreigner may own property within sixty miles of the border or within thirty miles of the sea; foreigners may not control a Mexican corporation formed for the purpose of holding such land unless they waive their citizenship rights with respect to such companies; great estates are prohibited, so that true agricultural industry is made virtually impossible; foreign plans for irrigation projects — the one hope of the Mexican farmer — are nipped and killed; most serious of all, such lands are virtually confiscated through nationalization projects which have already been applied to many great properties, some of them of foreigners, and have been kept from affecting others only by diplomatic protest.

FUTURE TRADE WITH THE UNITED STATES

The future growth and volume of Mexico's trade with the United States depends largely upon the condition of Mexico itself. A strong government, stability of laws, and protection of life and property are naturally the first essentials of permanent commercial relations; but a mere dictatorial government, assuring peace and quiet in the country largely because the dictator has the power of the army and has a sufficiently strong personality to control opposing factions, does not of itself lay

[1] Wallace Thompson, Trading with Mexico. Dodd, Mead & Company.

the foundation for strong future trade development in the country. A strong commercial power is not merely the product of a strong force of arms. The attitude of the people and the economic, political, and social conditions must be upon a sane foundation and have for their aim the steady development of all classes in the country. A hard-and-fast dictatorship makes for only a temporary peace, which usually lasts only as long as the reign of the dictator. Mexico, with its maladministration covering so long a period of years, will need time to educate its lower classes and to produce a social equilibrium by the natural development of a middle class, without which a democratic form of government rarely if ever succeeds.

Trade with the United States depends also upon proper shipping facilities and a coöperative spirit between the two nations as concerns privileges of trade, salesmen's licenses, insurance, and a satisfactory mode of financing and merchandising materials.

The monetary system affects trade, and the condition of exchange is always a factor for or against enlarging commercial relationships. Mexico, while nominally on the gold standard, has been in such a disturbed financial state that its bonds and securities on the American markets, as well as its exchange, have been greatly depreciated. American bankers have hesitated to go to Mexico to organize American banks, fearing that their institutions would have experiences similar to those which many American business enterprises have had when extended periods of insurrection and war have practically stopped trade and greatly limited the dealings of Mexico with the outside world.

MEXICO'S DEBTS

The external obligations of the Mexican government held by foreign investors approximate, together with the national railway debt and certain internal loans, the sum of 1,000,000,000 pesos, or about $500,000,000. Because of internal disturbances the interest accumulated and unpaid between the years 1913 and 1920 approximated the sum of 400,000,000 pesos, or about

$200,000,000. In addition to these obligations the Mexican government must make restitution to the bank of the specie fund and is in arrears on its agrarian debt. Refinancing plans have been made, and there is hope of arriving at some plan for the bringing about of financial equilibrium in this country. That it will take time and a highly intelligent supervision of all departments of life in Mexico goes without saying. The country must restore the confidence of the world at large, and especially of its nearest neighbor and best customer, the United States, by showing signs that it has not only put its house in order for the time being, but is starting upon a period of sane rehabilitation in its social, economic, and educational life.

CHAPTER XVI

THE WEST INDIES

GENERAL TREATMENT

The West Indies constitute one of the most important foreign trade regions for the United States. In the year 1923 our exports to this group amounted to $247,650,000 in value, and our imports to $405,332,000. Cuba sent to the United States sugar to the value of somewhat more than three fourths of the latter amount. These figures do not include shipments from Porto Rico or the Virgin Islands, which are included in the trade statistics of the United States.

The West Indies are usually divided into three groups: the Greater Antilles, the Lesser Antilles, and the Bahamas. The Greater Antilles include the four larger islands of Cuba, Haiti, Jamaica, and Porto Rico. Because of the special volume and importance of their trade with the United States, Cuba and Porto Rico are treated by themselves in this chapter, and another chapter is devoted to a description of the general conditions and commerce of the other West Indian islands and colonial possessions located in the region of the Caribbean Sea.

The Lesser Antilles include the Windward Islands and the Leeward Islands, a chain which runs in the form of an arch east and south from Porto Rico to the vicinity of the northeastern part of South America. They are the possessions of Great Britain, France, the Netherlands, and the United States, and have a population consisting chiefly of the descendants of former African slaves. The language used is a more or less corrupt form of French, Spanish, or English. The white people in these smaller islands generally use the language of their home country in official and business circles. The islands are subtropical in climate, with climatic variations depending upon altitude and distance from the coast.

367

The bulk of the trade of the Lesser Antilles is retained by the mother countries by means of good steamship communication, preferential tariffs, and the maintenance of branch banks or other business agencies for the financing of production and trade. Between 1920 and 1921 preferential tariff agreements were formed between Canada and the British possessions which tend to divert to Canada some of the trade that formerly went to the United States.

The Bahamas belong to Great Britain and consist of a large number of small, sandy islands, of little commercial importance, extending eastward off the Florida coast for 700 miles. Some twenty of these islands are inhabited and contain a population of about 50,000. Their chief market is the United States, and their export products include lumber, sponges, sisal, and a certain amount of fresh fruits and vegetables.

The Bermudas, while not geographically a part of the West Indies, are similar in their political and economic status and are usually classified with the West Indies in trade statistics.

The prosperity of the West Indies depends chiefly upon their agricultural products, of which sugar comes first, followed by coffee, cacao, tobacco, and tropical fruits. An important part of the resources of Jamaica and Haiti is made up of such forest products as mahogany, cedar, logwood, and various tropical hard woods.

A large number of the West Indies are mountainous, and there are deposits of gold, silver, manganese, copper, iron, lead, and coal, although comparatively little mining is carried on at present. Cuba has furnished considerable iron and copper, the mines being developed by American capital, and during the World War manganese was produced there.

Little manufacturing is carried on, most of the manufactured products being imported. What manufactures there are include the production of such domestic articles as soap, matches, distilled alcohol (a by-product of the sugar industry), confectionery, chocolate, and fruit sirups. Breweries and bottling factories are found, and the tobacco crop of Cuba is utilized to a great extent in the manufacture of cigars and other tobacco products in the factories of Habana.

In general the exports include such products as sugar, molasses, rum, coffee, cacao, coconuts, spices, indigo, logwood, mahogany, and fruits. Trinidad lends variety to this list by its exports of asphalt, petroleum, and manjak.

CUBA

GEOGRAPHY

Cuba, the largest of the West Indies, lies about 100 miles south of Key West in one of the great trade routes of the world. It has an area of 44,164 square miles, being somewhat smaller than the state of Pennsylvania. The island has 2000 miles of coast line and several good harbors. The Isle of Pines, with an area of 1180 square miles, lies 88 miles to the south and is governed by Cuba.

Cuba is traversed by several mountain ranges, which cross and intersect each other. The eastern portion of the island is particularly mountainous. One peak, Pico Turquino, has an altitude of 8320 feet and adds to the picturesqueness of the mountain and sea views of this tropical island. On the southern slopes of the mountains much tobacco is raised, and on the plateaus one finds excellent forests and grazing lands.

Bordering the coast of Cuba are lowlands where the large plantations are found. Much of this land is planted with sugar cane.

The climate of Cuba ranges from the warmth of the tropics on the seacoast to the temperate airs of the plateaus on the mountain tops. Moreover, Cuba has the trade winds, which modify its tropical warmth, making its climate balmy and delightful.

There are two seasons in Cuba as in Mexico, the wet and the dry season. The rainy season extends from May to November, and the remainder of the year comprises the dry season. The average rainfall is about 54 inches. The range of the temperature in Cuba is from 60 to 92 degrees Fahrenheit, and seldom if ever do the inhabitants suffer from the heat to such an extent as do the people of New York City, for example, during the summer months. The people adapt themselves to the climate by dress, food, living arrangements, and charming houses. Since the Spanish-American War, Cuba has put its house in order from the sanitary point of view, abandoned many of the medieval and backward tendencies and customs inherited from Spain, and now boasts of being the healthiest country in the world, with a death rate of only 12.54 per thousand.

Cuba's landlocked harbors, its 13,000,000 acres of forest lands, its unusually rich tropical vegetation, together with its mild and delightful climate, give it distinction among all the islands of the Caribbean Sea.

HISTORY

Historically Cuba is particularly significant. It was here, in 1492, that Christopher Columbus, on his way to find a western route to India, discovered the American world, though at the time he was not aware that it was an island. Columbus landed at what is now known as the Bay of Nuevitas, where he took possession of the country in the name of the king of Spain, calling it Juana in honor of Prince John, the king's son. Soon afterward this name was changed to Fernandina, and later to Santiago, the name of Spain's patron saint. Another name, Ave Maria, was applied subsequently, and finally the country was named Cuba, the name used by the aborigines at the time Columbus landed.

In the year 1511 Diego Columbus, the son of the famous explorer, left Spain, taking with him 300 or 400 people, for the purpose of colonizing Cuba. The first settlement was at Baracoa. This was followed, during the years intervening between 1514 and 1516, by settlements at Santiago, Trinidad, and San Cristobal de Habana. The latter settlement is now the city of Habana. The first Spanish governor was Diego Velasquez, who found plenty of work in his attempt to subdue the warlike Carib Indians.

These settlements were the foundation of a long series of conquests, political and military, not unmixed with piracies, extending to the invasion and capture of Habana in 1762 by the British

Admiral Lord Albemarle, at the time when Spain was fighting England and France. At the declaration of peace between England and Spain, Cuba was returned to its original conquerors.

The history of Cuba is a romantic and lively story of wars with Indians, multifold attacks of privateers and Caribbean pirates, and sporadic attempts at independence, one of the earliest dating from the beginning of the nineteenth century, when nearly all the colonies of Spain in the Western Hemisphere revolted, and many threw off the Spanish yoke.

The American intervention in 1898 was the means of making Cuba free, driving the Spaniards from their last colony in the New World. In May, 1902, Cuba inaugurated her first president, the United States withdrew from direct control of the island, and the Cuban people began what has proved to be a growing and successful island republic. The political relations, as well as the trade connections, of Cuba and the United States have made the island of particular interest to Americans since the Spanish-American War. At present the United States has the greater part of Cuba's trade, taking about 85 per cent of its exports and sending to Cuba about 65 per cent of the imports of the island.

PEOPLE

Columbus found in Cuba races of Indians similar to those inhabiting the other Central and South American regions at that time. These were called Caribs and Nahacs, and their chief means of livelihood were fishing, hunting, and agricultural activities of the crudest and most primitive type. Columbus narrates that he found these people living in comparative ease and happiness, worshiping a Great Spirit as their god, who, as they believed, protected them from dangers on earth and at death transferred them to the "Happy Hunting Ground," which, to their primitive minds, was merely an extension of their natural existence in this happy island of sunshine and natural beauty. The primitive life of these half-clad but happy savages was soon checked by their Spanish conquerors, and they, like their fellows in other parts of the American hemisphere, were deprived of their land and their heritage.

Out of the mixture of these early races — Spanish, Indians, and imported African negroes — there has grown up much the same amalgam as is found in certain parts of Brazil, the white races being dominant in leadership.

The present population of Cuba is about 3,123,210, half of whom are white, about one third negroes, and the remainder mostly mulattoes. The white population is composed largely of Spaniards who remained after the close of the Spanish-American War, Americans, and a goodly number of Germans, French, and English. There are, of course, many other nationalities represented, and European foreigners are to be found in considerable numbers in the larger cities and connected with some of the industrial enterprises. The language of the people is Spanish.

Negroes are not prohibited from holding public office in Cuba, and these have at times held important positions under the government. They have also proved to be good soldiers, and the indomitable General Maceo exemplifies the noble part the Cuban negroes have taken in the defense of the country.

The Cuban people are characterized by the usual Latin traits, in their case softened and made attractive by the charming air and mode of life of the tropics. There is a notable devotion to home life, large families, music, and a flair for politics. Contact with the United States has brought in many Northern recreations and amusements, like baseball, tennis, and golf. The noon siesta, from twelve to two, still survives, as in most semitropical countries, and those who go to Habana on business must needs remember that they visit a land whose inhabitants as a whole are not yet thoroughly used to the rushing, strenuous business civilization of the North, but still cling to their Old World customs. These people take the most pleasurable road to a given end, rather than the quickest, and never forget in their business or their play their love of the easy-going, care-free gladness in mere living. Cubans do not have their eyes on the clock; it is sufficient that the sun shines, that their families are about them, and that they are happy.

CITIES

While the population of Cuba is engaged largely in agricultural pursuits, there are a dozen or more flourishing cities carrying on extensive import and export trade; the following cities are most important:

Habana	363,500	Matanzas	62,000
Camagüey	98,000	Sancti Spiritus	58,000
Cienfuegos	95,000	Manzanillo	56,000
Santiago	70,000	Pinar del Rio	47,000
Guantanamo	68,000	Trinidad	40,000
Santa Clara	63,000	Cárdenas	32,000

Habana is particularly interesting historically. It is filled with many ancient churches and cathedrals, crumbling fortifications, quaint foreign cemeteries, and beautiful Spanish-American homes, with their carved balconies and spacious patios, all breathing the air of equatorial ease and *dolce far niente*. Morro Castle, "the castle of three kings," and its near neighbor La Cabaña (castle of St. Charles of the Cabin), La Fuerza, the city's oldest fortification, and Columbus Cathedral, are all reminders of the past. A modern Habana, however, is not lacking.

The city is located on an excellent harbor which admits vessels of the deepest draft. From this port vessels leave regularly for the United States and Europe. Habana is growing industrially and is famous for its cigar manufactures. Sugar and tobacco are its export products, and an extensive volume of business is carried on in both domestic and foreign trade. There are the famous country club, where Americans and foreigners are always present in goodly numbers, Mariano Beach, the Prado, the combined Broadway and Fifth Avenue of Habana, and the Malecón Drive along the sea. The National Theater, facing Central Park, is the third largest playhouse in the world.

Santiago is the second city and port of importance in Cuba. It is 540 miles from Habana. The city is located on a landlocked bay and has a good harbor. There are large deposits of iron ore near Santiago, and ore steamers leave this port for the United States.

GOVERNMENT

The government of Cuba is of the republican representative type, and the constitution is based on that of the United States. The president and vice president are elected for four years. There are a Senate and a House of Representatives, similar in form to our own.

Cuba became an independent republic as a result of the treaty of peace of December 10, 1898, at the end of the Spanish-American War. The country's advance to a preëminent place among the islands of the Caribbean Sea in the years which followed this treaty of peace was due, not simply to the natural resources of the island, but in a peculiar way to the political association with the United States and the close connection by trade and political agreements as outlined in this treaty. The United States created a provisional government for temporary control after the Spanish-American War, and a convention met, in November, 1900, to draft a constitution for the new republic. This constitution was adopted in February, 1901. Although it recognized no supervisory powers by the United States, by an act of our Congress, known as the Platt Amendment, inserted in the Army Appropriation Bill, March 2, 1901, an unusual political arrangement came about between our country and Cuba. This amendment authorized the president of the United States to withdraw the American troops, and to "leave the government and control of the island to its people," but Cuba was to place a clause in her constitution binding the nation to conclude with the United States a treaty with the following agreements:

1. No treaty was to be made which would impair the island's independence, nor was any portion of the island to be allowed to pass under the control of a foreign power.

2. No debts should be contracted or assumed beyond the ability of the island to pay.

3. The United States was to have the right to intervene to protect Cuban independence, to maintain a government which would protect life, liberty, and property, and to carry out the obligation undertaken by the United States in her treaty with Spain.

FIG. 31. Caballería Wharf at Habana, Cuba. A familiar scene at this great crossroads port of the West Indies

This modification of the Cuban constitution, together with certain other ratifications of acts of the United States during its temporary occupation of the island with relation to the cession of land for coaling or naval stations, sanitation, and the Isle of Pines, was accepted by Cuba, June 12, 1901. This agreement was also later incorporated in a convention between the United States and Cuba.

Events have proved how important to Cuba was the support of the United States in the stabilization of the political affairs of the island. The first president, Tomas Estrada Palma, inaugurated May 20, 1903, was caught in a current of widespread political corruption, intrigue, and revolution in 1906, when the United States intervened and Mr. William H. Taft was sent to Cuba by President Roosevelt to restore order, acting as provisional governor. In 1908 José Miguel Gomez was elected president of Cuba, and the country enjoyed comparative peace until 1912, when a revolution occurred under the leadership of Everisto Estenoz, the head of the Negro party. A fleet of eight cruisers was sent to Key West in case it should be necessary for the United States to occupy Cuba for a third time, but they were not needed. For the first time the Island Republic showed its capacity for changing from one president to another without disruption, and a candidate of the conservatives, General Mario Menocal, was chosen president.

While Cuba has advanced tremendously in her industrial life, she still faces obstacles present in many other Latin-American countries in the line of political administration. Many of these republics have been unfortunate in the attitude of their office-holders toward public responsibilities. An office has too often been considered a stepping-stone to personal power, or a chance for patronage and extravagant expenditure. After the Spanish-American War, Cuba started debt-free, and before the end of the decade of local control her public obligation had reached $62,083,100, while in 1914 this amount had risen to $67,620,000. The resources of the island are so great that this debt is comparatively small, but anyone who studies the manner of expenditure may be led to question the wisdom of the Cuban politician in the use of public funds.

Closely connected with the political and commercial relationships between the United States and Cuba, and involving the entire Caribbean section, was the establishment of a naval station at Guantanamo in eastern Cuba. By the terms of the Platt Amendment the following clause provided this privilege:

That to enable the United States to maintain the independence of Cuba and to protect the people thereof, as well as for its own defense, the government will sell or lease to the United States, lands necessary for coaling or naval stations at certain specified points, to be agreed upon by the president of the United States.

The agreement to carry out this clause was signed by the president of Cuba, January 16, 1903, and by the president of the United States on February 23 of the same year. Certain lands and harbors adjacent were transferred to the United States by Cuba for coaling and naval stations, the United States to pay an annual rental of $2,000,000 as long as the areas are occupied by its forces.

There is no doubt that the position of the United States was greatly strengthened in the West Indian section by this arrangement, which is both a practical and a protective plan for Cuba as well as for the United States.

Because of this arrangement in regard to Cuba by the United States the investment of capital by foreigners is far more feasible than it is in certain of the other republics, and very large amounts have been invested, particularly in sugar and tobacco plantations.

CURRENCY

England, Canada, Germany, and France are also financially interested in Cuba. Banking institutions are numerous, and modern facilities connect these banks with the United States, as well as with other nations. The monetary system of Cuba is on the gold basis, the unit being the gold *peso*, worth $1.00 in United States money. There is a silver fractional currency as well as coins resembling our nickel and one-cent piece, and of the same denominations. American money was formerly current in Cuba, and is usually accepted at its face value.

EDUCATION

In Cuba, as in other Latin-American countries, education has had a struggle to overcome the handicap inherited from Spain, which seemed to have no satisfactory constructive policy for the systematic education of the people of its colonies. It was not until the American occupation of Cuba, when $10,000,000 was spent on Cuban schools, that the republic began to see the results which always follow intelligent and nation-wide educational policies.

Primary education is compulsory today in Cuba, and many an old building has been converted into a school. The Americans erected an academy of sciences and also a school of arts and trades, at the combined cost of $300,000. Cuban teachers were sent to Harvard University and other educational institutions to be trained in modern methods, and Harvard at least has reciprocated by establishing in Habana a branch school where American students may study at first hand the Spanish language and Latin-American conditions as they exist in Cuba.

PRODUCTS AND INDUSTRIES

Agriculture

Sugar. Among the products of Cuba sugar is king. In fact, the island has been called the world's sugar bowl. The production of sugar cane in Cuba extends over wide areas, nearly all the provinces being important producers. Even the extreme eastern portion has of late seen important advances in sugar production. The introduction of large amounts of American capital and modern methods of sugar culture are largely responsible for the extension of sugar-cane acreage.

The average annual production of sugar in Cuba approximates 4,200,000 long tons, about 85 per cent of which is taken by the United States. Large quantities go to Europe and Canada. The larger part of Cuban sugar is exported in the raw state, but some of it is refined in Cuban refineries.

The reciprocity treaty negotiated in 1903 between the Cuban government and the United States gave great assistance to the sugar production on the island, and aided other products of export. This agreement furnished mutual concessions and tariff rates, making a free list for both countries. All Cuban products not on the free list were to be admitted at 20 per cent reduction from the American tariff rates, while in turn the United States sent its articles into Cuba at reductions varying from 20 to 40 per cent. The Brussels convention of 1903, which brought about the stoppage of grants for export bounties for the production of sugar in European countries, was another influence that tended to increase the Cuban sugar industry. The result of these two legislative activities brought to the United States seven out of every eight pounds produced and fourteen out of every fifteen pounds exported from Cuba.

The Platt Amendment, which brought about the confidence of investors in Cuba's stability, assuring them that political disturbances would be checked and controlled by the United States, also greatly assisted the sugar business in Cuba.

Tobacco. Cuba produces annually between $40,000,000 and $50,000,000 worth of tobacco. This crop ranks second to sugar in value. Cuban tobacco is noted for its fine flavor. Its production is somewhat localized, since certain kinds of soil are much better adapted to its culture than others. The industry is centered largely in Pinar del Rio, where the choice tobaccos of the Vuelta Abajo are grown. A large amount of this tobacco is made into cigars and cigarettes in Cuban factories. Tobacco and its manufactures make up about 10 per cent of Cuba's export trade. The United States and Argentina take most of the leaf tobacco, and the United States, the United Kingdom, and Spain, most of the cigars and cigarettes.

Fruits. The fruit industry, while comparatively young in Cuba, is growing. The export of oranges, pineapples, and bananas to the United States amounts to several million dollars annually.

Coffee and cacao. Cuba raises about 40 per cent of the coffee that it consumes. Much must be imported from Porto Rico and other parts of the world, and this in spite of the fact that the mountain valleys, slopes, and foothills of Cuba are admirably adapted to coffee culture.

There is some production of cacao in the valleys that lie between the mountain slopes. Small quantities are exported, chiefly to the United States.

Live-Stock Industry

High-grade cattle are being introduced into Cuba for breeding purposes, and the herds are being rapidly improved. There are over 4,000,000 head of cattle on the island. Hides and skins are an important export.

The climate of Cuba is well adapted to the raising of horses and mules. With the investment of necessary capital this may prove a profitable industry in the near future.

Mining

In a recent year more than 1000 mines were registered by the government of Cuba. These included iron, copper, gold, lead, mercury, zinc, coal, asbestos, asphalt, and manganese. Iron is the chief metal of export. Large deposits of this metal are found in the eastern part of Cuba. Iron to the value of from $2,000,000 to $4,000,000 is sent annually to the smelters of the United States. Copper, gold, asphalt, and manganese are exported in small quantities. The most valuable copper mine is in the province of Pinar del Rio.

Forest Industry

The forests of Cuba contain valuable supplies of mahogany and cedar, both of which enter into the export trade of the island. Much cedar is used at home in the manufacture of cigar boxes for Cuban cigars.

Exports and Imports

Cuba, with a population of little more than 3,000,000, imports annually goods to the amount of nearly $300,000,000, about 65 per cent of which is furnished by the United States.

The large importation of goods is due to the fact that the energies of the island are devoted almost exclusively to the production of sugar and tobacco, and little manufacturing is done, so that there is a heavy import trade in manufactured goods and in foods other than those produced at home. With the growth of the sugar industry the purchasing power of Cuba has greatly increased until at the present time the island ranks among the first six or seven countries in the export trade of the United States.

Manufactures of iron and steel, cotton, wood, paper, leather, chemical products, machinery, meats, breadstuffs, vegetables, and dairy products are among the important imports. Spain, the United Kingdom, Germany, France, and British India also send a considerable amount of merchandise to Cuba.

In recent years the exports of Cuba have approximated $425,000,000 annually, of which the United States buys more than 80 per cent, the United Kingdom about 11 per cent, and the Netherlands and France about 1 per cent each; Spain, the country that formerly controlled this trade with arbitrary exclusiveness, gets about one fourth of one per cent of Cuba's exports.

Sugar and its products, especially molasses, make up about 85 per cent of the export trade of Cuba. Tobacco ranks second, furnishing about 10 per cent of the total export trade. Fruits, iron ore, sponges, and tortoise shell are exported in small quantities.

TRANSPORTATION AND COMMUNICATION

The ocean shipping facilities of Cuba are good. Several steamers from the leading ports of the United States call at the island each week. There is weekly communication between Habana and New York, Boston, New Orleans, Mobile, and Galveston. Direct lines run between Habana and Key West, Miami, and Tampa (Florida). By utilizing the Key West Ferry a person can go direct to Habana from New York by sleeper, and freight can be shipped between these two cities without breaking bulk.

There are several local steamship routes giving service between Cuban ports, and between Cuba and the Isle of Pines, Mexico, Porto Rico, and the Dominican Republic.

The rivers of Cuba are short and offer little in the way of transportation facilities. On some of the streams small boats are used for transporting sugar for short distances to the various ports.

The highways of Cuba are poor. Only the provinces of Habana, Matanzas, and Pinar del Rio have a continuous highway system. The question of improved roads is receiving much attention. It is hoped that a central highway will be completed, with branch roads connecting all important places.

Railway travel in Cuba is convenient and very comfortable. There are about 3000 miles of steam railway and 250 miles of electric railway. Santiago, the metropolis of the eastern provinces, is connected by railway with Habana, the trip of 550 miles being made in about twenty-four hours. Branch railways connect the main lines with the ports, and in many cases with the sugar centrals. In addition to the railways already mentioned there are several thousand miles of railway belonging to the sugar plantations and used entirely for transportation connected with them.

The telephone and telegraph systems of the island are owned and operated by the government. Cuba is connected with other islands of the West Indies, and with the mainland, by cable.

For tourists as well as for those engaged in trade the interior of Cuba offers rich reward. Trains carry the traveler through fields of sugar cane, tobacco, and pineapples and other fruits, with here and there jungles of hard wood. Tropical forests of mahogany, lignum vitæ, and logwood reach almost to the railway track in some places, while in others tobacco and the cedar trees which are one day to make boxes for transporting the tobacco grow side by side. Cuba has still greater possibilities for development along all these lines, and, like other comparatively new countries, awaits capital and the peculiar vigor of foreign population and achievement for the fulfillment of its larger destiny.

PORTO RICO

Advantageous Relations with the United States

The island of Porto Rico became an American possession in the year 1898, and its progress during the last decade has been an object lesson to all the islands in the West Indies. It has revealed what order, security of possessions, and modern leadership can accomplish in an island which had the usual doubtful inheritance from the Spanish régime. Porto Rico's free-trade relations with the United States, and the introduction of American methods into almost all the departments of the island, have spelled progress commercially and economically, and in the matter of government there have been produced in a short time administrative conditions similar to those existing in the United States.

Geography

Porto Rico is the most easterly of the four Greater Antilles, and is located 70 nautical miles east of the island of Haiti, and 40 west of St. Thomas. It is 100 miles long and 40 miles wide, and has an area of 3435 square miles, being somewhat smaller than the island of Jamaica, but with a much larger population. Extending in an east-west direction through the central part of the island is a mountainous area made up of two main ranges, the Sierra de Luquillo and the Cordillera Central. El Yunque, with an altitude of 3483 feet, is a well-known peak in the Sierra de Luquillo, and there are several higher peaks in the Cordillera Central. On the lower slopes of the mountains and in the mountain valleys coffee and tobacco are grown.

Bordering the coast of Porto Rico are areas of low plains. On these coastal plains live most of the people of the island, and here the main agricultural crop, sugar cane, is grown.

The rivers of Porto Rico are valueless for navigation, but they furnish water for municipal purposes and for irrigation. The La Plata River furnishes power and light for many of the cities of the island.

Porto Rico's climate is delightful the year round, the temperature being lower than that of any other island in the tropics.

It is a land of continuous summer, tempered as to climate by the constant trade winds. The average annual temperature is about 76 degrees Fahrenheit. The nights are always pleasant and cool. There are no defined wet and dry seasons, but the rainfall increases from February to May. There is cool weather beginning in November and lasting until early in March, and this is the best time to visit the island.

HISTORY

Discovered by Columbus in 1493 and colonized by Ponce de Leon in 1509, Porto Rico is Spanish in temperament despite the fact that English is taught in most of the schools and education is compulsory. Doubtless within the next quarter of a century Porto Ricans will be able to speak English quite as well as Spanish, and the civilization of the United States, of which the island is now an integral part, will have placed its stamp upon all its activities.

PEOPLE

The inhabitants number 1,299,809, or about 378 people to the square mile. Three fourths of the population is rural. The people are chiefly descendants of the Spaniards, and the large percentage of whites is notable. The census figures of 1899 listed two thirds of the inhabitants as whites, one fifteenth as negroes, and the remainder as mestizos; there were 304,352 mestizos to 59,390 negroes and 75 Chinese. With such a population the United States had a far better chance of inaugurating modern methods than it would have had in some of the other islands inhabited by larger proportions of colored and mixed races. In Jamaica, for example, only about one person in 53 is white, about three fourths are negroes, and one fourth "colored East Indians" or Chinese. Porto Rico has fewer colored people than any other island of the West Indies except Cuba.

CITIES

San Juan, the most important city, with a population of 71,443, is located on the northern coast, 1399 nautical miles from New York. It has a pleasant climate with an average temperature of about 79 degrees Fahrenheit. San Juan is the best port on the island and has a good harbor. It is reached from New York by the New York and Porto Rico Steamship Company, ships leaving every Thursday and Saturday and arriving at San Juan on the fourth or fifth day. The Red D Line also serves San Juan and several other Porto Rican ports with a similar schedule. There are several other steamship lines making regular sailings between San Juan and West Indian ports, and also monthly and semimonthly steamship communication with France and Spain.

Among the banks located here are branches of the National City Bank of New York, the American Colonial Bank of Porto Rico, and the Royal Bank of Canada. A large trade, both import and export, is carried on, and many large wholesale firms carry important stocks, making direct importations. It is the logical place to establish business agencies. The chief products distributed through this port are sugar cane, coffee, tobacco, pineapples, and grapefruit. Among the local industrial plants are shipyards, coaling stations, cigar and cigarette factories, breweries, machine shops, ice plants, and bottling works. San Juan is the business headquarters for canvassing the entire island.

Ponce, next in importance to San Juan, with a population of 41,912, is easily reached by railway or automobile from all parts of the island. Its harbor is not so good as that of San Juan. It is poorly protected from high waves. Ponce is in the sugar-cane region and near an important coffee area. In the vicinity are several sugar centrals with which are connected large commissaries which furnish a great volume of business. Here also are large wholesale and retail firms doing a direct importing business. Ponce is next to San Juan in the importance of its manufactures.

Mayagüez, with a population of 19,124, lies at the western end of the island. It has a poor harbor but is connected with the coastal towns by railway. It is near the large coffee plantations. Mayagüez carries on a considerable business in the main products of the island.

Other important and growing cities which are visited by commercial agents are Cayey (5243), the center of the tobacco industry; **Bayamon** (10,411), in a citrus-fruit and pineapple area; **Arecibo** (10,039), in a rich sugar district; **Caguas** (12,149), in an important sugar-cane and tobacco region; **Humacao** (6183) and **Guayama** (8924), in a growing agricultural district.

The island of Vieques, a short distance from the eastern coast of Porto Rico, is becoming important from a business standpoint. There are sugar centrals which import considerable machinery from the United States.

GOVERNMENT

The Insular Board of the United States War Department controls the government of Porto Rico, and the governor is appointed by the president of the United States. The legislature consists of a Senate of 19 members and a House of Representatives of 39 members. A resident commissioner elected by the people every four years represents Porto Rico in the Congress of the United States.

By an act of Congress in 1917, known as the "Jones Act," American citizenship was granted to the people of the island.

PRODUCTS AND INDUSTRIES

Agriculture

Sugar cane. Although only about 25 per cent of the land is actually cultivated, agriculture is the chief industry of the island. Sugar cane, with a yearly value of $40,000,000, is by far the most important of the agricultural crops. It is grown largely on the coastal and river plains, though the upland areas are also becoming sugar-cane producers. Large sugar mills with modern machinery have replaced the old-fashioned mills run by mule power, water power, or wind power, and the vacuum-pan process is rapidly taking the place of the wasteful evaporating pan of other days. The prosperity of Porto Rico is largely dependent on the sugar-cane crop and the price of sugar.

Tobacco ranks next to sugar cane in value of Porto Rican crops. The island raises about 20,000,000 pounds annually. A considerable part of this is exported to the United States, and

Fig. 32. A modern sugar central at Guánica, Porto Rico. (Photograph from Janet M. Cummings)

the remainder is made into cigars and cigarettes in Porto Rico. The tobacco crop has been greatly increased since the annexation of the island by the United States, and the methods of culture have been improved. Most of the tobacco is grown in the Caguas and Cayey valleys.

Coffee, at one time the leading export of Porto Rico, has declined in importance, though the island still produces about 50,000,000 pounds annually. Coffee-growing has proved less profitable than sugar-cane growing. Porto Rican coffee is exported chiefly to foreign countries, though the United States is taking more now than formerly.

Fruits. This industry has increased two hundredfold in the past decade. The United States takes nearly all of the fruit that Porto Rico exports. This ready market and the establishment of refrigerator-ship service between the island and New York has done much to encourage the fruit-growers to plant large acreages of citrus fruits and pineapples. Bananas are raised in large quantities, but they are not exported. The canning of fruits is becoming an important industry of the island.

EXPORTS AND IMPORTS

The foreign trade of Porto Rico has had a remarkable growth in the past twenty-five years, increasing from $9,500,000 in 1900 to $189,433,000 in 1925. Of the latter amount about $99,000,000 were exports and $90,000,000 imports.

The standard of living in the island has risen during the American possession, and this has brought about a demand for better food, clothing, and luxuries. The favorable tariff position is of assistance to the trade with the United States, and the constant association with Americans has exerted a tremendous influence on the civilization in general. The entrance of American capital into the country has been a vital factor in the commercial progress of the island. Agricultural production has increased by leaps and bounds, and Porto Rico has large quantities of products to export. With the money received for its exports it is able to buy from other countries manufactured goods and the foods that cannot be produced at home.

As might be expected, most of the trade of Porto Rico is carried on with the United States. The island is a part of that country, and goods pass between the two duty free. Sugar is Porto Rico's leading export, and of this product the United States takes 99 per cent. Tobacco, the second export, is sent largely to the United States. Most of the coffee goes to Cuba and Spain, and the fruits and nuts are taken by the United States. Handmade wearing apparel has become in recent years one of Porto Rico's important exports.

The chief imports of Porto Rico in 1925 were rice, cotton goods, iron and steel manufactures, meats, boots and shoes, wheat flour, automobiles, lard, and machinery. Since Porto Rico is for the most part a nonmanufacturing country, it sends its raw materials abroad and imports its manufactured goods and its temperate-zone food products. In normal years about 90 per cent of the imports are furnished by the United States.

TRANSPORTATION AND COMMUNICATION

Except for the great military highway across the island, the Spanish government did not concern itself with roads in Porto Rico. Under American administration more than 600 miles of good roads have been built. They go around the island and cross it, thus connecting all the important places.

There are about 340 miles of railway in Porto Rico, more than half of which has been constructed since 1898. One railway almost encircles the island, and extensions of this line into the interior are being projected.

The island is well provided with telegraph and telephone service, there being about 2000 miles of wires. It has communication with the outside world by three cables, and through wireless stations at Cayey and San Juan.

CHAPTER XVII

FOREIGN POSSESSIONS IN THE WEST INDIES AND SOUTH AMERICA

BRITISH POSSESSIONS

The British islands of the Caribbean extend over 1900 miles, in a half circle from Trinidad, at the mouth of the Orinoco, to the Bahamas, off the coast of Florida. Jamaica is the largest of these islands and at one time was the richest and most desirable of the British West Indian possessions. British Guiana, on the northern coast of South America, is the largest of the Guianas, having an area greater than that of the Dutch and French sections combined.

These possessions are predominantly negro lands, although Jamaica and British Guiana have imported a considerable number of East Indians for labor. There are few white residents, and most of these are employed on the large plantations to superintend labor and cultivation. Sugar cane, which was once a lucrative product in this region, is again gaining in importance, while new industries such as fruit-raising in Jamaica and cacao production in Trinidad are developing rapidly. As compared with Porto Rico, however, these possessions, as a whole, have shown far less commercial progress. The introduction of new capital has been less than in Cuba and Porto Rico in recent years.

A readjustment of agricultural activities is going on throughout the British West Indies, owing largely to the increasing hold of the United States upon West Indian markets and to the growing dependence of the British West Indies upon the markets of the United States. This fact in particular was emphasized at the Canadian-West Indian conference, held in Ottawa in 1913, when Mr. George Foster, Canadian Minister of Trade and Commerce, spoke thus:

The United States has now within her own territory, or affiliated to her by special treaties, a tropical area which goes far toward satisfying her own wants; as these countries now have advantages which are not enjoyed by the British West India Islands, a complete reversal of the condition of things has taken place. We are more and more driven to come to each other for our mutual advantage.

JAMAICA

GEOGRAPHY

The island of Jamaica lies about 90 miles south of Cuba and 100 miles from Haiti. It has the following dependencies: Turks and Caicos islands, Cayman Islands, Morant Cays, and Pedro Cays.

Jamaica has an area of 4207 square miles, its greatest length being 144 miles and its greatest width 50 miles. Nearly all of this island is mountainous and hilly, and some of the peaks attain an altitude of from 5000 to 7000 feet. The most important chain is called the Blue Mountains. The valleys are many and fertile, and the island is well watered by small streams.

The climate varies according to the distance from the coast, that of the coastal regions being humid and warm and that of the higher sections dry and equable. There is more or less rain throughout the year, but the season of least rainfall is from December to April.

HISTORY

Jamaica was discovered by Columbus in 1494, during his second voyage. Until the middle of the seventeenth century it was ruled by the Spanish, with disastrous effect on the native population. In 1665 it was captured by a British expedition, and fifteen years later the British claims were confirmed by the Treaty of Madrid. The island proved a prize of great value to Great Britain, and was associated with many of the early adventurous exploits in the days of the buccaneers. For many years Jamaica paid to the British crown an annual "irrevocable revenue" amounting to £8000 in Jamaican currency, in addition to supporting itself. This price was paid to gain freedom from interference in lawmaking.

The prosperity of the island, greatly enhanced by the benefits of British rule, was affected adversely by the abolition of slavery in 1838 (which disturbed considerably both the social and the economic conditions), and also by the development of the beet-sugar trade. Bounty-fed beet sugar forced down the price of cane sugar, and cultivation of sugar cane became unprofitable.

People

The population of Jamaica is about 900,000, or nearly 214 inhabitants per square mile. About three fourths of this population is black, there are some 15,000 whites, and the remainder of the population is made up of East Indians, Mongolians, and other races. One half of the inhabitants are said to live almost a hand-to-mouth existence, and 100,000 are reported to have an average income of about twelve cents a day. The increase of the population during the last quarter of a century has been chiefly from the black race.

Cities

Kingston, the capital of the island, with a population of about 62,000, is the chief city of commercial importance and is the port of call for many steamship lines trading with the West Indies and South America. Kingston is 1457 nautical miles from New York and carries on a considerable volume of both wholesale and retail trade. There are many sugar, coffee, coconut, and banana plantations in the neighborhood, and some business is done in foodstuffs and hardware. The principal exports of this port are sugar, rum, coffee, dyewoods, and fruits.

Other smaller towns carrying on a fair amount of trade are **Spanish Town,** formerly the capital of Jamaica, which has a population of 8694; **Montego Bay,** with a population of about 6600; **Port Antonio,** where the United Fruit Company has done much to develop the surrounding district, with a population of approximately 8000; **Savanna-La-Mar,** with a population of 3500; and **St. Anns Bay,** a favorite winter resort for tourists, with a population of about 2500.

© Publishers' Photo Service

FIG. 33. A charming bit of Jamaica, showing a coconut grove, and straw-covered huts in which the laborers live

PRODUCTS AND INDUSTRIES

The crops of Jamaica covering the greatest acreage are bananas, sugar cane, coconuts, coffee, and cacao. The industries of the island are essentially agricultural, although there have been recent advances in the timber industry, and cattle-raising is promoted on a small scale.

Adverse tariffs and the lack of proper transportation hinders the cultivation of citrus fruit, but the sugar industry, with the use of modern methods such as are employed in Cuba and Porto Rico, is promising. In a recent year the products of the banana industry formed 55 per cent of the total export trade. Tobacco is grown, but government experiments have not been successful and there has been difficulty in marketing this product, owing to the character of the leaf.

The plantation system which has been in vogue in the island for generations has been gradually changed by the breaking up of the big estates into holdings ranging in value from $100 to $200. Between 1839 and 1896 more than five hundred estates were abandoned or divided, and sixty-four more were included in this list by 1909. There are still large possibilities of land tillage, since only about one seventh of the tillable land is in use.

EXPORTS AND IMPORTS

Bananas, sugar, coffee, logwood extract, coconuts, ginger, logwood, cigars, cacao, pimento, rum, copra, and oranges are the chief exports of Jamaica. The export of rum, which formerly constituted about 10 per cent of the island's foreign trade, has been reduced in late years by rising excise taxes in both England and Germany.

The United States is the chief market for Jamaican products, about three fifths of the products exported being sent to us, as compared with one fifth to the United Kingdom. In some years the United States has taken 99 per cent of the bananas and nearly all the other fruit exported. Jamaican coffee is not popular in North America, and most of this is exported to France. In 1923 Jamaica exported to the United States products valued at $6,626,000.

The United States also led in the import trade in 1923, sending merchandise valued at $8,837,000. The imports included such commodities as cotton goods, flour, coal, automobiles, and foodstuffs.

The commercial language of Jamaica is English, and both English and United States money is accepted. The volume of trade here, as in other islands of the West Indies, would be greatly increased by the lowering of freight rates and the raising of the standard of living.

TRANSPORTATION AND COMMUNICATION

Jamaica has two hundred miles of railway owned by the government, and in addition has steam and electric tramways. It has excellent roads reaching to all parts of the island. There are more than 2000 miles of telegraph and telephone lines here, and the island has wireless and cable connections.

TRINIDAD AND TOBAGO

GEOGRAPHY

Trinidad is the most southerly of the British West Indies, and is located 16 miles from the coast of Venezuela and directly north of the mouth of the Orinoco River. Its area is 1862 square miles, or somewhat less than that of the state of Delaware. There are three ranges of hills running east and west on the island, the highest point being 3000 feet above sea level. There are numerous rivers, but none of them are suitable for navigation.

The temperature is hot and humid, but the nights are cool, the heat being modified by refreshing breezes. The average temperature is 79 degrees Fahrenheit, but from January to March the temperature is sometimes as low as 65 degrees.

The island of Tobago, 20 nautical miles northeast of Trinidad, is under the administration of the latter. It has an area of 115 square miles. This island is in part mountainous; but the soil is fertile, and sugar, coffee, cacao, tobacco, and cotton are raised and exported. The population is of mixed blood.

People

The population of Trinidad is 365,000, or about 200 per square mile. One third of the inhabitants are East Indians or their descendants. There are about 200,000 negroes or partly colored inhabitants on the island. The remaining population is of mixed African and European blood, among the European elements being French, Spanish, and Portuguese. There are some Canadians, English, and Americans, and about 3000 Chinese, who are mostly small-shop people.

The population of Tobago is approximately 20,000.

Cities

Port of Spain, the capital and chief port of Trinidad, is situated on the western side of the island. It has a population of about 75,000, or, if its suburbs are included, of 100,000. It is an important city in the West Indies and is a port of call for many steamship lines. Numerous sugar and cacao estates are located in this vicinity, while the raising of coconuts and the exporting of asphalt and oil contribute to the wealth of the community. There are markets here for machinery, tools, and other implements useful in the industries carried on in the island.

Port of Spain is a trade exchange for the llano district of Venezuela by way of the Orinoco River and Ciudad Bolívar, and a great many products from that region are shipped to Europe from Port of Spain. The chief sources of the wealth of Tobago lie in tropical agricultural products, and most of the business is done through Port of Spain.

Products and Industries

Trinidad is an agricultural island, cacao being the chief source of profit. Tropical fruits abound and are exported, but better refrigerating facilities on steamships are needed to make this trade successful. Sugar, coconuts, and rice are among the resources of the island, and the outlook for plantation rubber is good.

Cacao, the king of products in Trinidad, is grown on about three fourths of the cultivated area and is shipped in the bean for manufacture, chiefly to the United States. The cacao estates, of which there are at least 500, are owned by a large number of residents. The owners are anxious to retain the American market, since over half of the products are sent to the United States. There is considerable American capital and control here, and the commercial ties are important for Trinidad.

Asphalt, which is found in the famous asphalt lake of Trinidad in almost unlimited supply, continues to be one of the chief resources. It was formerly the leading export. Crude petroleum is found here, and people believe that this resource promises to be a very important factor in making the island a strategic fuel-oil supply station in the Caribbean.

As a growing center for transshipment trade and for coaling Trinidad holds an important place. Its imports of coal from the United States in recent years have had an annual value of more than $250,000. In proportion to its population Trinidad has become one of the wealthiest islands of the West Indies. Both British currency and United States gold are legal tender here.

EXPORTS AND IMPORTS

The United Kingdom and the United States compete about equally for the foreign commerce of Trinidad and Tobago, each having about one third of the total trade. Cacao, sugar, coconuts and copra, petroleum and asphalt, tonka beans, and bitters are the chief exports from Trinidad. The tonka beans and part of the cacao are from Venezuela. In 1925 the exports of Trinidad and Tobago to the United States amounted to $6,000,000. Among the principal imports are coal, lumber, grain, and petroleum.

TRANSPORTATION AND COMMUNICATION

Trinidad has some 120 miles of railway lines. Owing to the importance of the island as an oil center, oil is burned on the railways. There are telegraph and telephone systems, and Trinidad and Tobago are connected by a wireless telegraph system. Other wireless communication is maintained.

BARBADOS

GEOGRAPHY

The island of Barbados, which has an area of 166 square miles, is a British possession lying to the east of the Windward Islands, about 97 miles east of St. Vincent.

The climate is healthful, with a temperature averaging 63 degrees Fahrenheit in winter and from 75 degrees to 96 degrees in summer. The island is favored by cool northeast trade winds, but during the rainy season, between May and October, the heat is more oppressive. What is called the "hurricane season" occurs in August and September. The annual rainfall varies from 46 to 87 inches.

PEOPLE

Barbados has a population of 157,000, or approximately 940 people per square mile. Like Jamaica, Barbados is chiefly a black colony, although there are some Europeans, most of them English. The population has been declining for some time because of the economic pressure due to its density. Labor conditions have been rather bad in recent years, since the laborers constantly left to go to Panama during the construction of the Panama Canal. Many of the people of Barbados work on the banana plantations of Central America and in the sugar-cane fields of Cuba.

CITIES

Barbados is a popular resort for tourists from both North and South America. **Bridgetown,** the capital and chief commercial center, has a population of 13,486. It is the port of call for many southbound steamers and is about 2000 nautical miles from New York. There is a considerable volume of trade carried on here, the currency used being British. In the main this trade is of retail character, consisting of general merchandise and estate stores, but there is some wholesale business. There are many sugar works here and various small manufacturing industries.

PRODUCTS AND INDUSTRIES

The first successful sugar colony of Great Britain in the West Indies, Barbados is sometimes called the "molasses island." About 70 per cent of the total area of the island is devoted to large-scale sugar production, and there are more than 300 sugar estates here. The enormous windmills used to grind much of the sugar cane are picturesque features of the landscape. Fully a third of the sugar estates use steam-driven machinery, however. Fancy molasses, made from the entire juice of the sugar cane, is an important product of Barbados. Some sea-island cotton is raised here, and nearly all the inhabitants have their own patches of land on which they raise such crops as yams, bananas, and breadfruit. The limestone soil of the island is rich, and careful fertilizing is practiced.

EXPORTS AND IMPORTS

The leading exports are sugar, molasses, cotton, and rum. Small shipments of fruits and vegetables are made, but as yet this trade is not of great importance. The greater part of the exports are sent to Canada, although the United Kingdom and the United States have an appreciable share in the trade. Much of the sugar, cotton, and rum of the island goes to the United Kingdom, while some sugar is purchased by the Netherlands. The preferential tariff on sugar in the United States has turned shipments to British ports, but the United States has a growing import trade with Barbados.

Foodstuffs, cotton goods, fertilizer, machinery, and timber are the principal imports into Barbados. Canada has a subsidized line of steamers to the island, and through a trade agreement between Barbados and Canada the former has granted a 50 per cent tariff reduction to Canadian products, and Canada has granted a 50 per cent preference on the duties on goods imported from Barbados.

In 1923 the export trade amounted to about $10,364,000 and the import to about $11,601,000. Of the total imports 33 per cent came from the United Kingdom, 24 per cent from Canada, and 19.6 per cent from the United States.

TRANSPORTATION AND COMMUNICATION

A short railway line, owned by the government, extends from Bridgetown to St. Andrews. There is no telegraph system in the interior of the island, but there is a good telephone system, most of the lines of which belong to a private company.

THE WINDWARD ISLANDS

The Windward Islands, British possessions in the same general region as Barbados, consist of Grenada, St. Vincent, St. Lucia, and the Grenadines. Their products are similar to those of other islands found in this section.

The exports of these islands go chiefly to British ports and to Canada. Two thirds of the arrowroot from St. Vincent and almost all the sea-island cotton are sent to the United Kingdom. The chief handicap of the United States in this trade is the lack of direct steamship connection. Canada has a direct line to the islands, and the United Kingdom has several steamship services.

The currency used here is, as a rule, the same as in England, and weights and measures are similar to those used in England and the United States. Cable service with the United States is maintained by the West India and Panama Cable Company. The telegraph and telephone systems are under government control.

GRENADA

Grenada, the southernmost of the Windward Islands, is 90 nautical miles north of Trinidad and 65 miles south of St. Vincent. It is a small island with an area of 120 square miles. The mean maximum temperature here at sea level is 90 degrees Fahrenheit, but in the mountains of the interior the temperature is lower. The rainy season lasts from June to December, with September and November as the rainiest months.

Grenada has approximately 70,000 inhabitants, or nearly 600 per square mile. The greater part of the population is negro or colored.

Although there are no large cities on the island, St. George, the capital and principal port, is usually visited by salesmen who canvass the smaller islands. It is situated on the southwestern coast of the island and has a population of 6000 (mostly black). The chief resources of St. George are cacao, nutmegs, and mace.

The principal products of Grenada are cacao, sugar, limes, coconuts, and rum. Mace, nutmeg, and lime juice are other products exported. The cacao industry is becoming the predominant one for the entire region.

St. Vincent

St. Vincent, which is 97 nautical miles west of Barbados, has an area of 140 square miles. It is a volcanic island, with irregular woody ridges running along its entire length. There are numerous small streams, but none of them are navigable.

During the rainy season, from August to November, the climate is usually hot and damp, but during the rest of the year it is healthful, with temperatures averaging between 60 degrees and 88 degrees Fahrenheit. The average annual rainfall is about 100 inches.

St. Vincent has 50,000 inhabitants, or about 357 to the square mile. The language is English, as in most of these British islands.

Kingstown, the capital, is located on the southwestern coast, and is about 1876 nautical miles from New York. The principal wealth of this town is gained from cassava, arrowroot, cotton, cacao, and sugar. There is a market here for machines and implements for agricultural purposes.

St. Vincent is noted for its sea-island cotton and its arrowroot. This island is said to grow the best long-staple cotton in the world, and one fourth of its cultivated land is devoted to this product. Arrowroot, which is a form of starch especially suited for use in the manufacture of chocolate, is the most distinctive product, however. St. Vincent holds a monopoly of the production of arrowroot for world trade, and in favorable years produces about 5,000,000 pounds. Cotton and arrowroot constitute about four fifths of the exports of the island.

St. Lucia

The island of St. Lucia, the most northerly of the Windward group, is situated 30 nautical miles northeast of St. Vincent. It has an area of 238 square miles. The island is crossed from north to south by a mountain range averaging 1500 feet in height, these mountains sloping down to the sea on either side. In the center of the island is Canaries Mountain, its highest point, which rises 3140 feet above sea level. The island has several rivers.

The climate here is mild and pleasant, and the nights are cool. The temperature averages between 80 degrees and 90 degrees Fahrenheit, and the annual rainfall is about 84 inches.

St. Lucia was long a British naval base, and was historically important in the conflict between France and England in this section of the Caribbean. In many respects St. Lucia is the most important in this chain of islands. It has a population of 54,600, or about 230 inhabitants to the square mile. Both English and French are spoken here.

Castries is the chief town of the island and has a population of 8000. It is 1747 nautical miles from New York and 37 miles from Fort de France, Martinique. It has an excellent harbor with good docking facilities, and the cultivation of sugar, limes, and other tropical fruits is carried on here. This port is usually visited by commercial agents who tour the West Indies.

The principal products of St. Lucia are sugar, rum, lime juice, cacao, vanilla beans, nutmegs, bay seeds, cloves, and logwood.

THE LEEWARD ISLANDS

The Leeward Islands, which extend the arc of Caribbean islands northwestward toward Porto Rico, also include outposts of the British Empire, largely inhabited by a black population. In appearance these green-clad islands are among the most beautiful in the West Indies. The principal islands of the group are described here.

MONTSERRAT

Montserrat is a small island with an area of 33 square miles. It is of volcanic origin. The highest point in its three groups of mountains is the peak of Soufrière, 12,200 feet above sea level. The climate is fairly cool and healthful, the average annual temperature being 78 degrees Fahrenheit. The annual rainfall averages from 40 to 80 inches.

Montserrat has a population of about 15,000. **Plymouth** is the principal town, with a population of about 1700. The trade here is small. Cotton, sugar, lime juice, cattle, and cotton seed are the chief products of the island. Most of the trade of Montserrat, as well as of the other islands in the group, is with Great Britain.

ST. KITTS (ST. CHRISTOPHER)

The island of St. Kitts, north of Montserrat, has an area of 65 square miles. Its temperature and rainfall are in general similar to those of Montserrat. The population of approximately 30,000 is largely negro, with a few Englishmen and native-born whites. A fair amount of trade is carried on at **Basse Terre,** the capital and principal town, which is located at the southwestern end of the island. The chief dependence here is upon tropical products, especially sugar. Sea-island cotton and corn are grown here.

The three islands of St. Kitts, Nevis, and Anguilla form one presidency.

NEVIS

Nevis, two miles from St. Kitts, has an area of 50 square miles and a population of 13,000. **Charlestown,** the principal town, has a population of 1500. The leading products of the island are sugar, sea-island cotton, corn, and coconuts.

BRITISH VIRGIN ISLANDS

The British group of Virgin Islands, consisting of some thirty small islands, is located close to the United States group of Virgin Islands. Their population numbers about 5000. Tortola Island has the largest number of inhabitants. The chief products of the islands are cotton, sugar, coconuts, and limes.

DOMINICA

The British island of Dominica, 30 nautical miles from Guadeloupe and the same distance from Martinique, has an area of 300 square miles and a population of 38,000, 1 per cent of which is white. This island is notable for the fact that it contains the last remnants of the Carib race found by Columbus in the West Indies when he discovered America.

Dominica is of volcanic formation and has a range of hills running north and south. The climate is healthful, the coastal temperatures averaging between 70 degrees and 90 degrees Fahrenheit. The annual rainfall varies between 80 and 250 inches in different parts of the island.

Roseau, the capital, is situated on the southeastern coast. It has a population of some 6000. There is steamship service to Dominica from New York by way of the British steamers of the Quebec Steamship Company, and other foreign lines visit this island.

The population of Dominica is increasing, and economic conditions are encouraging in view of the development of the lime industry. The principal market for limes is New York, and this market is growing rapidly, the United States holding second place in the export trade of the colony. Lime juice, both raw and concentrated, is a well-known product in British markets, and the island produces in normal years about 150,000 gallons of the raw and more than half a million gallons of the concentrated juice. Lime products form two thirds of all the exports. Among the other products are oranges, spices, coconuts, and hard wood.

ANTIGUA

Antigua is the British governmental headquarters of the Leeward Islands. It has an area of 108 square miles and a population of about 30,000, of which 80 per cent is composed of negroes. The island is comparatively level and the climate is agreeable.

The principal products of Antigua are sugar, molasses of a high grade, cotton, and pineapples, and its industries include the ginning of sea-island cotton and the manufacture of earthenware household utensils. Rum is one of its exports.

This island, together with St. Kitts, Nevis, and Montserrat, was well known in the days of the Caribbean buccaneers.

BAHAMA ISLANDS

The Bahamas consist of a large group of islands extending for 700 miles off the southeast coast of Florida. They have a total area of 4400 square miles. Only some twenty of the islands are inhabited, and the total population of these is estimated at 53,000. These islands were the headquarters of the blockade-running steamers during the Civil War, and Nassau was a leading transshipment port. In commercial importance the Bahamas are now at the bottom of the list among the British West Indies. Lying somewhat off the trade route for international commerce, they have suffered from the effects of a declining population. There has been a considerable emigration of the laboring classes to Florida. Only about one sixth of the population is of white blood.

Among the important islands of the group are New Providence, with a population of 13,000; Abaco, with 4500; Harbour, with 1000; San Salvador, with 5000; Long Island, with 4500; Andros, with 7500; the Caicos and Turks islands, with 5500; Grand Bahama, with 1800; and Eleuthera, with 6500.

Nassau, the capital and chief town of the Bahamas, is located on the island of New Providence and has a population of about 12,500. It is 145 nautical miles from Miami, Florida, and 960 nautical miles from New York. Its principal industry is the canning of pineapples. Nassau owes much of its importance to the fact that it is a great pleasure resort with a delightful climate. The annual temperature here averages 77 degrees Fahrenheit.

The principal industry of the Bahamas is that connected with sponges, but there have been some attempts to adapt the resources of the islands to the changed conditions of the world market. The sisal industry represents one of the attempts to adjust conditions to outside trade, and this product occupies second place among the exports of the islands. The raising of pineapples, tomatoes, and other fruits and vegetables is increasing. The tariff charges in the United States have hindered the growth of the citrus-fruit industries, but there is a large export of vegetables and pineapples for the early spring trade of this country. More than half of the imports of the islands, which consist chiefly of foodstuffs and manufactured articles, are furnished by the United States, and a large proportion of the exports are taken by it. American markets take practically all the hemp and one fourth of the sponges of the Bahamas.

The islands are served by two steamship lines from New York, by a line from Miami (Florida) to Nassau, and also by a Canadian line of steamers. The language, and also the currency, weights, and measures are English. Nassau has radio-telegraphic communication and a telephone system.

The Turks and Caicos islands represent the primitive conditions of certain of this group. They have a population of some 5500, of which about 300 people are white. There is only an occasional contact with the outside world, and the islands are without telegraph or telephone systems. A cable station is at Grand Turk. Turk Island salt, which once enjoyed so wide a reputation, is produced by the evaporation of sea water, and salt-raking is still the colony's leading source of income. Salt comprises 75 per cent of the export trade of the island, and three fourths of this amount goes to the United States.

BERMUDA ISLANDS

This group of British islands is located off the coast of the United States, about 518 miles east of Cape Hatteras and 668 miles from New York. Of the 360 islands in the group only 18 or 20 are inhabited, and of these only 5 are of any importance. These are Bermuda, Somerset, Ireland, St. George, and St. David. The total population is about 21,000, 73 per cent of which is negro. The temperature averages between 60 and 70 degrees Fahrenheit, and the annual rainfall is between 55 and 60 inches. Because of its delightful climate Bermuda is famous as a winter resort.

Hamilton is the capital and principal town of Bermuda, with a population of 3000. An American consul and vice consul are located here.

The chief means of subsistence, outside of the hotel business, is the raising of vegetables, which form 92 per cent of the exports. Among these are the famous Bermuda onions, and also potatoes, tomatoes, arrowroot, and lily bulbs. Ninety per cent of the vegetables of the Bermudas go to the United States, while this country furnishes two thirds of the imports. The United States buys more from the Bermudas and sends more to these islands than all other countries combined.

Bermuda is more and more dependent upon tourist trade and winter travel, a large part of which is provided by the United States. Some 28,000 tourists are estimated to spend upwards of $1,125,000 annually in the islands. Both English and United States currency is accepted here. The steamship service from New York and Canada is good, and there are two cable companies.

BRITISH GUIANA

Although the largest of the three Guianas, being about 90,000 square miles in extent, British Guiana is not so important as the Caribbean colonies of the United Kingdom. Here 300,000 people live on some 300 square miles of cultivated land, while the interior has hardly been touched, except by a few gold workers. From forest-covered lowlands along the coast the country gradually rises through grasslands to a highland region, where Mount Roraima is the highest peak. The climate is tropical and the average annual rainfall is 90 inches.

Commercially the country is far less important than it was a century ago, when the foreign trade was stated to be $100 per capita; now it is less than $30. Sugar is the leading product, the annual output being 100,000 tons. Rice is cultivated on small holdings in the lowlands, chiefly by East Indians, who form nearly one half of the population. Other agricultural products are cacao, coconuts, and coffee, while balata, dyewoods, and hard woods are the chief forest products. Gold, diamonds, and bauxite are among the mineral resources.

Georgetown, the capital of the colony, with a population of 55,000, is the principal city. It contains some mining industries, and its products are sugar, rice, gold, and diamonds. It is canvassed in connection with Trinidad.

The exports of British Guiana were valued at $18,000,000 in 1923, and the imports at $13,000,000. The bulk of the trade is with Great Britain and Canada. There are 98 miles of railway and 450 miles of river navigation in the colony, and telegraph, telephone, and cable communication is available.

FRENCH POSSESSIONS

The French possessions of the Caribbean region, and also the Dutch possessions, are of small significance save for the commercial and military importance attached to them. There will doubtless be changes in the character of the population in the future, and modern developments relating to the cultivation of tropical products are destined to advance the trade output of these colonial possessions. At best, the French and Dutch possessions of this region are fragmentary sections of the former holdings of France and the Netherlands in this hemisphere.

The policy of France with regard to her colonies, assuring their trade to the mother country, is in striking contrast with that of other European powers. Heavy duties are laid upon imports from foreign countries, and the French tariff rates are applied save for a few articles that France is unable to supply, these being imported from the United States. Free entry into France is given to goods from the French West Indian colonies. The island of Martinique sends to France sugar and rum, and these form about four fifths of the exports. The same is in general true of the export trade of Guadeloupe. The United States sends certain foodstuffs and lumber, which can be secured by these islands more cheaply than from France.

GUADELOUPE

The French island of Guadeloupe, located between Montserrat and Dominica, is one of the Lesser Antilles. It consists of two parts, separated by a narrow channel. The area of

Guadeloupe is 619 square miles, and 75 per cent of the population of more than 200,000 are negroes. Fully 35 per cent of the foreigners in this island were born in France, and the language is French and a patois. The annual temperature here averages between 81 degrees and 94 degrees Fahrenheit.

The principal towns are **Basse Terre,** the capital and seat of government, with a population of some 8000, and **Pointe à Pitre,** which is the chief town of the island, having a population of about 27,000. The harbor of Pointe à Pitre is said to be the finest in the West Indies. Commercial agents selling fertilizer, machinery, and agricultural implements visit Guadeloupe.

The chief products of Guadeloupe are sugar, rum, cacao, coffee, and vanilla beans, and some cotton, cassava, yams, and other crops are raised in smaller quantities. Sugar-refining and rum-distilling are the principal industries.

The currency used here is similar to that of France. Several steamship lines connect Guadeloupe with France and with New York, and there are telegraphic and wireless connections. There are highway transportation facilities in the interior.

MARTINIQUE

This French possession lies between the islands of Dominica and St. Lucia. It has an area of 385 square miles and a population of 244,000. The inhabitants are chiefly descendants of the French, and there are also many negroes. The language is French, a French patois being spoken by most of the people, and all business correspondence should be in French, as few of the inhabitants understand English or Spanish.

Fort de France is the capital and has a population of 30,000. It is 1787 nautical miles from New York. Nearly all the import business goes through this city. Business in this island is done largely by automobile. Fort de France is a coaling station as well as the headquarters of the Compagnie Générale Transatlantique, which has an intercolonial steamship service. The city is also served by the Furness Line, which has boats leaving frequently from New York. There is an excellent harbor here with large dry-dock and other facilities, and this port is visited by commercial travelers doing business in the various islands of the West Indies.

The products here resemble those of the other islands of the Windward and Leeward groups, with sugar cane and cacao leading. Other products are coffee, vanilla, pineapples, bananas, and oranges. There are a large number of sugar works and distilleries of rum on the island.

Transportation is furnished by motor cars, mail coaches, and steamers subsidized by the government, and there is telegraphic, wireless, and cable service. As in Guadeloupe, the currency used is French.

It is interesting to note that although the two islands of Guadeloupe and Martinique are less than one twentieth as large as Costa Rica, their foreign trade is larger than that of this Central American republic. These islands have not been self-supporting in recent years, however, and France has been forced to establish subsidies. The local governments have been more or less disturbed by scandals, and conditions are far from what they should be. There is a great difference between the present-day conditions and those of the days when sugar and slaves brought wealth to the owners of the plantations.

FRENCH GUIANA

French Guiana is even less important than these French islands, although it has an area of 32,000 square miles. Slavery was abolished here in 1848, and the large sugar estates of other years have fallen into decay. White colonists are conspicuously absent. Most of the settlements are along the coast, and the total population numbers not more than 50,000. The colony is used largely for a convict settlement, and there is a convict colony numbering about 6500. The climate is tropical, with much rain, and health conditions are not good.

The gold resources of this colony are the most important, and there are said to be between 10,000 and 15,000 men in the gold camps of the interior. Such agricultural products as sugar, coffee, and cacao are grown, but not in large quantities. The forest resources are as yet but little developed. There are few exports or imports save to and from France, and the cost of the penal establishment is about $100,000, while the total amount received from the home treasury is not far from $1,250,000.

Cayenne, the capital and principal commercial center, has a population of 13,500. It is situated at the mouth of the Cayenne River, near the island of the same name. It has no railway connections, for there are no railway lines in the colony, and is connected with the interior only by a few roads. The whole civilization here is belated.

DUTCH POSSESSIONS

At one time the Dutch had vast ambitions in the New World. They held in Brazil, as well as in the region of New York, some of the richest and most potential lands of the Western Hemisphere. Now their colonies are but remnants of their former possessions.

The traveler in northern Brazil will see certain indications of Dutch influence. The Dutch occupation of this section of Brazil was completed in 1640. A period of prosperity followed, lasting until 1654, when the Dutch were obliged to surrender on being defeated in war by the English. The chief contribution of the Dutch from this part of the world at this period was the sugar and rum which they sent to the European markets.

DUTCH GUIANA

The Dutch were more successful in their colonizing efforts in the region now known as Dutch Guiana. This section was gained only after many conflicts with the French as well as with the English, who in 1664 took from the Dutch their New Amsterdam colony. The present area of Dutch Guiana is 46,000 square miles, and its population, a large part of which is colored, is estimated at 91,000. There are a considerable number of Mohammedans and Hindus in the colony. The port of Paramaribo, the capital, has a population of about 40,000.

The commercial importance of Dutch Guiana, which was formerly the most prosperous of all the Guianas, is now, as far as foreign trade is concerned, about half that of British Guiana.

Dutch Guiana exports chiefly sugar, balata, coffee, and cacao. Some rice and bananas are raised, but these do not figure largely in the export trade. Gold is the only mineral obtained in any quantity. The Netherlands pursues a different policy with regard to foreign trade than does France, giving broader scope to her colonial possessions. As a result, Dutch Guiana receives more than one fourth of its imports from the United States, these imports consisting of breadstuffs, fish, meats, and petroleum. The colony sends about one third of its exports to the United States, — one half of its sugar exports, one fifth of the balata, and nearly all of the cacao and coffee.

Like French Guiana, Dutch Guiana depends upon the home treasury for partial support, the deficit in some years amounting to one million guilders. These three Guiana colonies are expensive luxuries for the countries possessing them, and their prosperity, perhaps more than that of possessions in the West Indies, depends upon the good will of the United States.

CURAÇAO

The Dutch also possess the island of Curaçao and its dependencies, Aruba and Bonaire, in addition to the islands of St. Martin (the northern half of which belongs to France), St. Eustatius, and Saba, all in the Leeward group. The Curaçao group lies off the main route of trade and has suffered the same adversity as other islands of the West Indies since the abolition of slave labor. The present population of the group is approximately 50,000. Curaçao is the largest and most important island, having an area of 210 square miles and a population of 34,000, largely negroes. Spanish is commonly spoken.

The climate here is most unfortunate, and the natural resources of the islands are few. The transshipment of goods destined for Venezuela forms the principal commercial interest. To add to the tragedy of these islands, lying helpless off the coast of Venezuela, the trade winds are blowing away the best soil, and heavy rains are assisting in the depletion of these remains of the Dutch possessions in the New World. In 1914 the sea was discolored six miles from the coast by the floods that carried away some of the most valuable portions of the islands. It is often unbearably hot here.

Some guano and phosphate are exported from these islands. Straw hats constitute one third of the exports, and a large proportion of the people depend upon this industry for their livelihood. At one time there was a large salt industry here, and Curaçao salt, similar to that of the Turks Islands, was sold throughout the world. In addition to the products named the islands produce goatskins, divi-divi, aloes, and various other crops. The United States takes over half the exports of this group, straw hats being the chief item, while we send to the islands more than half of their imports of meat and other foodstuffs, petroleum, and coal.

Willemstad, the capital and chief city of Curaçao, has a population of 11,000. Oil-refining is the principal industry of this town, as well as of the entire island of Curaçao.

There is steamship service to Bonaire and Aruba from Curaçao, and also to the Dutch islands in the Leeward group. Lines from the United States and Europe visit the island. Curaçao has cable and wireless connections.

Saba, St. Eustatius, and St. Martin are small and relatively unimportant. Agriculture and cattle-raising are their principal industries.

VIRGIN ISLANDS OF THE UNITED STATES

The Virgin Islands, a group of more than fifty islands forty miles east of Porto Rico, formerly known as the Danish West Indies, were purchased from Denmark by the United States in 1917. The total area of the group is 132 square miles. Only three of the islands — St. Thomas, St. Croix, and St. John — have any commercial importance.

The climate during the winter months is particularly enjoyable, and during the hottest months the temperature seldom goes beyond 91 degrees Fahrenheit. The population is about 26,000, of which 93 per cent of the inhabitants are negroes.

Among the principal towns of the Virgin Islands are **Christiansted,** on the island of St. Croix, with a population of 4600;

St. Thomas, formerly Charlotte Amalie, on the island of St. Thomas, with a population of 8000; and **Cruz Bay,** on the island of St. John. The latter town is noted for its industry of growing bay leaves and for the distillation of bay oil from which bay rum is made.

The products of the islands are chiefly agricultural and include sugar, bay rum, bay leaves, tropical fruits, limes, cotton, lime juice, and molasses. Goats, sheep, hogs, donkeys, and other small animals are raised. In 1924 the Virgin Islands exported to the United States products valued at $595,000, while in the same year products valued at $1,616,000 were imported from this country.

English is the principal language spoken here, and the currency and weights and measures are the same as in the United States. There is good steamship service, both foreign and local. From the island of St. Thomas telegraphic communication may be had with all the West Indies and with the western coast of South America. St. Thomas and St. Croix both have telephone service.

HAITI

A Unique Republic

The Republic of Haiti, occupying the western portion of the island of Haiti, is unique among all the Latin-American states. It is the one Latin-American country that can really be called a Black Republic. Nicaragua, in which the United States has taken certain supervisory control, may be called an Indian Republic, and the Dominican Republic may be called a Mulatto Republic, but in nearly all the other Central American and West Indian sections political and economic conditions are controlled by white men or by those having chiefly white ancestry.

In Haiti, on the contrary, people of the white race have been without influence in politics, and a white man is looked upon with prejudice, occupying a position similar to that of the negro in the United States from the point of view of the white population. Furthermore, Haiti, a republic created largely by ex-slaves, has been more or less of an international outcast, with a history so turbulent as to be comic at times. This island has experienced throughout its history almost every phase of disorder, revolution, and barbarity, and only in recent years (since, at the urgent request of the people, the United States has taken a hand at maintaining order in a kind of fiscal protectorate) has there been any great promise for the future of Haiti.

GEOGRAPHY

The Republic of Haiti has an area of 10,200 square miles. It is made up of a mixture of mountains and valleys. The mountains are low and are covered with pine trees. On their lower slopes forests of palms and mahogany grow. In the valleys tropical agriculture is carried on, with sugar cane, tobacco, cotton cacao, and the famous Haitian coffee as the principal crops. The peculiar formation of the island affords excellent harbors, and traffic between the various ports has been by water rather than by railway.

The climate is pleasant. The temperature ranges from 60 degrees in the coldest weather to 100 degrees in the hottest. There is a dry season lasting from December to March and a rainy season from April to November.

HISTORY

The history of Haiti is closely associated with that of its neighbor, the Dominican Republic. For two hundred years after the island was discovered by Columbus on his first voyage Haiti remained under Spanish control. French adventurers gradually gained control of the western half of Haiti, and in the Treaty of Ryswick, in 1697, Spain ceded to France a portion of the island, although the line of demarcation between the French and Spanish territory was not made until 1770.

During the seventeenth and eighteenth centuries Haiti was a country of large plantations, possessions of rich French landowners. The native Indian inhabitants having been exterminated during the first fifty years of the Spanish régime, slaves were imported from Africa for labor. The population was therefore overwhelmingly black, with only a few French landowners and overseers. Slavery was abolished in the year 1793, when France offered freedom to slaves who had enrolled in the army to fight against the English invaders of the country.

Doubtless the greatest man in Haitian annals was the "George Washington of the Haitian Army of Independence," Toussaint L'Ouverture, a black liberator of outstanding ability. A former runaway slave who led the black resistance against the English, he was made military governor by the French, and in 1801 he promulgated a constitution which was considered by Napoleon as rebellion. Toussaint was sent as a prisoner to France, where he died, and in December, 1803, the blacks of the island again rose under Dessalines and Christophie. This rising against the French proved successful; Haitian independence was declared by Dessalines on January 1, 1804, and he himself was proclaimed emperor. From this point onward the political history of Haiti is opéra bouffe, with short-lived emperors, presidents, and self-proclaimed black kings. In 1844 the Dominicans separated from Haiti and set up an independent republic.

Of the rulers of independent Haiti, whatever may have been their abilities, little can be said save that their offices were temporary and their lives tragic. Of the twenty-three Haitian presidents holding office up to 1915, three were assassinated, one committed suicide, one was blown up in his own palace, fifteen were driven out by revolutions, seeking safety in exile, and three died in office. Nissage Saget, president from 1870 to 1874, was uniquely distinguished in Haitian history by the fact that he lived through his term of office and died a natural death in his own country.

PEOPLE

The Republic of Haiti has a population estimated at 2,000,000, exclusive of 3000 foreign whites, or about 196 inhabitants to the square mile. It is one of the most densely populated of the Latin-American republics. The population is predominantly black. Probably 95 per cent of the inhabitants are negroes or possess negro blood. As a rule the people speak the French language or a patois.

CITIES

The capital of Haiti is **Port au Prince,** with a population of about 100,000. It is the most important port in the country and has a fine natural harbor, through which passes from 45 to 50 per cent of the foreign trade of the island.

Cape Haitien is the capital and chief city of the department of the North, and the second city in size and commercial importance. It has a good harbor and supplies a large agricultural region, being the chief port for the export of logwood.

Aux Cayes is the capital, chief city, and port of the department of the South. It is a source of supplies for many cities and towns in the southern coastal section.

All of these cities possess telephone and telegraph service, a number of excellent public buildings, and a flourishing trade, both export and import.

Other cities are **Gonaives, Jacmel, St. Marc, Jérémie,** and **Port de Paix.**

GOVERNMENT

The government of Haiti, while nominally under a new constitution which went into effect in June, 1918, is not what is usually considered that of an orderly republic, as has been suggested. The powers of government are vested in three branches — legislative, executive, and judicial. The Chamber of Deputies, or the legislative power, is composed of 40 members, and the Senate of 16 members. There are the usual secretaries of the cabinet, and the executive authority resides in the president, who is elected for four years and is eligible for immediate reëlection.

For a decade or more previous to the signing of a treaty in 1915 between Haiti and the United States, by which the United States assumed a kind of economic protectorate, the political conditions of Haiti had been growing steadily worse. The eight presidents had held office, on the average, for less than a year each, while revolutions and insurrections were almost continuous. Both Great Britain and France, and also Germany, threatened severe measures in order to get Haiti to pay the money due them, and it looked as though the republic would be unable either to govern itself or to find a way out of its revolutionary difficulties.

Early in the year 1915, after a French cruiser had landed marines at Cape Haitien to protect commerce, the United States sent Rear-Admiral William B. Caperton from Vera Cruz to Cape Haitien, where he took charge of the situation. About this time an even more unrestrained outbreak occurred at Port au Prince, followed by a "ten days reign of terror." Admiral Caperton landed marines on July 26 to protect the legation, but not without bloodshed. Six Haitians and two Americans were killed. The American battleship *Connecticut* was ordered to the port, an election was held under American auspices, and Admiral Caperton placed naval paymasters in charge of the customhouses and the port. There were still further insurrections and violation of the rules protecting the legations, and on September 4 Admiral Caperton proclaimed martial law. On September 15 the treaty for a protectorate was signed. The United States government now recognized the new Haitian government.

The treaty that was promptly signed by the Haitian Congress and sent to the United States was more comprehensive in character than the arrangement with the Dominican Republic. According to this convention the United States not only controlled the expenditure of all moneys but had the right to help Haiti in maintaining order. The following provisions were the chief ones of the convention :

1. A Haitian receivership of customs was to be created under American control. There was to be an American financial adviser.

2. There was to be a native Haitian rural and civil constabulary commanded by American officers.

3. The United States, through its customs control, was to manage all expenditures of public moneys. The receipts were to be devoted to the payment of the expenses of the receivership, to the interest and sinking fund of the public debt, to the maintenance of the constabulary, and to the Haitian government for the current expenses.

4. Haiti was to promise to cede no territory to any nation but the United States.

5. All revolutionary forces were to be disarmed.

6. The convention was to last ten years, and an equal additional period if its objects were not accomplished within that time.

Thus the United States has assumed a greater task than in the case of the Dominican Republic, with a population nearly twice as large, with a more turbulent people, and with greater economic responsibilities. As regards annexation and the general political motives of the United States, the words of Secretary of State John Hay, in a letter to Mr. J. N. Leger, the minister of Haiti in Washington, in February, 1905, are significant:

In reply to your inquiry addressed to me this morning, I take pleasure in assuring you that the government of the United States of America has no intention to annex either Haiti or San Domingo, nor does it desire to acquire their possessions either by force or by means of negotiations, and that even in case the citizens of one or the other republic should ask incorporation in the American union there would be no inclination on the part of the government or in public opinion to accept such a proposal. Our interest in harmony with your desires is that you should continue in peace, prosperous and independent.

CURRENCY

The Haitian unit of currency is the *gourde*, which is worth about 25 cents in United States currency. Paper notes of five, two, and one gourde, which fluctuate in value, are used, and nickel and copper coins are in circulation. United States currency is used in the republic, especially in the coast towns.

EDUCATION

There is free public elementary education in the republic, and since 1910 it has been compulsory. In recent years there has been a notable improvement in the rural schools. Private schools and lycées provide secondary education, and the University of Haiti, established in 1921, gives work of college grade.

PRODUCTS AND INDUSTRIES

Agriculture

Agriculture is the mainstay of the people of Haiti. Coffee is the leading agricultural product, 50,000,000 and more pounds being produced annually. The value of the coffee exported in some years makes up more than 50 per cent of the total foreign trade of the republic. Europe, especially France, takes most of the Haitian coffee.

Cotton is being raised and exported in increasing quantities. Haiti has cheap labor and cheap land, and with good seed and the proper cultivation of the soil it is thought that the cotton fiber may be improved and the output increased.

Sugar is also an important agricultural product, and considerable areas of land are given over to the raising of sugar cane. There are no sugar refineries, so the sugar is sent in the raw state to the United States and the United Kingdom. With the advent of capital and proper organization the sugar industry should promise well for the future.

Cacao, tobacco, and other tropical products are grown on a small scale.

EXPORTS AND IMPORTS

The total foreign trade of the Republic of Haiti has recently reached nearly $40,000,000 annually. It is quite evenly divided between exports and imports. France takes about 65 per cent by value of the exports, and the United States about 10 per cent. Denmark also uses a considerable amount of Haitian goods. The exports to France consist mostly of coffee and cotton, and those to the United States are chiefly sugar, logwood and logwood extract, coffee, and cacao.

About 80 per cent of the imports to the Republic of Haiti are supplied by the United States. The United Kingdom, France, and Germany are next in line. The chief articles of import are cotton cloth, foodstuffs, especially wheat flour, iron and steel manufactures, soap, tobacco manufactures, machinery, cement, and hides and skins.

With the coming of orderly conditions in the country and the elimination of the fear of revolutions which have plagued the land so long, Haiti should reveal increasing progress in its commercial and industrial life.

TRANSPORTATION AND COMMUNICATION

Railways in the Republic of Haiti are few, there being only about 150 miles. The several good ports make communication by sea easy, and there is regular steamship service from New York and the southern ports of the United States and from Europe. Direct lines of steamers also run between Cuban and Haitian ports.

Haiti has satisfactory telegraph and telephone service, and cable connections with Cuba, the Dominican Republic, the United States, and South America. A wireless station has been built at Port au Prince.

THE DOMINICAN REPUBLIC

POLITICAL UNREST

For more than one hundred years the island of Haiti has been a caldron of revolution, political intrigue, anarchy, and bankruptcy. From many points of view it has seemed a distressing experiment in self-rule. Until the United States, in 1905, took a supervisory hand, particularly in the control of the customhouse finances, this island had suffered from a succession of calamities at the hands of "Little Black Napoleons" and soldiers of fortune that has been without counterpart in any other section of the world.

GEOGRAPHY

The Dominican Republic occupies the eastern part of the island of Haiti. It has an area of 19,325 square miles and is about six times as large as the island of Porto Rico and almost as large as the states of Maryland and Massachusetts together.

Four nearly parallel mountain ranges in the central part of the republic separate the Cibao, a large fertile area on the north,

422   LATIN AMERICA—MEN AND MARKETS

from a vast southeastern plain. The highest peak of these mountains is Mt. Tina, with an altitude of 10,300 feet. This is also the highest peak in the West Indies.

The mountains are the source of several large rivers, in which are rapids and waterfalls making the rivers useless for navigation. There are a goodly number of deep-water bays and inlets furnishing fine harbors for large sea-going vessels.

The climate of the republic offers considerable diversity. Since there is little low-lying land, the climate is healthful, and cooler than its latitude might suggest. There is an almost constant sea breeze. The rainfall is quite sufficient for agriculture. The rainy months are from November to May in the northern regions. Comparatively little rain falls during the winter in the eastern and southern sections of the island. Here the rainy season is from June to October.

HISTORY

The known history of the island of Haiti, or Santo Domingo, as it was formerly called, began during the first voyage of Columbus, who discovered the island on December 6, 1492. The inhabitants at that time were peaceful Indians, who in a short time were almost annihilated by the Spanish colonists.

For more than a century Santo Domingo was a central base of operations for Spanish explorers, for the *conquistadores*, and for various French, Dutch, and English buccaneers, who found here a favorable rendezvous for their activities. The capital of the present Dominican Republic has been spoken of at that period as "the metropolis of the vast colonial empire of Spain." For several centuries France and Spain were successively in control of the island, or parts of it. In 1821 the Spanish-speaking section of this area declared its independence of Spain, and in 1822 the entire island came under the control of the Haitians, who governed it until 1844, when a Dominican Republic was formed. In 1861, after innumerable quarrels among the Dominicans, the republic petitioned Spain to take over its responsibilities and govern the island. Another revolution came in 1863, with subsequent unrest. This lasted until 1865, when the Spanish government was wise enough to withdraw its forces from the island and to lower its flag.

During the thirty years following 1865 there occurred in this republic many revolutions, while "twenty-five national administrations held power and fell." It was a time of lawless dictators, plundering and pillage, terrorized foreigners, social demoralization, and economic degeneracy. Paper money flooded the country, and domestic and foreign loans were contracted quite regardless of the ability of the country to pay.

One absolute dictator for seventeen years, Ulises Heureaux, who came into power in 1882 and was assassinated in 1899, brought a certain peace with despotism. There was little healthful growth under his rule, however, and the debt of the country was greatly increased. At the end of the nineteenth century it was stated that there were only ten miles of decent roadway in the republic, and that when a traveler came to a bridge it was the part of prudence to go around it. Business and industry were more or less at a standstill, and only the seaports, within the range of the guns of battleships, gave any indication of order. The opening years of the twentieth century, from 1899 to 1904, were even more deplorable, with the mere form of constitutional government controlled by dictators and the debt rising to mammoth proportions.

Foreign nations began to press for payment of their debts, and the state itself was threatened with disruption at this time. With the republic in such a deplorable state, President Morales, in 1905, appealed to the United States to save his country from its creditors and foreign interference. Although a considerable portion of our population advocated then, as many do now, our following the traditional policy of noninterference, yet our position in the Caribbean, in Cuba and Porto Rico particularly, made it essential not only to protect our interests against bad sanitation and the diseases for which the islands had become a breeding place, but also to follow the Monroe Doctrine in discouraging European colonization in the New World.

President Roosevelt presented a protocol to the Senate, providing that the United States should act as a kind of receiver for the country, assuming control of the customhouses and adjusting the claims of foreign creditors. This protocol not being ratified by the Senate, an executive agreement was put into force which did not involve the Senate's consent but was along similar lines and fulfilled a similar purpose. The Dominican government received 45 per cent of the receipts of customs for its expenses, and the other 55 per cent was used for meeting interest on loans, for paying the expenses of collecting customs, and for other purposes.

The result of the supervisory relation of the United States was that revolutions stopped, since it was useless to have revolutions when there was no money to be stolen; agriculture began again with fresh incentive on the part of the peasants; corruption among the officials ceased; soldiers received their pay for the first time; and the Dominican government showed greater prosperity under its 45 per cent customs receipts than when it retained the entire amount. A new treaty was drawn up in February, 1907, which was ratified by both governments, and by which the customs of the Dominican Republic were to be collected by a general receiver appointed by the president of the United States. Other provisions were similar to those of the previous temporary agreement. Between the years 1907 and 1914 the imports of the country rose from $4,948,961 to $6,729,007, while the exports increased from $7,628,356 to $10,588,787.

It is worthy of note that President Carlos F. Morales, who made the plea to the United States to exercise its control, held office until the end of his term in 1906 and went out of office without a revolution. He was allowed to live a life of peace in the republic after holding office, and finally died without being assassinated, — perhaps the most remarkable statement to be made about a president of the Dominican Republic at this time.

PEOPLE

The population of the Dominican Republic is approximately 897,500, or about 46 persons per square mile. For the most part the inhabitants are negroes or mulattoes, with a foreign white population numbering possibly 10,000. Although the Domini-

Fig. 34. Picturesque river scene in the Dominican Republic. The Ozama River and a bridge spanning it at Santo Domingo. (Courtesy of Pan-American Union)

can negro is not the most efficient laborer, it has been proved that when the country is orderly he becomes industrious.

The comparatively few white people of the republic are engaged in business and in the production of sugar and cacao. The political influence of the whites is very small. Spanish is the language spoken here.

CITIES

Santo Domingo, with a population of about 31,000, is the capital and a leading commercial city of the Dominican Republic. More than 40 per cent of the imports and about 20 per cent of the exports of the republic pass through the port of Santo Domingo. It is in a region of large sugar estates, and sugar is the leading export. It has direct steamship connections with New York and Porto Rico.

Santiago is the chief commercial city of the northern part of the republic. It is in the tobacco-growing region, and the manufacture of cigars and cigarettes is its main industry.

San Pedro de Macoris, in the southeastern part of the island, is at the mouth of the Higuamo River, along which many of the sugar centrals of the republic are located. Nearly 30 per cent of the foreign trade of the country goes through this port. It has steamship connections with New York, the southern part of the United States, and with other islands of the West Indies. The manufacture of raw sugar and of mahogany furniture are important industries.

Puerto Plata, the principal port of the north, is the port of entry for Santiago. A number of importing firms are located here, and the city ranks third among the Dominican ports in the value of its imports.

GOVERNMENT

The form of government is that of a republic, and executive authority resides in the president, who is assisted by a cabinet of seven ministers. The president is elected for a term of six years by indirect vote and is ineligible for a second successive term. Each of the twelve provinces has one senator and two deputies in the legislature.

The Dominican Republic possesses no vice president, Congress having the authority to appoint a national head in case of the death or disability of the president. The cabinet consists of secretaries of the various departments, — foreign affairs, interior, police, etc., — corresponding in a general way to those of the United States and of other Latin-American republics.

It must be remembered, however, that the term "republic" has been little more than a name here, and that the peaceful condition and prosperity of the country depend largely upon the offices of the United States government in appointing efficient and nonpartisan commissioners to take charge of the collection of customs and to assume such other duties as are required for the preservation of order and the natural growth of representative government.

The Dominican Republic is represented in Washington by a minister, by a consul-general for the United States in New York City, and by another consul-general in San Juan, Porto Rico. There are consuls in Boston and Philadelphia, and vice consuls in Baltimore, Mobile, Chicago, Wilmington, Norfolk, and other cities.

CURRENCY

The money standard of the Dominican Republic is the gold dollar of the United States. The Dominican peso is worth one fifth of the gold dollar. Currency of the United States circulates at face value here.

EDUCATION

Instruction in the primary schools is free, and there is a nominal compulsory attendance. There are upwards of 100,000 children in the schools, but there is much illiteracy. In addition to the primary schools there are secondary, technical, and normal schools

PRODUCTS AND INDUSTRIES

Agriculture

Agriculture is the chief industry of the Dominican Republic, and sugar the most important product. The soil is so rich that sugar cane grows here from the same root for from ten to twenty years. The large sugar estates are in the southern part of the republic. In the eastern and northern parts tobacco, cacao, and coffee are raised.

Tropical fruits such as pineapples, bananas, and alligator pears grow here in profusion.

Mining

The Dominican Republic is thought to be rich in minerals. Deposits of gold, copper, iron, and coal are known to exist, but little mining is being done. Much gold was formerly obtained from this portion of the island of Haiti.

Forest Industry

The mountains of the republic are covered with forests of hard woods and dyewoods. Logwood, lignum vitæ, and mahogany are produced in commercial quantities. The pods of the divi-divi tree are used in tanning.

EXPORTS AND IMPORTS

The foreign trade of the Dominican Republic in recent years has approximated $50,000,000 annually, and is quite evenly divided between imports and exports.

The United States supplies about 70 per cent of the imports, with Porto Rico and England next in importance. Cotton cloth and manufactures of cotton, iron and steel, rice, machinery, wheat flour, gasoline and kerosene, lard, and boots and shoes are the principal imports, and of all these except rice the United States furnishes the largest supply.

The United States takes the largest share of the Dominican exports, but Ireland, Canada, England, and the Netherlands are also good customers. Most of the cacao, some sugar and coffee, logwood, and hides are received by the United States. The raw sugar is sent largely to Canada, Ireland, England, and the Netherlands. Sugar comprises about 60 per cent of the total exports of the republic, and coffee, cacao, and tobacco are the next most important exports.

Transportation and Communication

The transportation facilities of the republic have been greatly improved in recent years, but they are still inadequate. There are approximately 150 miles of railway, part of which is owned by the government and the remainder by an English company. Private railways are owned and operated by some of the large sugar estates.

There is steamship service from New York, Cuba, Porto Rico, the Virgin Islands, and other West Indian points. European service is afforded by French, British, and occasional Spanish and Italian steamers.

The construction of highways has received considerable attention, and stretches of macadamized roads have been built. The old highways are passable in dry weather, but during the rainy seasons automobiles travel over them with difficulty. In some places the roads are only trails and wait for further improvement.

Cables connect the island with New York and Porto Rico. There are wireless stations in several cities. The telephone system is under civil service.

CHAPTER XVIII

TRADE PROBLEMS

WITH QUESTIONS FOR CLASS USE

Investment in foreign securities. Mr. John S. Drum, as president of the American Bankers' Association, made the following remarks in speaking before a large group of bankers:

It is useless to grow commodities we cannot use or sell. Foreign nations which need our commodities have only one thing to sell to obtain money with which to buy our goods, — that is, securities in their productive enterprises. And we, prominently the credit nation of the world, are the one people who can invest in these productive enterprises of other nations and thus enable them to trade with us.

It is what England and Holland and Belgium and France and all great trading nations of the Old World have done in building up markets for their products. Their foreign investments enabled foreign countries to produce more than before, and therefore increased their ability to buy.

Foreign trade is a reciprocal process. There must be buying as well as selling. Profit must attend both sides of the transaction or the trade is certain to be an ephemeral affair. The Latin-American republics require considerable money to enlarge their natural industries, to develop new territory by irrigation, to build new docks, to enlarge and construct proper harbors, and to install modern means of transportation and lighting. These and a score of other enterprises await capital acquired from foreign nations.

What is the best means of furnishing these republics with the necessary money for development purposes? The United States has made large loans to some of the South American republics since the World War, also to a few of the Central American and West Indian countries. Certain American firms have invested considerable sums of money in mining and agricultural projects in Latin America since the war. Which plan is better for all concerned, loans to these countries or business investment in their enterprises? In what Latin-American countries and in what lines of trade are investments safest today? What are the chief advantages that North American business men and manufacturers gain by placing capital in large agricultural developments like the cotton industry in Peru?

Firm prices. It is necessary that there should be a clear understanding between the American firm and its representative in Latin America concerning prices. There are many delays in transmission of messages, and in some cases troubled political conditions affect markets. There is keen competition in many commodities also, and orders for important products are cabled and placed "firm" while the salesman is on the ground. It is necessary that prices remain firm long enough for orders to be received at the home office and to be acknowledged by cable. How long must prices remain firm if the manufacturer lives in Dayton, Ohio, and the representative is in Buenos Aires? Suppose the salesman were in La Paz, Bolivia, and it were necessary to depend upon correspondence rather than cable, how long would the prices have to remain firm?

In the case of rapidly fluctuating prices there is often the understanding between the home office and the salesman that the prices quoted are good for forty-eight hours. Would this be sufficient for Manáos, Brazil?

Services of the bank in foreign trade transactions. Certain New York banks have branches in South America in some of the larger centers. The facilities that these branch banks enable the home bank to offer are very important to traders. Name some of these facilities.

The National City Bank of New York, which has established nearly one hundred branches abroad in the last few years, affords the following services:

1. Collection of drafts drawn on foreign houses.
2. Protests of drafts where drawer so instructs.
3. Securing of legal services in foreign countries through the bank's foreign attorneys.
4. Creation of foreign markets for dollar exchange.

5. Collection of credit data on foreign houses and furnishing of reports on credit conditions.

6. Furnishing of credit information to Latin-American houses through the branch banks concerning firms in the United States represented by salesmen in Latin America.

7. Study of foreign market conditions and collection of trade data, also furnishing of letters of introduction and letters of credit issued in New York on foreign branch banks.

What do you consider to be the chief advantage, to the American trader doing business with Latin America, of the use of an American bank instead of a British or German bank in one of these southern countries? The above facilities may be had to a great extent in foreign banks. Why establish American banking concerns abroad?

Is foreign trade essential to the United States? During a manufacturers' convention a few years ago it was stated that the United States did not need to send its materials abroad in order to do successful business and build up the country. To be sure, this statement was made by an inland manufacturer, who had no knowledge of or experience in foreign business. It was argued that the United States was self-sufficient, needing no outside trade connections or market. According to this view we could develop a larger output of sugar, cotton, and certain other tropical products in our southern states if we gave our attention to proper diversification of crops.

Those who adhere to this policy stress the significant fact that the United States has over one half the known coal of the world and two thirds of the world's cotton; with 7 per cent of the world's land and with only 8 per cent of the world's population the United States produces 50 per cent of the world's supply of basic raw materials and grains. Approximately 25 per cent of the world's wheat, 40 per cent of the world's lead, 50 per cent of the world's zinc, 60 per cent of the world's aluminum, 60 per cent of the world's copper, 65 per cent of the world's oil, and 75 per cent of the world's corn, all come from the United States.

Since we have so great a supply of the world's elemental products, there is a tendency among some conservative manufacturers to disparage the efforts which are being made to extend the foreign business of the United States.

What is the fallacy in this line of argument? Upon what products of Latin America is the United States absolutely dependent? What raw materials are found in Latin America that are not found or cannot be duplicated in the United States? Is it true that the percentage of American foreign trade, as is sometimes stated, determines whether the nation shall be prosperous or experience hard times?

Consideration as an element in foreign trade. A dealer in Ecuador sent by cable to New York, to one of the large exporting houses, a rush order for a very large number of cases of porous plasters; in giving the contents of the cases the customer stated gross instead of dozens. The manager of the exporting house receiving the order readily saw that the customer had evidently made a mistake and had ordered enough plasters to supply the whole of South America. Thinking there must be some mistake, the New York house shipped one twelfth of the order, calling the attention of the customer to what was thought to be a mistake. This act of consideration on the part of the exporter so pleased the Ecuadorian customer that he became permanently attached to the exporting house, never thereafter, in fact, purchasing goods from any other American firm.

What particular characteristics of the successful exporting house or manufacturing firm does this incident suggest?

W. C. Shaw, the head of a large jewelry firm in Washington, D.C., is quoted as saying:

The thing which most salesmen do not realize is that the amount of goods a man sells depends to a very great extent upon his *interest* in them, his *knowledge* about them, and his *imagination* concerning his goods and the customer.

What are the essential characteristics of a foreign salesman? of a successful export manager?

Germans in South America. Previous to the war the Germans were rapidly becoming the foremost traders with several of the countries in Latin America. Their success consisted largely in their ability to adapt their products to the South American requirements, both in price and in style; in the type of salesman or representative sent to Latin America, this representative usually having been trained for his work in some exporting house before leaving Germany; and also in the ability to speak Spanish or Portuguese, and in the knowledge of the customs and business traditions of the people with whom they were to deal. It is argued by some that salesmanship is the same thing, in whatever country the salesman may happen to be, — that the knowledge of the goods and his ability to sell them are the two all-important essentials.

In what respect is this opinion untrue of the needs of Latin America? What is the first essential for making an opening for selling American products in a Latin-American city? Is it essential for the manufacturer himself to know at first hand the country to which he is planning to send his goods?

The following foreign salesman's decalogue is taken from "Foreign Trade Markets and Methods." [1]

First: Thou shalt not address thy prospective purchaser in what is to him an alien tongue! (This is to lose your case before you begin to plead it.)

Second: Thou shalt not yell at thy customer as though you were in a boiler factory! (Foreigners are not usually deaf.)

Third: Thou shalt not try to hustle thy customer, be he Latin, Briton, Oriental, Spanish, or Portuguese-American! (This is one of the unpardonable sins of the foreign salesman.)

Fourth: Thou shalt not lie about thy goods, or thy firm, or thy income, or thy personal achievements! (Emerson said, "What you are makes so much noise that I can't hear what you say.")

Fifth: Thou shalt not wear clothes that herald thy approach by reason of the loudness of their color; neither shalt thou wear thy hat on thy head nor thy cigar in thy mouth when entering a foreigner's office!

Sixth: Thou shalt not wax aggressively patriotic in the presence of a foreigner, nor shalt thou draw invidious comparisons between Paris and New York or between Buenos Aires and Buffalo!

[1] Clayton Sedgwick Cooper, Foreign Trade Markets and Methods. D. Appleton and Company, New York, 1922.

Seventh: Thou shalt not call Latin Americans "thinly veiled Indians," or Orientals "yellow men," or East Indians "Eurasians," or Italians "Wops," or in any wise deal expansively with the color of thy customers' skins! (Remember that there is no color line in foreign trade.)

Eighth: Thou shalt not vaunt thyself or be puffed up! ......

Ninth: Thou shalt not bear false witness against thy competitor!

Tenth: Thou shalt not criticize adversely thy customer's morals, thy customer's clothes, his amusements, his food, his house, nor his women, nor his trade methods, nor his religion! (Mark Twain said that the chief irreverence is irreverence for another man's gods.)

The Monroe Doctrine. Certain writers (for example, Professor Archibald C. Coolidge, the director of the Harvard University Library, in his book "The United States as a World Power") have sided with those Latin Americans who are opponents of the Monroe Doctrine as applied to international or industrial problems between the United States and Latin America. On the other hand, a very large number of Latin Americans agree that the Monroe Doctrine has been an important factor in the development and maintenance of independent statehood on the part of the Central American and South American states.

In what way does the Monroe Doctrine affect commercial relationships between the United States and Latin America? Has the growth of certain countries in Latin America necessarily affected the significance and the utility or necessity of the Monroe Doctrine? [1]

Knowledge of advertising. When in the city of Lima a few years ago we found that an enterprising and pushing American advertising man had placed a large outdoor sign advertising his particular product immediately at the side of the famous Lima Cathedral. Upon being criticized for what certain of the Peruvians considered little short of vandalism, he defended himself by saying he had received permission to do this and that the discussion about it was drawing attention to his product and therefore revealing his wisdom.

[1] See J. Warshaw, The New Latin America (chapter on "The Monroe Doctrine"). Thomas Y. Crowell Company, New York, 1922.

What was wrong in the psychology of this advertiser? What is the chief difference between the methods of advertising in the two Americas? [1]

Foreign trade correspondence. Walter F. Wyman, in his book entitled "Direct Exporting," suggests ten points of distinction which characterize a successful letter written by a New York man to a Melbourne firm, showing ten "distinguishing trifles" that are very important for successful export correspondence with British clients.

An American firm has established a training school for those whose duty it is to correspond with clients or prospective purchasers in foreign countries. This firm considers it vitally important that each letter should reflect the spirit of the house and that the danger of cross purposes through correspondence by different departments of the same house be avoided. This firm lays particular emphasis upon the necessity of clear statements rather than ambiguous ones, and the terms of address at the beginning and end of the letter.

We have in mind an incident which cost a large American exporting house several hundred dollars in cables and other expense in filling an order, because the letter containing the request was vaguely worded and was open to several interpretations.

In business correspondence with Latin Americans, what particular elements should be emphasized? Should the principle of crisp and short directness characterizing American business letters be used with Latin Americans? Should English ever be used in writing to a Latin-American business house? What language should be used in business correspondence with Martinique? with Brazil? with Jamaica? with Chile?

Public holidays in Latin America. The Guaranty Trust Company of New York publishes a book entitled "Bank and Public Holidays throughout the World." Much time and money are lost in cables and in business on the part of Americans by the lack of knowledge of the Latin-American holidays. Many exporters have a list of holidays in their offices.

---

[1] See D. L. Brown, Advertising to the World (McCann Company, New York, 1921). See also booklets on advertising in Latin-American countries, published by the Bureau of Foreign and Domestic Commerce, Washington, D.C.

What are the important holidays to remember in dealing with countries like Peru, Colombia, Ecuador, and Chile, where the Roman Catholic Church influence is particularly strong?

What about trying to do business in Rio de Janeiro in the Mardi Gras season?

Packing for shipment. Among the most common criticisms brought against American manufacturers and exporters to Latin America are those referring to the fact that we have not paid proper attention to the packing of goods shipped to foreign countries. Among the points at issue are the size of the packages, the weight that can be carried by a mule or a llama, and the possibility of breakage in the transference from ship to lighters in unprotected seaports of the west coast of South America.

What would be the general method of baling, packing, and shipment of goods sent from the city of Buffalo, for example, to La Paz, Bolivia? [1]

Definition of foreign trade terms. The misunderstanding of foreign trade terms is said to be responsible for at least half of the difficulties arising among traders engaged in business with Latin America.

What are the exact obligations that trade terms such as "F. O. B.," "C. I. F.," "F. A. S.," and "C. & F." impose upon the seller? What obligations do these terms impose upon the buyer, the shipowner, and the banker?

Nine large foreign-trade organizations of the United States held a conference at the India House, New York, under the auspices of the National Foreign Trade Council, on December 16, 1919, for the purpose of agreeing upon uniformity of trade terms and the particular responsibilities involved in their use. The result of these decisions can be obtained by addressing the National Foreign Trade Council, India House, New York City. [2]

---

[1] See Ernst B. Filsinger, Commercial Travelers' Guide to Latin America (United States Department of Commerce, Washington, D. C.). See also literature on packing issued by the Bureau of Foreign and Domestic Commerce, Washington, D.C.

[2] See C. S. Cooper, Foreign Trade Markets and Methods, chap. vii ("Definitions of Foreign Trade Terms"). D. Appleton and Company, New York, 1922.

Direct or indirect exporting. What are the chief advantages gained by the American manufacturer who sells direct to his foreign customer rather than through a commission house? Would direct selling be feasible for a firm not having an agency or representative in Latin America? What are the detailed steps with which a manufacturer should be acquainted in sending a shipment from a city like Des Moines, Iowa, to Montevideo, Uruguay? [1]

Marine insurance. Many of the larger export houses are obliged to employ a special representative to handle the intricate matter of marine insurance upon their shipments to foreign countries. What are the responsibilities of the carrier? What is the significance of the following terms, commonly used in shipping circles relative to insurance: "W. A.," "S. P. A.," "F. P. A., 3%"? [2]

Trade with Mexico. Upon what conditions does the oil business in Mexico depend, and what solution do you think feasible for the present international and industrial problems associated with this vital industry in that distracted country? [3]

Latin-American markets. What, in the order of their importance, are the twenty most important exports of Latin-American countries, and from what countries are these exports shipped?

What are the twenty leading imports of Latin-American republics, and what percentage of these imports come from the United States? [4]

[1] See Benjamin Olney Hough, Practical Exporting (*American Exporter*, New York, 1920). See also the following: E. B. Filsinger, Exporting to Latin America (D. Appleton and Company, New York, 1916); A. A. Preciado, Exporting to the World (J. A. McCann, New York, 1920); F. Henius, The A B C of Foreign Trade (Bobbs-Merrill Company, Indianapolis, Indiana, 1920); Exporters' Encyclopædia (Exporters' Encyclopædia Company, New York, 1918); G. C. Vedder, American Methods in Foreign Trade (McGraw-Hill Book Company, New York, 1919); Trading with Latin America (Irving National Bank, New York); H. S. Shuey, Bibliography of Foreign Trade Publications (Ten Bosch Company, San Francisco, 1918).

[2] For a comprehensive account of marine-insurance procedure see Clayton S. Cooper's "Foreign Trade Markets and Methods," pp. 138–145. D. Appleton and Company, New York, 1922.

[3] See Wallace Thompson, Trading with Mexico, chap. viii ("The Romance of Mexican Oil"). Dodd, Mead & Company.

[4] See "Exporter's Gazetteer of Foreign Markets" (*American Exporter*, New York). See also Commerce Reports, issued by the Department of Commerce, Washington, D.C.

Languages. In what countries of Latin America can French be used? Where can it be used as a partial substitute for Spanish? Why should the trader be careful not to use Spanish or to send correspondence or catalogues in Spanish to Brazil? In what West Indian islands is English the commercial language? What are the best helps in getting a working knowledge of commercial Spanish? [1]

The house organ. What is the value of the house organ in promoting trade with Latin America? What magazines and newspapers are the best mediums for advertising American products in Latin America? [2]

Cables and trade with Latin America. Cables have been called "the nerves of foreign trade," and share with steamships and banks a definite responsibility in facilitating commerce. An extensive cable service with the various countries to the south of the United States has been established. The proper use of cables in promoting commerce with these countries is an art. The student of this subject should get in touch with the All America Cables Company, located in New York, for definite literature on this subject. What Latin-American republics have satisfactory cable connections? Which ones have wireless?

Consular service. What are the duties of an American consul in connection with trade with Latin America? What is a consular invoice and how is it obtained? In what cities and towns of Latin America are American consular agents to be found? [3]

---

[1] See J. Graham and G. A. S. Oliver, Spanish Commercial Practice (The Macmillan Company, New York, 1904–1906); G. R. MacDonald, Lessons in Spanish Commercial Correspondence (Isaac Pitman & Sons, 1918); E. da Cunha, Portuguese Self-Taught (G. E. Stechert & Co., New York); W. N. Cornett, French Commercial Correspondence (Casper, Milwaukee, 1914).

[2] See Grace Log (W. R. Grace & Company, 7 Hanover Square, New York); The Lamp (Standard Oil Company, 26 Broadway, New York); C. S. Cooper, Foreign Trade Markets and Methods, chap. xiii ("The House Organ in Foreign Trade"), and also chap. xiv ("Newspapers and Periodicals as Foreign Trade Builders") (D. Appleton and Company, New York, 1922).

[3] See "Consular Regulations of Foreign Countries: Canada and Latin America," Tariff Series No. 24 (1915) (Bureau of Foreign and Domestic Commerce, Washington, D.C.); John H. Latané, The Diplomatic Relations of the United States and Spanish America (Johns Hopkins Press, Baltimore, 1900). See also reports and literature of the State Department, Washington, D.C.

Automobiles in Brazil. An automobile manufacturer, who is an enthusiast over driving his own car, writes us from an inland city in the United States as follows:

I am meditating taking my car for an automobile trip through South America. I have an ambition to be the first man who has ever crossed South America from the east coast of Brazil to the west coast of Peru in a motor car. Please give me your opinion as to the advisability of such a trip.

We replied that no more heroic adventure had ever been planned since the days of Pizarro and the buccaneers, and that the only way that we could conceive of for him to cross Brazil with an automobile (from Recife to La Paz, for example) would be to suspend it from a Zeppelin or a strong army airplane, or possibly to take his machine apart and engage half a hundred Indians to carry it, together with the whole party, across on their backs.

He who would cross Brazil today from east to west would find awaiting him a little jaunt of several thousand miles across gigantic table-lands cut with irregular mountain chains, through tropical jungles to be penetrated only by means of the machete, and for his only road map (if he was especially fortunate) a faint and sometimes vanishing mule track, — nothing more. He would find also along the way savage tribes of Indians living in jungle fastnesses as impregnable as any to be found in Central Africa.

The ordinary traveler, after looking over the situation, would decide that it was more salutary and expeditious to place his automobile on a slow steamer and sail to the west coast of Peru via Cape Horn.

The automobile-trade problem in Brazil, as in certain other South American countries, is dependent upon the national highway problem. Strictly speaking, there are no international highways in South America today that compare with those built by the Peruvian Indians in the palmy sixteenth-century days of the ancient Inca, before Spanish conquest extinguished the art of road-making in South America. Moreover, in Brazil the railroads have appropriated many of the best highways, and there is the further problem of making roads that are permanent in a climate, with heavy tropical rains and seasonal floods.

Americans, however, do sell motor cars to Brazilians, and besides many continental cars of French, Italian, and German manufacture there is quite a wide variety of American cars.

In the year 1915, owing partly to the war, American automobile sales in Brazil amounted to more than four times those of all other nations combined. It should be noted, however, that German cars had decreased from 1060 in 1912 to 3 cars in 1915. French cars decreased in a similar proportion. Brazil has now become a good automobile market, and automobiles and accessories make up a considerable share of the imports of many Latin-American republics.

The market for automobiles in Brazil is limited, so far as any considerable quantity is concerned, to a dozen cities and a few of the larger towns. Low-priced cars are chiefly in demand, and these are used for utility purposes by the owners of large plantations of coffee, sugar, and other crops.

Rio de Janeiro carries on approximately 50 per cent of the export and import trade in automobiles, but an ever-increasing number of cars are found in the cities of São Paulo and Santos, as well as in the coastal cities of São Salvador, Recife, and Belem. Excellent machines are found also in the inland cities like Bello Horizonte in the state of Minas Geraes. The Brazilian automobile paradise is the capital, where, in addition to the government machines, which do not require registration, there are to be found several thousand registered automobiles.

To what extent will the increased steamship transportation to countries like Brazil affect the automobile trade in American cars? Is there any reason why Brazilians should prefer an Italian car to a car of similar price made in the United States? What are the profits on American cars sold in Brazil as compared with profits on the same cars sold in the United States? [1]

As the automobile trade is dependent upon the financial conditions of the country, how will this fact affect the trade at present in a country like Brazil?

[1] See booklet on motor vehicles issued by Bureau of Foreign and Domestic Commerce, Washington, D.C.

Foreign-trade houses. Problems of an American shipping house.
The foreign-trade firm of W. R. Grace & Company, whose
activity extends over seventy years of shipping, merchandising,
and export and import business (including banking and the
financing of shipments), has built up some of the largest branch
houses in Latin America, especially on the west coast of South
America. This firm has evolved from a commission-merchant
business into what is really a large merchandising house, own-
ing its own shipping lines, which run between the United States
and various South American ports.

What advantages would naturally accrue to a firm capable
of being its own carrier of merchandise to foreign countries?
Would the cost of buying and maintaining shipping lines be an
advisable undertaking for the average foreign-trade house?

What are some of the outstanding problems in relation to men
and methods confronting a large manufacturing firm? [1]

Cuban politics and United States trade. President Zayas of
the Cuban Republic made an appeal to President Coolidge
when a revolution was imminent in Cuba, in the spring of 1924,
asking that we place an embargo on arms and ammunition for
the Cuban rebels. The Cuban president also made a request
for an appropriation of $400,000 credit for the purchase of air-
planes from the United States.

Why did the Cuban president make such a demand, and what
was the obligation of the United States to consider it and to
preserve order in Cuba? [2]

What effect has the existence of this Platt Amendment had
upon the trade between Cuba and the United States?

Psychology and trade. To what extent does a psychological
knowledge of the South Americans affect trade? Germany, for
example, before the World War, was trading successfully with
the whole world, although it has been said that she lost the war,
and a large part of the foreign commerce built up by great
exertion during many years, because she failed in psychology
and did not get the viewpoint even of her nearest neighbors.

[1] See *Grace Log*. W. R. Grace & Company, 7 Hanover Square, New York.
[2] See the Platt Amendment, inserted in the Army Appropriation Bill, March 2,
1901.

Do you think that a salesman or a manager preparing to reside in South America should spend much time in studying the traditions, history, ideals, temperament, and mental proclivities of the people? What proportion of his time should he give to such subjects in comparison with preparation in methods of doing business, financing, and the mere merchandising of the particular product that he will handle? Is the problem of selling to Latin Americans more intimately bound up with the human elements of courtesy, behavior, and an attitude of culture than is the case in dealing with a European country like France or England?

Trade advisers. The eleventh national foreign-trade convention, held in Boston, Massachusetts, June 4-6, 1924, under the auspices of the National Foreign Trade Council, had a trade-adviser service. The object of this service was to bring every convention delegate having a foreign-trade problem into contact with an adviser who had successfully handled the same kind of problem.

What are the chief advisory sources concerning problems relating to foreign commerce? [1]

Agriculture in Peru. The Peruvian government plans to establish an agricultural school in the department of Cuzco and also experiment stations at Catas and Espinar.

What would be the special advantages of such a school on the ridge of the Andes? What would be some of the difficulties in teaching scientific methods of agriculture to the inhabitants of this region?

Panama hats. The value of toquilla straw hats (commonly called Panama hats) exported from Ecuador in 1900 was 327,489 sucres, and for the first six months of 1923 the figures were 1,718,227 sucres. What is this amount in American money? The United States is the best customer of Ecuador for these hats.

[1] See reports of the National Foreign Trade Council (India House, New York); of trade advisers of the Bureau of Foreign and Domestic Commerce, Washington, D.C.; of trade advisers of the Pan-American Union; of consuls and commercial attachés situated in countries in which the problems requiring solution occur; also export managers of the large commission and merchandising houses in New York City.

Is there any other Latin-American country or section surpassing Ecuador in this business? In what other sections of Latin America are Panama hats an item of trade? Has there been a noticeable increase in this export trade from Ecuador since the new sanitation processes in Guayaquil have been put into effect?[1]

Training for foreign commerce. The American Locomotive Company, located at Schenectady, New York, states through one of its representatives that the important elements in training for foreign service are as follows:

a. A thorough knowledge of the company's mechanical practice.

b. A knowledge of the essentials of its engineering practice.

c. The handling of responsible work in the home office which would give an appreciation of the relation of work in the foreign field to that of the industry.

d. The development of sound judgment in business relations.

e. A knowledge of modern salesmanship.

f. A clear understanding of the characteristics of people to be met with in the foreign field.

There is nothing said about college training as an essential.

Should a man expecting to enter foreign-trade pursuits begin to prepare himself while in college, and if so, with what kind of courses?

Does the American college or university with which you are familiar give courses that bear directly upon the training of men for business residence in Latin America?

What detailed steps should you suggest as necessary for a student to take in equipping himself for engineering practice in Central or South America?[2]

Why foreign investments in South America? Travelers to South America are frequently surprised to see how firm a foothold foreigners have gained in the business enterprises of these republics.

[1] See Commerce Report, issued by the Department of Commerce, Washington, D. C., and reports of the Rockefeller Foundation concerning work at Guayaquil.

[2] See C. S. Cooper's "Foreign Trade Markets and Methods," chap. v, for this entire subject of training for foreign commerce, in which the experience and advice of many of our large foreign-trade business firms is summarized, and in which the experience of a number of American universities specializing in courses on foreign trade is also presented.

Why do not South Americans do these things for themselves? In the cities of Rio de Janeiro and São Paulo, for instance, foreign capital has built the great hydroelectric power stations that furnish power for the tramways, electric lights, and many industries. The leadership of this business is in the hands of Americans, while the capital has been furnished largely by Canadians. Why should the Brazilians not endeavor to handle such business themselves, or purchase the rights of foreigners in enterprises which are so vital to the life and prosperity of the country?

Why does the Peruvian Corporation, with its British capital and control, have charge of the great railway systems in Peru?

What are the main causes that have brought American capital to promote large nitrate and copper interests on the west coast of South America and to invest in them? [1]

American versus British foreign trade in Latin America. In the book by L. C. Ford and Thomas F. Ford, "Foreign Trade of the United States," [2] Professor William Clarence Webster is quoted as follows:

While England has been losing her position as the world's workshop, she has been building up her capitalistic supremacy. Her capital has flowed into her colonies and nearly every country in the world. Consequently she has become the world's creditor, and wields the power that accompanies capitalistic supremacy. Her capitalists own vast tracts of land and work farms in nearly every country of the world; they also control railroads, manufacturing plants, and mines in many of the most strategic places on every continent. In this way England keeps her cows in Australia, Canada, and Argentina; cultivates her wheat in Manitoba, the United States, and India; grows her cotton in the United States, India, and Egypt; spins it not only at home but even in India, China, Egypt,

[1] See William H. Lough, Financial Developments in South American Countries, *Special Agents Series No. 103* (1915) (Bureau of Foreign and Domestic Commerce, Washington, D.C.); F. M. Halsey and G. B. Sherwell, Investments in Latin America, *Trade Information Bulletins Nos. 362, 382* (1925–1926) (Bureau of Foreign and Domestic Commerce); James H. Collins, Straight Business in South America (D. Appleton and Company, New York, 1920); C. Reginald Enock, Republics of South and Central America: Their Resources, Industry, Sociology, and Future (Charles Scribner's Sons, New York, 1913).

[2] L. C. and T. F. Ford, Foreign Trade of the United States. Charles Scribner's Sons.

and Mexico; makes her machinery in Germany and the United States. Thus not only her many colonies but the whole world has become a part of her domain through the power of her capital.

In general we may say that the United Kingdom of Great Britain is primarily dependent upon her foreign-trade activity, and she has become a past master in trade procedure relative to credits, open accounts, packing, financing, and shipping her goods. Her chief imports from Latin America are raw materials for her factories and certain foodstuffs, and her exports to Latin America are for the most part included in such large items as coal, manufactures of iron and steel, woolens, cotton, and chemicals.

In what way are the interests of England identical with those of the United States in Latin-American trade? In what respects are they different?

Is it necessary for the United States to compete with England in "capitalistic supremacy" in Latin America? If so, along what lines? Are both England and the United States dependent upon these South American and Central American republics?

Latin-American cities and ports. Make a list of the twenty-five most important port cities of Latin America from the point of view of volume of export and import business.

BIBLIOGRAPHY

GENERAL REFERENCES

ADAMS, FREDERICK UPHAM. Conquest of the Tropics. 1914.

AKERS, C. E. A History of South America, 1854–1904. 1904.

ALLEN, NELLIE B. South America. 1918.

ASPINALL, ALGERNON E. The British West Indies. 1912.

ASPINALL, ALGERNON E. Pocket Guide to the West Indies, British Guiana, British Honduras, the Bermudas, the Spanish Main, and the Panama Canal. 1914.

ASPINALL, ALGERNON E. West Indies and Guiana. 1914.

AUGHINBAUGH, W. E. Selling Latin America. 1915.

BINGHAM, HIRAM. Across South America. 1911.

BLAND, J. O. P. Men, Manners, and Morals in South America. 1920.

BONSAL, STEPHEN. The American Mediterranean. 1912.

BRYCE, JAMES. South America: Observations and Impressions. 1914.

CARPENTER, F. G. South America. 1900.

CLARK, F. E. The Continent of Opportunity: South American Republics. 1907.

CLEMENCEAU, GEORGES. South America To-day. 1911.

COLLINS, JAMES H. Straight Business in South America. 1920.

COOPER, CLAYTON SEDGWICK. Understanding South America. 1918.

DAWSON, T. C. The South American Republics. 1903.

ENOCK, C. REGINALD. The Republics of South and Central America. 1913.

FILSINGER, ERNST B. Commercial Travelers' Guide to Latin America (Second Revised Edition). 1926.

FILSINGER, ERNST B. Exporting to Latin America. 1916.

GARCÍA CALDERÓN, F. Latin America: Its Rise and Progress. 1913.

HALSEY, FREDERIC M. Investments in Latin America and the British West Indies. United States Department of Commerce. 1918.

HALSEY, FREDERIC M. Railway Expansion in Latin America. 1916.

HARRIS, GARRARD, and various American consular officers. The West Indies as an Export Field. United States Department of Commerce. 1917.

HILL, ROBERT T. Cuba and Porto Rico and Other Islands of the West Indies. 1898.

HOUGH, B. OLNEY. Practical Exporting. 1920.

HUMBOLDT, ALEXANDER VON. Personal Narrative of Travels to the Equinoctial Regions of America during the Years 1799–1804. 1822.

JONES, CHESTER LLOYD. Caribbean Interests of the United States. 1916.

LATANÉ, J. H. The United States and Latin America. 1920.

447

MERRIAM, R. B. The Rise of the Spanish Empire in the Old World and the New. 1918–1925.
MOORE, JOHN BASSETT. American Diplomacy: Its Spirit and Achievements. 1905.
OBER, F. A. Guide to the West Indies and Bermudas. 1908.
OBER, F. A. Our West Indian Neighbors. 1904.
PAXSON, F. L. The Independence of the South American Republics. 1903.
PECK, ANNIE S. Industrial and Commercial South America. 1922.
PECK, ANNIE S. The South American Tour (Revised Edition). 1924.
ROBERTSON, WILLIAM SPENCE. Rise of the Spanish-American Republics. 1918.
ROSS, E. A. South of Panama. 1915.
SHEPHERD, W. R. Historical Atlas. 1911.
SHEPHERD, W. R. Latin America. 1914.
STUART, GRAHAM H. Latin America and the United States. 1922.
VERRILL, A. H. Getting Together with Latin America. 1918.
WILSON, OTTO. South America as an Export Field. United States Department of Commerce. 1914.
ZAHM, J. A. Through South America's Southland. 1916.
Commerce Reports. United States Department of Commerce.
Pan American Union Bulletins.
Publications of the Bureau of Foreign and Domestic Commerce. United States Department of Commerce.
Reports of the National Foreign Trade Council.
South American Yearbook. Annual.
Statesman's Year-Book. Annual.
Statistical Abstract for the Colonies. Annual.

ARGENTINA

FRANCK, HARRY A. Working North from Patagonia. 1921.
FRASER, JOHN FOSTER. The Amazing Argentine. 1914.
HOLLAND, W. J. To the River Plate and Back. 1913.
KOEBEL, W. H. Modern Argentina. 1907.
MÉROU, M. GARCÍA. Historia de la República Argentina. 1899.
PENNINGTON, A. STEWART. The Argentine Republic. 1910.
ROSS, G. Argentina and Uruguay. 1916.
ROWE, L. S. The Federal System of the Argentine Republic. 1921.

BOLIVIA

CONWAY, W. MARTIN. The Bolivian Andes. 1901.
PARKER, WILLIAM B. Bolivians of To-day. 1922.
SANGER, J. W. Advertising Methods in Chile, Peru, and Bolivia. United States Department of Commerce. 1919.
SCHURZ, W. L. Bolivia: A Commercial and Industrial Handbook. United States Department of Commerce. 1921.
WALLE, PAUL. Bolivia. 1914.

BRAZIL

BATES, HENRY WALTER. A Naturalist on the Amazon. 1910.
BULEY, E. C. North Brazil. 1914.
BULEY, E. C. South Brazil. 1914.
COOPER, CLAYTON SEDGWICK. The Brazilians and their Country. 1917.
DENIS, PIERRE. Brazil. 1911.
DOMVILLE-FIFE, CHARLES W. The United States of Brazil. 1911.
ELLIOTT, L. E. Brazil Today and Tomorrow. 1917.
FOUNTAIN, PAUL. The River Amazon. 1914.
OAKENFULL, J. C. Brazil in 1909. 1909.
TOMLINSON, H. M. The Sea and the Jungle. 1913.
Yearbook of American Chamber of Commerce for Brazil and American Business Directory. 1920.

CENTRAL AMERICA

BANCROFT, HUBERT HOWE. History of the Pacific States of North America, Vols. I–III, "Central America, 1501–1887." 1883–1890.
DOMVILLE-FIFE, CHARLES W. Guatemala and the States of Central America. 1913.
HARRIS, GARRARD. Central America as an Export Field. United States Department of Commerce. 1916.
KOEBEL, W. H. Central America. 1917.
LEA, H. C. "Hidalgo and Morelos," in American Historical Review, Vol. IV (1898–1899), pp. 636–651.
MARTIN, P. F. Salvador of the Twentieth Century. 1911.
MUNRO, DANA G. The Five Republics of Central America. 1918.
PALMER, FREDERICK. Central America and its Problems. 1910.
Gaceta Oficial de Honduras.

CHILE

BERTRAND, ALEJANDRO. The Chilean Nitrate Industry, Technology, and Economics.
ELLIOT, G. F. S. Chile. 1907.
KOEBEL, W. H. Modern Chile. 1913.
LLOYD, REGINALD. Twentieth-Century Impression of Chile. 1915.
MILLS, GEORGE J. Chile. 1915.
PARKER, WILLIAM B. Chileans of Today. 1920.
ROWE, L. S. Early Effects of the European War upon the Finance, Commerce, and Industry of Chile. 1918.
SANGER, J. W. Advertising Methods in Chile, Peru, and Bolivia. United States Department of Commerce. 1919.

COLOMBIA

BELL, P. L. Colombia: A Commercial and Industrial Handbook. United States Department of Commerce. 1921.

BINGHAM, HIRAM. The Journal of an Expedition across Venezuela and Colombia. 1909.

BUNAU-VARILLA, P. Panama: The Creation, Destruction, and Resurrection. 1914.

ELDER, P. J. Colombia. 1913.

JOHNSON, EMORY R. The Panama Canal and Commerce. 1916.

LEVINE, V. Colombia. 1914.

SCRUGGS, W. L. The Colombian and Venezuelan Republics. 1905.

CUBA

AUSTIN, H. A. "Cuba's Future," in *North American Review*, Vol. CLXXXIX (1909), pp. 857–863.

BEVERIDGE, ALBERT J. "Cuba and Congress," in *North American Review*, Vol. CLXXII (1901), pp. 535–550.

BROOKS, SYDNEY. "An English View of Cuba," in *Forum*, Vol. XLVI (1911), pp. 461–470.

EWING, W. W. Markets for Construction Materials and Machinery in Cuba. United States Department of Commerce. 1917.

FORBES-LINDSAY, C. H. A. Cuba and her People of To-day. 1911.

HILL, ROBERT T. Cuba and Porto Rico and Other Islands of the West Indies. 1898.

JOHNSTON, SIR HARRY. "An Englishman's Impression of American Rule in Cuba," in *McClure's*, Vol. XXXIII (1909), pp. 496–504.

PALMER, T. G. "Sugar at a Glance," Senate Documents, Vol. XXXIII, Document 890. Sixty-second Congress, Second Session.

PARKER, W. B. Cubans of To-day. 1919.

PORTER, R. P. Industrial Cuba. 1899.

RENO, GEORGE. Cuba: Havana. 1915.

ROBINSON, A. G. Cuba, Old and New. 1915.

ROBINSON, A. G. Cuba and the Intervention. 1905.

ROBINSON, A. G. "Cuban Constitution Making," in *Independent*, Vol. LIII (1901), pp. 435–438.

SANGER, J. W. Advertising in Cuba. United States Department of Commerce. 1919.

TUCKER, W. A. Textiles in Cuba. United States Department of Commerce. 1917.

VERRILL, A. H. Cuba Past and Present. 1914.

WOOD, LEONARD. Cuba. General descriptive data prepared in September, 1914.

WOOD, LEONARD. "The Origin and Purpose of the Platt Amendment," in *American Journal of International Law*, Vol. VIII (1914), pp. 585–591.

WRIGHT, I. A. Cuba. 1910.

Customs Tariff of Cuba. United States Department of Commerce. 1911.

ECUADOR

ENOCK, C. REGINALD. Ecuador. 1914.
VEATCH, ARTHUR CLIFFORD. Quito to Bogotá. 1917.
Report of Rockefeller Foundation relative to the improvement of health
conditions of the Port of Guayaquil.

GUADELOUPE AND MARTINIQUE

Annuaire de la Guadeloupe et Dépendances.
Annuaire de la Martinique.

THE GUIANAS

LEECHMAN, ALLEYNE. British Guiana Handbook. 1913.
RODWAY, J. Guiana: British, Dutch, and French. 1912.
British Guiana: Blue Book of the Colony and Colonial Report. Annual.
Dutch Guiana: Jaarcijfers voor het Koninkrijk der Nederlanden Kolonien
(Annual Report for the Kingdom of the Netherlands Colonies). Annual
series.
French Guiana: Statistiques du Commerce des Colonies Françaises.
Annual.

HAITI

ST. JOHN, SIR SPENSER. Hayti, or the Black Republic. 1884.
The Blue Book of Haiti. Printed in English and Spanish.
Le Moniteur. Official newspaper of the government.
United States Senate Committee's Hearings on Haiti and Santo Domingo,
Parts I, II, and III. 1921.

JAMAICA

BROCK, HERMAN G. Market for Boots and Shoes in Jamaica. United States
Department of Commerce. 1917.
CUNDALL, FRANK. Jamaica in 1912: A Handbook of Information.
GARDNER, W. J. History of Jamaica from its Discovery by Christopher
Columbus to 1872. 1909.
STANFORD, E. Handbook of Jamaica. Annual.
TUCKER, W. A. Textiles in Porto Rico and Jamaica. United States
Department of Commerce. 1917.
Jamaica Gazette.

MEXICO

Books and literature dealing with various phases of Mexican life and
activities are not so numerous or satisfactory as those dealing with certain
other Latin-American countries. The following books, selected with particular regard for the subjects treated in the text, are recommended.

BANCROFT, HUBERT HOWE. History of the Pacific States of North America, Vols. IV–IX, "Mexico, 1516–1887." 1883–1890.
BARRON, CLARENCE W. The Mexican Problem. 1917.
ITURBIDE, AGUSTIN DE. Memorias. English translation by M. J. Quinn.
ITURBIDE, AGUSTIN DE. A Statement of Some of the Principal Events in the Public Life of Agustin de Iturbide, written by himself. 1824.
JONES, CHESTER LLOYD. Mexico and its Reconstruction. 1921.
O'SHAUGHNESSEY, EDITH. A Diplomat's Wife in Mexico. 1916.
PRESCOTT, W. H. The Conquest of Mexico.
THOMPSON, WALLACE. Trading with Mexico. 1921.
New Classified Business and Commercial Directory of Mexico City and State. Revised to 1921.
Terry's Guide to Mexico. 1922.

PANAMA

BUNAU-VARILLA, P. Panama: The Creation, Destruction, and Resurrection. 1914.
JOHNSON, EMORY R. The Panama Canal and Commerce. 1916.
MILLER, G. A. Prowling about Panama. 1919.
Boletin de Estadística: Panama. Annual.

PARAGUAY

CHARLEVOIX, P. F. X. DE. Histoire de Paraguay. 1756.
DOBRIZHOFFER, MARTIN. An Account of the Abipones, an Equestrian People of Paraguay. 1822.
GRAHAM, R. B. C. A Vanished Arcadia. 1901. An account of the Jesuit Missions in Paraguay.
HARDY, M. R. Paraguay.
WASHBURN, C. A. History of Paraguay. 1871.
WHITE, EDWARD LUCAS. El Supremo. 1916.

PERU

CRAWFORD, M. DE C. Peruvian Fabrics. 1916.
FRANCK, HARRY A. Vagabonding down the Andes. 1917.
HELPS, SIR ARTHUR. Life of Pizarro, with Some Account of his Associates in the Conquest of Peru. 1869.
MARKHAM, C. R. A History of Peru. 1892.
PARKER, WILLIAM B. Peruvians of Today. 1919.
PRESCOTT, W. H. The Conquest of Peru.
SALOMON, ALBERTO. Peru: Potentialities of Economic Development.
SANGER, J. W. Advertising Methods in Chile, Peru, and Bolivia. United States Department of Commerce. 1919.
VIVIAN, E. C. H. Peru. 1914.
Peruvian Yearbook (*West Coast Leader*), Centennial Number. 1921.

PORTO RICO

ALLEN, C. H. "How Civil Government was Established in Porto Rico," in *North American Review*, Vol. CLXXIV (1902), pp. 159–174.

HILL, ROBERT T. Cuba and Porto Rico and Other Islands of the West Indies. 1898.

ROWE, L. S. The United States and Porto Rico. 1904.

VERRILL, A. H. Porto Rico Past and Present and San Domingo of Today. 1914.

URUGUAY

DODDS, JAMES. Records of the Scottish Settlers in the River Plate and their Churches. 1897.

DOMVILLE-FIFE, CHARLES W. The United States of Brazil; with a Chapter on the Republic of Uruguay. 1911.

FRANCK, HARRY A. Working North from Patagonia. 1921.

HOLLAND, W. J. To the River Plate and Back. 1913.

HUDSON, W. H. The Purple Land. 1916.

KOEBEL, W. H. The Romance of the River Plate. 1914.

KOEBEL, W. H. Uruguay. 1911.

MURRAY, J. H. Travels in Uruguay.

ROSS, G. Argentina and Uruguay. 1916.

STANFORD. The Republic of Uruguay. 1883.

The Conquest of the River Plate, 1535 to 1555. Translated by Luis L. Dominguez (Hakluyt Society). 1891.

VENEZUELA

BELL, P. L. Venezuela: A Commercial and Industrial Handbook with a Chapter on the Dutch West Indies. United States Department of Commerce. 1922.

BINGHAM, HIRAM. The Journal of an Expedition across Venezuela and Colombia. 1909.

DALTON, L. V. Venezuela. 1912.

EWING, W. W. Markets for Construction Materials and Machinery in Venezuela. United States Department of Commerce. 1917.

SCRUGGS, W. L. The Colombian and Venezuelan Republics. 1905.

Customs Tariff of Venezuela. United States Department of Commerce.

Venezuela. An economic report presented by students of the School of Foreign Service as an aid to the foreign trade of the United States. Published by Georgetown University, Washington, D. C. 1921.

INDEX

Acajutla (ä kä ho͞ot'lä), 332, 334

Advertising, knowledge of, 435

Agricultural implements, importation of, 106, 160, 409

Agricultural industries, 46, 47, 272. *See also* Agriculture

Agriculture: Argentina, 137, 138, 155, 159; Bolivia, 90, 91, 98, 102, 105 f., 108; Brazil, 196, 197, 220, 224, 226, 229, 230, 235 ff.; British Honduras, 329; British West Indies, 390 ff.; Chile, 111, 120, 122, 126, 129, 134; Colombia, 272, 276 ff.; Costa Rica, 306; Cuba, 378 ff.; Dominican Republic, 427 f.; Dutch West Indies, 411 f.; Ecuador, 36, 38, 49; French West Indies, 408 f.; Galapagos Islands, 58; Guatemala, 339 f.; Haiti, 420; Honduras, 324; Mexico, 351, 353, 358; Nicaragua, 314; Panama, 294; Paraguay, 182, 188, 190, 192; Peru, 81, 83, 443; Porto Rico, 386 f.; Salvador, 333; Uruguay, 167, 173, 176 f.; Venezuela, 256, 260

Aguas Calientes (ä'gwäs kä lē ĕn'täs), 353

Alagoas (ä lä gō'äs), 218

Alfalfa, production of, 83, 129, 138

Almagro, Diego de, 15, 60, 112

Alpaca wool, exportation of, 79, 84, 87, 106

Aluminium, deposits of, 296

Amapala (ä mä pä'lä), 322 f., 325, 326

Amazonas (ä mä zō'näs), 217

Ambato (äm bä'tō), 47, 49, 57

American business man, Latin-American idea of, 23 f.

American versus British trade in Latin America, 445 f.

Ammunition, importation of, 106, 243

Antigua (än tē'gwä), 404 f.

Antimony, exportation of, 106

Antofagasta (än tō fä gäs'tä), 98, 107, 117, 131, 133

Arequipa (ä rä kē'pä), 77, 81

Argentina: army and navy, 158; cities, 147 ff.; competition for trade, 162 f.; currency, 158; education, 158 f.; exports and imports, 160; general description, 135 ff.; geography, 137 ff.; government, 155 ff.; history, 141 ff.; people, 142 ff.; products and industries, 159 ff.; transportation and communication, 160 f.

Arica (ä rē'kä), 100, 107, 116, 124, 131, 133, 134

Artigas (är tē'gäs), 173

Asbestos, deposits of, 296, 380

Asphalt, deposits of, 261, 262, 380; exportation of, 263, 369, 396, 397

Asunción (ä so͞on syōn'), 152, 186, 189, 190, 193

Automobiles, importation of, 106, 160, 177, 243, 263, 296, 362, 389; in Brazil, 440 f.

Aviation: Bolivia, 101; Brazil, 234, 250; Colombia, 275, 280; Guatemala, 339; Peru, 80; Venezuela, 258, 259

Ayacucho (ä yä ko͞o'chō), 78

Bahama Islands, 367, 368, 405 f.

Bahia (bä ē'ä), 212, 218, 242

Bahia Blanca (blän'kä), 155

Bahia de Caraques (dä kä rä'käs), 47

455

456   LATIN AMERICA — MEN AND MARKETS

Balata, exportation of, 261, 262, 294, 412; production of, 78, 258, 261, 294, 407

Balboa, 293

Balsa wood, 54, 306

Balsam, 221, 272, 332, 334

Bananas, exportation of, 54, 281, 296, 302, 306, 308, 311, 321, 324, 325, 330, 340, 379, 394; production of, 54, 230, 277 ff., 294, 302, 304, 305, 306, 324, 328, 329, 338, 339, 392, 394, 410, 428

Bank, services of, in foreign trade transactions, 431 f.

Barbados: cities, 398; exports and imports, 399; geography, 398; people, 398; products and industries, 399; transportation and communication, 400

Barley, exportation of, 160; production of, 98, 105, 121, 176, 278

Barquisimeto (bär kē sē mä′tō), 258

Barranquilla (bär rän kē′lyä with trilled r), 271 f., 277, 281

Basse Terre (bäs′târ′), 403

Beans, production of, 229, 235, 340

Belem (bā lĕm′), 217, 218, 222, 243, 245, 246

Belize (bĕ lēz′), 328, 330

Bello Horizonte (bā′lyō ō rē zôn′tä), 229

Bermuda Islands, 406 f.

Bismuth, exportation of, 106; production of, 87, 105

Bluefields, 311 f., 315, 316

Bocas del Toro (bō′käs dĕl tō′rō), 289, 297

Bogotá (bō gō tä′), 267, 268, 269 f., 275, 276, 281

Bolivar (coin), 259

Bolívar, Simón, 15, 32, 34, 66, 92, 93, 253, 269, 288

Bolivia: army, 101; cities, 96 ff.; currency, 101; education, 101 f.; exports and imports, 106 f.; future tendencies, 108 f.; geography, 90 ff.; government, 101; history, 92 f.; land of opportunity, 90; people, 93 ff.; products and industries, 102 ff.; transportation and communication, 107 f.

Boliviano, 101

Boots and shoes. See Shoes

Borax, 118, 129

Brazil: army and navy, 233 f.; cities

and states, 217 ff.; currency, 234; education, 234 f.; exports and imports, 243 ff.; geography, 195 ff.; government, 232 f.; history, 199 ff.; people, 207 ff.; products and industries, 235 ff.; transportation and communication, 244 ff.

Breweries, 45, 120, 121, 122, 136, 231, 351, 361, 368, 385

Bricks, 136, 351

Bridgetown, 398

British Guiana (gē ä′nä), 390, 407 f.

British Honduras, 300, 301; cities, 328; currency, 329; education, 329; exports and imports, 329; geography, 326 f.; government, 328; history, 327 f.; people, 328; products and industries, 329; transportation and communication, 330

British possessions in Latin America: Antigua, 404 f.; Bahama Islands, 405 f.; Barbados, 398 ff.; Bermuda Islands, 406 f.; British Guiana, 407 f.; British Virgin Islands, 403; Dominica, 404; Grenada, 400 f.; Jamaica, 391 ff.; Leeward Islands, 402; Montserrat, 403; Nevis, 403; St. Kitts, 403; St. Lucia, 402; St. Vincent, 401; Trinidad and Tobago, 395 ff.; Windward Islands, 400

British Virgin Islands, 403

Buenaventura (bwā nä vĕn tōō′rä), 274, 277, 280

Buenos Aires (bwā′nōs ī′rās), 97, 100, 118, 122, 131, 133, 136, 141, 143, 147 ff., 154, 159, 162, 172, 173, 183, 186, 193, 245

Business in Latin America, approach to, 8 ff.; methods of doing, 6 ff.; type of man in, 8

Cables. See Wireless and telegraph service

Caboclo, 32, 236

Cabot, Sebastian, 141, 183

Cacao, exportation of, 45, 47, 56, 222, 229, 244, 256, 260, 262, 296, 306, 308, 369, 380, 397, 412, 420, 428; production of, 36, 49, 50, 77, 78, 83, 106, 197, 217, 218, 235, 238, 255, 258, 272, 278, 294, 302, 304, 305, 306, 312, 337, 340, 368, 380, 390, 394, 396, 401, 402, 407, 409, 410, 420, 428

Cali (kä′lē), 274, 281
Callao (kä lyä′ō), 61, 68, 74, 77 f.
Candles, manufacture of, 45, 136, 153, 351
Caracas (kä rä′käs), 255, 259, 260, 264, 266
Carriages, manufacture of, 153 ; importation of, 160
Cartagena (kär tä hä′nä), 268, 272, 276, 277, 280, 281
Casein, exportation of, 159, 160
Castries (käs trē′), 402
Cattle, exportation of, 79, 228, 261, 281 ; raising of, 46, 47, 54, 58, 98, 106, 120, 122, 129, 153, 155, 173, 175, 182, 188, 191, 197, 218, 220, 221, 222, 223, 229, 235, 238, 240, 256, 258, 260 f., 294, 305, 312, 321, 325, 332, 334, 337, 340, 358, 380, 394, 403
Cattle products, 152, 180, 230, 278. *See also* Hides and skins, Leather, Meat
Cayenne (kä ĕn′), 411
Ceará (oñ ä rä′), 220
Cedar, exportation of, 340, 380 ; production of, 222, 272, 306, 329, 340, 360, 368, 380
Ceiba (sä′bä), 321
Cement, importation of, 243, 420 ; production of, 136, 255
Centavo, 48, 80, 125, 189, 276, 313
Central America, general description of, 300 ff.
Cereals, production of, 46, 47, 77, 120, 197, 223, 224, 228, 278, 302. *See also* Barley, Corn, Maize, Oats, Wheat
Cerro de Pasco (sĕr′rō *with trilled* r, dä päs′kō), 79, 86, 87
Champerico (chäm pä rē′kō), 338
Charlestown, 403
Chemicals, importation of, 106, 163, 243, 315, 334, 381
Chicle, exportation of, 330 ; production of, 78, 329, 340
Chihuahua (chē wä′wä), 353
Chile : army and navy, 124 ; cities, 116 ff. ; currency, 125 ; education, 125 ; exports and imports, 130 ; geography, 110 ff. ; government, 123 ; history, 112 f. ; people, 113 ff. ; press, 124 f. ; products and industries, 125 ff. ; relations with United States, 134 ; transportation and communication, 130 ff.

Chileans, characteristics of, 114 ff.
Chocolate, manufacture of, 100, 270, 353
Cholos, 95
Cigarettes, exportation of, 296 ; manufacture of, 192, 256, 271, 332, 351, 361, 385
Cigars, exportation of, 394 ; manufacture of, 258, 271, 332, 337, 351, 353, 368, 373, 385, 426
Ciudad Bolívar (syōō thäth′ bō lē′vär), 258, 259, 264, 266
Coal, importation of, 55, 128, 177, 230, 242, 243, 360, 397, 413 ; production of, 55, 87, 121, 123, 128, 136, 177, 230, 235, 242, 262, 280, 296, 360, 368, 380, 428
Cobalt, 78
Coban (kō′bän), 338
Cochabamba (kō chä bäm′bä), 97 f., 101
Coconuts, exportation of, 296, 330, 369, 394, 397 ; production of, 294, 304, 305, 312, 321, 328, 329, 392, 396, 401, 403, 404, 407
Coffee, exportation of, 45, 79, 105, 225, 229, 244, 256, 260, 262, 271, 272, 277, 281, 306, 308, 311, 321, 324, 325, 332, 333, 334, 340, 362, 369, 385, 388, 389, 392, 394, 412, 420, 428 ; importation of, 160, 379 ; production of, 50 f., 83, 106, 197, 202, 223, 224, 226, 230, 235, 255, 258, 260, 270, 274, 294, 302, 304, 305, 306, 312, 324, 332, 333, 337, 338, 339, 358, 368, 379, 385, 388, 392, 394, 407, 409, 410, 420, 428
Colombia : army, 275 f. ; cities, 269 ff. ; currency, 276 ; education, 276 ; exports and imports, 281 ; geography, 267 f. ; government, 275 ; history, 268 f. ; people, 269 ; products and industries, 276 ff. ; transportation and communication, 280 f.
Colon (coin), 305, 333
Colón (kō lōn′), 289, 296, 297
Colonia (kō lō′nyä), 173
Colonial period, 26, 28 ff.
Colonial policy of Spain, 30 ff.
Columbus, Christopher, 26, 27, 199, 253, 268, 286, 300, 310, 319, 370, 384, 391, 422
Communication. *See* Transportation and communication
Concepción (kôn sĕp syōn′) (Chile), 112, 121

Concepción (Paraguay), 186 f., 193
Condor (kôn dôr'), 48
Consular service, 439
Conto (kôn'tō), 234
Copper, exportation of, 78, 87, 106, 107,
    117, 128, 130, 362; importation of,
    160; production of, 55, 86, 98, 102,
    118, 120, 121, 128, 136, 154, 159, 177,
    221, 235, 258, 262, 280, 296, 321, 334,
    340, 358, 360, 368, 380, 428
Copra, exportation of, 394, 397
Coquimbo (kō kēm'bō), 66, 111, 118,
    131
Cordoba, 313
Córdoba (kôr'dō bä), 153 f., 159
Corinto (kō rēn'tō), 311, 316
Corn, exportation of, 160, 229; produc-
    tion of, 98, 129, 176, 231, 235, 260,
    278, 312, 325, 333, 403
Coronel (kō rō něl'), 121, 131
Correspondence, foreign trade, 436
Cortez, Hernando, 15, 26, 28, 300, 319,
    344, 347
Corumbá (kō rōōm bä'), 193, 221
Costa Rica, 300; army and navy, 305;
    cities, 304 f.; currency, 305; educa-
    tion, 305 f.; exports and imports,
    308; geography, 303; government,
    305; history, 303 f.; people, 304;
    products and industries, 306 ff.;
    transportation and communication,
    308
Cotton, exportation of, 45, 52, 78, 79,
    87, 218, 238, 244, 400, 420; produc-
    tion of, 47, 49, 52, 78, 79, 83, 182, 197,
    218, 220, 221, 223, 224, 228, 231, 235,
    238, 260, 271, 278, 333, 340, 358, 399,
    401, 403, 404, 409, 414
Cotton goods, importation of, 271, 272,
    302, 315, 325, 334, 340, 362, 381, 389,
    399, 420, 428; manufacture of, 52, 83,
    220, 229, 256, 270, 271, 332, 351, 352,
    353, 361
Credentials, form of, 7; need of, 6
Cristobal (krēs tō bäl'), 290
Cruzeiro (krōō zä'rōō), 234
Cuba, 367, 368; cities, 373; currency,
    377; education, 378; exports and
    imports, 380 f.; geography, 369 f.;
    government, 374 ff.; history, 370 f.;
    people, 371 f.; products and indus-
    tries, 378 ff.; transportation and com-
    munication, 381 f.

Cuban politics and United States trade,
    442
Cuenca (kwĕn'kä), 46 f., 49
Curaçao (kōō rä sä'ō), 412 f.
Curitibá (kōō rē tē bä'), 230
Currency: Argentina, 158; Bolivia,
    101; Brazil, 234; British Honduras,
    329; Chile, 125; Colombia, 276;
    Costa Rica, 305; Cuba, 377; Domini-
    can Republic, 427; Ecuador, 48;
    French West Indies, 409; Guate-
    mala, 339; Haiti, 419; Honduras,
    324; Mexico, 356; Nicaragua, 313;
    Panama, 293; Paraguay, 189; Peru,
    80; Salvador, 333; Uruguay, 174;
    Venezuela, 259
Cuyabá (kōō yä bä'), 193, 221
Cuzco (kōōs'kō), 68, 70, 77, 78, 81

Dairy products, importation of, 315,
    362, 381, 389
Dairying, 126, 176, 223, 230
David, 290, 297
Diamonds, exportation of, 218, 408;
    production of, 218, 220, 228, 235, 242,
    262, 407, 408; black, 218, 228
Discovery, period of, 25 ff.
Dominica, 404
Dominican Republic: cities, 426; cur-
    rency, 427; education, 427; exports
    and imports, 428; geography, 421 f.;
    government, 426; history, 422 ff.;
    people, 424 f.; political unrest, 421;
    products and industries, 427; trans-
    portation and communication, 429
Drugs, production of, 54, 83, 84, 105
Drugs and medicines, importation of,
    315, 334
Dutch Guiana, 411 f.
Dutch possessions in Latin America:
    Curaçao, 412 f.; Dutch Guiana, 411 f.
Dyewoods, production of, 261, 278, 294,
    312, 360, 402, 428

Ecuador: army and navy, 48; cities,
    43 ff.; commercial future, 57 f.; cur-
    rency, 48; education, 49; exports
    and imports, 56; geography, 36 ff.;
    government, 47; history, 39 f.;
    people, 41 ff.; products and indus-
    tries, 49 ff.; transportation and com-
    munication, 56 f.
Education: Argentina, 158; Bolivia,

101 f.; Brazil, 234 f.; British Honduras, 329; Chile, 125; Colombia, 276; Costa Rica, 305 f.; Cuba, 378; Dominican Republic, 427; Ecuador, 49; Guatemala, 339; Haiti, 419; Honduras, 324; Mexico, 357; Nicaragua, 314; Panama, 293; Paraguay, 189; Peru, 80 f.; Salvador, 333; Uruguay, 175; Venezuela, 259
Electrical machinery and supplies, importation of, 106, 163
Emeralds, 279
Encarnación (ĕn kär nä syōn'), 188, 193
Esmeraldas (ĕs mĕ räl'däs), 47
Espirito Santo (ĕs pē'rē tōō sän'tōō), 229
Eten (ā'tĕn), 79
Explosives, importation of, 106, 243
Exporting, direct, 438; indirect, 438
Exports: Argentina,160; Bolivia,106 f.; Brazil, 243 ff.; British Honduras, 329; British West Indies, 390 ff., Central America, 302; Chile, 130; Colombia, 281; Costa Rica, 308; Cuba, 380 f.; Dutch West Indies, 412 f.; Ecuador, 56; French West Indies, 408 ff.; Guatemala, 340; Haiti, 420; Honduras, 325; Mexico, 362; Nicaragua, 315; Panama, 296 f.; Paraguay, 192 f.; Peru, 87 f.; Porto Rico, 388 f.; Salvador, 334; Uruguay, 177 ff.; Venezuela, 262; Virgin Islands, 414

Fertilizer, importation of, 399, 409
Florianopolis (flō rē ä nō'pō lēs), 230 f.
Flour, importation of, 263, 296, 315, 334, 362, 389, 420, 428; manufacture of, 120, 122, 136, 153, 225, 228, 270, 338, 351, 353, 361
Foodstuffs, importation of, 88, 106, 107, 177, 193, 243, 281, 302, 308, 315, 325, 340, 381, 389, 399, 412, 413, 420
Foreign investments in South America, 444 f.
Foreign possessions in West Indies and South America: British, 390 ff.; Dutch, 411 ff.; French, 408 ff.; United States, 413 f.
Foreign securities, investment in, 430 f.
Foreign trade, consideration as an element in, 433; psychology and, 442 f.; training for, 444
Foreign-trade advisers, 443

Foreign-trade correspondence, 436
Foreign-trade houses, 442
Foreign-trade terms, 437
Forest products, 54, 84, 106, 130, 159, 191, 223, 226, 240, 261, 278, 294, 334, 360, 380. See also Rubber, Timber, etc.
Fortaleza (fôr tä lä'zä), 220
Fort de France (fôr de fräNs), 409 f.
Foundries, 120, 153, 225
Fray Bentos (frī bĕn'tōs), 173
French Guiana, 410 f.
French possessions in Latin America: French Guiana, 410 f.; Guadeloupe, 408 f.; Martinique, 409 f.
Fruit, exportation of, 121, 368, 379, 381, 389, 392, 396, 406; production of, 120, 126, 129, 140, 154, 173, 197, 228, 278, 312, 379, 388, 390, 396, 406, 428. See also Bananas, Oranges, Pineapples, etc.
Fur industries, 122
Fur-bearing animals, 123, 177
Furniture, importation of, 160; manufacture of, 153, 192, 225, 361

Galapagos Islands (gä lä'pä gôs), 58
Gasoline and kerosene, importation of, 296, 428
Gaucho, 146 f., 170, 201
Germans, success of, in Latin America, 1, 433 f.
Glass, importation of, 243; manufacture of, 136, 225, 255, 352
Goats, raising of, 105, 175, 340
Goatskins, exportation of, 54, 261
Gold, exportation of, 45, 78, 87, 106, 263, 271, 272, 274, 281, 308, 311, 334; production of, 47, 55, 62, 77, 86, 102, 105, 123, 128, 136, 154, 159, 177, 202, 220, 228, 229, 235, 242, 258, 262, 279, 296, 302, 306, 321, 334, 340, 358, 360, 368, 380, 407, 408, 410, 412, 428
Gourde, 419
Goyaz (gō yäsh'), 220, 240
Gracias (grä'syäs), 322
Grain, exportation of, 153, 155, 160, 162, 221; importation of, 397; production of, 126, 129, 153, 155, 332, 337. See also Corn, Wheat, etc.
Granada (grä nä'dä), 312
Grapes, raising of, 126, 129, 154
Grazing. See Cattle, Sheep, Live stock

Greater Antilles, 367
Grenada, 400 f.
Guadalajara (gwä thä lä hä′rä), 351 f.
Guadeloupe (gô dĕ lōōp′), 408 f.
Guano, exportation of, 413; production of, 62, 77, 81
Guatemala (gwä tä mä′lä), 300; army, 339; cities, 337 f.; currency, 339; education, 339; exports and imports, 340; geography, 335; government, 338 f.; history, 336 f.; people, 337; products and industries, 339 f.; transportation and communication, 340 f.
Guatemala City, 335, 337, 339, 341
Guayaquil (gwī ä kēl′), 43 ff., 49, 55, 56, 57
Gums. See Forest products

Habana, 370, 373
Haiti, 367, 368; cities, 417; currency, 419; education, 419 f.; exports and imports, 420 f.; geography, 415; government, 417 f.; history, 415 f.; people, 416; products and industries, 420; transportation and communication, 421; unique republic, 414 f.
Hamilton, 407
Hardware, importation of, 106, 160, 163, 193, 243, 353
Henequen, exportation of, 334, 362; production of, 333, 358
Herva maté. See Maté
Hides and skins, exportation of, 54, 79, 106, 118, 121, 123, 160, 162, 172, 177, 191, 218, 220, 221, 222, 228, 229, 235, 240, 244, 256, 261, 263, 271 f., 278, 281, 294, 296, 308, 325, 334, 340, 428; importation of, 420; production of, 58, 78, 84, 153, 176, 221, 255, 274, 312, 321, 332, 337, 380
Historical background of Latin America: discovery, 25 ff.; colonial period, 26, 28 ff.; liberation period, 26, 33 f.; republican period, 26, 34 f.
Holidays in Latin America, 436 f.
Honduras, 300; army and navy, 323; cities, 321; currency, 324; education, 324; exports and imports, 325; geography, 318; government, 323; history, 319 f.; people, 320 f.; products and industries, 324 f.; transportation and communication, 325 f.
Horses, raising of, 106, 122, 175, 380

Imports: Argentina, 160, 163; Bolivia, 106 f.; Brazil, 243 ff.; British Honduras, 329; British West Indies, 390 ff.; Central America, 302; Chile, 130; Colombia, 281; Costa Rica, 308; Cuba, 380 f.; Dutch West Indies, 412 f.; Ecuador, 56; French West Indies, 408 ff.; Guatemala, 340; Haiti, 420; Honduras, 325; Mexico, 362; Nicaragua, 315; Panama, 296 f.; Paraguay, 192 f.; Peru, 87 f.; Porto Rico, 388 f.; Salvador, 334; Uruguay, 177 ff.; Venezuela, 262
Incas, 66, 67, 69, 78, 81, 86, 89, 92, 102, 148, 183, 201, 211
Independence, period of, 26, 33 f.
Indians, as elements in population, 32, 42, 66, 68, 69, 91, 93 ff., 113, 114, 135, 140, 144, 168, 185, 208, 209, 210, 211, 254 f., 269, 289, 304, 311, 320 f., 331, 337, 347, 350, 372; fought by whites, 92, 112, 141, 167, 182, 201, 253, 268, 310, 344, 422; treatment of, by whites, 60, 61, 67, 81, 95, 211 f., 350, 371
Indigo, exportation of, 334; production of, 182, 332
Industries. See Agricultural industries, Manufacturing, Mining
Insurance, marine, 438
Iodine, 117, 128, 130
Iquique (ē kē′kä), 116 f., 131, 133
Iquitos (ē kē′tōs), 78, 217
Iron, exportation of, 130, 373, 380, 381; production of, 55, 118, 129, 196, 221, 229, 235, 242, 262, 280, 334, 368, 373, 380, 428
Iron and steel products, importation of, 88, 160, 163, 243, 302, 315, 325, 334, 340, 381, 389, 420, 428
Ivory. See Vegetable ivory

Jamaica, 367, 368; cities, 392; exports and imports, 394 f.; geography, 391; history, 391 f.; people, 392; products and industries, 394; transportation and communication, 395
Jujuy (hōō hwē′), 155
Jute, importation of, 243, 340; manufacture of, 220, 225, 228

Kapok, 52 f.
Kingston, 392
Kingstown, 401

La Guaira (lä gwī'rä), 256, 264
La Libertad (lä lē bĕr täth'), 332
Languages. *See* Portuguese language, Spanish language
La Paz (lä päs'), 77, 91, 92, 93, 94, 96 f., 98, 100, 101, 107, 108, 117, 133, 152
La Plata (lä plä'tä), 154, 159
Lard, importation of, 107, 334, 389, 428
Latin America and United States, 1 ff.
Latin Americans, characteristics of, 3 ff., 15 ff.; individualism of, 15 ff.; intellectual and artistic traits of, 10 ff.; racial inheritances of, 17 f.; understanding the, 1 ff.
La Union (lä ōō nyōn'), 332
Lead, exportation of, 106, 362; production of, 55, 98, 280, 296, 334, 340, 358, 360, 368, 380
Leather, importation of, 334, 340, 381; manufacture of, 126, 130, 136, 361
Leeward Islands, 367, 402
León (lā ōn'), 312
Lesser Antilles, 367
Liberation period, 26, 33 ff.
Libra, 80
Lima (lē'mä), 60, 61, 62, 63, 64, 67, 68, 70, 72, 74 ff., 77, 79, 81, 83, 88, 112, 287
Lime juice, exportation of, 401, 404; production of, 402, 403, 414
Limes, exportation of, 404; production of, 402, 403, 414
Limon (lē mōn'), 304, 308
Linseed, exportation of, 159, 160, 177; production of, 153, 176
Literature in Latin America, 11
Live-stock industry, 54, 78, 84, 106, 129 f., 135, 173, 175 f., 191, 231, 235, 239 f., 260, 294, 325, 358, 380. *See also* Cattle, Hides, *etc.*
Llama, raising of, 84, 94, 106
Llama wool, 84
Logwood, exportation of, 394, 402, 420, 428
Los Andes (lōs än'däs), 120
Lota (lō'tä), 121
Lumber, exportation of, 218, 240 f., 368; importation of, 106, 160, 325, 362, 397; production of, 154, 312, 334, 340, 360

Maceió (mä sä yō'), 218
Machinery, importation of, 107, 160,

193, 263, 302, 334, 340, 381, 389, 399, 409, 420, 428
Magellan, Ferdinand, 141, 183
Mahogany, exportation of, 278, 296, 325, 330, 369, 380; production of, 130, 222, 278, 306, 329, 338, 340, 360, 368, 380, 428
Maize, 84, 154, 218
Managua (mä nä'gwä), 312
Manáos (mä nä'ōs), 217 f.
Manganese, exportation of, 228, 242; production of, 129, 177, 196, 218, 229, 235, 280, 296, 306, 368, 380
Manioc, exportation of, 54, 229; production of, 54, 235
Manizales (mä nē sä'läs), 272
Manual labor, attitude toward, 17
Manufacturing: Argentina, 136, 153; Barbados, 398; Bolivia, 100; Brazil, 224, 226, 242 f.; Chile, 120, 126; Mexico, 351 f., 361; Paraguay, 192; Peru, 74, 83; Venezuela, 256; West Indies, 368
Maracaibo (mä rä kī'bō), 256 f., 259, 260, 264
Maranhão (mä rän youN'), 220 f.
Mar del Plata (mär dĕl plä'tä), 155
Marine insurance, 438
Markets, Latin-American, 438
Martinique (mär tē nēk'), 409
Matagalpa (mä tä gäl'pä), 312
Matches, manufacture of, 192, 225, 255, 351, 361, 368
Maté, exportation of, 192, 242, 244; production of, 188, 191 f., 221, 230, 242
Matto Grosso (mät'ōō grōs'ōō), 221, 240
Mayagüez (mä yä gwäs'), 385
Meat, exportation of, 129, 160, 172, 176, 177, 191, 235, 244; packing of, 136, 173, 176, 192, 228, 235, 240
Meat products, importation of, 315, 362, 381, 389, 412, 413
Medellín (mä dĕ lyēn'), 270 f., 276, 281
Mendoza (mĕn dō'sä), 154, 183
Mercedes (mĕr sä'däs), 173
Mercury, deposits of, 55, 87, 334, 380
Merida (mä'rē dä), 353
Mestizo, 32, 41, 69, 95, 269, 331, 347, 350, 384
Mexico: army and navy, 357; cities, 351 ff.; currency, 356 f.; debts, 365 f., 438; education, 357; foreign concessions in Mexico, 363 f.; future trade

with United States, 364 f.; geography, 342 ff.; government, 354 ff.; history, 344 ff.; immigration, 348 f.; imports and exports, 362; land monopoly in, 347 f.; people, 347 f.; products and industries, 357 ff.; transportation and communication, 363

Mexico City, 351, 357

Milreis (mĭl'rās), 234

Minas Geraes (mē'näsh zhä rīsh'), 228, 235, 242

Mineral earths, 56

Mineral springs, 228, 229

Minerals. *See* Mining

Mining: Argentina, 138, 155, 159; Bolivia, 98, 100, 102, 108; Brazil, 196, 197, 242; Chile, 126 ff., 134; Colombia, 279 f.; Cuba, 380; Ecuador, 47, 55 f.; Mexico, 353, 360; Nicaragua, 312; Panama, 296; Peru, 72, 84; Venezuela, 261 f. *See also* Gold, Iron, Silver, *etc.*

Miranda, Francisco, 15, 32

Molasses, exportation of, 381, 399, 404, 414

Mollendo (mô lyĕn'dō), 77, 78, 79, 107

Molybdenum, 87

Monazite sand, production of, 218, 228, 242

Money. *See* Currency

Monterrey (mōn tĕr rā'), 352

Montevideo (mōn tä vē thä'ō), 148, 152, 170 ff., 175, 178, 179, 180, 186, 221, 245

Montserrat, 403

Mules, raising of, 106, 175, 380

Nassau (năs'ô), 405

Natal (nä täl'), 223

Negroes, as element in population, 32, 43, 70, 113, 135, 143, 168, 208, 209, 210, 211, 236, 254, 269, 274, 289, 304, 308, 311, 320, 321, 328, 372, 384, 390, 396, 409, 413, 414 ff., 424

Nevis, 403

Nicaragua: army and navy, 313; cities, 311 ff.; currency, 313; education, 314; exports and imports, 315; geography, 300 ff.; government, 313; history, 310; people, 311; products and industries, 314 f.; relations with United States, 316 f.; transportation and communication, 315 f.

Nispero, 294, 329

Nitrates, exportation of, 116, 117, 128, 130; production of, 62, 81, 110, 111, 126

Nutmeg, 401, 402

Nuts, exportation of, 222, 389; production of, 217, 221, 235

Oats, exportation of, 160, 177; production of, 121, 176, 231

Oil. *See* Petroleum

Oil cake, 218

Oil seeds, 244

Oranges, exportation of, 325, 379, 394; production of, 49, 190, 218, 321, 404, 410

Orizaba (ō rē sä'bä), 353

Oruro (ō rōō'rō), 100, 101, 133

Pacasmayo (pä käs mä'yō), 79

Packing for shipment, 437

Paita (pī'tä), 79

Panama: army and navy, 292 f.; Canal Zone, 284 f.; cities, 289 f.; currency, 293; education, 293; exports and imports, 296 f.; friendly relations with United States, 299; geography, 283 f.; government, 291 f.; history, 286 ff.; link between the two Americas, 282 f.; people, 289; products and industries, 294 ff.; strategic republic, 282; trade requirements, 297 f.; transportation and communication, 296 f.

Panama Canal, 3, 18, 35, 57, 77, 122, 269, 282, 284 f., 297, 302, 363

Panama City, 286, 287, 289, 290, 296

Panama hats, exportation of, 45, 52, 56, 274, 443; manufacture of, 36, 50, 51, 79, 271

Pan-American Union, 1, 7, 206

Paper, importation of, 160, 243, 263, 340, 381; manufacture of, 126, 153, 255, 361

Pará (pä rä'), 78, 222

Paraguay: army and navy, 189; cities, 186 ff.; currency, 189; education, 189; exports and imports, 192 f.; future, 194; geography, 181 f.; government, 188 f.; history, 183 ff.; people, 185; products and industries, 190 ff.; transportation and communication, 193

Paraná (pä rä nä'), 155, 196, 230, 240

Paysandú (pī sän dōō'), 173
Pearls, 262, 296
Pernambuco (pĕr näm bōō'kō), 203, 204, 222 f., 238
Peru: army and navy, 80; characteristics of people, 70 ff.; cities, 74 ff.; currency, 80; education, 80 f.; exports and imports, 87 f.; geography, 63 ff.; government, 79 ff.; history, 66 ff.; land of extremes, 62 f.; land of splendor and tragedy, 59 ff.; people, 68 ff.; products and industries, 81 ff.; transportation and communication, 88 f.
Peso, 125, 174, 189, 276, 293, 324, 339, 356, 377, 427
Petroleum, exportation of, 84, 87, 262, 352, 362, 369; importation of, 160, 177, 362, 397, 412, 413; production of, 55, 79, 84, 100, 104, 129, 159, 177, 256, 261, 279 f., 358, 360 f., 362, 397
Phosphate, exportation of, 419, production of, 262
Pimentel (pē mĕn tĕl'), 79
Pine, importation of, 160; production of, 130, 230, 240, 241, 360
Pineapples, exportation of, 379, 385; production of, 218, 305, 306, 386, 404, 405, 406, 410, 428
Pizarro, Francisco, 15, 26, 28, 33, 39, 66, 67, 72, 76, 92, 102, 112, 201, 286
Platinum, exportation of, 272, 274; production of, 55 f., 279
Plymouth, 403
Pointe à Pitre (pwănt'ä pē'tr'), 409
Politics, individualism in, 16
Ponce (pōn'sä), 385
Port au Prince (pôr tō präNs'), 417
Porto Alegre (pôr'tŏö ä la'grĕ), 231 f.
Port of Spain, 396
Porto Rico, 367; advantageous relations with United States, 383; cities, 384 ff.; exports and imports, 388 f.; geography, 383 f.; government, 386; history, 384; people, 384; products and industries, 386 ff.; transportation and communication, 389
Portugal, influence of, on history of Brazil, 200
Portuguese language, use of, 12, 14; in Brazil, 209, 216
Potatoes, importation of, 177; production of, 84, 105, 235

Potosí (pō tō sē'), 98
Prices, firm, 431
Printing and literature, 11
Psychology and trade, 442
Puebla (pwä'blä), 352
Puerto Barrios (pwĕr'tō bär'rē ōs), 338
Puerto Cabello (kä bĕ'lyō), 256, 261, 264
Puerto Colombia (kō lôm'byä), 271, 281
Puerto Plata (plä'tä), 426
Punta Arenas (pōōn'tä ä rä'näs), 122 f., 124, 129, 131, 134
Puntarenas (pōōn tä rä'näs), 305

Quebracho (kä brä'chō), exportation of, 160, 162, 188, 191; production of, 54, 136, 140, 155, 159, 191, 192, 240
Quezaltenango (kä säl tä nän'gō), 335, 337 f.
Quito (kē'tō), 46

Railways: Argentina, 160 f.; Bolivia, 107; Brazil, 196, 247 ff.; British Honduras, 330; Chile, 131 ff.; Colombia, 280; Costa Rica, 308; Cuba, 382; Dominican Republic, 429; Ecuador, 56 f.; Guatemala, 341; Haiti, 421; Honduras, 326; Mexico, 363; Nicaragua, 316; Panama, 296; Paraguay, 193; Peru, 88; Porto Rico, 389; Salvador, 334; Uruguay, 178; Venezuela, 264
Recife (rä sē'fä), 223
Religion, 21 ff., 73, 115 f., 144, 158, 169, 204, 213
Republican period, 26, 34 f.
Resins. See Forest products
Retalhuleu (rä tä lōō lä'ōō), 338
Rice, exportation of, 54, 218, 229; importation of, 160, 263, 296, 315, 389, 428; production of, 36, 54, 78, 79, 83, 231, 235, 332, 333, 340, 396, 407, 408
Rio de Janeiro (rē'ō dä zhä nā'rō), 152, 178, 196, 197, 217, 226, 230, 235, 244, 245, 246, 250
Rio Grande do Sul, 196, 231, 232
Roads. See Transportation and communication
Rosario (rō sä'ryō), 153
Roseau (rō zō'), 404
Roto, 114
Rubber, exportation of, 56, 106, 222, 228, 242, 244, 294, 362; production of, 55, 77, 78, 84, 106, 196, 198, 217,

8

220, 221, 224, 240, 241 f., 261, 272, 278, 305, 312, 321, 340

Rum, exportation of, 369, 392, 394, 399, 401, 408; production of, 78, 401, 409, 410

St. Kitts, 403
St. Lucia, 402
St. Vincent, 401
Salaverry (sä lä věr're), 79, 82
Salesmanship, requirements for good, 8 ff.
Salt, exportation of, 117, 159; production of, 47, 105, 129, 159, 243, 280
Salta (säl'tä), 155
Saltillo (säl te'lyō), 353
Salto (säl'tō), 173
Salvador: army, 332 f.; cities, 332; currency, 333; education, 333; exports and imports, 334; geography, 330 f.; government, 332; history, 331; people, 331; products and industries, 333 f.; transportation and communication, 334 f.
San Cristóbal (sän krēs tō'bäl), 258, 260
San José (sän hō sä'), 304
San Juan (sän hwän'), 384 f.
San Juan del Sur (děl soōr'), 312
San Luis Potosí (sän loō ēs' pō tō sē'), 353
San Martín, José de, 15, 32, 34, 68, 112, 142
San Pedro (sän pä'drō), 322
San Pedro de Macoris (dä mä kō'rēs), 426
San Salvador (sän säl vä dōr'), 332, 333
Santa Ana (sän'tä ä'nä), 332
Santa Catharina (kä tä rē'nä), 230
Santa Cruz (krōōs'), 100
Santa Fe (fā'), 155
Santa Rosa (rō'sä), 321
Santiago (sän tē ä'gō) (Chile), 114, 118 f., 125, 132, 133, 152
Santiago (Cuba), 373
Santiago (Dominican Republic), 426
Santiago (Panama), 290
Santo Domingo (sän'tō dō mēn'gō), 426
Santos (sän'tōōsh), 197, 225 f., 235
São Luiz (souN loō ēzh'), 221
São Paulo (pou'loō), 196, 224 f., 235, 236, 238
São Salvador (säl vä dōr'), 218 f., 238
Sarsaparilla, 217, 329

Sawmills, 45, 136, 231. See also Lumber
Schools. See Education
Sheep, production of, 54, 94, 106, 122 f., 125, 129, 140, 175
Sheep's wool, exportation of, 79, 84, 87
Shipbuilding, 45, 126, 228
Shipping, packing for, 437
Shipping facilities, 308, 340 f., 381. See also Waterways
Shoes, importation of, 296, 362, 389, 428; manufacture of, 45, 120, 122, 126, 136, 153, 192, 243, 255, 270, 351
Silver, exportation of, 78, 87, 106, 118, 325, 334; production of, 55, 77, 86, 92, 98, 102, 105, 120, 129, 154, 159, 258, 262, 272, 296, 302, 306, 308, 321, 334, 340, 358, 360, 368
Sisal, 353, 368, 405
Skins. See Hides and skins
Soap, importation of, 420; manufacture of, 45, 136, 153, 192, 255, 256, 270, 332, 351, 353, 368
Sole (sō'lä), 80
Spain, colonial policy of, 30 ff.
Spanish language, use of, 10, 14, 25; Argentina, 136, 143, 146; British Honduras, 328; Chile, 113; Colombia, 269; Costa Rica, 304; Cuba, 378; Dominican Republic, 426; Ecuador, 41; Mexico, 357; Nicaragua, 311; Panama, 289; Paraguay, 185; Peru, 70
Spanish possessions in America, extent of, 29
Spices, exportation of, 394, 401, 402
Sponges, exportation of, 368, 381, 406; production of, 405, 406
Steel. See Iron and steel products
Straw hats, manufacture of, 36, 47, 50. See also Panama hats
Sucre (coin), 48
Sucre (soō'krä) (Bolivia), 100, 101
Sucre, General, 66, 78, 92, 93
Sugar, exportation of, 83, 87, 218, 221, 229, 238, 260, 262, 306, 308, 325, 334, 340, 373, 378, 381, 389, 392, 394, 397, 399, 408, 412, 420, 426, 428; importation of, 160, 177; production of, 36, 46, 47, 49, 58, 77, 78, 79, 82, 100, 154, 182, 190, 196, 197, 218, 223, 224, 226, 230, 231, 235, 238, 255, 258, 260, 278, 294, 302, 304, 312, 324, 332, 333, 337, 338, 339, 368, 373, 378, 385, 386, 390,

392, 394, 396, 399, 401, 402, 403, 404, 407, 408, 409, 410, 414, 420, 426, 427, 428; refining of, 45, 82, 100, 136, 153, 154, 186, 192, 202, 220, 228, 272, 312, 361, 378, 386, 398
Sulphur, 56, 58, 87

Tagua nut, exportation of, 49, 294; production of, 51, 278. *See also* Vegetable ivory
Talara (tä lä′rä), 79
Talca (täl′kä), 120
Talcahuano (täl kä wä′nō), 121, 124, 131
Tampico (tăm pē′kō), 352 f., 363
Tannin, exportation of, 191; production of, 140, 240, 261
Tanning, 45, 47, 100, 120, 121, 122, 130, 153, 186, 232, 255, 337, 351, 428
Tegucigalpa (tū gōō sē gäl′pä), 321
Telegraph. *See* Wireless and telegraph service
Textiles, importation of, 88, 107, 130, 160, 193, 271, 281, 296, 302, 325, 420, 428; manufacture of, 47, 83, 121, 126, 228, 229, 231, 243, 255, 332, 337, 352, 353, 361
Timber, importation of, 399; production of, 78, 130, 173, 196, 217, 221, 229, 232, 271, 278, 311, 394, 428
Time, attitude of Latin Americans toward, 4 ff.
Tin, exportation of, 102, 106, 107; importation of, 160, 243; production of, 98, 100, 102, 104
Tobacco, exportation of, 54, 79, 190, 193, 218, 229, 230, 244, 272, 373, 379, 381, 385, 386, 389; importation of, 160; production of, 49, 54, 79, 84, 120, 154, 182, 190, 218, 220, 223, 224, 228, 231, 235, 238 f., 243, 255, 258, 260, 271, 278, 325, 332, 340, 368, 379, 385, 386, 420, 426, 428
Tobago, 395 ff.
Tools, importation of, 160, 163, 243
Tortoise shell, 312, 381
Trade problems, 430 ff.
Training for foreign commerce, 444
Transportation and communication: Argentina, 160 f.; Bolivia, 107 f.; Brazil, 244 ff.; British Honduras, 330; Chile, 130 ff.; Colombia, 280 f.; Costa Rica, 308; Cuba, 381 f.; Dominican Republic, 429; Ecuador,

56 f.; Guatemala, 340 f.; Haiti, 421; Honduras, 325 f.; Mexico, 363; Nicaragua, 315 f.; Panama, 296 f.; Paraguay, 193; Peru, 88 f.; Porto Rico, 389; Salvador, 334; Uruguay, 178 f.; Venezuela, 263 ff.
Trinidad and Tobago: cities, 396; exports and imports, 397; geography, 395; people, 396; products and industries, 396 f.; transportation and communication, 397
Trujillo (trōō hē′lyō), 78, 81, 83
Tucumán (tōō kōō män′), 154, 159
Tumaco (tōō mä′kō), 274
Tungsten, exportation of, 106, 159; production of, 87, 98, 102, 136, 159

United States possessions in Latin America, 413 f.
Universities, 10 f., 16 f. *See also* Education
Uruguay (yōō′rōō gwä): army and navy, 174; cities, 170 ff.; currency, 174 f.; economic conditions, 179 f.; education, 175; exports and imports, 177 ff.; geography, 166 f.; government, 173 f.; history, 167 f.; "little Belgium of the New World," 166; people, 168 ff.; products and industries, 175 ff.; transportation and communication, 178 f.
Uyuni (ōō yōō′nē), 98 f.

Valdivia, 112, 121
Valencia (vä lĕn′syä), 256
Valparaiso (väl pä rī′sō), 115, 116, 117, 118, 120, 122, 124, 131, 132, 133
Vanadium, 86 f.
Vanilla, 329, 402, 409, 410
Vegetable ivory, 45, 47, 49, 51, 56, 78, 83, 272, 296. *See also* Tagua nut
Vegetables, exportation of, 129, 368; production of, 121, 129, 140, 260, 278
Venezuela: army and navy, 259; cities, 255 ff.; currency, 259; economic progress, 266; education, 259; exports and imports, 262; geography, 251 ff.; government, 258 f.; handicaps, 251; history, 253 ff.; people, 254 f.; products and industries, 260 ff.; transportation and communication, 263 ff.
Vera Cruz (vä′rä krōōs′), 353, 363
Victoria, 229

Villa Rica (vē′lyä rē′kä), 188
Vineyards, 129, 154. *See also* Grapes
Virgin Islands, British, 403
Virgin Islands of the United States, 413 f.

Waterways: Bolivia, 108; Brazil, 244 ff.; British Honduras, 330; Chile, 130 f.; Colombia, 280; Cuba, 382; Dominican Republic, 429; Ecuador, 56; Guatemala, 340 f.; Honduras, 325 f.; Nicaragua, 315; Panama, 297; Paraguay, 193; Salvador, 335; Venezuela, 263 f.
Wax, carnauba, 220, 240
West Indies, general treatment of, 367 ff.
Whaling, 121, 218
Wheat, exportation of, 160, 177; importation of, 243, 296; production of, 83, 84, 98, 105, 121, 129, 153, 176, 230, 231, 235, 260, 270, 278, 337, 340
Willemstad (wĭ′lĕm stät), 413
Windward Islands, 367, 400
Wine, importation of, 106; production of, 47, 120, 121, 126, 136
Wireless and telegraph service, 439; Argentina, 162; Brazil, 249 f.; British Honduras, 330; Chile, 133 f.; Colombia, 280 f.; Costa Rica, 308; Cuba, 382; Dominican Republic, 429; Ecuador, 57; Guatemala, 341; Haiti, 421; Honduras, 326; Mexico, 363; Nicaragua, 316; Panama, 297; Paraguay, 193; Porto Rico, 389; Salvador, 326; Uruguay, 179; Venezuela, 266
Women, attitude toward, in Latin America, 18 f.
Woodworking, 120, 121
Wool, exportation of, 79, 84, 87, 106, 118, 121, 123, 130, 155, 159, 160, 162, 172, 177, 235, 240; importation of, 243; production of, 78, 129, 176
Woolen goods, importation of, 243; manufacture of, 122, 232, 270, 271, 361

Yerba maté. *See* Maté

Zinc, exportation of, 362; production of, 87, 280, 358, 380